The globalization of business

In recent years economic activity has become increasingly globalized. One of the main instruments behind this process is the multinational enterprise. In *The Globalization of Business*, John Dunning explores the latest issues in the world of international business and looks ahead to the remaining years of this century identifying the likely challenges of the future.

Against a background discussion of global strategy and current theoretical frameworks, Dunning looks at diverse aspects of multi-national activity. What are the challenges posed by the technological, political and economic developments of the 1990s for international business? What are the implications of the opening up of new territories such as in central and eastern Europe and parts of China for both established and newly emerging multinational enterprises? To what extent are the competitive advantages of nation states increasingly coming to depend on the presence of multinational activity? What are the new forms of international business involvement and how do they affect our theorizing about foreign direct investment and multinational activity? What are the implications of the globalization of markets and production for the domestic economic policies of governments? This state-of-the-art collection of essays will be vital reading to students of international business and policy makers alike.

John Dunning is State of New Jersey Professor of International Business at Rutgers University and Emeritus Professor of International Business at the University of Reading. He is one of the best known and most distinguished experts in the growing field of international business.

Other titles by the same author:

American Investment in British Manufacturing Industry, London: Allen & Unwin, 1958 (reprinted by Arno Press, New York, 1976).
Studies in International Investment, London: Allen & Unwin, 1970.
An Economic Study of the City of London (with E.V. Morgan), London: Allen & Unwin, 1970.
Economic Analysis and the Multinational Enterprise, London: Allen & Unwin, 1974.
International Production and the Multinational Enterprise, London: Allen & Unwin, 1981.
The World's Largest Industrial Enterprises 1962–82 (with R.D. Pearce), Farnham: Gower Press, 1985.
Japanese Participation in British Industry, London: Croom Helm, 1986 (2nd edition 1989).
Explaining International Production, London: Unwin Hyman, 1988.
Multinationals, Technology and Competitiveness, London: Unwin Hyman, 1988.
Multinational Enterprises and the Global Economy, Reading, Mass. and Wokingham, England: Addison Wesley, 1992.

The globalization of business
The challenge of the 1990s

John H. Dunning

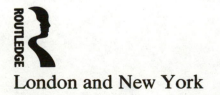

London and New York

First published 1993
by Routledge
11 New Fetter Lane, London EC4P 4EE

Simultaneously published in the USA and Canada
by Routledge
29 West 35th Street, New York, NY 10001

©1993 John H. Dunning

Typeset in 10/12pt Times by Solidus (Bristol) Ltd, Bristol
Printed and bound in Great Britain by
Mackays of Chatham PLC, Chatham, Kent

British Library Cataloguing in Publication Data
A catalogue record for this book is available from the British
Library

ISBN 0–415–09610–3
    0–415–09611–1

Library of Congress Cataloging in Publication Data

A catalogue record for this book is available
from the Library of Congress

Contents

Part I Challenges for teaching and research in international business

Introduction

Part II Challenges for theorizing about MNEs and MNE activity

Introduction

Part III Challenges to established patterns of MNE activity

Introduction

Tables

Figures

Preface

This volume brings together several articles and contributions to books I have written over the past five years. All of these contributions relate to a common theme, viz. the globalization of the world economy, and the ways in which Multinational Enterprises (MNEs) have influenced that globalization and responded to it.

All of the originally published material has been extensively revised and updated, so as to give the volume cohesion and a sense of direction. In addition, Chapters 3 and 4 have not previously been published. The book is divided into four parts, which correspond to four sets of challenges posed by recent (and likely future) events in the global economy. The first is primarily addressed to the academic community and concerns the teaching and research in international business. The second – also mainly scholastic in its thrust – deals with the implications of the new economic international environment for our theorizing about MNEs and MNE activity.

The third and longest part of the volume describes and analyzes the main changes which have actually occurred in globalization of production and markets in the last two decades or more and speculates a little about the likely course of future events over the rest of the decade. Part IV deals with a critically important topic, viz. the changing interface between the operations of MNEs and the way in which national and regional governments organize their economic activities in the light of the growing interdependence between nation states. In the 1990s, this interface is likely to be an amalgam of both strategic competition and strategic cooperation between governments; and is likely to demand a reappraisal and modification of existing regimes of international governance.

John H. Dunning

Acknowledgements

I am grateful to several journals and the publishers of books, in which earlier versions of some of the chapters first appeared, for permission to make use of the material. Two of the studies were originally co-authored; one with Michele Gittleman who at the time of writing was a Research Officer at the UN Center on Transnational Corporations, and one with Philip Gugler of the University of Friborg. I much appreciate the contribution of these colleagues to this monograph.

Most of the typing for this volume was cheerfully and expertly undertaken by Mrs Phyllis Miller of the Graduate School of Management, Rutgers University; and to her I extend my warmest appreciation. I would also like to thank Mrs Melanie Waller of the Department of Economics, University of Reading who also shared in the preparation of the final two chapters.

Acknowledgement is also due to the copyright holders for their kind permission to reprint the following contributions. Chapter 1 is a revised version of an article of the same name first published in the *Journal of International Business Studies*, Vol. 31, Summer 1989 (pp. 1–30). Chapter 2 was first published as a chapter of the same name in a book edited by Brian Toyne and Douglas Nigh, *The Institutional Status of International Business*, London, Greenwood, 1993. Chapter 5 was first published as an article of the same name in *Transnational Corporations*, Vol. 1, No. 1, 1992 (pp. 135–68). Chapter 6 was first published as a jointly authored chapter of the same name in an edited volume by M. W. Klein and P. J. Welfens, *Multinationals in the New Europe and Global Trade*, Berlin and New York, Springer-Verlag. Chapter 7 is a revised version of an article of that name first published in *International Economic Journal*, Vol. 6, No. 1, Spring 1992 (pp. 59–82). Chapter 8 first appeared as a chapter in a book edited by R. Culpan entitled *Multinational Strategic Alliance*, International Business Press, Binghampton, New York, 1993. Chapter 9 is an updated and extended version of an article published in *Development and International Cooperation*, Vol. 7, No. 12, June 1991 (pp. 21–40). Chapter 10 is a much extended version of a chapter of that name in a volume edited by Y. Aharoni entitled *Coalitions and Competition: The Globalization of Professional Services*, London and New York, Routledge, 1993. Chapter 11 is an updated and expanded version of a chapter of the same name in a volume edited by Lars Oxelheim, *The Global Race for International Investment in the 1990s*, Berlin and New York, Springer-Verlag, 1993. Chapter 12 first appeared in the *CTC Reporter*, No. 31, Spring 1991 (p. 207). Chapter 13 is a revised version of an article of that name first published by *Millennium (Journal of International Studies)*, Vol. 20, No. 2, Summer 1991 (pp. 225–44). Chapter 14 was first published as a chapter in P. J. Buckley (ed.) *New Directions in International Business*, Aldershot, Edward Elgar, 1992. Chapter 15 was first published as a chapter of that name in a volume edited by J. C. Cantwell, *Multinational Investment in Modern Europe*, Aldershot, Edward Elgar, 1992.

John H. Dunning
University of Reading

Part I
Challenges for teaching and research in international business

Introduction

In this first part of the volume, attention is given to the challenges now facing international business as an academic discipline. Chapter 1 traces the emergence and growth of teaching and research on international business since the 1960s, to the present day. It argues that all too little attention has been paid to those aspects of international business which are unique to the cross-border operations of firms; and that only by approaching the subject matter from an interdisciplinary perspective can this deficiency be properly remedied. The chapter concludes by setting out some of the ways in which individual scholars, university departments and graduate schools, and the professional body of international business teachers and researchers – the Academy of International Business – might best respond to these challenges in the 1990s.

1 The study of international business: a plea for a more interdisciplinary approach[1]

INTRODUCTION

It is almost a truism to say that the practice of international business (IB) is only as successful as the human and physical resources available to the practitioners and the way in which these are procured, organized and translated into marketable products. Likewise, the effectiveness of our scholastic efforts to study and teach international business is entirely dependent on our capability to marshal and organize the necessary human and other assets so as to supply a range of end products which are acceptable to the academic community of which we are part, our paymasters and the main purchasers of our products, viz., the business community. Of course, the determinants of success of the practice and study of IB are inter-related; and, in our particular pursuit for excellence, there is no unique or sure-fire recipe for success.

But, I observe, that in an ever increasingly complex world of international business, which is dominated by rapid and far-reaching changes in technology and by environmental turbulence, this is no less true of successful practitioners. Rarely, in seeking to identify the reasons for business achievement, is one able to find a single common denominator. Sometimes excellence is primarily based on innovatory ingenuity; sometimes on the access to or control of key inputs or markets; sometimes on aggressive or novel methods of advertising and marketing; sometimes on super-efficient capital budgeting; sometimes on dynamic and imaginative entrepreneurship; sometimes on the diversity of operational experiences and capabilities; and sometimes on an unusual aptitude to manage both intra- and inter-firm human relationships. But in most cases, success is founded on some amalgam of these, and it is the way in which these discrete – though increasingly interdependent – advantages are combined with each other and with complementary assets in different countries and cultures, which contemporary research suggests is the key competitive advantage of international firms. Call it what you will – e.g. a holistic and integrated approach to the creation and organisation of business wealth – the success of the modern international corporation is increasingly determined by the ability to organize natural resources, information, money and people across national boundaries, both within, and between organizations.

What's new in this, one may ask. In principle, nothing. What is perhaps new, is the high degree of diversification of modern IB in its products, production processes and markets. *Inter alia*, this is revealed by the increasing role of transaction-related business activities. By transaction-related activities, I mean all activities other than those directly associated with the actual act of producing or consuming goods and services. In the case of single product firms competing in perfect markets, transaction costs are zero. As firms become multi-activity and markets become imperfect, transaction costs assume a greater significance, and, in some cases, the proficiency of transaction-driven activities may determine the success or failure of an enterprise.

Essentially transaction costs comprise the costs of organization and the costs of strategy. They include the functions of coordinating the procurement and disposition of inputs; those of production scheduling and inventory control; those of monitoring, controlling and inspecting performance and product quality; those of establishing networks of suppliers and managing industrial relations; those to do with the logistics of the movement of people, assets and materials; those to do with marketing and final product and post-sales activities; those to do with the acquisition and use of information; and those to do with the management of all kinds of risk. As these tasks become more important, so transaction, relative to production, costs will rise. As new cross-border alliances are concluded and networks formed; as generic technologies, which are capable of being put to multiple uses, become more important; and as markets and production outlets become culturally more sensitive, then the demands on organizational capabilities become dimensionally very different from those facing the single product firm. Multinationals both fashion change and are fashioned by it. But the prosperous firms are those best able to exploit technological advances and learning experiences to their own benefits; to adapt their strategic postures and ownership patterns to meet competitive pressures; to manage diversity and environmental turbulence; and to identify and seize new economic opportunities.

THE CHALLENGE TO INTERNATIONAL BUSINESS STUDY: MEASURES OF SUCCESS

So much for our brief excursion into the changing determinants of the success of IB. Let me now turn to some of the implications of these changes for the study, and particularly the organization of the study, of IB.

I believe that for the most part, the challenges and opportunities now facing the international business community are well acknowledged and understood by scholars. Ours is a pragmatically oriented discipline and, more than our colleagues in most other disciplines, we keep abreast of the most important developments in our subject. A high proportion of IB teachers act as business consultants. Many are regular contributors to journals, periodicals and newspapers, read (or at least purchased by!) the business community. Through our research activities, conferences, seminars, executive training programs and professional contacts, we are afforded a good insight into the workings of international companies and their interaction with the economies in which they operate. At the same time, I am not persuaded that the way in which we presently organize the study of IB is best suited to the needs of the 1990s. Let me explain what I mean.

Historically, the study of IB (IBS) has gone through two phases and is now entering a third. The first phase lasted from the mid-1950s to the late 1960s. This was a time in which the subject was taught and researched by a small group of senior scholars, most of whom played a key role in the formation and early development of the AIB (Academy of International Business). These scholars were primarily interested in IB *per se*, and although their initial training and professional orientation was rooted in one of the established functional fields of business, their perspective and vision was essentially cross-disciplinary. I am sure these scholars – most of whom are still active members of the Academy today – would be the first to admit that the tools and technical apparatus they brought to analyzing the behavior of international companies were relatively undeveloped and unsophisticated; but, in emphasizing the distinctive features of the international or foreign dimension of business, they were inevitably drawn into issues that were not only of interest to disciplines outside their own, but which needed to be approached and studied in a coordinated way. Since, at this time, there were few research-oriented business schools outside the US[2] (and what there were, were strongly American influenced), it was not surprising that these scholars were of US origin.

However, in the main, the efforts of these scholars met with only limited success. Partly, this was because, since most US businesses were largely domestically oriented, the study of their activities followed suit; and partly because the methodologies and techniques of IBS lacked analytical rigor. The authors addressed several functional issues from an international perspective; and their orientation of interest was primarily, though not exclusively, pedagogic. Trained usually in management economics or marketing, they argued for a more international approach to the teaching of business, but in so doing they did not hesitate to embrace an interdisciplinary perspective.

The second phase, which proceeded in conjunction with the first as IB became a subject in its own right, was more research driven. It was led by a rather different group of scholars who were interested in some international aspects of their particular subject. More often than not, these scholars were outside business schools, and were non-American. By and large, their research was policy-oriented. For example, the growth of outward direct investment from the US in the 1950s and 1960s triggered off a variety of host and home countries' studies on the economic consequences of that investment,[3] while the first major project of multinationals *per se* was conducted by Ray Vernon and his colleagues at Harvard.[4] These studies were mainly undertaken by economists; and this discipline, and that of finance, also spawned a galaxy of theories – and, I might add, largely unidisciplinary theories – about the motivation for, and determinants of, foreign direct investment and the multinational enterprise (MNE).[5] But it is perhaps worth observing that, with one or two major exceptions, these scholars were not in the mainstream of international economics, industrial organization or the theory of the firm; and, indeed, they did not draw upon received theoretical constructs. The international textbooks gave short shrift to the subject of direct foreign investment until the 1970s. It was the fourth edition of Kindleberger's *International Economics* in 1968 that gave the first attention to foreign direct investment; and even the 1985 edition of Caves and Jones allocated only 10 of 537 pages to the subject. The industrial organization literature paid even less attention to the structure, conduct and performance of international markets; and one would be hard put to find any reference to transaction costs and market failure in any textbook on the theory of the firm before the late 1970s.[6] At the same time, the stirrings of discontent with existing paradigms in these branches of economics, and quite independently, the new thinking on organizational form and control, typified by the work of Alfred Chandler and Oliver Williamson,[7] were providing the lynch pins for some of the most exciting theoretical advances of the later 1970s and early 1980s.

If most of the research on IB issues was being undertaken within particular disciplines, the period produced intense debates, both between and within disciplines, about the organization of IB study. For the most part, the argument centered on whether IB – and particularly the teaching of IB – should be developed as a new and self-contained discipline or whether each of the functional areas comprising business studies should be internationalized; a debate which is still very much alive today. The AIB, and its members, have taken the lead in analyzing the comparative merits of the alternative modalities without coming to any definitive conclusions as to which is the preferred one.[8] So much seems to rest on university- or school-specific characteristics, the interests and the personalities of those involved, and the knowledge, motivation and leadership of the Dean. The arguments for and against organizing IB studies via an extension of the functional areas, compared with integrating these within a single IB department, are well known and do not need to be rehearsed here; except, it is perhaps worth underlining that the options are not mutually exclusive. But I think the fact that much of the research on IB in the 1970s was unidisciplined, and was US led, tended to favor the first rather than the second option, which, in any case, was easier to accommodate within existing organizational structures. In this sense, at least, the organization of IB study paralleled that of much of IB, which in the 1960s and 1970s grafted on the international dimension to an organizational responsibility based on product divisions. Thus most business schools carved up the teaching of IB by disciplinary area, while a few developed geographical specializations. As for the AIB itself – apart from gathering information and acting as a forum for debate, I do not think it advanced a particular view, even though individual members of the Academy did so.

As I see it, we have now reached a new watershed in the evolution of IBS. It has been brought about by changes in both exogenous variables and those endogenous to the profession. These changes are having, are likely to continue to have, widespread implications for IBS at all levels. They affect the training and career prospects of individual scholars; the composition of, and relationships between disciplines; the organization of schools or faculties; and the function of IBS as a whole. The question I now want to address is: What might be, or should be, the role of AIB not only in responding to these developments but helping to fashion them?

External factors

The main external factor influencing IBS has undoubtedly been the globalization of economic activity, and the realization, by the business community and governments alike, that both are competing for resources and customers in a market environment in which one's own strategy both influences, and is influenced by, one's major foreign competitors. In such a scenario, governments need to adopt globally oriented macro-organizational strategies, while firms, particularly in industries dominated by MNEs, need to adopt globally oriented micro-organizational strategies. This, in turn, requires a reappraisal of existing macro- and micro-economic policies, and a much greater understanding of both the workings of the international economy and the variables affecting the internationalization of business activity. And by internationalization I mean the totality of cross-border activities, be they production or trade in assets, goods or services; and be they within the same institution or between independent economic agents. An understanding of the forces making for Japanese direct investment in the US is just as relevant to our understanding of IB as how best non-resident firms might break into the Central and East European market, or react to the new investment policies introduced by the Indian government, or to the latest debt crisis in Latin America, or to the changes in the political climate in Mexico or the Middle East, or to the implications of the completion of Europe's internal market at the end of 1992.

From the perspective of the student of IB, I believe the change required is a fundamental shift in the way in which we examine the foreign related variables affecting business. Initially, just as in the practice of IB, the study of IB – which, I repeat, was largely US dominated – took the study of domestic business and gave it an international dimension with the least possible change. If it was acknowledged that there were some differences in selling to or producing in Belgium, Peru or Thailand compared with selling to or producing in Kansas, Oregon and Louisiana, these were considered relatively minor. Or, to put it differently, the achievement of business goals was perceived to be a *culture-free* phenomenon. Such a perception led to ill-conceived attitudes and inappropriate behavior. For example, it encouraged a parochial and ethnocentric approach by both American business and the American government. The argument in the 1950s and early 1960s seemed to run something like this. US industry in the US is efficient; its technology, management and marketing skills are the best in the world. Therefore when US industry goes abroad, US products, skills and production methods should follow it. A similar rationale drove macro-organizational strategy, although, since the US was more or less a self-sufficient economy, such a policy was entirely domestically oriented. From the perspective of a hegemonic power, any reaction of other firms or governments to what the US firms or the US government did or did not do was assumed to be of negligible significance.

In the later 1960s and 1970s, micro-business policy was differently focused. There was an increasing recognition, earlier acknowledged by some older European MNEs, that, because of country-specific differences in factor endowments, consumer tastes, institutions, culture and government policies, foreign subsidiaries needed to be organized differently than their domestic counterparts. There was a move towards polycentrism and the development of multidomestic MNEs; increasingly decisions in such firms were decentralized and local managers appointed to manage local operations. A third phase of organizational development followed in the late 1970s and early 1980s. This was aided and abetted by regional integration, techno-logical developments and the geographical diversification of MNE activity. It led to a geocentric strategy in which the operations of the various subsidiaries were geared to a common goal and coordinated by a central plan. Yet, initially at least, even this strategy, while accepting that the internationalization of an enterprise required some organizational modifications to allow for differences in institutional arrangements and political and ideological perceptions, presumed that, at the end of the day, these differences could be readily accom-modated in the search for new markets and for greater efficiency.

In the late 1980s, this philosophy was being increasingly ques-tioned; and, since that time, efficiency-seeking MNEs have increasingly accepted the need to adapt their strategies to meet the particular and specific needs of the countries in which they operate. It is not just that international transactions are more important to almost all national economies; the very character of trade and invest-ment has undergone important changes. Let me identify just four of particular interest to the IB student. First, exchange rates are more volatile. Compare the 1960s with fixed exchange rates which could be considered exogenous. Firms could plan foreign operations. The gyrations of the major currencies since the mid-1980s have reinforced the importance of this extra-domestic variable which had huge re-percussions for risk management.

Second, and even more pervasive, has been the growing role of government as a factor influencing the location of economic activity by international companies. I will not dwell in detail on this thesis here,[9] but it is based upon three hypotheses. The first is that industry is becoming more footloose in its choice of location as its dependence on natural and, for the most part immobile, factor endowments is becoming reduced. *Inter alia*, this reduced dependence is shown by the decreasing proportion of raw material and unskilled labor to total production costs. Second, and partly as a consequence of the first, the role of government in shaping locational costs and benefits is increasing. This is being accomplished not only by the more obvious instruments such as investment incentives, tariffs, and the performance requirements expected of foreign affiliates, but by a gamut of macro- and micro-organizational measures, ranging from education and health programs, through competition and mergers policy to industrial relations legislation; but, perhaps most important of all, by fashioning an economic ethos acceptable to the major wealth-creating agents in society. By such means, the locational attractions of countries may be increased or decreased. As the policies, regulations and incentives of government are *country* specific, it follows that an examination of the character and rationale of these must be an important part of any international business study.

Third, the role of technology as a factor affecting internationalization has also become more important. This is for four reasons. First, technology is generally mobile across national boundaries, whether it be within the same firms or between different firms. Second, because of the escalation in the costs of product or process innovation, firms have not only had to look to world markets to sell their products, but have had to conclude strategic alliances with other firms to recoup the benefits of joint supply and specialization along the value-added chain, and/or to share risks and exploit scale economies at a given point on the value-added chain. Third, within the industrialized world, at least, the amount of intra-industry trade in all kinds of knowledge and information has risen rapidly. No one nation has a technological hegemony; each has something the other needs. Fourth, such technology has affected the organization of cross-border transactions. Not only has it pushed back further the geographical boundaries of both firms and markets; it has had considerable implications for the economic strategies of national governments (Dunning, 1988).

The net result of these and other trends – including a resurgence of interest in environmental issues and national cultural identity – is that international business is now on the political agenda of most countries. Developments such as the North American Free Trade Area (NAFTA), the rapid industrialization of the Pacific Rim countries, and the changing political and industrial map of Europe – to name but three – are forcing a reappraisal of the role of IB – particularly in North America and Europe. In a variety of guises, such as the US Trade Bill which has authorized over $10 million for the setting up of new international business centers, to the establishment of the Ontario Centre for IB in Canada, and the initiative of the Economic and Social Research Council in the UK in fostering research into the implications of the global economy for international regimes, e.g. GATT, the interest in IBS, as a possible means of improving international competitiveness, is wide-spread.

Internal factors

At the same time – and partly as a consequence of the above – the study of IB, and of business in general, is itself changing. A reading of the literature, and conversations with other scholars, suggests several reasons for this. The first is that the subject of IB has achieved a certain amount of intellectual maturity, and, indeed, academic respectability. One sign of this is that it has started to evolve theories and paradigms of its own; another is that its own interpretation and application of existing paradigms has had some appeal outside the disciplines which make up IB. A third is that IBS has begun to attract some of the sharpest minds of a new generation of academia. In economics, some of the most interesting work is currently being done on strategic trade theory, international market structures, technology transfer, and the multinational firm. In organizational theory, the focus is on network analysis, on intra- and interfirm cooperative relationships, on the organization of technological galaxies, and on the coordination and control of interdependent assets. In marketing, renewed attention is being given to the entry strategies of firms into foreign markets, and to identifying the generic competitive advantages which allow firms to penetrate their rivals' markets. In management theory, the emphasis of interest has shifted from domestic to global business strategies and all this implies; witness, for example, some recent work of Porter (1986, 1990), Doz and Prahalad (1987), Bartlett and Ghoshal (1989) and Westney and Ghoshal (1992). In finance, scholars are paying increasing attention to questions of risk and management of financial assets in a world dominated by volatile exchange rates. Between several disciplines, there is evidence of an increasing cross-fertilization of ideas and paradigms (Robbins, 1985; Boddewyn, 1993, Dunning, 1988). Each of these approaches or lines of study has been sparked off by an interest in issues or problems specific to IB, or by new lines of thought or research in the mainstream discipline, that are perceived to be especially relevant to cross-border economic activities.

At the same time, scholars have been forced to look outside their particular neck of the woods for answers to problems which, in a domestic context, might be capable of a unidisciplinary solution. Take a question like the location of value-added activity by US firms. Within the US thi: can be largely explained by economic variables. Not so when one looks outside the US to discuss the merits of siting an electronics factory in (say) Korea cf. Thailand or Ireland cf. The Netherlands. Here political, cultural, legal, institutional and language considerations may play a crucial role. Or take another example. How should a business acquire and organize the technology it needs to produce a particular range of products? As recently as 20 years ago, only a rudimentary knowledge of a limited range of technologies was required. Not so today, when an understanding of the interaction between a variety of generic technologies and the materials on which they are based may be key ingredients to success. No less far-reaching have been advances in the organizational techniques and modes open to MNEs, as they affect, for example, both the ownership and control of resources and markets. As these latter advances, I believe, offer the most promising lessons for the future organization of IBS, I will return to consider them further a little later.

At a macro-disciplinary level, we are now seeing the various professional associations taking a key interest in international issues. Some associations, e.g. the Academy of Management, have set up International Affairs Committees while others which have long had such committees, have begun to take them more seriously. At the same time, new journals, with intriguing titles such as *Journal of Global Marketing, Journal of International Financial Management and Accounting* and *Journal of International Technology,* have begun to appear. The International Studies Association, ASCSB and latterly the Association of American Colleges have been extremely active in encouraging the internationalization of a wide range of academic curricula. All these, and many other developments I have not mentioned, have important implications for the content and the study of IB.

TRANSACTION COSTS

I now turn to the one piece of theorizing or model-building in this chapter. It is concerned with the transaction costs of international economic activity and how the changing role of these costs is affecting the organization of IB and IBS. The literature on transaction costs tends to concentrate on the costs of alternative modalities for organizing the exchange of goods and services; but, taking a broader perspective, such costs might be thought to include all those associated with the buying or selling of a good or service, other than those incurred in actual acts in production or consumption.[10] To the consumer, these might include the time and costs (including search, evaluation and negotiating costs) he has to incur prior to the purchase of a product; the uncertainty he faces as to whether the product will satisfy his needs; and the post-purchasing costs of servicing, repairs and maintainance, including the costs of seeking out and obtaining the necessary services at the right quality. To the producer, transaction costs include the costs of coordination of inputs to the value-added process, which are both internal and external to the firm. They include those of search costs for the appropriate inputs, of monitoring the quality of these inputs and of intermediate products, of minimizing disturbances to the flow of output, of creating and sustaining cooperative interfirm working relationships, and of managing the uncertainty of markets. It is worth noting that most of these costs dramatically rise as a firm diversifies its output or production outlets, and as the number of inputs required to produce a given product increases.

The literature identifies three kinds of transactional costs which producers and consumers[11] may have to incur if they use markets as a means of exchange. There are those which stem from the uncertainty surrounding the outcome of an exchange, the terms of which have already been agreed to; those which arise from the external affects of a transaction; and those which occur when the presence of scale economies is incompatible with a perfect market situation. It is to save on these costs or potential costs, or to capture the benefits of common governance of separate but interrelated activities that lead producers to internalize markets. But by so doing they also incur costs. These are coordinating costs and are essentially to do with the management of intrafirm relationships and, in other than spot markets, with extrafirm relationships as well. Indeed as the number and complexity of relationships increase, so too are transactional costs likely to rise. The question is how best to organize relationships to produce a given set of products at the lowest production and transaction costs.

The exogenous and endogenous forces affecting the internationalization of business activity I have just described have had a dramatic impact not only on the production capabilities of firms and the consumption opportunities of consumers; but on the transaction costs incurred in production and consumption. As a result, the study of the disciplines making up IB, and IB as a discipline in itself, have had to pay more attention to the ownership and organization of transactions as factors influencing the industrial and geographical distribution of business activity.[12] The demands of modern technology and the internationalization of consumer tastes are necessitating strategic alliances among producers. The specific characteristics of foreign (cf. domestic) production are such that their impact is likely to be felt on the transaction costs of MNEs rather than on their production costs. Obvious examples include the risks and uncertainties associated with environmental instability, e.g. fluctuating exchange rates, intercountry cultural differences, and the role of government both in influencing these and as a force in its own right.

Let me now draw the threads of my argument together. First, as a matter of fact, the relative importance of foreign trade and production is increasing in almost all major economies (World Bank, 1991; UNCTC, 1988; UN, 1992); and, with it, the foreign component of national economic decision taking at a macro- and micro-level Second, the uniquely foreign attributes of the practice of IB are becoming more important; hence IB is becoming a more distinctive subject for study. Third, we have suggested that the impact of the foreignness is predominantly shown in the transaction costs incurred by the participating firms; and that, due to the complexity and nature of IB, the ratio of transaction costs is increasing relative to production costs.

What does this all mean for IB scholarly research and teaching? First, imagine if you will, a world without transaction costs. In such a scenario, there would be little or no need for an interdisciplinary approach to IBS. The theories and paradigms would be subject or functional specific; indeed, one supposes that this is why the study of business, as an academic discipline, was initially broken down into economics, management, finance, marketing and so on in the first place. This is not to say there would be no cross-functional linkages; clearly there would be, e.g. between economics and marketing, finance and management and so on. However, the introduction of transaction costs, which themselves often reflect the existence of non-economic forces affecting the efficiency of markets, suggests the need for a mode of study which is not just multidisciplinary, but interdisciplinary. By interdisciplinary in this context, I mean a holistic and integrated approach to a study of IB and its constituent subject areas, the primary purpose of which is to advance our understanding of the former as a discipline in its own right. *Inter alia* such an approach would capture certain externalities of common governance, which the individual disiplines working independently could not. *Interdisciplinary studies when properly organized lower the transaction costs of IB study.*

This, then, is the final piece of the jigsaw. Due to both exogenous and endogenous factors, the practice of IB is involving an increasing ratio of transaction to total costs. But in order to study and explain this phenomenon, IB scholars need not only to draw upon different disciplines but to do so in a coordinated way. Hopefully this will lead to the emergence of paradigms and theories which are not only multidisciplinary in their applications, but when approached from the viewpoint of the study of IB as a whole, yield special and unique benefits of their own.

IMPLICATIONS: CHALLENGE AND PROBLEMS

If developments in the practice and study of IB are anything like I suggest, then clearly there are both opportunities and challenges to us both as individual scholars and collectively as AIB. The *opportunities* mainly stem from the tremendous demand for knowledge about IB. These are exemplified by the surge of demand both for undergraduate and graduate courses in IB, and for executive training programs, workshops, conferences and the like. In several countries too, the funds for IB research have also dramatically increased, both from governments and international agencies and from private institutions. In-house training and research on matters to do with IB have also mushroomed. Less clear is the impact of internal or autonomous demand by the producing institutions, i.e. the universities and business schools. True, some faculties and schools have sought to create the demand for more internationalization of their curricula. Naturally, such bodies as the AIB have long encouraged and assisted such efforts; by contrast, it appears to me that most other professional associations are responding to (rather than taking the lead in creating) the demand for the internationalization of their subject matter.

The *challenges and problems* are essentially supply oriented. I want to identify four of these. The first is resources, mainly human resources. The demand for first-rate teachers and researchers in IB still outweighs the supply at all levels. For whatever reason, we are not attracting a sufficient share of the top brains from the disciplines comprising IB. Whatever its interest and practical applicability, the intellectual prestige of IB as an area for academic study is insufficient to outweigh the attractions of a career in the private sector or to tempt academics to specialize in IB research. I believe this is changing but slowly. The number of good Ph.D candidates pursuing IB studies is inadequate; our discipline still has difficulty in recruiting the best of these and other newly graduated doctorates; while the number of mainstream scholars of the highest calibre who apply their expertise to IB-related problems remains all too small. There is also the problem of retaining staff once recruited; the ease at which good faculty can move into business or elsewhere in the public sector is well known to all of us. Our first challenge, then, is to improve the quantity and quality of our human resources.

The second challenge is that of competition. Perhaps, here, we need to distinguish between scholars and disciplines with a peripheral or passing interest in IB and those who regard IB as their mainstream academic pursuit. For there appears to be a burgeoning of interest in IB topics by some younger unidisciplinary scholars who see IB providing a rewarding area for research. I do not think the results of such research have yet found their way into the journals, but I do see some evidence of an increase in articles that might have been of interest to *JIBS* being published in some of the more application-oriented specialist journals such as *Strategic Management Journal, Journal of Economic and Organisational Behaviour, Sloan Management Review, Managerial and Decision Economics, Weltwirtschaftliches Archiv, Journal of Marketing*, etc.; and some issue-oriented journals, e.g. *The Service Industries Journal* and the *International Journal of Technology Management.* I also observe – with mixed feelings I might add – the launching of several new journals with an international perspective, e.g. *Journal of Global Marketing, Pacific Review, Journal of International Consumer Marketing*; and also of special issues of journals dealing with IB issues, e.g. as recently produced by the *International Trade Journal,* and the *Journal of Common Market Studies.* More generally, there are stirrings within the disciplines to focus more on the international dimension of their subjects. As yet, this is primarily an 'awareness' factor at work; but it could develop into a major change of emphasis; and, if it does, it could offer a challenge to our own Academy, in as much as it is perceived to offer an alternative academic forum for analyzing and discussing issues germane to IB. How far would (or will) economists, organizational and financial theorists, marketing scholars, business analysts, political scientists and so on, need AIB, if their own professional associations fully embrace the international dimensions of their subject?

The third, and I think perhaps the greatest, challenge is within the profession of IB itself. Is the organization of IBS efficient? If not, why not? Is its ownership (i.e. who, in fact, are its researchers and teachers, and in control of its organization) appropriate? Is it properly focused to meet the needs of its customers in the 1990s? Let me tackle the problem from three levels, viz. that of the *individual scholar*, the *school or faculty*, and *the AIB*. First, the individual scholar level. Take a newly qualified Ph.D student. The question arises as to whether IB is recruiting the appropriate and best quality Ph.Ds. I doubt it. Should we (do we?) insist upon a Ph.D in international business as a necessary qualification for a faculty position in that subject area? Is it not possible to recruit the best Ph.Ds from outside IB and encourage them to research and teach IB? With those already trained in IB, how can they best be guided to improve their techniques, methodologies, and to be imaginative and productive research workers. Some work that the Academy – and more particularly the Fellows of the Academy and the regional chapters – is doing in the training at the doctoral level is to be applauded, but I believe that more post doctoral tutorage is required, particularly in the interdisciplinary aspects of the subject. But in some cases, the issue is an academic [*sic*] one, as the recruiters are in the functional and not the IB areas. Here, I believe one touches upon one of the crucial yet sensitive areas of ownership rights and organizational responsibility. If business schools recruit on the basis of academic qualifications, technical merit and the potential for making a contribution to knowledge in a particular discipline, and if existing departments prefer to recruit in areas in which they already have a strong reputation – which is likely to reflect the academic and personal predilections of the existing faculty – there could well be a self-perpetuating barrier to entry to hiring new faculty trained or with interests in IB. Worse still, one can easily get into a 'vicious' knowledge-creating circle as the choice of subjects studied for a doctorate degree will reflect the interests of the existing faculty. So, fewer Ph.Ds in IB are trained because of shortage of qualified or interested supervisors; and this leads to fewer good potential IB scholars and so on. I shall suggest a possible way out of the impasse in a moment, but, for now, will simply observe that we should not rule out the possibility of training in at least some areas of IB coming *after* recruitment to faculty, even though it might mean that the productivity of the person appointed might be lower in the short run.

The next level of analysis is the school, and, within the school, the disciplines making up IB. In the past 20 years, AIB has been at the fore in trying to identify the best method of internationalizing the business curricula. It has carried out several surveys – the last one was published in 1986[13] (Thanapoulos, 1986). It concluded that 262 schools, or 81 per cent of those approached, taught one or more courses in IB, but that still only 68 schools offered a major in IB at an undergraduate level, 50 at an MBA level and 20 at a doctoral level. In the schools which did offer a range of courses in IB, the pedagogic model varied considerably. The majority tended to prefer a functional approach, by which the kind of courses taught in a traditional business curriculum were also offered at an international level. Few programs appeared to start off by looking at IB as a study in its own right, and then working backwards to identifying the kind of courses which might make up an integrated syllabus. Few appeared to tackle subjects outside the business arena, yet which are no less relevant to the practitioners of IB. Languages, social anthropology, political science, law, business history and economic geography, each have much to contribute to an understanding of IB; but in the early 1980s only a handful of business schools embraced these in their curriculum, although things are quite rapidly changing and seem likely to continue to change. Currently there are many initiatives, from the ASCSB downwards, to integrating liberal arts and, occasionally, some technologically or science-based subjects, with business studies.

The situation is worse outside the United States. In Canada, for example, in the early 1980s only one school offered a major or degree in IB; now there are at least three schools which offer such courses; in France, Sweden, Switzerland and the UK the situation is better; and in most of the prestigious business schools, IB comprises between a third and 40 per cent of an MBA curriculum. In Germany and Japan, IB is usually taught in university economics, finance or accounting departments, but in both countries, in-house training provided by MNEs plays a much more important role. In developing countries, the interest is generally following the US pattern. India has a strong tradition in teaching commerce and there are several strong management schools that are now internationalizing their curricula; one indeed – IMI (India) – teaches only internationally-oriented management. In East Asia, where most of the faculty in business schools have North American Ph.Ds, the curriculum is strongly US influenced, but in some schools, e.g. in Singapore, Korea, Hong Kong and Thailand, IB is the most important component of an MBA curriculum. Teaching and research on IB subjects in Latin America is generally a long way behind. In Africa, business subjects appear to be mainly taught in management colleges and at a post-experience level; though some departments of economics or political economy, e.g. at the Universities of Nigeria and Zimbabwe, have incorporated MNE-related material into their syllabi.

But quantity is not as important as quality. It may be that there should be tiers or divisions of academic institutions. At the top of the pyramid, or in the first division, would be relatively few institutions in each country concentrating on a broad spectrum of research and Ph.D and post professional teaching programmes. These might be followed by a larger number of schools, well renowned in their own way, pursuing a variety of niche strategies, which could be issue or functionally oriented. A third group of institutions would offer MBA courses but conduct only limited research; while the base of the pyramid would be made up of schools which offered at least some training in IB, but primarily at an undergraduate level. No less relevant is *what* is taught and *how* it is studied and how IB relates to the larger program of which it is part. All too frequently, the international dimension is tacked on to the end of a course which is nationally oriented. This applies to all subjects, as taught in most countries. Only some of the smaller nations, e.g. Sweden and Switzerland in Europe, Singapore and Hong Kong in Asia, take an international perspective from the start, simply because their economic prosperity so much depends on events that occur outside their national boundaries.

Circumstances are changing, but it remains to be seen how disciplines will react. My guess is that many will take the easy way out and graft on the international dimension to unidisciplinary domestically-oriented courses. Others will take matters further and widen the curricula to include language, law, political science, etc., and, in a few cases, engineering and technology-related subjects. The more entrepreneurial and far seeing of the new entrants and established schools will attempt to offer distinctive IB programs, which, depending on the interests, resources and motivation of the faculty, may either be functional or issue based, or a mixture of the two. I suspect that most will opt for the former, simply because the perceived transactional costs of an issue-based interdisciplinary approach are regarded as too high. These costs include both the provision of the necessary academic infrastructure and interdisciplinary communication and monitoring costs. A lack of knowledge of how best to coordinate the contributions of the various disciplines, the uncertainty of the benefits of such integration and the reluctance to experiment by faculty with

new organizational structures, may deter all but a few very determined schools. But I hope it will not deter all, for it is here where I
believe much of the best work on IB is likely to be done in the future.

On the other hand, I think the chances of interdisciplinary collaboration are more promising at a research level. The mushrooming of
research centers or institutes on issues such as IB in developing
countries, strategic alliances and network analysis, economic integration, international entrepreneurship, cross-cultural management,
competitiveness, and international technology management, and of
those which tackle a variety of issues from a regional or industrial
perspective, are testimony to this. While these often draw people
from various disciplines within the same school or university, and
provide a useful mode for the cross-fertilization of ideas, there is a
temptation to adopt a 'me too' or 'copy cat' attitude towards the
setting up of these institutions, with the result that already scarce
resources are even more thinly spread. Such centers or institutes can
provide a focal point for the sharing of interests and the cross-
fertilization of ideas of people from different disciplines; and where
the research is properly integrated, they can be a useful tool for interdisciplinary training at the highest intellectual level. Indeed clusters of
such centers within an institution or between institutions could help
produce a network of research and doctoral training facilities. In this
respect, I believe the AIB could provide a useful role as an information clearinghouse.

At the same time, there is also a need for the centers to be accorded
full academic status, and to be fully supported by the functional
disciplines which they comprise. All too frequently, scholars whose
research directions lie outside those which are the primary focus of
their own departments or schools are treated as second class citizens.
Even worse, because their interests are issue rather than technique
oriented and they do not publish in the mainstream journals, they are
assumed to lack intellectual rigor, and, hence, academic distinction.
This is particularly evident when appointment, tenure and promotion
questions are discussed. I believe the present state of peer judgment
in departments, which, on occasions, borders on arrogance (in my
own discipline, it is seen in the attitude taken by some economics
departments to economists working in business schools) to be a
strongly inhibiting factor for interdisciplinary research.

The problem does not just rest with the discipline itself. The upper
echelons of decision takers in the university or schools may have even
less knowledge about the value of a particular piece of interdisciplinary research; in any case they may be strongly influenced by

recommendations of departmental chairmen and deans. And when appointments and promotions are considered by university committees, these are again usually represented by unidisciplinary scholars; while external assessors may well be chosen from outside the mainstream of a person's discipline.

The final level of analysis is the Academy itself. What *is* its role – and what might its role be? Like many other trade associations, the AIB has no legislative power; it cannot impel individuals or institutions to behave in a particular way. The best it can do is inform, educate and advise; to act on behalf of its members to advance their educational interests and career prospects; to offer a forum for the presentation and discussion of research results, and of pedagogic issues; and to provide support and guidance to those who seek to advance the teaching and research of IB in their own institutions. I think that the AIB has a pretty good track record in performing these functions. Paralleling the evolution of a multinational enterprise, it has grown from its ethnocentric origins in 1959 to a fully fledged globally-oriented organization in the early 1990s. In the past, it has adopted an incremental approach to its tasks and functions; but just as the study of our subject matter is at a watershed, so too may the role of AIB itself need a fundamental reappraisal. It also is faced with its own distinctive opportunities and challenges. Indeed, the last decade of the twentieth century *could* provide the most exciting yet in the Academy's short history; but it will need a bold, imaginative and well conceived strategy if it is to exploit its comparative advantages and offer distinctive benefits to its members and to the study of international business in general.

SOME SUGGESTIONS FOR SOLVING PROBLEMS

Space does not permit me to deal with all the issues facing the Academy. Suffice for me to offer two bullet-type comments, before concentrating on a matter which, I believe, should be given especial attention by the Academy. The bullet remarks, which I shall present as propositions, though all too familiar, I think they merit repeating in the light of the growing interest of IBS outside of AIB.

1   The Academy should continue its efforts to encourage an internationalization of its membership and of its sphere of influence. At the moment the globalization of the study of IB is lagging that of the practice of IB. In mid-1992 72 per cent of the AIB membership was North American, a much greater proportion than the proportion of trade and direct investment accounted for

by US and Canadian international companies. I regarded the London meeting as an organizational breakthrough. I must add however that I was disappointed that the two subsequent annual meetings in the US did not elicit a better response from the European members. For whatever reason, the numbers of Americans attending the annual EIBA meetings is considerably higher than that of Europeans attending AIB meetings. We must continue to publicize AIB as *the* international association of teachers and researchers in IB. In some respects the meeting in Singapore in 1989 was an even more significant step forward. The Pacific–Asian region embraces the fastest growing economies in the world, and much of the growth is internationally led. Cross-border trade and investment plays a more important role in most East Asia economies than in Europe or the Americas, and international business is high on the agenda of most business and management schools in the region. We must make a greater effort to involve our Asian colleagues more fully in the work of the Academy, and, in particular, to assist in the setting up of more regional chapters and the promotion of regional meetings.

2   The Academy should widen its constituency by interesting scholars who, while not teaching IB *per se*, have much to contribute to our understanding of IB. I'm thinking both of scholars who pursue disciplines, which not only help fashion the environment of IB – e.g. law, political science, international relations, sociology – but those interested in issues of space and time, e.g. economic geography and business and economic history, and those working on the commercial and international applications of science and technology. The book *European Multinationals in Core Technologies* by Rob Van Tulder and Gerd Junne illustrates the kind of interdisciplinary blending I have in mind – in this case between technology, business strategy and international relations. Another, *Corporate Strategy and the Search for Ethics* by Edward Freeman and Daniel Gilbert, bravely tackles the interface between ethics and management. The AIB should encourage the membership of such cross-disciplinary researchers, and for them to submit papers to *JIBS* (which I was delighted to see become a quarterly publication in 1990). But it is not the commonality of issues that should determine the membership of our constituency. We should go beyond issues and seek to see how far it is possible to find unifying concepts, methodologies and paradigms.[14]

I now turn to the kernel of my remarks, which are concerned with the very *raison d'être* of the Academy; what its basic objectives should be; and how far these need to be modified or realigned in the light of the growing interest by unidisciplinary associations in international issues. Let me first present one scenario which I think is entirely possible even though it may be improbable. It is certainly one that I imagine would not appeal to most AIB members. Suppose the American Academy of Management, Academy of Marketing Science, American Finance Association, Administrative Science Association and the American Economic Association (I hope you will forgive a rather ethnocentric approach to the point I want to make) were each successful both in encouraging their members to internationalize their research and teaching, and in providing a forum for the exchange of information and ideas. Suppose that the house journals of these associations allocated 30 per cent, 40 per cent, 50 per cent of their space to papers on international issues; or were to launch an additional, but specifically internationally research-oriented, journal. Suppose, further, that the disciplines changed the orientation of their teaching from treating the foreign operations of firms as an extension of their domestic operations, to treating the domestic firm as a special case of the firm *per se*, whatever the geographical distribution of its activities might be. Suppose, too, that schools or departments began to offer a premium to faculty researching the international dimension of these disciplines. Suppose finally that, as a result of all these things, scholars who are currently members of the AIB because its goals, rubric and facilities meet their needs and aspirations, discover that these same needs and aspirations can now be met by their own unidisciplinary associations; and, in consequence, either withdrew from the AIB, or played a less active role in its affairs. Then, under such a scenario (what I might call the *substitution* scenario), AIB would be very considerably weakened, as indeed would its house journal. To those who think this scenario is an implausible one, and point to the fact that the leading activists of the internationalization movement within disciplines are staunch members of AIB, I would point to the ranking of business-related journals in the peer evaluation stakes, and also to the growing number of IB-related publications in well-respected journals other than JIBS.

The second scenario is what may be called the *room for all* or *status quo* scenario. Here one might speculate that the growth of interest in IBS will redound to the strength of both the unidisciplinary organizations and the AIB; but that, broadly speaking, each will coexist without any dramatic change in its functions or responsibilities. Supporters of this scenario would see no need for any change in the interests on policy of AIB.

The third scenario suggests the need for a *niche* strategy by the AIB; and argues for a reorientation of the Academy's academic thrust. The case for this scenario is based upon the validity of two propositions. The first is that the extension of unidisciplinary studies to incorporate the international dimension will lead to some re-direction of interests of some of the members, or potential members, from the AIB to their own disciplines. I see this particularly likely to occur in the more technically oriented subject areas, e.g. finance and accounting. The second proposition is that, since both the practice and study of IB is becoming increasingly multidisciplinary, the AIB – precisely because it deals with issues which transcend disciplinary boundaries – has a distinctive role to play in fostering and providing a forum for the promotion and results of interdisciplinary studies. Indeed I would argue that some of the most promising research now being undertaken in IB is at the intersection of (parts of) organization theory and economics, finance and strategic management, and marketing and cross-cultural studies.

Earlier in this chapter I suggested that not only were foreign or country-specific variables becoming more significant in affecting the location and behavior of international companies, but that these elements were more likely to affect the transaction costs than the production costs of business activity. Because of this, I suggested that although primarily an economic or business concept, the determination of the nature and extent of transaction costs depended on both economic and non-economic variables, which needed to be treated from an interdisciplinary perspective. I finally suggested that these relationships were interdependent, in the sense that it was often impossible to isolate the political, legal, cultural, organizational, managerial, *et al.* components of transaction costs. In consequence, to understand the nature and practice of decision taking in international companies, one needed to develop a cross-disciplinary (or supra-disciplinary) paradigmatic approach; and it was this (more than issues *per se*) that provided the bonding material for interdisciplinary studies.

The AIB has always been, or at least has aimed to be, a cross-disciplinary organization. I am not persuaded, however, that in spite of efforts of past presidents and program chairmen, the Academy is yet a truly inter- (as opposed to a multi-) disciplinary association, in the sense that it acts as a forum for the analysis of IB issues from different, but complementary disciplinary perspectives. Perhaps this reflects the isolationist persuasion of some of the constituent subjects, but, also I think, the fact that the focus of interest (at least of US business scholars) has been domestically rather than the internationally oriented. I also think it reflects a lack of a common methodology of approach, which has resulted in intellectual iconoclasm. An analysis of the programs in past annual meetings of the AIB shows a marked tendency to compartmentalize sessions by functional specialization, apart from a few sessions dealing with themes of general interest. In almost every respect, these sessions could be said to be miniatures of the kind of sessions that the unidisciplinary professional meetings could put on – and, in fact, are now putting on. Indeed it is not unknown for the same paper to be presented at both these meetings and the AIB! It was my purpose in suggesting the theme for the San Diego annual meeting, in 1988, that, for one year at least, we got away from this kind of segmentation and focused more on issues and paradigms at the confluence of two or more disciplines. I did so partly because I believed the important issues in IB needed a multidisciplinary input; partly because I thought the comparative advantage of AIB, relative to its sister associations, would increasingly rest in the area of interdisciplinary studies; partly because I believe that there is more intellectual commonality among us than many business scholars realize; and partly, because I wished to encourage the Academy to rethink its role in the light of the current and likely future developments I have outlined.

Just in case anyone should misunderstand me, I am not proposing that we should all become multidisciplinary in our expertise or interests; although I do think it important that, as our teaching and research cross over traditional disciplinary boundaries, we will need to read and study well outside our own area of training. But what I am suggesting is that disciplinary parochialism and educational insularity (to use David Blake's expressions [Blake, 1987]) have no place in the teaching of IB; and that the kind of problems we are interested in solving require joint intellectual inputs, which, when properly organized, provide an output greater than if the inputs were provided separately. This, indeed, is the quintessence of any holistic program of study. And I am also of the opinion that international business departments at universities and business schools, and the AIB among the professional associations, have an important – indeed unique – organizational task in minimizing the transaction costs of such studies. For while I would contend that it is the perceived high transaction costs of the kind of scenario I have portrayed that has so far prevented us from a realignment of our teaching and research alliances, I also believe that the costs of not seeking to capture the benefits of cross-disciplinary integration may be even greater. For without such a focus of interest, I think there is a real danger of the component disciplines of IB splintering off and scholars reinforcing their prime allegiance to their unidisciplinary parents. AIB would then be left as a 'hollow' association.

SOME POLICY PRESCRIPTIONS

Finally, I want to return very briefly to some of the challenges I identified earlier, and in the light of what I have just said, ask what, if anything, the AIB can do about them. First, recruitment and training. I think the AIB must promote the distinctive intellectual character (and difficulties) of its subject matter and of IBS in general, so as to convince those in authority in our universities to recognize the challenges of the subject and the capabilities of those who pursue their studies (sometimes in collaboration with scholars in other disciplines) outside their own subject area and publish their results in other than mainstream journals. At the same time, I would urge AIB members, and especially, I might say, its leading scholars, to publish in mainstream unidisciplinary journals and to take a lead within their own schools and departments in influencing decisions which have implications for IBS. Concurrently AIB members need to recruit more of the leading scholars in the disciplines making up IB to the AIB, by offering them an interdisciplinary perspective which they are unable to obtain from other sources. At a different level, we need to publicize the work of and unique characteristics of AIB to the deans of business schools and of faculties in which AIB members work. The ASCSB itself has its own international affairs committee on which the president of AIB sits as an ex officio member. In spite of the valiant efforts of the committee to date, too many deans appear to be unfamiliar with the intellectual content of IBS, and its contribution to mainstream business studies or, indeed, of the work of the AIB. They also seem too easily persuaded in their role as faculty recruiters, and members of promotion committees by the chairmen of unidisciplinary departments who, themselves, may have even less knowledge, and certainly less interest, in IB. We must preach the value of IB as a subject in its own right and one of critical relevance to modern management, and the need for those who contribute to it to be rewarded accordingly.

On training, I hope the AIB – and more especially the regional chapters – will continue and extend their 'on the job' training for younger faculty members. At the same time the AIB, possibly jointly with sister associations, might consider a series of interdisciplinary doctoral or post-doctoral seminars. Could we, the AIB, consider promoting such a tutorial with the Academy of Management or the equivalent associations in finance, marketing, sociology and organization? Or, should we perhaps arrange more joint sessions at our annual meetings with associations like the AEA or AMA? Should we, or our regional chapters, attempt to become more seriously involved with international or regional studies associations? This idea of jointly organized meetings extends well beyond the training functions, of course; and, in the future, I hope the Executive Board of AIB will actively encourage joint sessions with some at least of its sister associations, including those covering subjects outside the mainstream of business, e.g. business history, economics, geography, law and political science.

Second, the AIB, through its publicity, annual meetings, training programs, regional chapters, newsletters and *JIBS*, and the research of its members, must preach the interdisciplinary message. It is possible I am exaggerating the role of cross-disciplinary research. I certainly don't mean to downplay the unique contributions of the individual disciplines; and I accept that most of the monographs and articles on IB will continue to reflect a unidisciplinary perspective. But if AIB does have a distinct role to play, and if it is to play it effectively, then it must give much more attention to integrating the various interest groups and work programs, including those subject areas I have already mentioned as not being part of business schools. If it is possible, and in the not too distant future, I would like to see *JIBS* publishing a 'state of the art' issue on *Interdisciplinary Paradigms and Issues in International Business*. I also hope that the regional chapters will focus more on conference topics that allow interdisciplinary contributions; and not hesitate to ask specialists in areas germane to IBS, who have not worked in the international arena, to apply their mind to some of the issues of common interest and concern. By such means, the quality of IBS will improve, and as it does, I believe that some of the challenges currently facing its practitioners will disappear.

Third, I hope that AIB will lend what support it can to a rigorous restructuring of the teaching and research in IB. This it will primarily have to do through its members, acting either in their personal capacity or as members of other like-minded associations. But the Academy can play its part, as it has done already, by collecting and interpreting data on new experiments in teaching IB, and by organizational as well as pedagogic and research-based discussion sessions at conferences and seminars, especially those related to cross-disciplinary teaching and research projects. I am fully aware of the difficulties of running interdisciplinary teaching programs. At the same time it is not unreasonable to suppose that students reading for the Ph.Ds or those attending executive training programs should have an intellectual capacity and curiosity which extends beyond the confines of their own subject interests and be able to assimilate techniques and methodologies that cut across disciplines. Surely in pursuing this kind of training at least we should be bold enough to present an interdisciplinary perspective.

I do not go along with the proposition that you have to have a degree in law to appreciate the legal implications of transfer pricing or the elements of interfirm cooperative agreements; or that you need a training in political science to discern the major political ramifications of IB for the sovereignty of nation states; or that you have to master all branches of economics to comprehend the rudiments of transaction costs and market failure; or that you need a formal qualification in social anthropology to value the importance of culture as a variable influencing business practices or government intervention in industry; or that you need to have read social ecology or business history to understand fully the emergence and growth of MNEs, and their changing interaction with their environment.[15] I believe that any Ph.D student worth his salt should be able to pick up enough of the technical apparatus of any subject area, while maintaining and advancing his own special interests, to benefit fully from an interdisciplinary approach to at least some parts of his program of studies. For myself, I find it much more rewarding to teach a group of students from different disciplinary backgrounds, interested and well motivated in IB, to discuss questions of (say) the implications of cross-border strategic alliances for acquisition and merger policy; the impact of biotechnology on the organization of the international pharmaceutical industry; the ethical implications of Bhopal and Piper Alpha (the North Sea oil rig disaster in 1988); or the impact of culture on cross-border transaction costs, than I do to teach students all of whom have a first class degree in economics only interested in model-building or utilizing their econometrics, but who know little, and usually want to know little, about the variables *they* want to take as given. There must be room for academic excellence by grafting on, and integrating the relevant parts of other disciplines with a particular disciplinary specialization; and this should be the common meeting point of all scholars of IB. This I believe is what AIB should be about, and what its members should seek to encourage. I know a few scholars and departments have moved along this path with success; the rest of us need their help and guidance, as well as that of others who have been less successful, in helping to form our own strategy.

Finally, and perhaps more controversially, I think AIB must gain more allies for what it is seeking to do in the academic community from outside that community, and especially from international business itself. I appreciate that AIB wants to remain independent of any factions or special-interest groups, and this I fully endorse. But I wonder if we, as an organization promoting IBS, are doing enough to publicize the relevance and cogency of our subject to the business community, or are benefitting from an exchange of ideas as much as we might. Of course, most of us are involved with business corporations, sometimes at the most senior level. We act for them as consultants; we serve with them on government task forces and commissions; we mine them for money and information. At our universities, we use them on policy-oriented committees and advisory boards, and welcome them as guest lecturers; and occasionally at academic conferences we invite them to present papers or act as discussants. But between AIB and the business community I see a communication gap. There are still too few executives, economists or other professionals working in MNEs who are members of AIB. Too often we think of the corporate managers as being interested only in making decisions on day-to-day and firm-specific issues; and they think of our research and teaching as being overtly esoteric, too general, and of little immediate relevance to decision taking. I can't believe either of us is so naive not to recognize there is so much more we can contribute to each other's interests and concerns, and that beneath apparent differences in goals and perspectives, IB practice and study – or what might be loosely called the art and science of IB – have a great deal in common.

We do well also to remember that the practice of IB has gone through waves of organizational and ownership change, as has the methodology and logistics of decision taking. There still remains room for the functional specialist; technical qualifications and skills are still much valued assets, especially in finance and marketing. I also accept that in their recruitment of MBAs most of the leading MNEs do not give a high priority to IB skills. At the same time there are pressures for undergraduate and graduate business programmes to include some language training, some teaching on cross-cultural communications, and at least the rudiments of the international political and legal environment. By contrast, at an executive (and particularly senior management) training level, the skills required are more those of adaptability, interpersonal relationships, negotiating with governments, leadership and entrepreneurship, each of which requires an input from a variety of disciplines. This, in turn, I believe, reflects the fact that the practice of IB is increasingly involving the input of specialists from a variety of disciplines. How else might one explain the growing number of lawyers, psychologists, sociologists, political scientists and organizational theorists being employed by such companies?

CONCLUSION

In conclusion I would like to make one final parallel between the practice and study of IB. Contemporary research suggests that the possession of a core asset or assets (a particular product or technology, or access to essential inputs) is not, by itself, sufficient to ensure business success.[16] To fulfil their potential – to appropriate their full economic rent – core assets must be properly coordinated with a network of complementary assets at different points of the value-added chain. A failure to control properly the quality of components, or to make the necessary modifications to machinery or equipment, or to develop or acquire adequate and efficient distribution channels, might turn a brilliant innovation into a commercial disaster. Moreover, the importance of such complementary assets is likely to increase where these assets serve different core assets and/or where the core assets become mature or imitated by competitors. It is also likely to be the case that the complementary assets play a more important role in the success of international than domestic business.

Apply this concept, if you will, to IBS. Assume the discipline of the scholar is his core asset; assume too that to be exploited efficiently, this may require to be combined with other disciplines – these are his complementary assets. If, as in the *practice* of IB, the role of complementary assets – which essentially are those that arise from the economies of common governance – are becoming more important due *inter alia* to the increasing role played by transactional relationships in the success of the firm; so in the *study* of IB, if the property rights of the unidisciplinary scholar are to be fully appropriated, he (or she) may need to combine this knowledge with the insights of other disciplines much more systematically in the future than he (or she) has done in the past. Finally if the kind of common paradigmatic approach I have suggested in this chapter helps to bring the disciplines together, it will surely offer a fruitful avenue both for a more constructive dialogue between those concerned with the future of IBS, and for a more stimulating environment and better career prospects for our members.

Part II
Challenges for theorizing about MNEs and MNE activity

Introduction

In this part of the volume we identify and consider three new thrusts of research by scholars in their theorizing about the determinants and effects of MNE activity. They are by no means the only areas of new research,* but they represent some of the new thinking of the present author over the past five years or so.

The first thrust concerns the extension of the internalization paradigm to explain the *raison d'être* both of the changing form of governance by MNEs and of cooperative agreements; and also to consider more carefully those aspects of transaction costs which are uniquely associated with the trans-border activity of firms. In discussing these issues, Chapter 2 also examines the role of one particular variable influencing the form of international business to which scholars are now paying increasing attention, viz. culture. To what extent is culture a location bound asset; and if and when it is transferrable across national boundaries, what is the organizational mode by which this is best achieved?

The second thrust concerns the efforts of international business (IB) scholars to dynamize the theory of MNEs and MNE activity. Chapter 3 reviews some of these efforts to date, and concludes that apart from a limited amount of model building, most progress is still limited to the conceptualization of the main issues involved. The nature of the interface between the competitive advantages of firms and those of countries over time is gaining rather more attention; and an analysis of the determinants influencing this interaction is set out in Chapter 3. The role of strategy, which until recently has been the preserve of business analysts, is now engaging the interest of the economist and organizational theorist. In Chapter 4 we identify

*For an excellent review of the contemporary state of the art on this subject see Toyne and Nigh, 1993.

strategic change as a 'dynamized add on' variable to the eclectic paradigm of international production, and attempt to show the process by which autonomous or induced strategic change link the OLI configuration facing firms in one period of time and that of another period of time. Chapter 3 also traces the interaction between different kinds of FDI and the stages of economic development a country might pass through; and, indeed, the extent to which inbound and outbound MNEs may affect the speed and pattern of development.

The third theoretical thrust concerns the determinants of impact of MNE activity on the competitiveness and economic restructuring of countries. Chapter 5 takes Michael Porter's 'diamond of competitive advantage' (Porter, 1990) and specifically introduces a multinational business activity (MBA) variable into it. More particularly, it theorizes about the likely affects of outward and inward direct investment on the ingredients of competitiveness; and observes that *inter alia* this will critically vary according to the nature of the MNE activity and the specific locational characteristics (including government policies) of the countries which are home and host to this activity. As more and more governments are placing national competitiveness higher on their political agenda and as the role of MNEs is becoming more important in the global economy (UNCTC, 1991), the way in which each affects the other seems likely to become a top research issue of the 1990s.

2 Micro- and macro-organizational aspects of MNEs and MNE activity

INTRODUCTION

The contributions by economists to our understanding of the determinants of foreign production and the growth of the multinational enterprise have taken two different but complementary forms. The first attempts to identify and explain the unique characteristics of the MNE *qua* MNE; while the second has tried to explain the determinants of the foreign value-added activities of MNEs irrespective of whether they are due to their multinationality. Over the years, the distinction between these approaches has become increasingly blurred with the result that some of the richness of the two strands of thought has become devalued in unnecessary and fruitless controversy. In this chapter, we shall take as given the reader's knowledge of the basic tenets of the micro-theories of the MNE and the more macro-oriented theories of MNE activity, including theories of foreign direct investment (FDI);[1] and shall concentrate on what the author perceives to be some of the more exciting challenges and pressing needs for research in each area over the next decade or so.

THE ECONOMICS OF THE MNE:
A MICRO-ORGANIZATIONAL PERSPECTIVE

Apart from the pure modelling of the MNE – a task which, no doubt, will continue to fascinate the economist way into the twenty-first century – and what, to some pure theorists, is the only legitimate contribution he can make to the debate – it is likely that, in the future, economic analysis, by itself, will play a less dominant role in theorizing about the MNE than it has done in the past. At the same time, economic analysis, in conjunction with other disciplines, especially organizational theory, seems set to offer several new and existing insights into both the determinants of MNE behavior and the inter-action between MNEs and other economic agents.

It seems probable that an increasing number of cross-disciplinary strategic alliances will be concluded in the 1990s. This is because in order, to understand properly the form, content and consequences of the emerging globalization of economic activity, the international business (IB) scholar needs to be much more eclectic in his intellec-tual foraging. In particular, although the word can be easily over-played, culture – by which is meant the ethos of a particular group of people, as revealed, *inter alia*, by their attitudes, ideologies, values and social mores, and the private and public institutional framework which gives expression to this ethos – is likely to become center-stage in much of IB research over the next decade or more.

Most surely, the most significant contribution by micro-economists to our understanding of the MNE, *qua* MNE, is the application of internalization theory (or, as it is sometimes more appropriately called, the internalization paradigm) to explain cross-border hier-archical transactions. Yet, in many ways, such an analytical perspec-tive, which stems from the twin disciplinary stables of Ronald Coase and Oliver Wiliamson, although developed to explain the emergence and growth of the MNE, has made greater inroads into the theory of the multi-activity firm than the theory of MNE *per se.* This is because, true to its neoclassical tradition, its main tenets take some of the more interesting influences on the behavior of MNEs, *qua* MNEs, as exogenous variables; the result of which is that many of the aspects of market failure, which are uniquely cross-border, have received less attention than those which are not.[2]

There are, of course, exceptions. The response of firms to im-perfections in international capital and exchange markets has long occupied the attention of finance scholars. But, industrial organiza-tion theory, as extended to explain the interface between the behavior of firms and the structure of regional or global market structures in which they compete, has made very little allowance for the kind of parameters that are fixed when the firm operates in a country, but must be considered variable between countries, or between groups of countries. The MNE is different from the uninational multi-activity firm precisely because it operates within different national or location bound environs. Indeed, as an organizational entity or system of cross-border relational interactions, one of the main tasks of an MNE is to understand, reconcile and assimilate into its own corporate culture, a miscellany of disparate country or regional ideologies, perceptions, laws and regulations, in a way which best advances its global strategies.[3] Behind the identification and evaluation of the different kinds of cross-border market failure which may both prompt the internationalization of value-added activity and determine its form, lies the questions 'Why?', or 'What causes markets to fail?'. Are these market impurities technical and *culture neutral,* or do they arise specifically because of the costs of establishing and maintaining transactional and other commercial relationships which, more often than not, are *culture related.*

Different perceptions of time and punctuality in Spain, Jordan, India and Canada may affect the interfirm transaction costs of the procurement of (say) a CTV set. Differences in values of workers toward authority, incentives, loyalty, teamwork and commitment in Japan, the US and Nigeria may affect the costs of maintaining labor productivity and discourage or encourage shirking. Differences in laws and regulations in Sweden, Pakistan and Columbia, with respect, e.g. to the environment, mergers and property rights may create a 'constitutional uncertainty' in trade and FDI, which poses coordination problems of a special type for interacting economic agents.[4]

While the determinants of some of these culturally related transaction costs are idiosyncratic – or even firm specific – others may be generalized about; and it is the identification and evaluation of these generalizations which has prompted multidisciplinary coalitions among scholars, with the objectives and form of the alliances being determined by the 'lead' discipline. Taking, as an example, economics as the lead discipline, the economist needs to join forces with management, organizational and legal scholars, and these, in turn, may need an input from other disciplines interested in the make-up of a country's culture,[5] and the way in which particular systems of governance can handle them.

Intrafirm relationships

It is our contention that such a networking of scholars is necessary better to appreciate and explain both intra- and interrelationship firms now being forged, and, indeed, the interface between the two.

One of the features of the last decade, which seems set to dominate intellectual discussion in the 1990s, is the nature of the dynamic interplay between cooperative and combative transnational modes. For example, organizational scholars are now questioning the concept of the *hierarchy* as the main mechanism for organizing commercial, non-market transactions, at least in large global firms. In pointing to MNEs such as IBM, SKF and ICI, in which key resources and capabilities are geographically dispersed, cross-border flows of knowledge, information and ideas are multidimensional, communication is lateral, and there is a strong sense of shared values and mission among the different parts of the organization, the interplay of decision taking is better described as a *heterarchy*.[6]

Yet, if the cross-border costs of internal decision taking, which are culturally related, increase as one moves from a series of dyadic and unidimensional relationships to a network of cooperative relationships geared to advancing the global strategy of the hierarchical core; the complications which arise in balancing the economies of organizational integration with that of organizational localization, in situations where intrafirm communication is multidimensional, lateral and between multiple centers of decision taking are even more daunting. This is one reason why the systems approach taken by Mark Casson and others in dissecting the core attributes of large MNEs of the 1990s offers considerable promise for economic and business analysts.[7]

At the same time, the identification and measurement of culturally related transaction costs, and an analysis of the way in which these might be surmounted, circumvented or minimized, remain largely unchartered territory. Many of the empirical advances so far made in this area rest on the differences perceived between the microorganizational practices of Japanese MNEs and those of their Western counterparts.[8] While some attention has been given to the organizational differences between European and North American MNEs, most scholarly effort has so far sought to explain technical, rather than culturally related, differences, and rarely have these been embodied into either particular or general theories of MNE behavior. Indeed one suspects that this may be one of the reasons why scholars, businessmen and politicians have made so little headway in explaining much of the conflict which arose between MNEs and the governments of host developing countries in the 1960s and 1970s. Frequently, in their negotiations, the two parties were on completely different cultural wavelengths, and, because of this, they misunderstood or mistrusted the other's objectives and actions.

As an increasing number of MNEs are now emerging from a non-North Transatlantic culture, and as more cooperative ventures are involving partners from South East Asia, Latin America and Eastern Europe, one might expect a greater diversity of cultural interaction, which might be expected to raise intrafirm transaction or relational costs[9] – except where the introduction of new, and culture free, organizational methods may lessen hierarchical or heterarchical tensions.

It is not the purpose of this chapter to detail the intercountry, cultural differences which might add to intrafirm organization costs. Instead we wish to explore the premise that firms which are best able to identify and reconcile such differences, and utilize them to their gain, are likely to acquire a noticeable competitive advantage in the global marketplace. Borrowing from Lipsey (1991), we shall refer to such ownership (O) specific advantages as cultural competitive advantages, or – and Part III will explore this notion in more detail as is more relevant to the macro-theory of MNE activity – the comparative advantage of national cultures or attitudes.

The outcome of such MNE management may show itself in various ways, well beyond the organization of decision taking *per se*. These include the types of innovatory and product strategy adopted, the location of production and the methods of advertising and training methods employed. In particular, the techniques and capability of an MNE to transfer its intrafirm domestic organizational capabilities to a foreign location may rest on the transaction costs associated with the adaptation of these methods, or the costs of replanting them in an unfamiliar or uncongenial environment. The literature recognizes that organizational methods, particularly those which may require substantial modification to well established practices (e.g. industrial relations procedures), take much longer and are likely to be more expensive to transplant than machine intensive production techniques and processes (Kogut, 1990; Kogut and Parkinson, 1993); and that the extent and speed of the transfer is likely to vary according to the cultural distance between the investing and recipient country and the experience of the investing firm in the foreign country (Franke, Hofstede and Bond, 1991).

Studies of the governance of Japanese and US corporate activity have highlighted the differences in the cross-border market failure experienced by the two groups of firms and their organizational responses to them.[10] As to the major differences, two, in particular, might be highlighted. These are first the production systems employed, and second the structuring of the internal labor market (which includes such considerations as the recruitment, training and allocation of labor within the firm, compensation and promotion systems and their incentive and motivational effects) (Lincoln, 1993).[11]

As to the first, we may compare and contrast the Toyota Production System (TPS) adopted by some of the large Japanese MNEs in fabricating (and especially in the motor vehicles sectors), and the Mass Production System (MPS) – sometimes call 'Fordism' – which their US counterparts pioneered later this century.[12] Each differently affects both the production and relational costs of value-added activity. At the same time, each system demands adherence to a different set of rights, objections and responsibilities, the nature and character of which is at least partly culture specific, even though this specificity may not necessarily be linked to a particular country.[13]

Second, Japanese firms appear to strive to minimize relational costs by encouraging a sense of group loyalty, commitment to equality and a strong work ethos; the Americans rely more on the 'carrot' of monetary incentives, the 'stick' of unemployment, and the written contract between the two or more parties to an agreement.

The options available to US and Japanese MNEs to respond to unfamiliar cultural environments are broadly the same. First, they might try to avoid potential combative situations altogether, by adapting to local customs (this is likely to be practiced where the conflicts are relatively unimportant, and/or can only be resolved by the localization of organizational methods). Second, they may avoid conflict by exercising direct control over the areas where such conflict is serious enough to undermine the long-term strategy of the firm. However, the emphasis on these alternative routes differs in the two groups of firms. While, e.g. in the past, US affiliates have largely conformed to local personnel practices (except in respect of incentives), Japanese MNEs while being prepared to localize their wage systems, have strongly inculcated the management of their affiliates with the philosophy of Japanese working practices and industrial relations. Moreover, while US MNEs prefer US expatriates to be in charge of their sales and marketing functions, Japanese MNEs are more likely to have Japanese nationals employed in either the top or second-to-top position in finance and accounting, production and in the purchasing department (Dunning, 1993a).

Of course, the extent and complexity of intrarelational transactions, both between different parts of an MNE system and within a particular affiliate, will vary with the extent and form of foreign value added activities. In the main, the globalization of Japanese MNEs is still in its infancy. In 1989, the foreign production of their leading industrial companies averaged less than 10 per cent of their total production; the corresponding figure for US MNEs was 29 per cent. Probably less than 2 per cent of the total R&D undertaken by Japanese MNEs is currently conducted outside Japan: the corresponding figure for US MNEs in 1990 was 13 per cent.[14] Up to now, the local value-added content of Japanese affiliates in most European countries is considerably less than that of US or other European

MNEs. As this rises – and it is rising – both the number of trans-actions and the likelihood of higher relational transaction costs are also likely to grow. Thus, the real test of the capability of Japanese MNEs to internationalize the kind of competitive cultural advantages that initially helped them establish a premier position in some world markets remains to be seen (Gittleman and Dunning, 1992; Dunning, 1993b).

In general, however, there are several reasons to believe that, relative to pure production costs,[15] the transaction costs of economic activity will continue to rise in the 1990s – whatever their organiza-tional form may take. We have also suggested that part of the trans-action costs of firms associated specifically with their cross-border operations will also become relatively more significant; and that any systemic economies of scope, scale or flexibility may well be outweighed by the costs of culture specific intrafirm decision taking. Whether or not this does, in fact, occur depends on the ability of firms from different cultures to overcome the relational costs of technological advances and environmental change; and the pace and pattern of the globalization of production. Any advances in the theory of the MNE, *qua* MNE, must then surely await a better under-standing of (a) the content of these costs, (b) how they vary according to the particular characteristics of countries, industries and firms and (c) what is the appropriate organizational route for replacing surmounting or minimizing them, relative to the benefits they confer.

Interfirm relationships

In some ways, however, a more needful area of research, and certainly a no less challenging one, is that which arises from the growth of cross-border strategic business alliances (SBAs). Although not new, the motivation and character of these non-equity ventures has changed over the last decade. As with FDI – at least within the Triad – the objective of many SBAs is to *acquire* a competitive advantage; while the selection of partners, the concordance of management goals, attitudes and strategies, and the synergy of capabilities have become more important ingredients of success.

Interfirm alliances are of especial interest to the scholar of the MNE because they open up new organizational modes which possess some of the features of markets and hierarchies, but also some of their own. Although they are part of a hierarchical strategy of the participating firm and may be driven by market imperatives (particularly in the final goods markets), they do not fit neatly into Williamsonian or Coasian paradigms.

Both the rationale for and the implications of SBAs, for our theorizing about the MNE, have been discussed extensively in the literature[16] and this chapter will not repeat what has already been written. Instead, it will make just two points. The first is that, viewing the multi-activity firm as an initiator and organizer of a system of transactional linkages, increasing attention is now being given to the nature and form of these linkages *as a competitive or ownership (O) specific advantage in its own right*. Second, in our complex technological age, it would seem that not only are fewer and fewer transactions of intermediate products being conducted at arms length, but that the nature of the interface between differently owned firms – be it one between buyers, sellers, or buyer and seller – is increasingly taking on the characteristics of an intrafirm relationship.

This *de facto* convergence between the two sets of relationships reflects changes in both. On the one hand – as in a marriage – the real binding force of an interfirm alliance rests not in the formal terms of the agreement, but on the trust and forbearance established between the two parties. On the other, as we have already seen, the complexities of organizing a global firm suggests that an authoritarian hierarchical relationship is giving way – in part at least – to a cooperative heterarchical relationship. Such a relationship is governed less by authority and more by the need to benefit from a sharing exchange of ideas, knowledge, values between parts of a heterarchy, so that the heterarchy, as a system, may flourish.

Obviously, the notion of intra- and interfirm cooperation – replacing interfirm contractual or intrafirm hierarchical relationships – can be pushed too far; and it is easy to wax lyrical about the benefits of cooperation while, in practice, intra- and intercorporate rivalry conflict and strife abound. But, two points might be made. The first is that technological developments and changes in the world economic environment are exerting an increasing pressure on firms to cooperate along and between value-added chains if they are to compete effectively in the global marketplace. The second is that the organization and management of transaction intensive assets is becoming as important a competitive advantage as that of the 'harder' assets of resources, technology and human skills.

In this approach, which is echoed in the writings of various scholars, one is clearly influenced by the difference between the Japanese (or should we call it the Far Eastern?) way of conducting business relationships and most of the US and European way. Again, the literature is replete with examples of the way in which the Japanese MNEs conduct their interfirm relationships, especially with their supplier and industrial customers in such sectors as engineering and cars.[17] Words such as trust, loyalty, commitment, reciprocity, forbearance slip easily off the tongue, but those who have observed, not just the Japanese way, but that of all successful MNEs, cannot but be impressed by the attention given to the minimizing of culturally related transaction costs – including, in this instance, intercorporate cultural differences – as a prime target for success.

A recent analysis of the influence of alternative mechanism of interfirm transactions and governance on the success of firms – and particularly of Japanese car firms in Asia – is set out by Okada (1991). He argues very strongly that the cooperative interface between Japanese MNEs and their suppliers, not just in the *production* of car components, but in the *innovation* of new products, production processes and organizational structures stands out in marked contrast to the arms length and often adversarial relationships which frequently exist between US firms and their suppliers.[18] This point is reinforced by Jay Stowsky (1987) in his study of the semiconductor production equipment sector in the US in which he argues that rather than adopting a cooperative stance towards the design and manufacture of components and subassemblies, contracting firms view their suppliers as potential (if not actual) competitors.

But what, specifically, do the changing mechanisms of cooperative interaction (Okada prefers this word to transactions) have to do with the theory of the MNE, *qua* MNE? Simply this – and let me state it in terms of the emerging globalization of Japanese business. If one accepts that at least part of the success of Japanese firms in world markets is due to the way in which they handle their domestic (i.e. intra-Japan) interfirm relationships, the question arises that as and when the Japanese engage in foreign production, can they successfully export these relationships, and/or adapt them to the cultures of the host countries? Or, putting it rather differently, if the Japanese modes of governance are successful both inside and out of Japan, to what extent can US and European firms emulate or improve on them, or, indeed, innovate new methods even more appropriate to their own corporate needs?

One thing seems to be sure. The theory of the MNE needs to embrace more explicitly both intrafirm and interfirm relationships. While the markets versus hierarchies conundrum remains central; the focus of the 1990s seems likely to shift to the alternative forms of interactions formed by, or within, hierarchies (or heterarchies) and the way in which these affect the competitive position of the parti-cipating firms. And, it is precisely in this area of research that a juxtaposition of different disciplinary approaches is needed, even though the *tools* of the economist, provided by internalization theory, transaction costs, agency theory, and modern industrial organization theory offer an excellent framework for analysis.

MACRO-ORGANIZATIONAL THEORIES

In contrast to scholars concerned with explaining the conduct and behavior of MNEs, *qua* MNEs, others are more interested in explaining the growth of the foreign value-added activities of MNEs. Clearly, MNEs possess many characteristics *other* than their multi-nationality *per se*, although, as firms become more global, the attribu-tion of their behavior to any one set of characteristics is becoming increasingly difficult. However, any explanation of a country's changing propensity to be home or host to MNE related activity needs to consider other variables than those which interest the micro-theorist.[19] Moreover, at a meso- or macro-level of analysis, some variables which are exogenous to the micro-theorist themselves require explanation.

Here again, however, the features which distinguish the deter-minants of the foreign from the domestic value activities of MNEs lie in the different national environments in which they produce, and, just as the economist needs to join forces with organizational *et al.* scholars to understand the way in which firms organize their cross-border activities, so some appreciation of the theory of political science is necessary to inject an element of reality into explanations of MNE activity. For the purposes of our discussion, we shall deliber-ately confine the boundaries of political science to the role of the State as a form of governance of economic activity, and geared to the political goals of the authorities currently in power.

If the internalization paradigm, modified by an appropriate theory of strategic behavior, is the contribution of the economist to explaining the distinctive characteristics of FDI or the MNE, the eclectic paradigm, as modified by the introduction of a theory of political economy is at least a good starting point to explaining all kinds of MNE activity. But, it is only a starting point and in the light of both technological and environmental change, needs frequent reconsideration and reformulation. In particular, we would foresee progress along three fronts. The first concerns the dynamics or developmental aspects of international production. There are various strands to this emphasis. Some interesting work is currently being done by Ozawa (1992a) and others on the interaction between inbound and outbound MNE activity and the course of economic development and restructuring.[20] This includes the evaluation of the relevant O specific advantages of MNEs and location bound assets of countries; and the way in which MNEs choose to organize the inter-action between these two sets of advantages, in the light of their international strategies – as countries proceed through various stages or phases of development – as, for example, identified by economic historians (Rostow, 1959), business analysts (Porter, 1990) and development economists (Chenery, Robinson and Syrquin, 1986). Add to the staging of a country's development that of the internation-alization or multinationalization process of firms, and one has the rudiments of a theory of the development and the restructuring of MNE activity.

A second and related line of progress concerns the suggestion by some scholars (e.g. Lipsey, 1991) to more explicitly take account of a nation's culture as a component of its comparative advantages; and to acknowledge that as a country moves through various stages of its development, and, depending on its structure of resources and capa-bilities, the demands on the entrepreneurial and work culture of its people change. The culture best suited to advancing the needs of producers and consumers in the information and service economy of the 1990s is not the same as that needed for a mass production manu-facturing economy of the 1960s and 1970s, or that for the early stages of contemporary industrialization. The ability of a country to identify and sustain the culture most appropriate to its resources and capabilities, and to make the necessary adaptations to that culture as its resources and capabilitis (and the market for them) change, will give it an important head start on its competitors as a location for MNE activity.

The third front of progress, and again it is related to the other two, rests in the theory of asset accumulation and/or agglomeration in explaining both the changing composition of the universe of MNEs and ability of countries to attract inbound MNE activity. Here one is involved, at a micro- or macro-level, with the way in which firms network with each other to the benefit or cost of the strategic groups or countries of which they are part. The relevant analytical techniques are partly those of the economics of technological change, in the Schumpeterian tradition (e.g. Pavitt, 1987; Cantwell, 1989, 1990); and partly those of the economies of geographical agglomeration (Porter, 1990). However, the concept of technological accumulation needs to be widened to include all kinds of firm specific resources, including those of organization, learning and experience, those to do with establishing and nurturing cooperative interfirm relationships (Okada, 1991); and those which relate to the degree to which a firm can sustain its privileged asset position (Dierickx and Cool, 1989).[21] It could then be hypothesized that the growth of MNE activity is positively related to the capacity of MNEs to accumulate and effectively control an international portfolio of competitive advantages in the most cost effective way.[22]

At the same time, the location of MNE activity and its competitiveness, *vis-à-vis* indigenous firms, is also likely to be influenced by the ability of countries to offer and build up the (complementary) assets required by MNEs. Certainly, in the advanced industrial nations, there is reason to suppose that the availability of technological and social infrastructure necessary to support the core assets of MNEs is a powerful inducement both to attract inward investment and to facilitate outward investment.

The interaction between MNE activity and the accumulated assets of a nation, via e.g. technological transfer and competitive stimulus, has long been of interest to scholars, but is only now beginning to be formalized. In Dunning, 1993c, the author has attempted to set out how this interaction *may* vary between the phases of development of a country. While, without knowledge about the kind of MNE activity and the locational characteristics of the countries concerned, the path of international production cannot be predicted, it is possible to identify and evaluate the variables likely to influence the changes in the accumulated inward and outward inestment stock over time.

Advances in the explanation of MNE activity seem likely to focus as much on factors exogenous to MNEs as on those endogenous to it. In a lecture delivered at the University of Lund, Sweden in 1989 (later published in Dunning, 1990) I argued that perhaps too much emphasis had been given in the 1970s and 1980s to organizational issues and too little to changes in the external environment, in influencing both the extent and form of MNE activity. This theme is taken up in Chapter 3 of this volume, which identifies three critically important variables. The first is the course of world economic development itself; the second is technological progress which was, itself, partly influenced by multinationality of firms, and the third was the role of governments in affecting the ownership, locational and internalization (OLI) configuration facing firms.[23] We propose for the remainder of the chapter to limit our comments to the last factor, which is also the third of the strands of thought to which reference was earlier made.

While, by their actions, governments affect and are affected by the behavior of all firms, it might reasonably be hypothesized that, in a world increasingly dominated by MNE activity, these actions should take account of both the presence of such activity and their likely consequences on it. While the theory acknowledges this, it is perhaps not given the explicit attention it should. For, in a variety of ways, governments shape both the competitive advantages of domestic MNEs and the attraction of their location bound assets to inbound investors. As most dramatically revealed in the course of the last decade, they can fundamentally influence the way in which economic activity is organized, and also the ethos of their constituents towards such wealth influencing variables as savings, work, innovation, entrepreneurship, income distribution, quality of demand and so on.

While scholars like Porter (1990) would prefer to view governments as setting the framework within which a country's competitive advantages are created and sustained, because their actions may (but not necessarily will) represent an alternative organizational form of the governance of resource allocation to that offered by markets or firms, and/or may considerably influence the conduct of both firms and markets, we consider this variable to deserve special attention.[24] While this has been the case for many years, it may be argued that, in a global economy where the capabilities for production have to be created as well as the goods and services arising from such capabilities, where these capabilities can be moved across national boundaries with increasing ease and where the markets for intermediate and final products are becoming more costly to create and to operate efficiently, then the responsibility of national governments is increased. If this is correct, then any theory of MNE activity which does not explicitly seek to understand and explain the role of governments, not just as another variable, but, like the market, as an organizational entity is, in its own right, bound to be deficient.

The way in which the distribution of the governance of economic activity between governments, firms and markets impinges on the competitive strengths and weaknesses of firms and countries in their final goods market, and the strategic and organizational response of MNEs to these advantages, offers several challenges to the economist. Several well established analytical tools are available to him. Though mainly applied to explaining the choice between markets and hierarchies, transaction cost analysis can no less be applied to the reasons for which, and the extent to which, governments, directly or indirectly, may influence resource allocation.[25] The principles underlying strategic trade policy can be extended to other areas of government germane to MNE activity.

At the same time, these tools require the complementary assets of other scholars. It is impossible, for example, simply to transfer Japanese or Korean government policies out of their environment to (say) Spain or Nigeria and expect them to work. Some knowledge of the competitive theory of government behavior and of political institutions is necessary, not to mention wider issues of culture identified earlier. All this may not be good news to the 'pure' economist; however, for many years now, the IB scholar has argued for an interdisciplinary approach to his subject, simply because the key difference between international and domestic business issues lies in the legal, political and cultural characteristics which separate nations from each other.

CONCLUSIONS

This rather speculative chapter has tried to identify some – and only some – of the lacunae in the theories of MNE and MNE activity, and to suggest some of the avenues for further research in the 1990s. The chapter has suggested that the changing characteristics of intra- and interfirm relationships are requiring an extension and/or reappraisal of certain aspects of internalization theory; while the future explanations of the extent and location of MNE activity require more systematic treatment of the role of cultural and government related variables in affecting the OLI configuration facing MNEs and their strategic response to it. In both parts of the chapter, the need for an interdisciplinary approach has been stressed. Lest I might be accused of watering down the intellectual content of a single discipline, let me say that this is far from my intention. What I have in mind is for the assets of a core discipline, e.g. organization theory, economics, political science, marketing *et al.*, to be combined with the complementary assets of related disciplines. Only then will a systemic and holistic explanation of our subject matter be a realistic possibility.

3 The changing dynamics of international production[1]

INTRODUCTION

The dynamic interface between the internationalization of business enterprises and the environment of which they are a part has not engaged the recent interest of academic scholars as much as some other areas of international business (IB) research, e.g. the theory of the multinational enterprise (MNE). It is a difficult, even a messy, subject area to get to grips with, partly because it inevitably crosses disciplinary boundaries, and partly because it is unamenable to our tried and tested analytical techniques. But a series of dramatic events in the global economic scenario since the mid-1980s have forced researchers to give more attention to the way in which these events have affected not just the growth and form of foreign production, but the very path or trajectory of the internationalization process itself.

It is, perhaps, pertinent to observe that in the kind of world in which we live, any particular MNE one might like to consider is never likely to be in equilibrium, in the sense that it can be said to have achieved all the goals it sets itself. Similarly, at any particular moment of time, a country's competitive advantage is likely to be moving towards, or away from, its optimum position. Yet, most theories of international production which have emerged over the past 30 years[2] have tended to offer a snapshot explanation of the level and structure of the foreign value added activities of firms, or how these have changed between two points of time, i.e. a comparison between two or more snapshot views. Certainly, this would seem to apply to those theories which are of the Hymer-Kindleberger tradition, and also to some macro-economic approaches, e.g. that of Kiyoshi Kojima (1978, 1982, 1990).

Scholars from a business school tradition have always been more realistic and time-conscious in their study of firms; indeed some of the earliest writings on IB focused on the internationalization process *per se*.[3] But, such work, at least prior to some of the recent writings of marketing analysts such as Anderson and Gatignon in the US, Johanson, Wiedersheim and Vahlne in Sweden, and Luostarinen in Finland, was largely descriptive or qualitative.

One exception to this criticism were the studies of the Harvard Business School in the 1960s. The product cycle thesis (Vernon, 1966) was, perhaps, the first academic exercise in the dynamics of FDI. Moreover, its findings about the timing of new investments by US MNEs led to some early attempts to model the oligopolistic behavior of firms in international markets. The seminal thesis of Knickerbocker (1973), was taken up and extended by Flowers (1976) and Graham (1975) in their examination of the trans-Atlantic investment strategies of large US and European firms. More recently, Graham (1986, 1991) has tried to formalize some of the determinants of the strategies and to relate them to the extant theory of internalization.

Graham's current research is just one example of an attempt to bridge the approaches of some main stream economic and business school writings on the theory of the multinational enterprise. Another is the work of Michael Porter and some business school analysts. Porter distinguishes between the competitiveness of firms and that of countries, the interaction between which is the subject of one of his latest volumes (Porter, 1990). Earlier, in 1985, Bruce Kogut had considered these distinctions and their implications for the internationalization process (Kogut, 1985a, 1985b); while other papers by the same author (Kogut, 1983, 1987, 1990) traced both the changing nature of the competitive advantages of MNEs as their activities became increasingly global in dimension, and the way in which such enterprises both cope with, and turn to their own benefit, cross-border environmental volatility. Doz (1986) and Prahalad and Doz (1987) have related the types of organizational strategies MNEs might pursue in response to differential national economic policies.

There has been only a limited amount of work done on the dynamics of a country's international investment position, although reference might be made to the concept of the investment development path or cycle (Dunning, 1988a); to some research by Ozawa (1989) on the changing characteristics of Japan's outward investment; to some recent modelling of the MNE (Hill and Kim, 1988); and, to the dynamic interplay between inward direct investment and the accumulation of technological and organizational assets by indigenous economic agents or (to use an Italian expression) operators (Cantwell, 1989; Dunning and Cantwell, 1990).

This chapter considers some aspects of the process of the inter-action between MNEs and the economies of which they are part over the past two or three decades, by introducing an 'over time' variable into the eclectic paradigm of international production (Dunning, 1988a, 1993); and to see whether we can draw any lessons from this analysis for the likely direction of multinationalization in the 1990s. The 'over time' related variable we shall use in our framework of thought is that of 'strategic change' (St). In particular, we shall be concerned with the strategic path of the 'representative' firm (to use Marshall's expression), which is to be interpreted as a firm's learning experience and its continuous reaction to the success or failure of its past strategies, as revealed by their impact on its current ownership specific advantages, However, in the latter part of this chapter we will also consider the interaction between the actions of governments in response to the changing competitive advantages of countries for which they are responsible.[4]

The eclectic paradigm of MNE activity avows that at any given point of time, the level and composition of a firm's foreign produc-tion (FP) reflects its strategic response to first, the level and structure of its ownership specific (O) or competitive advantages; second the locational (L) or competitive advantages of the countries in which these advantages might be created, acquired, or exploited; and third to the opportunities open to the firm to internalize the market for its O advantages between the home and selected host countries. Assuming some kind of time lag is required to implement the firm's strategy then one could write

$FP_t = (f)\ OLI_{t-1}$ where

(f) represents the strategic response of the firm.

A firm's foreign production may change either because of a change in the configuration of its OLI advantages, or because it pursues a different strategy towards its existing configuration of OLI advantage changes. Let us denote any such strategic change as St. Consider first the factors which might influence a change in the L advantages offered by a particular country. Now, most of these variables are likely to be exogenously determined, although, as oligopsonists or monopsonists, MNEs may sometimes be able to affect their value (e.g. by lobbying or their negotiating or bargaining strategies with governments[5]). So, assuming a single period of time, viz. t to t+1, then:

$$\text{then } L_{t+1} = f\ (OLI_t\ S_{Lt}\ \dot{S}_{Lt}\ \rightarrow\ _{t+1}\ \dot{EXN}_{Lt \rightarrow t+1} \cdots \tag{1}$$

where $\dot{S}t$ is any change in the firm's strategy between time t and t+1, and $E\dot{X}N$ = any change in other endogenous or exogenous variables likely to affect L between time t−1 and t.

Similarly a firm's ownership (O) advantages at time t+1 represents the stock of its wealth creating and cost-reducing assets at that time, the value of which is, at least, partly determined by the cumulation of its past strategies towards, e.g. product development, organizational structure, acquisitions, vertical integration, risk management, marketing policy, foreign production, and so on; and partly by any changes in other endogenous and exogenous variables which might affect its O advantages between t and t+1.

$$\text{i.e. } O_{t+1} = f\,(OLI_t, S_{Ot}\,\dot{S}_{Ot} \to {}_{t+1} E\dot{X}N_{Ot} \to {}_{t+1}) \cdots \qquad (2)$$

Finally, the advantages of internalizing the market for its O specific assets (and any others it may seek to acquire) (i.e. its I advantages) will also depend on its past strategies to concluding intra- or interfirm transactions of intermediate products, and any changes in these strategies.

$$\text{i.e. } I_{t+1} = f\,(OLI\,S_{It}\,\dot{S}_{It} \to {}_{t+1} E\dot{X}N_{It} \to {}_{t+1} \cdots \qquad (3)$$

Combining the three previous equations we then have

$$OLI_{t+1} = f\,(OLL_t\,S_{OLIt}\,\dot{S}_{OLI} \to {}_{t+1} E\dot{X}N_{OLIt} \to {}_{t+1}) \cdots \qquad (4)$$

International production, at a future moment of time (t+1), then represents the accumulation of the strategic responses of firms to past OLI configurations, and to changes in these configurations induced by changes in the external environment and non-strategic endogenous variables. The strategic and non-strategic response of firms to their current OLI configurations (and actual or expected changes in these configurations) will determine the future pattern of their international production.

In examining the process of change in international production, it is useful to distinguish between *strategy led* and *strategy initiating* changes of firms. The former represent the response of firms to changes in the value of all those variables outside of their control, which may affect their behavior; and the latter, actions initiated by the firms themselves to alter either their OLI configurations or their strategy towards such configurations (e.g. as part of a learning process or a reevaluation of risk).

In practice, of course, it may be difficult to separate the effects of these endogenous and exogenous variables as there is a constant and iterative interaction between them. However, conceptually, it is worth trying to do so. The following section of this chapter, then, looks at some of the more important endogenous variables which have influenced the process of internationalization over the past two or more decades, and the third section (p. 61) at some of the more significant exogenous changes. In conclusion we examine the interaction between the two sets of forces, and attempt to draw some implications for our theorizing about the dynamics of international business activity.

ENDOGENOUS VARIABLES INFLUENCING STRATEGIC CHANGE

Decisions implemented by a firm to advance its strategic objectives will have both first order and second order effects. The former comprise those which impinge on its own O specific advantages; on its ability or willingness to internalize the markets for these advantages; and on how it responds to exogenous locational variables. The latter embrace the consequences of a firm's actions on the other players or operators in the economies in which it produces or the market it serves, e.g. its competitors, suppliers and customers, which may, in turn, affect its own competitive positions and strategic choices.

A firm's strategic options will mainly depend on its economic and behavioral characteristics, and on the number and kind of markets in which it operates. For example, a single product firm competing in a perfect market can pursue only one strategy. In order to earn the opportunity cost on its capital, it must behave as a profit maximizer. Moreover, it is completely constrained in the output it produces and the price it charges for that output. Even when supply and demand conditions change, the reactions of the firm are predetermined.

In an imperfectly competitive situation, a firm has two sets of choices. The one is whether to aim to maximize profits or to achieve some other objective or set of objectives. Faced with the prospects of earning a higher than average profit in a high risk situation or an average profit in a zero risk situation, two firms may behave differently because of their different attitudes toward risk aversion. The other is, given the objective or set of objectives chosen, what is the optimum strategy for the firm to achieve these objectives? The more numerous and varied the ways in which a firm may reach its goals, the greater its strategic leverage is likely to be, even though, *ex post*, there may have been only one best way to have reached these goals. Uncertainty may either constrain or widen choice depending on the entrepreneurial attitude of the firm's decision takers towards risk-bearing. Competition may also play a dual role; but, broadly speaking, the greater the similarity of a firm to other members of its own or related strategic groups (McGee and Thomas, 1986) the less its freedom of action is likely to be.

Clearly, however, in practice, firms do have some flexibility in their strategic choices, if for no other reason than that they are not supplying identical products to consumers. Take, for example, a toothpaste firm which discovers that one of its competitors has discovered a new ingredient which is guaranteed to eliminate gingivitis. What might its strategic reaction be? There are a large number of options; and the outcome of each may involve some degree of uncertainty. The firm could step up its advertising, or reduce the price, of its product. It could try to improve the quality of its existing brand. It could acquire another toothpaste company, hoping to strengthen its asset base and/or capture additional scale or scope economies. It could reexamine the geography of its foreign investment portfolio. It could consider diversifying into other products, or hiving off some of its peripheral activities to fund more resources for toothpaste production and marketing. It could increase its own R&D to discover its own cure for gum disease or related ailments. It could try to conclude some kind of cooperative alliance with the innovating firm or with another firm working on similar lines. The possible options are many and varied, even though *ex post* there may be only one optimal strategy.

Of course, to identify the possible strategic options open to firms is one thing; to predict the one most likely to be chosen is another. Economists have not, in general, paid much attention to the determinants of the growth paths or trajectories of firms. The strategic management literature is, so far, mainly descriptive or taxonomic, although some progress has been made both in identifying the key competitive strategies open to firms and the types of firms likely to pursue particular strategies or sets of strategies.[6] There has also been some work on the organization and the management of cross-border technological innovatory activities (Bartlett and Ghoshal, 1989). But, there has been little serious work done on the dynamics of structural change or on the way in which this change affects the internationalization of firms.

What then has been the direction of recent research into the dynamics of international business? Reference has already been made to the dynamics of entry strategy into international markets. In particular, interest has centered on the determinants of entry modes

(Anderson and Gatignon, 1986); and, here, the transaction cost theory seems to have evolved as the dominant paradigm. Another group of scholars has focused on the export versus foreign production and/or licensing choice, e.g. Hirsch (1976) but apart from the early studies by the Harvard School, only Buckley and Casson (1981) and Hill and Kim (1988) have introduced strategy related variables or a time dimension into their analytical frameworks.

The literature on the dynamics of international transfer and dissemination of technology has followed a similar approach. Magee's appropriability theory (Magee, 1981) and the work of Davidson and McFeteridge (1985) on the conditions under which technology is transferred across national boundaries, each point to a kind of technology cycle, by which a new and idiosyncratic technology is initially exploited by the innovating firm itself, but, as it becomes mature and standardized, is more likely to be transferred through a licensing or some other form of non-equity cooperative agreement.[7]

Other studies on the internationalization of firms have focused on the dynamics of foreign production *per se*. There have been various strands to this research. Much of the organizational and business history literature is concerned with patterns and organizational growth of multinational business. The ideas contained in Mira Wilkin's classic study on the growth of American multinational firms (Wilkins, 1974) and Howard Perlmutter's seminal article on the different types of organizational strategy (Perlmutter, 1969) have been extended to explaining the path of multinationalization from a simple freestanding or monocentric FDI through polycentric multi-domestic operations to a global and systemic network of value added activities.

Another group of scholars has sought to examine and explain the trajectory of a firm's foreign value-added activities, and, in particular, the conditions under which it may engage in backward integration (activities) from simple assembling operations, or forward integration from primary production. Some attention has also been given to tracing the path by which foreign affiliates may move from replicating at least some of the goods and/or services produced by their parent companies for the local market, to supplying a more specialized range of products for regional or world markets; and to how these changes in output composition and the value-added produced by foreign affiliates may affect the locus of decision taking within the MNE. All this research adds grist to our understanding of the metabolic or biological growth of multinational business.

At the same time, none of these studies – as far as we are aware –

explicitly examines the nature of the growth trajectories of firms, or the factors which might cause them to alter direction. Most studies, too, focus on a firm's response to discrete changes in its external environment over time, and do not concern themselves with the dynamic interplay between endogenous and exogenous variables.

The exception is the work of scholars who view MNEs as strategic oligopolists competing in global markets. Here, there is assumed to be a continual interplay between the major players in a market. Firm A takes some action, and in so doing, makes some assumptions about the likely response of firms B and C. But, firms B and C may react in a different way than that anticipated by firm A. This will then cause a shift in the value of the exogenous variables facing firm A, which, in turn, may prompt that firm to further modify its competitive strategies. Given such market conditions, the path of a firm or group of firms towards the goals it (or they) seeks to achieve is never smooth; rather it is a series of iterations of strategic action and reaction.

The common feature of all these studies is that they focus on a particular strategy of the MNE, and attempt to give it some kind of time dimension. But most of them are very micro-oriented and tend to take exogenous variables as a constant. Reinterpreted in the language of the eclectic paradigm, they are mainly concerned with the effect the internationalization process has on the O advantages of firms, and how these, in turn, may influence its organizational and locational strategies. The value of the studies is that they suggest that there are some fairly well recognizable routes of the internationalization process; and that the choice of routes firms might travel may be explained by reference to a number of firm, industry and country specific characteristics.

What next about the more general theories of international production? How far can they be modified to embrace dynamic elements? Peter Buckley (1988) has suggested that the injection of time into the theory of the multinational enterprise might help bridge any differences which exist between the eclectic and internalization paradigms – presumably because in any dynamic theory, a change in O advantages, which may legitimately be assumed to be endogenous in any static theory, must itself be explained. Mark Casson believes that the critical link between changes in a firms' competitive position over time lies in the theory of entrepreneurship (Casson, 1987).

Our own stance would be to focus on the continuous interplay between OLI variables and strategic change; and, in particular, to try to incorporate the effects which strategy may have on the endogenous variables affecting a firm's foreign value-added activities into the eclectic paradigm. In contrast to the internalization theorists, however, we believe that the *main* emphasis of any dynamic theory should be addressed to explaining the changing competitive advantages of firms. Such advantages may not only be protected or promoted by successful innovation, but by the ability of firms to choose the optimum location and to exploit differences in country specific costs and benefits; and by their opting for the right modality of the creation or use of the ownership advantages – be it the market, their own hierarchies, or cooperation with other economic agents. On this last point, this does not necessarily mean that an MNE, faced with market failure, will always seek to internalize these markets; in some cases, it may find it more cost effective to try and to reduce (or persuade governments to reduce) the market imperfections with which it is faced.

To illustrate the ideas expressed in the previous paragraph, consider some of the work currently being done by scholars on the relationship between inward direct investment and the innovatory capability of the recipient countries. Here, the usual hypothesis investigated is that the combination of the competitive advantages of foreign firms and the locational advantages of the countries which are host to their affiliates at time 't' may set up a chain of interrelated consequences, which will impact on the inward direct investment position and innovatory capacity of those countries in time t + 1. We will illustrate this with reference to just one piece of research (Dunning and Cantwell, 1990; Dunning, 1988b), which was concerned primarily with examining the interface between the strategy of multinationals, market structure and the technological competence of the industry in which they operate; but it is just the tip of the iceberg of some extremely interesting work now being done by some US and European scholars.[8]

The Cantwell and Dunning study looked at the impact of US direct investment in the UK on the path of the competitiveness of two industries, viz. motor vehicles and pharmaceuticals, the first which, until recently as least, had a very bad record,[9] and the second which is one of Britain's post-war success stories. In the first case, the presence and behavior of the US subsidiaries – Ford, General Motors and Chrysler – while initially stimulating the competitiveness of the UK motor vehicle industry, was eventually associated with a deterioration in that competitiveness to such an extent that the UK, once the leading exporter of cars in Europe, was, by the mid-1980s, the largest net importer of cars. Moreover, between 1978 and 1986, UK car producers registered comparatively fewer patents in the US than those of any other of their major European competitors (Cantwell and Hodson, 1991).

This series of events was not only (or even mainly) the result of the changing strategy of the US owned car producers towards their UK operations – particularly as a result of the formation of the European Economic Community (EC) – which caused each of the foreign producers to restructure their European operations. A protectionist government policy towards the car industry, unsophisticated UK consumers, a lethargic attitude by domestic car assemblers and component suppliers towards quality control, delivery dates and product and process innovation, outdated organizational procedures and poor industrial relations, and a failure of the leading car producers to capture a major share of the international market were no less significant causes.

Nevertheless, a reorientation in the managerial strategies of the three foreign owned companies set in train a series of events which, given the changes taking place in the exogenous environment in which cars were produced, eventually resulted in a declustering of value-added activities in the UK, and an erosion of its innovatory capabilities and competitive advantages. At a time when the European car industry was introducing many new models, utilizing innovatory production techniques and upgrading the quality of its output, this led to a further weakening of the UK as a locational base for both the car companies and their component suppliers which were becoming increasingly mobile in their siting of their European production. Here, then, the dynamic interaction and the strategic response of US owned car producers to changes in their exogenous environment was such as to put in train a downward spiral in the technological capabilities of the industry, and the attractions of the UK as a locational base.

The story of the pharmaceutical industry is a very different one. Here the presence of foreign based companies induced a spirited revitalization in the competitiveness of UK owned companies (some of which were already strong international producers – unlike the UK car makers). This resurgence in competitiveness was encouraged by a congenial and positive ambience for high value activity, including that fostered by the National Health Service, which exerted strong quality control over the drugs it purchased; the government's pricing scheme for ethical drugs and its active suppot of R&D; the first rate university research and clinical testing procedures offered by the UK; an excellent rapport between the medical profession and the health care industry; and strong indigenous production capabilities throughout the value-added chain and in other parts of the chemical industry.

These forces ensured a positive dynamic interaction between foreign and domestically owned companies. In the early 1980s, the UK based firms undertook 13 per cent of the world's R&D in pharmaceuticals while UK consumers bought only 4 per cent of the world's output of pharmaceuticals. For many years now, the UK has had substantial revealed comparative advantage in the patenting of new drugs and as a base for R&D by foreign owned firms (Cantwell and Hodson, 1991).[10] It is also the second largest international direct investor in pharmaceuticals. In this case, the sequence of events was that the presence and strategy of foreign owned multinationals helped to strengthen rather than weaken the competitive advantages of indigenous firms. This, in turn, led to intensification of the innovatory capabilities of the industry, and the attractiveness of the UK to high value inward investment.[11] There was no need for Government protection, as occurred in the car industry. Intense competition among the leading pharmaceutical MNEs, an excellent technological infrastructure, agglomerative economies and high standards of demand set by UK consumers were sufficient inducements to sustain and encourage entrepreneurial vision and the upgrading of human and physical capital in the industry.

EXOGENOUS VARIABLES INFLUENCING DYNAMIC CHANGE

We now turn to discuss some of the exogenous variables which have helped fashion the dynamics of international business activity over the past three decades. Changes in the value of such variables are even more difficult to hypothesize about than those endogenous to firms. One might recall, for example, the very low risk rating given to Iran by the leading risk analysts like Frost and Sullivan just before the Revolution in 1979; and who could have predicted, three years ago, the quite dramatic happenings now occurring in Central and Eastern Europe? At the same time, there is no reason to suppose the world is entering an era of political or economic stability; and although, in some instances, the course of world events may have only a marginal impact on economic development and the competitiveness of firms, others, as vividly demonstrated by recent events in India, China, Yugoslavia, Nicaragua and the Philippines, may be quite decisive. We now briefly consider three such variables affecting the role of MNE business in the world economy, viz. *economic development, techno-logical advance* and *the role of Government.*[12]

Economic development

For the past two decades the global economy has been undergoing a major realignment. According to observers like Kenichi Ohmae (Ohmae, 1985, 1987), the economy of the Western world is now dominated by a Triad of trading blocs. Western Europe, Japan and North America, between them, account for 75 per cent of the world's output and trade, and its companies account for about 80 per cent of all international production (UNCTC, 1991). Each of these blocs has its own geographical hinterland, in and between which there are particularly close trading and investment relationships. These hinter-lands probably account for another 10 per cent–12 per cent of the world's output.

Although the contribution of the various sectors of economic activity to gross national product varies between the member countries of the Triad; the industrial structure of each has increas-ingly converged over the past 30 years, during which period Japan has emerged as a major economic power and *Pax Americana* has passed the way of *Pax Britannica* 70 years earlier. Both technological advances and Government action have been responsible for this situation, and, barring unpredictable events or unusually inept macro-economic management, it is likely that this trend will continue in the foreseeable future. It seems also reasonable to suppose that at least some of the countries in the hinterland of the Triad countries will themselves become part of its core in the next decade. Taiwan and Korea in Asia and Brazil and Mexico in Latin America, Hungary and Czechoslovakia in Europe are examples. As more economies become industrialized and better off, the significance of trans-frontier trade and investment, which has always been strongly income-elastic, is likely to increase; although the geographical composition of the leading MNEs is, itself, likely to change.

Within both developed and developing economies, too, the role of both producer and consumer services in the value-added process has steadily increased.[13] However, even in the most advanced industrial countries, it is neither appropriate nor desirable to talk about de-industrialization, notwithstanding the fact that, in many developed countries at least, the numbers employed in manufacturing industry has fallen. The truth is that the interaction between the goods and services sectors is becoming increasingly complementary, with the one supporting rather than replacing the other. What also seems clear is that the composition of output – be it of goods or services – in the emerging global economy is becoming increasingly determined by the disposition and productivity of 'created' or 'engineered' resources rather than those of 'natural' resources. *Inter alia* this is shown by the marked fall in the percentage of primary goods and unskilled labor in the value-added of most products.

Since the quintessence of the MNE is that it is a purveyor, producer, organizer, user and transferor of 'created' factor endowments – especially of human capital, technology and information – it may be expected that these developments will favor its further growth. Much will depend, of course, on the extent to which the new information-based economy lowers or raises barriers to entry into particular markets; and whether it generates its own cross-border economies of scale and scope.

Technology

It is almost a truism to say that contemporary world economic growth is driven by advances in technological and organizational capacity. But, it is worth reminding ourselves that this is still a relatively new phenomenon, and that technology is not the only resource which is expanding. The active work force of the world is still very much on the increase, although the distribution of the increase is heavily skewed towards the Asian and Latin American countries. Moreover, in certain parts of the world, even large areas of land are being reclaimed. And, most exciting of all, but this is a development which must await the next century, is the exploitation of the huge riches of the sea bed.

In the paragraphs which follow, we shall highlight just four features about technology and innovatory activity which are especially relevant to an understanding of the dynamics of MNE activity. First, there has been a marked acceleration in all forms of expenditure on technology creation over the last decade. In 1990, all the leading industrial nations devoted a higher percentage of their GNP to non-defense R&D expenditure than they did ten years earlier – and in Japan and West Germany's case dramatically so (National Science Foundation, 1991); while between 1975 and 1986 the number of scientists and engineers engaged on R&D[14] increased by 50.1 per cent from 1,032 thousand to 1,558 thousand. In the decade ending in 1990, patents registered in the US by the five leading industrial nations, rose from 54.8 thousand to 102.1 thousand (or by 86.3 per cent). (US Department of Commerce 1992.)

Second, technology has become much more expensive. The R&D of many biotechnology, pharmaceutical, industrial, electronics and telecommunications companies is now measured in $ billions rather than $ millions.

Third, technology is becoming less industry or activity specific and more systemic in its application (Stopford and Baden Fuller, 1992). At the same time, advances in product and process development are needed to draw upon multiple technologis. Increasingly, the competitive advantages of firms seems to be shifting from the ownership of technological capacity *per se* to the ability to manage and coordinate such capacity.

Fourth, technological advances have spread both across value-added chains, and between different stages of the same chain. Information technology, in particular, has led to far reaching changes in the organization of economic activity. In some cases, it has reduced hierarchical or heterarchical costs, or has exposed the weakness of markets as a resource allocative mechanism. In others, it has helped encourage process and product specialization among firms, and aided market efficiency. In still others, it has fostered cross-border alliances and networks between firms. In the 1990s, we see an increasing tendency for firms to concentrate their assets in their core competences, and hive off the rest, unless they offer considerable synergistic economies (Pralahad and Hamel, 1990). At the same time, in order to maintain their competitive edge, these firms are having to look beyond their borders for assets and acquisition routes. Moreover, as demonstrated by some recent take-overs of US glass and cement companies by Mexican firms, and US fish and chicken processing companies by Thai and Indonesian firms (Haude, 1991), this restructuring of activities is not confined to developed country MNEs.

Each of these changes is basically irreversible, although not all its consequences are. Among the effects on international production which appear irreversible are the organization of the creation, acquisition and deployment of technology and human resources, and advances in transport, communication and information processing techniques, which favor both the multinationalization and the rationalization of value-added activities. Similarly, it is difficult to see the huge costs of innovatory activities being reduced in the immediate future, or of much dilution in the concentration of activity among the leading global oligopolists.

Advances in technology also have enormous implications for the international allocation of economic activity. First, they may affect the productivity and costs of individual factor inputs. Second, they may introduce completely new products with different spatial needs to those they replace. Third, they may affect the nature of the production process by altering the relative significance of natural and created factor endowments. Fourth, they may affect transport and communication costs. Fifth, they may affect the propensity of firms to spatially integrate their value-added activities. Sixth, they may affect the advantages of firms to cluster their activities in close proximity of each other. And seventh, they may affect the dynamics of market structure and the competitive process.

As far as the dynamics of international business are concerned, technological change (depending on how it impacts on value-added activities, may have either a centripetal (pulling in) or a centrifugal (pushing out) effects. Even if it encourages the decentralization of production, however, its impact on the competitive advantages of countries may be different. Thus, a fall in transport costs may allow firms to take better advantage of lower real labor costs in some developing countries, while the introduction of computer aided design and manufacturing equipment might encourage more spatial integration of activities along the value-added chain in advanced industrial economies.

On balance, within the OECD area at least, it would seem that, while recent technological advances have tended to favor more centralization of fundamental research activities by MNEs,[15] they are also leading to the dispersion of applied or specialized technological excellence between the US, Japan and Western Europe. An examination of the patents registered in the US by the world's largest companies, according to the location within the company at the discoveries were made, confirms that an increasing proportion of innovations of MNEs are originating from the foreign subsidiaries of MNEs – mostly elsewhere in the Triad (Cantwell and Hodson, 1991).[16] This suggests that firms, both at the cutting edge of new technology and imitators or followers in the technological innovation, are increasingly seeking a presence in each of the main innovatory centers of the world.

Sometimes, this presence takes the form of the setting up of listening or monitoring posts, sometimes of acquiring firms with complementary R&D activities to those engaged in by the acquiring firm, and sometimes that of specialized R&D facilities intended to produce innovations and ideas for the rest of the organization. To give just one or two examples, in Japan's Tsukuba Science City – a world class center for R&D – no less than eleven foreign owned chemical and pharmaceutical companies have set up research facilities (*Japan Update*, 1990); SKF, a world leader in ball bearings, has its R&D headquarters in The Netherlands, while German plastics processing machinery companies and Swiss surveying equipments have located research laboratories in the US to develop electronic controls (Porter, 1990).

The picture in developing countries is more obscure. It is our understanding that the increase in innovatory capacity in developed countries has not increased the transfer of 'hard' technologies to many developing economies, although some East Asian countries have created their own specialized clusters of technological competence. The point here is that differential technological growth may change the strategic grouping of countries. Korea, Taiwan, Hong Kong and Singapore, for example, are becoming more like Japan, West Germany and Italy and less like Kenya, Ecuador and Sri Lanka. At the same time, new forms of telecommunications have aided the transfer of some forms of 'soft' technology, e.g. computer soft-ware, managerial and organizational technologies, which by lowering cross-border hierarchical and interfirm transaction costs are helping developing countries both to upgrade their indigenous resources and to attract more inward direct investment.

Technological change, then, has widespread implications for all aspects of international business activity. Its specific impact on the MNE has been first to lower the marginal costs of cross-border common governance and networking. Second, because of the increasing cost of innovations, their increasingly generic characteristics, and the faster rate of dissemination and obsolescence of many technologies, MNEs are being encouraged both to specialize more in the kinds of R&D they undertake, and to conclude more cross-border alliances to capture synergistic, scale and risk sharing benefits. Hence, we see the emergence of galaxies or networks of MNEs – centered around a group of core activities – with firms within the galaxies being differentiated by the particular technological packages they create, assemble and manage, and the particular relationships they have with other members of the galaxy.[17]

The role of government

We finally consider the role of government as an exogenous variable influencing the dynamics of international production, although some writers (e.g. Rugman, 1989; Franko, 1989) have argued that, as governments increasingly take on the role as protectors or promoters of the competitive advantages of their firms, they will become more sensitive to the lobbying of these same firms.[18]

However, it is one thing to describe and explain the way in which governments may interact with international business. It is altogether another to predict the nature of the interaction, and how this may change over time. But one thing is sure. Were we able to model government involvement in economic affairs in the early 1990s, that model would be very different from that of 15 years ago; and, no doubt, today's model may be inappropriate by the turn of the century. It also seems that no one model can hope to capture all aspects of government behavior simply because such behavior displays a feature which makes scientific prediction impossible, viz. it is inconsistent in the objectives it seeks to achieve, or in the priority it assigns to these objectives.

Can one point to any changes in government–business relations in the 1980s that helps better understanding of the dynamics of international production? We think so because we believe that inexorably, *in the long run*, government policies are as much fashioned, or indeed controlled, by changes in the two exogenous variables we have discussed, as they are shapers of these variables. Indeed, we would argue, that in most of the developed world, their ultimate (but not immediate) power to effect the economic destiny of their citizens and institutions is eroding all the time. For countries which have not yet achieved a Rostowian take-off (which is now at a very different point in development than when the concept was first put forward by its author in 1959), the situation is different; and whatever government is in office, and for so long as it remains in office, it has considerable latitude to affect the disposition and productivity of, at least, its domestic resources and capabilities.

We might identify three factors likely to influence the future path and pattern of government involvement, and its interaction with MNE activity.

The first is the increasing influence of governments on the institutional framework and economic milieu for value-added activity within their countries, and especially that undertaken by firms which have a choice of where to locate their activities. This may seem to be a strange claim to make at a time when, throughout the world, and as enlarged upon in Part IV of this volume, the trend seems to be towards less government intervention, more deregulation and liberalization of markets and more privatization. Yet, if one examines the factors leading MNEs to site their manufacturing and service activities in different countries, those they most frequently identify are government related or influenced (Dunning, 1991). Increasingly less important are basic factor endowments, e.g. natural resources and unskilled, or even semi-skilled, labor inputs. As we have already suggested, apart from in the primary product sectors, both these inputs are accounting for a decreasing proportion of the output of a particular activity. Increasingly more important are the costs and availability of created assets, including all kinds of information, and the capacity to assimilate, interpret and use this information, innovatory capacity, scientific, technical and professional personnel, a first rate transport and telecommunications system, a favorable tax environment, a culture which encourages entrepreneurship and wealth creation, a cooperative and well motivated labor force, a sophisticated domestic market, a commitment to excellence in product quality and production standards, a sound macro-economic policy, and a constructive and symbiotic working partnership between the main wealth creating institutions and government.

While each of these variables affects the revenue and *production* costs of firms, they much more influence their *transactional* costs and benefits; and it is these latter elements which governments, directly or indirectly, are increasingly shaping. Chapters 12 and 13 will take up this point in more detail. Here we will simply emphasize that, in an age in which the economic prosperity of the advanced industrialized countries is becoming increasingly dependent upon the quantity and quality of innovatory capacity and organizational skills, the role of governments, via myriad regulatory and policy instruments, is becoming a more, rather than less, critical one. And this role is *not* simply one of liberalizing or deregulating markets, the reason being that much of market failure facing global firms is not that arising from government imposed distortions, but is intrinsic or endemic in the market system *per se.*

Second, there is increasing reason to suppose that governments – some voluntarily and others involuntarily – are being forced to adopt more positive strategies to advance their competitive capabilities, and the upgrading of their indigenous resources, and, in some cases, to protect their firms from the results of the unacceptable actions and policies of other governments. *De facto*, governments are assuming the role of strategic oligopolists, in a world economy dominated by the activities of large integrated multinationals.

The explicit acceptance by governments of this role is presently confined to some East Asian nations. In the main, Western governments tend to confine their micro-economic management to providing selective grants, subsidies or fiscal incentives to firms, industries or regions; to supplying some informational services to international traders; subsidizing some kinds of R&D and training programs, and participating in international fora to ensure a level playing field in the arena of trade and foreign investment. Sometimes, too, governments may take direct countervailing action against the behavior of foreign firms which are perceived to operate against their national interests, e.g. by means of anti-dumping legislation against exporters, or the imposition of performance requirements on inward investors. Although these may add up to an impressive package of measures, more often than not, the policies are piecemeal and uncoordinated, and are primarily intended to achieve goals other than that of advancing national competitiveness.

The most persuasive illustration of a systemic approach to competitiveness and international business is most certainly that of the Japanese. Throughout the last 30 years, the Japanese government, by a variety of means, has directly and consistently influenced the value-added activities of its firms. In so doing, it has attempted not to replace the market, but to work with the market to achieve what it perceives to be a structure of resource usage, consistent with the dictates of comparative dynamic advantage. In the early post-war period, viz. up to the mid-1960s, government intervention was direct and all pervasive. Today, though it is more subtle and selective, it is still based upon a holistic economic strategy, geared to a continuous upgrading of indigenous innovatory capacity, and to sustaining and advancing the competitiveness of Japanese firms in world markets.

Terutomo Ozawa has characterized post-war Japanese industrial and trade policy as one of 'collaborative symbiosis' between government and industry, the aim of which is directed to promoting dynamic growth and efficient structural adaptation (Ozawa, 1989). Ozawa contrasts this with the fragmentary, disjointed and frequently changing economic policies of most Western nations which, more often than not, he argues, have led to conflict and disharmony between the public and private sector. This strategy has several familiar features; but before summarizing these, it is worth noting that the Japanese 'miracle' would not have come about, or come about so quickly, had Western industrial nations not been prepared to allow Japanese producers unrestricted access to their markets, natural resources, technology and educational facilities.

According to Ozawa's research, and that of Michael Porter, which tells a similar story (Porter, 1990), the fundamental platform of post-war Japanese competitive strategy has been the pursuance of a continual restructuring of its industrial output by making substantial investments in human capital and innovatory activities; and by promoting the appropriate entrepreneurial and work ethos to achieve this goal. Inward and outward direct investment has been an integral part of that strategy rather than an adjunct to it. In the first years of its post-war development, Japan concentrated on building up its heavy metal and chemical industries. However, this made enormous demands on intermediate products which the country was at a comparative disadvantage to supply. Hence, outbound investment by Japanese MNEs was directed towards sustaining a reliable supply of the necessary raw materials and energy. Later, Japan moved to produce less resource consuming and more knowledge intensive goods. To do this, she needed Western technology, which she achieved via inward direct investment, by way of the reverse engineering of imported capital goods, by licensing and other non-equity agreements with Western firms, and by the training of Japanese scientists and engineers in the US and Europe.

As she reconfigured her industries, Japan did not just surrender her interests in sectors in which her comparative advantage was declining. Instead, backed by low interest loans and tax breaks from the government, strong technical and financial assistance from the *Sogo Shosha* (who themselves were usually given preferential treatment by the Japanese banks), by the Japan Overseas Development Corporation, and by one of the earliest investment guarantee programs, Japanese firms were urged to transfer their labor intensive activities to developing countries; and, in so doing, practiced what Ozawa calls a Salvation Army or 'hand my clothes down' strategy.

At the same time, Japan invested abroad to gain access to the latest innovatory and technological know-how, while, subsequently, with shortages of labor and rising living standards pushing up wages at home, she found her exports falling. So she further realigned her domestic sector, while concurrently, rather than relinquishing overseas markets to her competitors, her firms were encouraged to set up off-shore facilities to manufacture the products previously supplied by Japanese factories. Protectionism and an ever rising trade surplus made for even more capital exports. The more comprehensive Japan's development strategy became, the more she has been prepared to assist her own firms and foreign governments to promote that strategy, and also to use developing countries as procurement bases for the manufacture of more labor intensive products and processes.

In the meantime, although Japan has begun to take a more liberal stance towards inward MNE activity and cross-border strategic alliances, and is finding her neighbors less willing to sell cutting edge technology to her without maintaining some control over it, she remains a substantial creditor on her international direct investment accounts. In March 1991, the value of Japan's outward direct investment stake was $320 billion, 14 times that of her inward investment stake of $17 billion.

The above example neatly illustrates our contention that in examining the dynamics of MNE activity it is necessary to take account of the dynamics of the interaction between both endogenous and exogenous variables, and, irrespective of the latter, to take particular account of the way in which governments may directly or indirectly affect the value of the OLI variables, and the strategic response of firms to them.

We offer just one other figure to put the Japanese story into perspective. West Germany was in a similar, although perhaps not quite such a catastrophic, situation to Japan after the last war. But, the ways in which the German government set about achieving its economic objectives, and the role it assigned to inward and outward direct investment was quite different. True, there *was* an economic miracle in West Germany, and this was accomplished a decade earlier than in Japan. But, it was staged in a very different way. In as much as international investment figured as part of the German economic strategy at all, it was to use inward foreign capital, skills and know-how as the best and quickest way to advance its own economic capabilities. In consequence, there were no restrictions on inward direct investment; while outward investment, which did not occur to any real extent until the 1960s, has never been part of any coordinated or supportive government industrial or trade strategy. The result of this policy was that the accumulated German outward direct investment in 1990 was D155 billion, only D23 billion more than the stock of inward investment of D132 billion.

Finally, on the role of governments affecting the dynamics of international production, at least passing mention should be given to the formation of regional customs unions, and the conclusion of bilateral or multilateral trading agreements. The interaction between corporate and regional integration is explored in more detail in Dunning and Robson, 1988 and UN, 1993; while Chapter 7 of this volume explains the impact of EC integration on transatlantic investment flows. Suffice here to underline the point that these intergovernment initiatives – which, as we have already suggested, are often prompted by the MNEs themselves – may dramatically affect the pattern and pace of international business activity and have widespread affects on the competitive advantages of both firms and countries.

CONCLUSIONS

Let us now draw the threads of this chapter together. A review of the dynamics of international production over the last 20 to 30 years suggests a number of characteristics. The first is the movement towards the globalization of production and markets by the leading MNEs, and a more integrated governance of their operations, especially in the advanced industrial nations of the world. At the same time, there is evidence that firms are adjusting their product and marketing strategies to take better account of specific factor endowments and consumer needs.

Second, we observe a variety of structural changes, in both the geographical and industrial composition of MNE activity. Especially noticeable are the growth of Japanese outward investment, the rise in inward investment in the US, the increase in two-way intra-industry investment, and the increased role of A&Ms (acquisitions and mergers) as a form of entry.[19]

These characteristics reflect the interaction of a strategically activist role by firms and other changes in the endogenous variables which will affect the level and structure of international production in a later period of time, and also of developments in the economic and political environment which may cause companies to reappraise their existing strategies. At the same time, as the following chapter will show, a firm's foreign production profile might alter due to changes in the value of endogenous and exogenous variables without any change in strategy on its part. In practice, it is difficult to disentangle the various determinants of the changing pattern of international production. This is due to the complex interplay between the behavior of MNEs and the exogenous variables which both affect and are affected by that behavior.

Chapter 4 will discuss these issues in more detail and particularly the ways in which a change in the strategy of MNEs may affect its long-term competitive advantages, and its organizational and locational preferences. While in some cases, the process of change is predictable from received theory – this, for example, would apply to most of the changing characteristics of international production over the last 20 to 30 years – others are not so. These include the timing of a major technological breakthrough or a change in entrepreneurship or management style, which, in turn, may affect the pace and path of predictable change.

The direction of some exogenous changes is also forecastable, as is their effect on international production. Economic development is one of these, and the role of created factor endowments of technology and human capital is another. Few futurologists in the 1960s, however, could have predicted either the pace or the effect of such changes, especially over the past decade; and the enormous ramifications (some of which are still to be worked out) for international business. Government strategies are the least easy to incorporate into any dynamic model; yet even here, as far as the developed countries are concerned, technological and economic forces, including the globalization of business itself, may well compel governments of advanced industrial nations to coordinate their micro-organizational strategies in a way similar to that of their macro-economic policies. There also seems to be a trend towards the conclusion of an increasing number of cooperative alliances between firms of different countries; and there is no question but that such arrangements have major affects on the ownership and organization of cross-border production.

Over the past 30 years, we have seen a continuous interaction between changes in exogenous and (non-strategic) endogenous variables and the strategic actions and reactions of firms, with the balance between a pro-active and reactive strategy shifting to affect the dynamics of international business operations. In the 1950s and 1960s the running was very much determined by exogenous variables, with FDI following changes in demand and supply conditions. Most firms pursued ethnocentric or polycentric strategies towards their foreign affiliates; and most, apart from those in resource based sectors, acted as part of a group of multi-domestic or multi-local production units. But, the recovery of the world economy, the setting up of the EC and other customs unions, and advances in transport and telecommunications technology have caused firms to modify their locational and organizational strategies, and sometimes their innovatory policies as well. The changing attitudes of governments in developing countries have also led both foreign and domestic firms to reappraise their attitudes towards joint ventures and strategic alliances.

The late 1970s and 1980s witnessed a marked change in the economic climate towards international business activity, and a considerable acceleration in the technological capacity of firms. Corporate strategies have both responded to such developments and helped fashion them. Governments have become more active in affecting the dynamic restructuring of international production in several ways. At the same time, sharp differences between (Far) Eastern and Western government strategies towards competitiveness have begun to reveal themselves (Porter, 1990). In the West, policies have been mainly directed at disengaging the government from the marketplace; although in the international arena, there has also been increasing pressure for selective protectionism. By contrast, in the Far East, the philosophy evolved has been one of symbiosis between governments and the private sector to promote a systemic economic strategy geared to a continual upgrading of productivity of domestic resources and of competitive advantage in international markets.

These policies suggest that exogenous factors, or, more correctly, an interplay between endogenous and exogenous factors, are once again playing an important role in the dynamics of international business. They are doing so primarily through their effects on cross-border comparative production costs, and on the domestic transaction costs of economic activity. These, in turn, both induce a response on the part of firms and cause them to reappraise their competitive strategies.

The interface between MNE activity and the competitive advantages of the countries in which they operate over a longer period of time has been examined by the author in another recently published volume (Dunning, 1992). In this study an attempt was made to relate different types of FDI to the different stages of economic development countries might go through, and to trace how changes in the propensity of firms to invest in (or out of) particular countries might affect their own competitive advantages, and hence the future attractiveness as a home or host to MNE activity.

The main thrust of our thesis is set out in Figure 3.1. This charts the possible impact of an inward MNE activity on the recipient country, and how that may, in turn, affect the competitiveness of the investing companies. It also considers how autonomous (i.e. non-FDI induced) changes may also impact on the O advantages of these same enterprises and countries. In this figure, we consider just two stages of development (or economic restructuring in the case of developed countries) of a particular country, t1 and tn.

Consider, first, the top half of the chart. In stage t1, existing and potential foreign investors are faced with a given set of OLI configurations. These, we assume, will lead to some new FDI. As a direct consequence of this investment (identified as FDI led change), a train of events will be set in motion which affect the trajectory of the

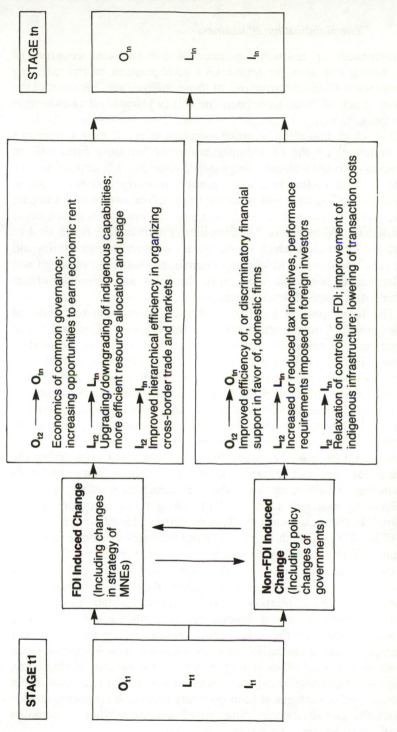

Figure 3.1 Some dynamics of the stages of growth and the eclectic paradigm (only two stages illustrated).

development or restructuring path of the recipient country (or countries), and also the future OLI configuration of the investing firms. Some of the determinants of these changes are illustrated in the figure. Each of these have been (or will be) described elsewhere in this book.[20]

The chart makes no *a priori* assumption as to *how* a country's development or the OLI configuration of investing firms will be affected. We have already emphasized that this will depend on the kind of FDI undertaken, and country, industry and firm specific variables leading to it, and resulting from it. The nature of the impact will also vary according to which stages of development are being considered. What Figure 3.1 does illustrate, however, is the kind of iterative interaction which might occur between foreign MNEs and the host countries in which they operate, the outcome of which will influence, to some extent at least, the form and character of the latter's next stage of development.

The lower part of the figure identifies some non-FDI induced changes which might affect the O advantages of firms and the L advantages of countries; and also, in the light of these, the relative merits of markets, hierarchies and cooperative ventures as modalities for the cross-border organization of the former. It is the combination of these two kinds of changes which will determine the configuration of the OLI variables facing the foreign investors in stage tn, and also the ESP of host countries, the extent and structure of which will identify its trajectory of development.

It would be possible to produce a similar chart considering the interaction between outward investment and a home country's economic development and also to incorporate other variables influencing changes in the OLI tn configuration into the existing chart.[21] In the former case, the kind of outward investment, the extent to which it is substitutable for, or complementary to, domestic invest-ment, and the conditions in which it is made, are among the critical factors influencing the extent to which it impacts favorably or un-favorably on domestic economic welfare. Again, it may be demon-strated that the contribution of MNE activity to a nation's economic and social objectives will depend not only on the nature of these objectives, but on the stage of its economic development. For example, while in the earlier stages of a country's development, some kinds of outbound MNE activity may be at the expense of upgrading domestic technological capability and may lead to a reduction in the competitive advantages of both investing firms and countries, in later stages the globalization of value-added activity is often essential to maintain or advance those same advantages.

Finally, we would observe that the globalization of technology and the escalating costs of innovation are causing new patterns of organization, including those between firms of different nationality. The dynamics of organizational change, and its interface with the level and pattern of MNE, is a subject which is only now commanding serious attention by scholars.[22] We hope that it will be one of the growth areas of academic research in the 1990s.

4 Global strategy and the theory of international production

INTRODUCTION

There is a slow, but discernible, convergence between the literature on global strategic management and that of the theory of international production. Though the language and analytical approach of the two schools of thought continues to differ, the message of each is similar. This is demonstrated particularly in the work of some younger scholars who have been trained in, or are at least familiar with, the concepts and techniques of both disciplines.[1]

It is the purpose of this chapter to attempt to review some of the similarities and differences between the approaches of the strategic management analyst and the economic theorist towards explaining the globalization of production, and to consider the possibilities of integrating some of their thoughts and findings. Writing as an economist with a long-standing interest in international business, the views of the author on these particular issues will inevitably reflect his own predilections and prejudices. In particular, this chapter seeks to see how far the economist's approach to understanding the determinants of foreign value-added activities of firms might be improved upon by taking more explicit account of the work of business scholars. No doubt the latter would wish to start from the opposite end, and see how far economic principles might be usefully incorporated into their thinking. Apart from the fact that we do not feel qualified to undertake this latter task, it would probably be accepted by both groups of scholars that the theory of international production is in a rather more advanced stage than the theory of global strategic management.[2]

DIFFERENCES BETWEEN THE ECONOMIST'S AND THE BUSINESS ANALYST'S APPROACH TO EXPLAINING INTERNATIONAL PRODUCTION

The main stream economic theories

Economists define international production as production owned or controlled by multinational enterprises (MNEs). The MNE is an enterprise which engages in foreign value-added activities and internalizes intermediate product markets across national boundaries. Until comparatively recently, economists were primarily interested in explaining foreign direct investment as a means of transferring resources, e.g. capital, management and technology, between countries but within the same firm. Nowadays, their domain of interest is more focused on the organization of cross-border activities, including non-equity collaborative alliances.

Over the past three decades, a variety of explanations have been forwarded to explain the level and pattern of MNE activity. Recent reviews are contained in Dunning (1989, 1992, 1993) and Cantwell (1991). Some scholars have directed their interest to explaining particular kinds or aspects of MNE related activity. Others have attempted to formulate more general theories or paradigms – either of the MNE or the value-added activities undertaken by such enterprises. Each, to a varying degree, implicitly incorporate strategy related variables in their explanations, but only a few, notably Knickerbocker's 'follow my leader', Graham's 'exchange of threats' and Lessard's and Rugman's 'risk diversification' hypotheses, have focused more explicitly on the strategy of firms as a separately identifiable explanatory variable.[3]

Up to now, most economic theories of foreign production have been directed to explaining such production at discrete points of time rather than its path of change between these points of time. Exceptions include Vernon's product cycle theory (Vernon, 1966, 1979) which relates the changing propensity of firms to engage in foreign direct investment as the product they produced moved from its innovatory to its mature or standardized form; Buckley and Casson's analysis of the optimal timing of a switch in the mode of servicing as foreign market from exports to foreign investment (Buckley and Casson, 1981); and Dunning's investment development cycle or path, which traces the changing propensity of countries to be inward or outward direct investors according to their stages of economic development (Dunning, 1988). Mention might also be made of the exploratory attempts of Mark Casson to incorporate entrepreneurship into the theory of foreign direct investment (Casson, 1987, 1988). At the same time, most of these contributions have paid only passing attention to the alternative strategies open to firms in penetrating foreign markets (apart from the export v. foreign direct investment option); and, like most of the other explanations by economists, they were predicated on the assumption that firms were profit or wealth maximizers.

Since the mid-1970s, there have been three attempts by economists to offer generalized explanations of international production.[4] These might be called the macro-economic, the internalization, and the eclectic paradigmatic explanations. Each should be considered as complementary rather than competitive to each other, and to the partial explanations earlier put forward. Since the latter two approaches address themselves to the behavior of groups of firms (rather than that of countries), and appear to offer the most promise for incorporating the thinking of the strategic business analyst, we will concentrate our attention on these.[5]

The internalization school

Scholars of this school of thought are primarily interested in the MNE as a particular kind of multi-activity firm. Their central proposition is that the existence of the cross-border value-added activities by firms stems from the failure of intermediate product markets to operate efficiently. FDI seeks to improve upon the market as a transactional mechanism. The replacement or internalization of such markets by hierarchies leads to an extension of the boundaries of the firm. Most of the internalization literature[6] is concerned with identifying the kinds of cross-border market failure which might lead to, or increase, MNE activity, and with the evaluation of the transactional costs and benefits associated with these alternative organizational routes.

In several respects, the internalization theory of foreign production offers a promising basis for the inclusion of strategic related variables. Like the management analyst, the internalization economist fully embraces the concept of uncertainty in his analysis of market failure; indeed the reduction or counteracting of uncertainty is viewed as one of the critical reasons for the emergence and growth of multinational activity.[7] Like the management analyst too, the internalization economist focuses his attention on the conduct and behavior of the firm as a unit of analysis, and on the alternative strategies open to it in the pursuance of its objectives.[8]

At the same time, the purview of interest of the two groups of scholars is rather different. The internalization economist is primarily interested in explaining the organization of the cross-border value-added activities. The strategic management analyst is interested in evaluating the determinants of all aspects of decision taking to do with the creation and deployment of a firm's competitive advantages in international markets. To the internalization economist, most competitive advantages of MNEs (other than those which derive from their multinationality as such) are taken as given; to the business strategist they are something to be explained. To the internalization economist, the key question is 'Under what situations will multi-national hierarchies replace international markets?' To the business strategist it is to analyze why some firms, rather than others, are successful at becoming global players, and sustaining or advancing their global market shares.

The eclectic paradigm

The eclectic paradigm of international production sets out a generalized framework for explaining the level and pattern of the cross-border value-added activities of firms. It postulates that, at any given point of time, the stock of foreign assets, owned and controlled by multinational firms, is determined by (a) the extent and nature of the ownership specific or competitive advantages of those *firms, vis-à-vis* those of uninational firms, (b) the extent and nature of the location bound endowments and markets offered by *countries* to firms to create or add further value to these competitive advantages, and (c) the extent to which the market for these advantages, including those which arise from multinationality *per se,* are best internalized by the firm itself, rather than marketed directly to foreign firms.

The paradigm suggests that the configuration of these ownership, location and internalization (OLI) advantages will vary according to country, nature of activity, and firm specific characteristics; but that the propensity of corporations to engage in foreign production will be the most pronounced the greater their (relative) competitive advantages, and the more they find it profitable to create or add value to these advantages themselves from a foreign location. Some of the more important OLI variables identified by the eclectic paradigm are set out in the appendix to this chapter.

Although the eclectic paradigm addresses itself to explaining the foreign production of *firms,* rather than that of a particular firm, and draws on a wider range of economic tools than does internalization theory, in several respects it has more in common with the interests of the strategic management analyst. Most importantly, perhaps, it takes both the competitive advantage of firms and those of countries as something to be explained, although it accepts that some of these former advantages may arise from the common governance of value-added activities and the internalization of cross-border markets. In the identification of these advantages, there is very little difference (except in presentation, emphasis and language) between the kind of ownership specific advantages of firms, and locational advantages of countries listed by such scholars as Porter (1986, 1990), Kogut (1983, 1985), Doz (1986, 1988), Ghoshal (1987), Hamel and Prahalad (1987), and those in my own writings.

For reasons already suggested, the attention given to the concept of market failure by the strategic management literature is somewhat less. At the same time, the advantages which arise from the common ownership of activities across national boundaries are fully recognized by business scholars. Porter (1990), for example, distinguishes between *nation* or *location* based advantages and *system* based advantages of firms; while, in an earlier study (Porter, 1986), he identified the *configuration* and *coordination* options open to firms, identifying the latter as those which other scholars would refer to as the economies of common governance or scope. Kogut (1983) explicitly distinguishes between the O specific advantages which are often a necessary prerequisite for the initial act of foreign production, and those which arise as a direct consequence of foreign production, or the growth in it. These latter benefits include the spreading of environmental risk, the capacity to maximize global efficiency by engaging in product and process specialization, and intrafirm trade; the opportunities to arbitrage cross-border information, financial and factor markets, and/or to exercise additional leverage in negotiating with national governments or indigenous economic agents; and the learning and experience gains which may stem from operating in different environments (Kogut, 1985).

In his suggestion for an organizing framework to study the issues of global strategic management, Ghoshal (1987) sets out two matrices. One relates the objectives of firms to different kinds of competitive advantage (p. 428) and the other the economies in product and market diversification to some components of common governance (p. 435). The latter is almost a perfect rationale for the hierarchical coordination of discrete value-added activities to capture the extra market benefits arising from them (Caves, 1980b), while the former sets out some of the gains from geographical diversification, which parallel those identified by Kogut and Porter, but which arise primarily because of the capacity of multinationals to exploit cross-border market imperfections.

There are, however, important differences in emphasis between the eclectic paradigm and the strategic management literature in explaining the globalization of business. The most important among these is that like most other economic models, the eclectic paradigm is interested in identifying and evaluating the most significant variables affecting the level and patterns of international production, or changes in international production, rather than those affecting the strategic action of firms to achieve such production.

Second, while the eclectic paradigm acknowledges the significance of firm specific characteristics in determining international production, its main focus is on country and industry characteristics. For example, the theory is interested in explaining why there tends to be more globalization of production in the pharmaceutical and petroleum industries than in the iron and steel or railway sectors, or why the industrial or geographical distribution of Japanese and Taiwanese MNEs is different from that of its Canadian or French counterparts. By contrast, the strategic business analyst's attention is more likely to be directed to answering such questions as why the global sourcing strategy of Toshiba is different from that of BMW, or why the marketing strategy of Nestlé is more 'niche' oriented than that of Unilever. From the economist's perspective, strategy related variables are more often treated as part of the 'unexplained' (or unexplainable) variables, whereas they are the main subject of interest to the business analyst.

Third, the eclectic paradigm is usually couched in static or comparative static terms. Though some attempt has to be made to theorize about the changing international OLI configuration facing, or engineered by, firms or industries over time,[9] for the most part, economists have been content to explain the international allocation of MNE activity at a given point of time or between points of time. Moreover, no real attempt has been made either to explicitly incorporate the interaction between firms into the eclectic framework – and particularly the feedback effects of a firm's actions on the behavior of its competitors – nor to acknowledge the fact that the capabilities of firms in implementing their chosen strategies may be very different. Finally, it is only recently that the eclectic paradigm has acknowledged that firms may invest abroad (particularly via the acquisition and merger route) to protect or gain a competitive position rather than to exploit existing O specific advantages.[10]

INCORPORATING STRATEGY INTO THE ECLECTIC PARADIGM OF INTERNATIONAL PRODUCTION

We now turn to consider how the eclectic paradigm, and, for that matter, internalization theory as well, might better take account of the strategic actions and reactions of firms. We have suggested that, insofar as they directly affect the foreign value-added activities of firms, many of the strategy related variables considered by business analysts have already been identified by the eclectic paradigm; but others, which impact indirectly though affecting the behavior of firms, may require more attention than they have so far been given.[11] What, however, is missing is the incorporation of strategy *per se* as an explanatory variable. How, if at all, might this be done?

First, we would reiterate the point that a firm's choice of options is only a point of issue where the markets in which it competes are imperfect. Such imperfections may be *structural* (i.e. they are brought about by market distorting actions on the part of the participants in the market) or *endemic* (they reflect the inability of the market to fulfil certain tasks required of it). Pure market failure is a situation in which, due to the presence of uncertainty, or to technological imperatives, or to the fact that the consequences of some transaction spill-over to institutions or individuals who are not party to those transactions, it is impossible to create the conditions of a perfect market in which each firm produces at its lowest average cost while equating marginal cost to price. Once, however, market failure arises, a firm's range of behavioral options increases. For example, there can be no generalized 'optimal' trade-off between a set of possible outcomes to a firm's strategic behavior and the profits associated with these outcomes because the estimation and valuation of the uncertainties involved are, themselves, likely to be firm specific! Similarly, once the choice of product differentiation is introduced as a possible corporate strategy, one is immediately faced with the possibility of multiple profit or wealth maximizing strategies, e.g. to supply a superior quality product at a higher price versus a lower quality product at a lower price.

The way in which we would suggest strategic choice might be incorporated into the eclectic paradigm of international production is to introduce a 'dynamized add-on' independent variable.[12] The variable we propose to use in our framework of thought is that of strategic change (S_t). We shall define strategy as a 'change in the conduct of firms designed to advance their long-term objectives, which specifically takes heed of the estimated likely reactions of other decision taking units in response to that change'.

We shall identify two kinds of strategic change. The first is a change in the way in which a firm or group of firms seeks or seek to achieve its (their) long-term objectives, given any particular configuration of any OLI advantages (i.e. a *strategy initiating,* or autonomous strategic, change). The second is a change in strategy occasioned by a change in that configuration (i.e. a *strategy induced* change). To illustrate and simplify our analysis, we shall consider just one period of time viz. $t-1 \rightarrow t$; and examine how a strategic variable or set of strategic variables might be incorporated into the tripod of OLI variables affecting the level and structure of foreign production. We shall also assume that the goals of firms remain unchanged over this time, i.e. their reaction to a *given set* of OLI advantages is constant.

Take first the ownership or competitive advantages of a firm. At any given point of time t, these advantages (O_t) represent its current stock of income generating or cost reducing technological and organizational assets, the nature and structure of which are a function of its past ownership advantages, and the overall strategic response to such advantages. Such a response is likely to be multifaceted and to include actions taken with respect to, for example, innovation, organizational structures, acquisitions and interfirm alliances, product diversification, vertical integration, sourcing exchange risks and foreign production. So, assuming just one time period '$t-1 \rightarrow t$',

$$O_t = f\,(OLI_{t-1}\ S_{Ot-1}\ \dot{S}_{Ot-1 \rightarrow t}\ E\dot{X}N_{Ot-1 \rightarrow t}) \cdots \tag{1}$$

where EXN represents changes in the value of any exogenous or non-strategic endogenous variables over time $t-1 \rightarrow t$.

Similarly, the competitive or locational specific attractions of countries for the value-added activities of a firm at time t (L_t) is a function of its OLI configuration in time $t-1$ (as each of these variables may interact to affect a firm's locational choice at that time), changes in the locational advantages of countries, as affected by changes in the value of non-strategic related variables, and any changes in the autonomous strategy of a firm which may affect its location. So:

$$L_t\ f\,(OLI_{t-1},\ S_{Lt-1},\ \dot{S}_{Lt-1 \rightarrow t}\ E\dot{X}N_{Lt-1 \rightarrow t}) \cdots \tag{2}$$

This equation, then, suggests that the geographical distribution of a firm's current production is dependent, in part at least, on changes in either its autonomous locational strategy or that which is the result of changes in non-strategic related variables which may themselves induce a change in its strategy over the time $t-1 \rightarrow t$.

Finally, the way in which a firm organizes the creation or development of its O advantages (or others it may seek to acquire) and relates these to the advantages of countries (i.e. its choice of whether or not to internalize or increase its internalization of cross-border intermediate product markets) will depend upon its transnational deployment of past OLI advantages and any changes in strategy which might occur over the time period under consideration. Hence:

$$I_t = f\,(OLI_{t-1}\ S_{It-1}\ \dot{S}_{It-1 \to t}\ \dot{EXN}_{It-1 \to t})\ \ldots \tag{3}$$

Combining the three previous equations and aggregating for all firms, we arrive at a general equation:

$$OLI_t^* = f\,(OLI_{t-1}^*\ S_{OLIt-1}^*\ \dot{S}_{OLIt-1 \to t}^*\ \dot{EXN}_{OLIt-1 \to t}^*)\ \ldots \tag{4}$$

where $*$ = all firms.

International production in time t then represents the totality of the strategic responses of firms to past OLI configurations and to changes in these configurations brought about by changes in the external environment and non-strategic endogenous variables. Indeed, the strategic responses of firms to their current (or expected future) OLI variables, together with autonomous strategic changes, will determine their future pattern of international production.

It is worth noting that unless the firm is in equilibrium at time $t-1$ and that there are no learning or other strategic responses still in the pipeline at that time (i.e. $S_{OLIt-1 \to t}$ is zero), OLI $_t$ will be different than OLI $_{t-1}$, and hence so also will be the level and structure of international production. In this event, any changes in foreign production are assumed to be caused solely by changes in the value of exogenous or non-strategic endogenous variables which might affect the OLI configuration (e.g. a product innovation, a reduction in cross-border transport costs, a more cost-effective advertising campaign, better protection of property rights, a new inroad into the firm's market by its competitors, and so on).

It may also be observed that we have chosen to treat strategic change as a time related variable; but that at a given moment of time, we have not included the response of a firm to its past OLI configuration as an independent variable. This implies that we have assigned objectives to a firm which are independent of the OLI variables affecting these objectives, and that these goals are consistent over time, and similar between firms. For those who feel uncomfortable with this procedure, it would be acceptable to formulate an additional hypothesis which treated foreign production as the independent variable, and the OLI configuration and the goals of firms as dependent variables. Thus, at time t for a group of firms

$$IP_t = f(OLI_t, G_t) \ldots \tag{5}$$

where G = the goals of the firms at time t. A change in the goals of firms over time $t-1 \rightarrow t$ could then either be explicitly incorporated into equations 1 through 4, or be assumed to affect their strategic actions and reactions over that time period, and hence its OLI, at time t.

HYPOTHESIZING ABOUT STRATEGY RELATED VARIABLES

Strategy induced variables

The primary purpose of the eclectic paradigm is to identify the kind of OLI advantages likely to affect international production, and to hypothesize about the significance of these variables. However, on this second point, much will depend upon the nature of the products produced, by which firms they are produced, and where they are produced. An operationally testable explanation of *resource based* investment will draw upon a different set of OLI variables than will that of *market seeking* investment or an investment which is part of a *global, cost-minimizing or asset acquiring* strategy. Similarly, the relevance of a particular configuration of OLI variables affecting the foreign value-added activities of Italian or Korean MNEs may be different than those influencing Canadian or UK multinationals. Finally, the O specific advantages of firms and the L advantages of countries, and the way in which firms coordinate their cross-border value-added activities based on these advantages, are likely to vary according to such variables as the size of the enterprise, whether the investment is a greenfield or an acquisition, whether it is first-time or sequential, and whether it is just one or one of many foreign ventures.

All this suggests that, within a general paradigmatic framework, a number of self-contained, and for the most part, complementary, operationally testable theories may be generated. Indeed, much of the research of trade and industrial organizational economists has been directed to identifying and evaluating the most significant, explanatory variables, and, it might be added, with some success.[13]

However, all of these studies assume that, faced with the same OLI advantages and normalizing for country, industry and (non-strategic) firm specific characteristics, firms will react in a similar way to these advantages. Implicitly or explicitly, firms are assumed to be wealth or profit maximizers. Neither does any of the empirical research attempt to incorporate strategic variables *per se* into the OLI configuration of firms. Only strategy related theories, such as those already identified and which are designed to answer very specific questions about the oligopolistic behavior of firms, come near to doing this.

Is it then possible to suggest strategy induced variables, which could be incorporated with OLI variables, into the eclectic paradigm; and also to theorize more explicitly about which particular strategy variables are likely to affect particular types of international production? Can one predict ways in which strategic change may affect the (future) value of OLI variables?

Consider, for example, the case of a profit maximizing firm producing a single product (say a pharmaceutical drug) in a mono-polistically competitive market. The firm is faced with a particular OLI configuration, on the basis of which it finds it profitable to export part of its output to an independent distributing and marketing outlet in another country. Assume, too, that the firm's cost and pricing strategy is consistent with its long-term economic goals, and that this strategy does not affect its future OLI configuration. Finally, assume that the firm has all the information it needs about domestic and foreign markets, suppliers, customers and government policies, and that it undertakes no innovatory activities. In every sense then, the firm's output is in equilibrium with its OLI configuration, and the strategy management of that configuration (which in one sense, of course, might be considered as an O advantage in its own right) is consistent with maintaining this equilibrium. This latter assumption is the one built into the eclectic paradigm.

Now suppose this equilibrium is disturbed by the importing country imposing a substantial tariff on the drug supplied by the foreign firm. The immediate affect of this is to decrease the attractiveness of domestic production (i.e. by raising the cost of supplying the foreign market by exports). The question then is, should the firm opt out of the market altogether or try to supply it by other means, and, if the latter, by what means? In turn, to answer these questions, other issues need to be explored. Among these are the effect the options may have on the firm's O advantages (e.g. on its ability to exploit scale and scope economies); and if some of these produce negative results, how might they be overcome and at what cost? The primary interest of the international business economist is to identify the way in which the first best solution to these questions affects the level and pattern of global production. Rarely, if ever, is he or she concerned with the path by which a firm makes a choice from the alternative options open to it.

As a first step to incorporating strategy in the OLI paradigm, one then needs to identify the options available to firms to any change in the OLI configuration. However, the real significance of strategy is where the outcome of pursuing alternative options is uncertain, and where there is no clearly identifiable optimum way of achieving particular goals or even of identifying the trade-off between goals. Taking the above example as a case in point, there may be some uncertainty as to the future policy of the importing government, not only towards the purchase of foreign goods, but towards inward direct investment or licensing. There may be some doubt as to the extent to which local licensors are likely to adhere to any contract for producing the drug under license. There may also be some question over the contestability of domestic markets and the effect of new entrants on the profitability of existing investment. While, in part, the likely response to these uncertainties may be gauged from the existing OLI configuration of firms, it is the latters' idiosyncratic character-istics, and their perception of their position in the strategic groups with which they identify, which is likely to determine the actual strategies pursued.

Consider next a situation in which the value of locational variables changes. A firm may have a set of options open to it to adjust to these changes. Each option is likely to vary according to the type of foreign production being considered. Each option is likely to have a different outcome. Each outcome is likely to generate different costs and benefits which it is impossible to predict in advance. Often, too, the consequences of alternative options are interactive. Only if we know the firm's assessment of the degree of risk involved, and if its trade-off between risk and profitability is known, will it be possible to gauge its optimum locational strategy.

Now, assume there is a change in the firm's O specific advantages. Suppose, for example, it invents a new fermentation process which halves the cost of producing the drug. How might this affect its foreign production? Since the firm is not currently producing over-seas it may be that the answer is 'not at all'; it may simply increase its exports. But, this will not necessarily be the case. Depending on its price elasticity, the demand for the product might rise in the importing country to allow local production to become economically viable. Or, it could be that, because of the nature of the inputs it requires, the fermentation process can be more economically under-taken in a foreign country than at home. At the same time, it might be in the firm's strategic interest to license, or otherwise collaborate with, a foreign firm to produce the drug. Again, while it is possible to identify the options available to the firm, the strategy it actually chooses will rest on its perception of, and attitude towards, the anticipated costs and benefits of the options, and, not least, how these may impinge upon its main competitors (or potential competitors).

Finally, the circumstances surrounding a firm's I related advantages may change. Suppose, for example, the firm finds that the foreign distributing and marketing company to which it is exporting its products has become unreliable, or the quality of its services has fallen, or it raises its prices. Suppose, too, that, at the same time, the firm's own knowledge and experience of the local market has improved, and/or it perceives that local customers require it to modify its product to meet their particular needs. Then, the firm may decide to undertake the distributing and marketing functions itself. But, again, this might not be its only option and, even if it were, the firm still has a choice as to whether it should set up a greenfield marketing venture or buy an existing venture. Or should it enter into a cooperative alliance with a local competitor or with another marketing and distribution company? What effect might each of these possible actions have on its O advantages, and so on? Each option carries an uncertain outcome, and thus requires some appreciation of the strategy of a firm.

We have introduced the most simple of changes in the OLI configuration of firms; and we have assumed away many of the interesting options open to firms. For example, suppose our pharmaceutical company was producing in an oligopolistic market. Then, not only might its OLI configuration be directly affected by the behavior of its major competitors, but, considering any change in its own strategy, it would have to take account of the likely impact of this strategy on its competitors, and how, in turn, their responses may affect its own competitive position. We have also assumed that the firm is a single product and non-innovating enterprise. Clearly, not only are multiproduct and innovating firms likely to have more options in reacting to changes in their OLI variables; the chances are they will also interact with the strategy of a larger number of other firms, both along and between value-added chains.

Strategy initiating variables

Up to this point we have considered strategic induced changes being brought about by changes in the configuration of the OLI variables of firms (i.e. those exogenous to their strategies). Earlier in this chapter we also identified strategy initiating changes. These pro-active changes may be made for a variety of reasons, the most common of which are, first, to improve the O specific advantages of firms (to reduce those of competitors); second, to influence the L attractions of particular countries (in some cases by lobbying governments to take action to help achieve this goal); and third, to reduce the trans-action costs of markets and/or improve the transaction efficiencies of single or collaborative hierarchies. Such autonomous changes in strategy are often sparked off by a change in the ownership of the firm or the composition of its senior management. They may be forced on a company by a failure of previous strategies; or they may be made in anticipation of new technological advances or organiza-tional restructuring. Expected changes in the external environment, e.g. a reorientation in government economic policy, may also neces-sitate a change in strategy. A possible configuration in the structure and composition of competition, and the global strategies of rivals may have a similar effect.

There are two key consequences of strategic initiating changes. The first is that they may result in a particular OLI configuration being responded to in a different way. In this case there will be a direct effect on international production. For example, a greater reluctance to embrace political risks might result in less FDI in politically unstable regimes; while, in anticipation of the effects of the formation of the European Economic Community (EC) in 1958, many US firms began integrating their production facilities within its six founding members.

Second, they may, themselves, impinge upon the OLI configura-tion and, by doing so, affect the level and pattern of international production. A conscious decision to invest more in innovatory activities, or to reduce product diversification and specialize on core value-added activities, or to develop a niche marketing strategy, or to boost up and/or change the format of advertising campaigns, or to introduce new sourcing policies or wage systems, or to decentralize more decision taking activities to regional offices, are just a few examples of autonomous changes in strategy that may affect OLI configuration and, thus, the foreign production of firms.

To what extent is it possible to generalize about the likely form of strategic initiating changes and their effect on international produc-tion? As regards the first question, several writers, e.g. Porter (1986), Doz (1986), Hedlund (1986), Bartlett and Ghoshal (1990) and Teece, Pisano and Shuen (1990), have sought to demonstrate how changes in endogenously determined variables such as the creation and management of technological capabilities and organizational systems, and the revitalization of entrepreneurship, and exogenously determined variables such as the emergence of Japan as a major international competitor, the trend towards less regulated market economies and regional economic integration, and the changing structure of global competition, have affected the direction of the global product and marketing strategies of firms – including their strategies towards foreign production *per se*. Similarly, researchers have identified some of the likely changes in the ownership and locational preferences of firms which have followed, or may be expected to follow, the dismantling of trade barriers in the EC (UN, 1993); from more relaxed Government policies towards inward foreign direct investment (Contractor, 1990); from the competitive pressures to innovate and upgrade the quality of output (Cantwell, 1989); or from the liberalization and deregulation of many service or service related markets (Giersch, 1989; UNCTC, 1988).

As to how these changes are likely to impact on the OLI configuration of firms and, through these, foreign production there has been less substantial research. There is, however, a great deal of casual evidence. For example, a change in the character and geography of European production by US manufacturing affiliates, following the formation of the EC in 1958, led to an increase in the competitive advantages of US firms by offering new opportunities for product rationalization and the economies of common governance. At the same time, it also resulted in a shift in the location of production by US firms to the EC from the United States, and increased the extent to which US firms internalized their exports of technology and management skills to their EC based subsidiaries.

In conclusion, autonomous strategic changes may sometimes affect the level and pattern of international production directly, and sometimes indirectly, through their affect on the firm's OLI configuration. Strategy induced changes are a response to changes in the OLI configuration, which will also impact directly on international production. In each case, strategy is the 'dynamic add-on' variable which links past and current as well as current and future levels of production to existing and future OLI advantages. While changes in international production may and do occur without strategic change, many changes are a direct consequence of it.

Explaining differences in the global strategy of firms

So far in this chapter we have illustrated some ways in which strategy might be incorporated into the variables influencing the foreign decision by the average or representative firm. In doing so, we have argued that the direction of a firm's future strategy is related to its current OLI configuration (which, in turn, is partly the result of its past strategies). *It follows, then, that if firms possess a different configuration of OLI advantages, they are likely to pursue different strategies towards the deployment of these advantages.* Indeed, a good deal of the management literature has sought to identify and explain these strategies, and to examine how far they can be linked to the particular characteristics of firms.

Consider, first, the kind of strategic initiating changes which different kinds of MNEs might introduce. It may, for example, be reasonable to hypothesize that firms, which are leaders in their particular industry in product innovation, are likely to opt for a product differentiation strategy, while those which see their main advantage in supplying low cost products are more likely to pursue a cost minimizing strategy (Porter, 1980, 1985). Integrated MNEs which operate in a large number of countries are likely to pursue different finance raising and international sourcing strategies than those which produce in only one or two countries and who organize their affiliates on an 'every tub on its own bottom' basis. New MNEs seeking to establish a global marketing presence in sectors in which there is a surplus of production capacity are likely to follow very different market entry strategies than those in rapidly growing industries. MNEs which have already decentralized their R&D facilities to several foreign countries and/or adapted their products to local needs, are likely to evolve different innovating strategies than those who centralize these facilities, and/or aim to produce a world product. Given then, a knowledge about the OLI configuration of firms, it should not be difficult, at least, to narrow down the likely choice of strategic initiating changes open to it, and indeed, to classify MNEs accordingly.

Similarly, it may be possible to offer some generalizations about the form of the strategic response of firms to changes in the value of non-strategic variables, according to the character and mix of their OLI configuration. Thus, firms which are particularly adept at supplying and marketing low-cost standardized products are likely to respond differently to regional economic integration than those supplying high quality products to niche markets. MNEs which have a special knowledge of (say) production conditions in Latin America are likely to react differently to locational strategies in respect to changes in these conditions than firms whose main production experience is confined to the Far East. MNEs which compete in a tight oligopolistic market structure, or which have developed close bonds with their industrial customers, are likely to respond differently to a reduction in cross-border market failure than firms which operate in monopolistic competitive markets or which maintain an arms length relationship with their customers.

These illustrations could be multiplied many times. They all point to the conclusion that hypothesizing about the factors which may determine strategy is not very different from hypothesizing about the contextual variables which determine the shape of the OLI configuration affecting particular firms. These we have identified as *industry* (or *activity*), *country* and *firm* specific variables; and the value of each of these is likely to influence both the strategic options open to firms, and their response to them. Alternatively, we might take the OLI configuration as a given variable and relate (future) strategic behavior to that variable. Much depends upon one's starting point of analysis and the extent to which one believes strategic decision taking impacts on the OLI variables or the OLI variables impact on strategy! The answer is likely to be 'both', depending on the time frame one is taking. Thus, we might have:

$$S_{t \to t+1} \, f\,(OLI_t) \text{ or } OLI_t = f\,(S_{t-1 \to t}) \tag{6}$$

We accept, of course, that an explanation of the differences in the strategic behavior by firms based upon their reactions to a particular OLI configuration may not give a complete explanation of such conduct. However, in the context of global strategy, it does have the major advantage that research has already demonstrated its robustness as a framework for analyzing the international operations of firms.

This brings us to another point. Our main subject of explanation is the *foreign* value-added activities of firms. At the same time, as has been pointed out elsewhere (Dunning, 1977, 1988, 1993), these activities may be influenced by variables which affect the ability of such firms to compete in foreign markets independently of whether they engage in foreign production, and by those which are a direct consequence of internalizing cross-border markets. Indeed, it is an important premise of the internalization paradigm that these latter advantages are both a necessary and sufficient condition for FDI to occur.

Similarly, in explaining the global strategy of firms, it is reasonable for the strategic management analyst to direct his attention to those aspects of their behavior which arise from their multinationality *per se*. Hence, for example, the distinction is made by Doz (1986) between integrated MNEs and nationally responsive MNEs; and much of the author's analysis is concerned with identifying differences in the production and marketing strategies pursued by two types of firms. Likewise, Porter's conceptual framework (Porter, 1986) and Teece's distinction between firms pursuing entrance deterring strategies and those pursuing resource and capabilities enhancing strategies (Teece, Pisano and Shuen, 1990) can be readily applied to identifying the managerial responses to a particular OLI configuration facing MNEs, and how these differ according to the degree of multinationality of such firms and their governance structures. Indeed, in their monograph, Bartlett and Ghoshal (1990) specifically address the way in which the globalization of production by firms might affect their organizational capabilities and mentalities, and how these, in turn, may impact on management structures.

CONCLUDING REMARKS: A FIRST CUT AT A SYNTHESIS

The question then remains. How can strategic behavior best be embodied into the economist's approach to international production? First, we have suggested that at the paradigmatic level, strategy specific variables may be incorporated as 'dynamic add-ons' to the OLI configuration of variables, which currently offer a generalized or eclectic framework for explaining the foreign value-added activities of firms. We have also suggested that it is possible to hypothesize about the autonomous or induced strategies likely to be pursued by MNEs according to the configuration of the OLI advantages with which they are faced.

Second, we have argued that, just as any operationally testable *theory* of international production must specify the *kind* of foreign production being considered,[14] so likewise any attempt to theorize about the effect of strategy on foreign production must do the same. Thus, the strategies of firms considering resource based investment are likely to be different from those considering market seeking, cost minimizing or strategic asset acquiring investments, or from those wishing to acquire new competitive advantages. By the same token, different generic product, innovation or marketing strategies will have a different impact on the future OLI configuration of MNEs.

Third, we have asserted that the significance of particular OLI variables will also vary according to the products being produced, the countries of origin and destination, and firm specific factors. So, too, might the relevance of any combination of strategic variables also vary; and it is the task of the business analyst to identify and evaluate these.

One final problem needs mentioning. Most of the OLI variables (or proxies for them) identified by the eclectic paradigm are, to some degree or another, measurable. Strategic variables are, perhaps, less so. How does one quantifiably compare a cost minimizing strategy with a product differentiation strategy? Or an innovating aggressive as compared with an imitating defensive strategy? Or a segmented compared with a general product line strategy? The fact is that most strategic actions can be measured only indirectly, e.g. by their effects. But, this raises another difficulty, namely how to attribute the effect, or effects, associated with a strategic action to that action? Indeed, one can easily fall into the trap of tautological reasoning, viz. the OLI configuration determines strategy yet strategy determines the OLI configuration.

However, by treating strategy as a time related or dynamic variable, this particular trap can be avoided. The challenge which then remains is how to isolate the strategic from the other variables that might affect the future OLI configuration of firms – a problem which most economists avoid by treating strategic success (or failure) as a residual. By the same token, economists, *de facto*, regard the strategic response to a particular OLI configuration as a residual variable in explaining foreign production.

At the end of the day, whether this matters or not obviously rests on the size of the unexplained variable. This, in turn, will depend on how correctly one has identified and specified the appropriate OLI variables and the particular kind of production one wishes to explain.

For example, firms from a particular country or industry which adopt global sourcing strategies are likely to exhibit a very different profile of international production to those which prefer to buy their inputs from local suppliers. The choice of whether to decentralize or centralize R&D facilities is also likely to be closely related to particular innovatory capacities of a firm, which markets its serves, and of how it views the relative advantages of using or internalizing the market for foreign sourced R&D. Firms which engage in product specialization in different countries are likely to be those which have important systemic or common governance advantages, and which supply products which face few barriers to trade and whose transport costs are relatively insignificant. Firms which conclude international coalitions presumably do so because they perceive that this is the best way to exploit or strengthen their existing ownership advantages, *vis-à-vis* their competitors. Firms which practice a strategy of international cost leadership are likely to do so because they have strong competitive advantages in either acquiring cheap and efficient factor inputs or in scale economies. The strategies pursued by firms towards human resource recruitment, deployment and training are likely to reflect the relative importance attached to this management function and the capabilities of their personnel managers.

If the above analysis is correct, what is left to be explained is strategy or strategic change *which is unrelated to the existing OLI variables affecting the firm.* Earlier (pp. 90–2) we gave some examples of autonomous strategic change, which leads, rather than reacts to, any given OLI configuration – but, at the same time, may affect the pattern and structure of international production. Of the strategies which it might be difficult to trace back to the OLI configuration, those which are uncertainty or risk related are perhaps the most significant. Even here, however, there are aspects of entrepreneurial risk strategy, e.g. the measurement of risk, and the choice of options to protect against, counteract, or reduce risk, which may be gauged from knowledge about the OLI configuration.

In as much as intelligent entrepreneurship is, itself, a firm specific advantage and is likely to affect corporate attitudes to uncertainty bearing, there remains only those risks which essentially reflect the attitudes of individual decision takers. That these can be important is witnessed by the dramatic changes in both functional and overall management strategies which often follow a change in the senior management (and especially the Chief Executive) and/or boards of directors of corporations. Indeed, one might hypothesize that, more than any other factor, apart from those strategic related variables embodied in the OLI configuration of firms, the perception of, and attitudes towards, risk taking by the key decision takers in a corporation are the most critical variables determining strategy. And, at the end of the day, because these are, at least partly, culture specific, it may be the difficulty of embodying these in any general theory of the firm – or that of global business strategy – which constrains the extent to which the economist's and strategic analyst's approach to understanding and explaining foreign production can be integrated.

Appendix

An extended version of the eclectic paradigm of international production*

1. *Ownership-Specific Advantages* (of enterprise of one nationality [or affiliates of same] over those of another)
   a. Property right and/or intangible asset advantages.
      Product innovations, production management, organizational and marketing systems, innovatory capacity, noncodifiable knowledge, 'bank' of human capital experience, marketing, finance, knowhow, etc.
   b. Advantages of common governance.
   i. Those that branch plants of established enterprises may enjoy over *de novo* firms.
      Those due mainly to size, product diversity and learning experiences of enterprise, e.g. economies of scope and specialization. Exclusive or favored access to inputs, e.g. labor, natural resources, finance, information. Ability to obtain inputs on favored terms (due, e.g. to size or monopsonistic influence). Exclusive or favored access to product markets. Access to resources of parent company at marginal cost. Synergistic economies (not only in production, but in purchasing, marketing, finance, etc. arrangements).
   ii. Which specifically arise because of multinationality. Multinationality enhances operational flexibility by offering wider opportunities for arbitraging and production shifting. More favored access to and/or better knowledge about international markets, e.g. for information, finance, labor, etc. Ability to take advantage of geographic differences in factor endowments, government intervention, markets, etc. Ability to diversify or reduce risks, e.g. in different currency areas and creation of options and/or political and cultural scenarios. Ability to learn from societal differences in organizational and managerial processes and systems. Balancing economies of integration with ability to respond to differences in country specific needs and advantages.

2. *Internalization Incentive Advantages* (i.e. to protect against or exploit market failure)

*These variables are culled from a variety of sources, but see especially Dunning (1981, 1988, 1993) and Ghoshal (1987).

Avoidance of search and negotiating costs.
To avoid costs of moral hazard and adverse selection, and to protect reputation of internalizing firm.
To avoid cost of broken contracts and ensuing litigation.
Buyer uncertainty (about nature and value of inputs [e.g. technology] being sold).
When market does not permit price discrimination.
Need of seller to protect quality of intermediate or final products.
To capture economies of interdependent activities (see b. above).
To compensate for absence of future markets.
To avoid or exploit government intervention (e.g. quotas, tariffs, price controls, tax differences, etc.).
To control supplies and conditions of sale of inputs (including technology).
To control market outlets (including those which might be used by competitors).
To be able to engage in practices, e.g. cross-subsidization, predatory pricing, leads and lags, transfer pricing, etc. as a competitive (or anticompetitive) strategy.

3. *Location Specific Variables* (these may favor home or host countries).
    Special distribution of natural and created resource endowments and markets.
    Input prices, quality and productivity, e.g., labor, energy, materials, components, semifinished goods.
    International transport and communications costs.
    Investment incentives and disincentives (including performance requirements, etc.)
    Artificial barriers (e.g. import controls) to trade in goods and services.
    Societal and infrastructure provisions (commercial, legal, educational, transport and communication).
    Cross-country ideological, language, cultural, business, political, etc. differences.
    Economics of centralization of R&D production and marketing.
    Economic system and policies of government: the institutional framework for resource allocation.

4	*Dynamic 'Add-on'* Strategy Related Variables (Some illustrations)	Extent and form of innovation – and in what direction? Is the firm aiming to develop core or diversified competencies?
	Technology and Innovation	Is the firm primarily an innovator or an imitator? Does the firm internalize or externalize the R&D function? To centralize or decentralize R&D? Nature of foreign R&D activities. Form and nature of technology transfer.
	Product	Degree of product specialization or diversification.

	High quality or low cost product? Product line broadening or upgrading? Degree of vertical integration. Degree of geographical specialization of plants. Extent to which products are adapted for local consumption.
Sourcing	The 'make' or 'buy' decision. Single or multiple sourcing? To source locally or import? Form of relationship with suppliers. Quality control exercised over intermediate products.
Production	Methods of manufacturing (batch, mass production, flexible manufacturing). Extent to which production processes are adopted in foreign subsidiaries. Work practices. Quality control and inspection procedures.
Human Resource Management	Recruitment policy (e.g. extent to which this is centralized or decentralized). Patterns of industrial relations. Methods of wage payments, productivity incentives, and fringe benefits. Worker participation in decision making process. Training programs. Policy towards employment of local nationals in foreign subsidiaries.
Marketing and Distribution	Geographical market orientation. Broad liner, innovator, nicher or synergist. Distribution channels. 'Do it yourself' or use agents? Control over markets served by foreign subsidiaries. Extent of intrafirm trade. Advertising *et al.* promotional techniques.
Organization	M, U or matrix form? Ethnocentric, polycentric or geocentric attitudes towards foreign operations. Multidomestic, global or transnational

	orientation of MNEs towards foreign affiliates.
	Organizational structure of foreign affiliates.
	Degree of control or influence exerted over decision taking by affiliates.
	How far are local managers included in centralized decision taking process?
Finance and Accounting	Techniques of capital budgeting and evaluation of investment projects.
	Sourcing of finance.
	Transnational accounting, budgetary, and planning control procedures.
Ownership	Extent of ownership of foreign subsidiaries.
	Policies towards strategic alliances – with whom and what form?
	Strategy towards joint ventures and non-equity associations.
Locational Issues	Attitudes towards foreign production and geographical risk diversification
	Leverage and arbitrage opportunities.
	Behavior of competitors, supplies, customers, etc.
	Nature of interface with home and foreign governments; negotiating and bargaining strengths and tactics of the two parties.

5 The competitive advantage of countries and MNE activity

INTRODUCTION

The dynamic interplay between the competitive advantages of countries and those enterprises of a particular nationality is a subject commanding the increasing attention by students of the MNE. Indeed, it has been suggested that a fuller understanding of the nature, content and determinants of this interaction, as it affects the globalization of production and markets, may provide the basis for one of the next advances in the theory of foreign value-added activity[1] (Dunning, 1990).

Since the mid-1970s, the focus of scholars interested in explaining the existence and growth of the MNE has been directed to identifying and evaluating the relative costs and benefits of organizing the cross-border transactions of intermediate products by hierarchies or markets. In the early 1990s, however, renewed attention[2] is being given to explaining the origin and composition of the resources and capabilities[3] of corporations to engage in production outside their national boundaries and to the determinants of their success in managing and organizing the international portfolio of resources rather than ownership or control. Faced with the same economic conditions and prospects, why are some firms significant global players and others are not? Why is the share of international direct investment accounted for by Japanese companies rising so rapidly? Why is Europe claiming a larger share of US based MNE activity than it used to? What explains the rapid growth of the participation of foreign owned firms in the United States? What determines which developing countries will emerge as important international investors? Why do firms conclude strategic alliances with some firms, but avoid them with others? Why is foreign direct investment (FDI) in services rising more rapidly than that in goods?

These are just some of the questions now demanding answers by MNE researchers. What is their response? Well, one response by the scholar of the MNE, *qua MNE*,[4] is that only part of the explanation for the growth of foreign owned production may have to do with the increasing propensity of firms to internalize their cross-border transactions. For example, a particular competitive advantage which may help to explain the capability of a firm to supply a particular market, or set of markets, is not, in itself, a sufficient reason for that firm to create, or add value to, that advantage from a foreign located facility.

Take, for example, a pharmaceutical patent as a competitive advantage of a UK MNE. The *origin* of that advantage is likely to be determined by a combination of factors, including the amount of resources the company allocates to innovatory activities, the quality and motivation of R&D personnel, the organization and technical efficiency of the R&D department, and the successful commercialization of that R&D. The *outcome* of that advantage is that it may enable the UK firm to increase its penetration of the world drug market. Is the possession of this advantage an explanation for any increase in foreign production, which might directly arise from such an advantage; or, is it simply to be taken as an exogenous variable which may or may not lead to such production?

Supposing, next, it can be shown that it pays the UK firm to produce the new pharmaceutical product for worldwide distribution from its German plant rather than to export it from its UK plant. Is this an explanation of international production; or is it rather an explanation of the location of economic activity, *given* its ownership? Or, is the explanation of MNE activity concerned only with the circumstances in which a firm engages in foreign value-added activity rather than the next best option open to it, *given* its resources and capabilities and the locational opportunities open to it?

If this latter is thought to be the main focus of interest, then Michael Porter's book *The Competitive Advantage of Nations* will be of limited appeal.[5] If, however, it is perceived that, for example, part of Japanese direct investment in the US car industry is due to the success of Japanese owned firms in producing highly saleable motor vehicles, irrespective of the mode by which this advantage is exploited, and that the reasons for such a success are, themselves, part of the explanation for their foreign activities, then much of the Porter monograph is highly relevant to the student of the MNE.

Our own view is that Michael Porter has rendered a very considerable service in identifying many of the explanatory variables which help us better appreciate some *country specific* explanations of the changing pattern of international production by MNEs. In particular, his extensive field research has advanced our knowledge of why corporations domiciled in some countries have been successful in penetrating foreign markets in some product areas but not in others; and also why some countries have been able to attract inbound MNE activity in some value-added activities but not in others. The book also offers a penetrating insight as to why, in some countries and sectors, the activities of MNEs help stimulate the technological and organizational efficiency of local firms, and why, in other cases, they inhibit it. More generally, many of the ideas and concepts articulated by Porter help enrich our understanding of the dynamic interplay between the strategy of MNEs and the competitive advantages of countries in which they operate.

THE 'DIAMOND' OF COMPETITIVE ADVANTAGE

By now, most readers of this volume will be familiar with the main analytical tools used by Porter in his latest book, viz. the diamond of competitive advantage. By competitive advantage, Porter means the ability of a country – or more specifically indigenous firms of a country – to use its location-bound resources in a way which will enable it (them) to be competitive in international markets. Porter likens the determinants of this ability to a diamond which comprises a set of attributes which 'shape the environment in which local firms compete, and which promote or impede the creation of competitive market' (Porter, 1990: 71). He goes on to argue that the diamond is a naturally reinforcing system, with each of its determinants being contingent on the state of the other (ibid.: 72)

According to Porter, the strength, composition and sustainability of a nation's competitive advantage will be demonstrated by the value of its national product[6] and/or the rate of growth of that product, *relative to that of its leading competitors*. The extent to which a country is successful in achieving this goal then depends on the kind of goods and services produced by its enterprises, and the efficiency at which they are supplied. This, in turn, Porter suggests, rests on the extent and quality of, and the interaction between, four sets of attributes:

1 The quantity and quality of demand for goods and services by its domestic consumers.
2 The level and composition of its natural resources and created factor capabilities.[7]

3 The domestic rivalry of wealth producing agencies, i.e. the nature and extent of interfirm competition.
4 The extent to which its firms are able to benefit from agglomerative or external economies by being spatially grouped in clusters of related activities.

Surrounding and influencing these variables are two others, viz. the role of government and chance. Excluding the MBA component (to be discussed later), Figure 5.1 sets out Porter's depiction of the 'structure' of the diamond.

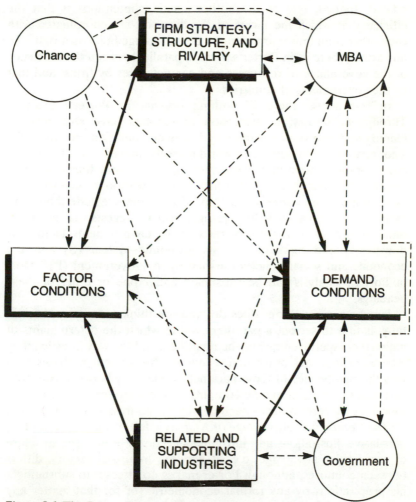

Figure 5.1 The Porter diamond: the complete system.

The main objective of Porter's work is twofold. First, it is to show that these facets of the diamond, and the way in which they interact, will vary between countries. Second, it is to suggest that the principal ways in which countries may improve their competitiveness are to upgrade the quantity or quality of their resources and capabilities and/or to utilize their existing resources and capabilities more efficiently.

Much of Michael Porter's treatise, which extends to over 800 pages, is directed to providing the reader with examples of the ways in which the various facets of the diamond are systemically interrelated. Indeed, one of the author's main contentions is that the efficiency at which the facets of the diamond are coordinated with each other is an important competitive advantage in its own right. To this extent, there is, in Porter's mind, a parallel between the efficiency of the governance of resources and competencies by firms, and that by the governments of countries.

In one sense, there is nothing original in Porter's analysis. Throughout history, a succession of scholars have attempted to identify and evaluate the supply and demand conditions necessary for a country to be competitive in world markets. Indeed, most have been more comprehensive than Porter, who identifies only four sources of competitive advantage and pays little or no attention to such variables as investment and entrepreneurship.[8] The scholars include those who focus on the so called ESP paradigm, which suggests that an economic prosperity of a country rests on its environment (factor endowments) and markets (E), its economic system (S) and the economic and social policies pursued by its Government (P).[9] Most of Porter's analysis can be subsumed under one or other of these headings.

However, what Porter does do, and, we think, does very successfully, is first to set out a paradigm within which the determinants of national competitiveness may be identified, and the way in which they interrelate with each other, and second to offer some hypotheses as to why the significance of these parameters may vary between countries and sectors. The monograph contains eight country case studies[10] and four industry case studies – each of which is addressed to these issues.

The Competitive Advantage of Nations is full of short case studies, persuasive illustrations and intriguing anecdotes of why the structure of competitive advantage, e.g. as between industrial sectors, differs between countries, although Porter makes no attempt to substantiate his propositions by any formal econometric (or for that matter any other) testing! Indeed, on several occasions, the reader feels that the author comes near to rationalizing his arguments, and that, had he chosen to do so, he could have provided illustrations which point to the opposite of the conclusions he draws.

One of the most interesting chapters of the book concerns the role of governments. Porter prefers to consider government not as an attribute of the diamond, but as a fashioner of its structure and efficiency. This makes sense! Although, as producers and consumers, governments may directly affect the supply and demand of both immobile and mobile resources and capabilities affecting competitiveness, they alone have the ultimate responsibility for shaping the framework, or system, under which these resources and capabilities are organized. They set the 'rules of the game' and set the signals, which trigger a response by firms, which determine whether national competitiveness is advanced or not. Moreover, in a variety of ways, they affect the ability and motivation of a nation's citizens and firms, for example to save, to be entrepreneurial, to work efficiently, to accept new ideas and attitudes and to upgrade human and technological capacity. By affecting exchange rates, by participating (or not) in supra-national trading schemes, and by their policies and regulations towards FDI, they may influence the extent to which, and the form in which, a country is involved in international commerce.

It is not the purpose of this chapter to give a detailed critique of Porter's work, but rather to examine its relevance to our understanding of international business activity. In several places, the author addresses himself to the ways in which outward and inward direct investment by MNEs may affect both their own competitiveness and that of the countries in which they operate. In general, however, he seems to believe that the main thrust to improving national competitiveness must come from a better use of indigenous resources and capabilities by domestic corporations. Indeed, Porter frequently cautions governments from relying too much on the affiliates of foreign MNEs to fulfil this task.

While, in principle, we would not wish to take issue with Porter on this point, the fact that between 30 per cent and 40 per cent of the sales of the leading industrial MNEs are now produced outside their national boundaries, and that the value of these sales now considerably exceeds that of international trade, suggests to us that more explicit attention should be given to the ways in which the transnationalization of business activity could affect the nature and character of the diamond of competitive advantage of the countries involved. Certainly, there is ample evidence that the technological and organizational assets of MNEs are influenced by the configuration of the diamonds of the foreign countries in which they produce, and that this, in turn, may impinge upon the competitiveness of the resources and capabilities of their home countries.[11]

Indeed, we would submit that in the global economy of the 1990s, it is entirely appropriate to consider a country's involvement in foreign trade and commerce as a separate exogenous variable affecting the facets of the diamond in the same way in which Porter treats the role of government. However, for the purpose of this chapter, we shall consider only the foreign production of domestic owned firms and the domestic production of foreign based MNEs as they affect the shape of particular national diamonds.

THE ACTIVITIES OF MNEs AS AN ADDITIONAL EXOGENOUS VARIABLE AFFECTING THE DIAMOND

Let us then treat the foreign business activities of MNEs, i.e. the foreign output of domestic MNEs and the domestic output of foreign non-resident owned companies, as an exogenous factor, along with chance and government, affecting the diamond of competitive advantage. Figure 5.1 introduces this new component, i.e. multi-national business activity (MBA) into the Porter schema. How might this affect the strength and composition of a nation's competitive advantage?

First, let us briefly remind ourselves of the distinctive features of MNEs, i.e. those which might be attributed specifically to their transnationality. Consider, for example, some of the unique characteristics of *inward* direct investment. First, it is likely to provide a different package of resources and capabilities (e.g. finance capital, technology, management skills, etc.) than that provided by domestic investors. This is partly because these are being imported from a country which has a different combination of competitive advantages, and partly because some of these assets, at least, are likely to be specific to the firm which owns them. Japanese owned subsidiaries in the UK, for example, draw upon a different set of resources and capabilities (or the same resources and capabilities at different prices) than do UK owned firms. Put another way, the sourcing and marketing opportunities and the production and organizational capabilities of the two groups of firms are likely to be different.

Second, the use made of these assets is likely to be different, partly because the firm is foreign owned, and partly because of the distinctive characteristics of multinationality *per se*, for example, those to do with the international arbitraging of resources and capabilities and the spreading of risks of environmental volatility (Kogut, 1985). *Inter alia*, this suggests that decisions taken by the local subsidiary of an MNE might be different than if it were domestically owned, and that a decision on local resource allocation by a uninational firm might be different than if that firm operated a global network of subsidiaries.

It is the balance between the asset transfer and the control of the use of these assets that is the essence of the uniqueness of MNE activity; although, depending upon the macro-economic situation in the home and host country and the assumptions made about government macro-organizational policies, it is possible that inward investment might also affect the *level* of economic activity.

Consider next some unique features of *outward* direct investment. There are at least three distinguishing attributes of MNEs compared with uninational (or international trading) firms. The first is the additional options to the former in the geographical configuration of their value-added activities. Second, MNEs have more opportunity to diversify their assets and economic activity to reduce exchange and other risks of producing in different countries. Third, MNEs find it easier to gain access to foreign resources, markets, economic systems, business relationships, infrastructure and forms of competition. Indeed (borrowing from Porter's terminology), an important competitive advantage of MNEs is their unique ability to draw upon and make use of different national diamonds of competitive advantage.

Given these (and other) distinguishing characteristics of cross-border business activity, how might it affect the competitiveness of countries? The answer will mainly rest on the values of three contextual variables. The first relates to the *nature* of the MNE activity. Here, the relevant questions include: Is it market seeking, resource seeking, efficiency seeking (e.g. cost reducing) or strategic asset seeking in its intent? Is it primarily to protect or exploit an existing competitive advantage or to acquire a new advantage? Is the investment a greenfield investment or an acquisition of existing assets? Is it a 100 per cent subsidiary or a joint venture? Is it an initial or sequential investment? Is it a stand alone or an integrated investment?

The second group of variables relate to the content and structure of the *existing* competitive advantages of a country. Is domestic rivalry, prior to outward or inward investment, weak or strong? Are its factor endowments plentiful or not? Are domestic consumers demanding more differentiated products or not? What role do governments play in upgrading or standardizing product quality? And so on.

The third main variable, which affects and is affected by the second, are the economic signals provided by governments. To what extent, and in what way, might (or do) governments, directly or indirectly, influence both the competitiveness of the resources and capabilities within their jurisdiction, and the actions of their own, and/or foreign, MNEs?

Clearly, the significance of each of these three variables will depend on (home and host) *country* (or region), *firm* and *activity* specific circumstances; and while, at any given moment of time, they might be independent of each other, over time they are closely interlinked. For example, FDI may both impact on the technological capabilities of rival domestic firms and be affected by them. However, for the purpose of our analysis, it may be appropriate to consider the impact of a change of inward or outward investment on *the existing competitive advantages of firms and industries.*

We would make one other general point. In most analyses of the impact of MBA on national competitiveness, inward and outward direct investment are considered independently of each other. Although each kind of investment has its distinctive consequences, there is some merit in considering these as opposite sides of the same coin. This is especially so when looking at the macro-organizational dynamics of competitiveness. Though there is no necessary connection between a change in inward investment and the propensity of domestic firms to engage in outward investment (i.e. it may affect only domestic resource allocation), in practice, in a world in which four-fifths of MNE activity is within the advanced industrial countries, and is primarily intra-industry in character, the volume and structure of outward and inward direct investment are likely to be closely interwoven, and governed by broadly similar factors.

The evidence suggests, however, that the relationship between the two is not straightforward (Dunning, 1985). Indeed, a fascinating topic for additional research (and one not really tackled at all by Porter) is the identification of the circumstances in which changes in the level and/or structure of outward and inward MBA move in similar directions (i.e. are complementary to each other), and those in which they move in opposite directions (i.e. are substitutable for each other).[12]

For the purpose of this chapter, however, we will try and analyze some of the implications of a spontaneous or induced change in outward and inward MNE activity on each of the four facets of the diamond of competitive advantage, both directly and indirectly through their repercussions on the actions of government. Again, we shall concentrate on just one or two aspects of each of the four facets. We would also reiterate that the facets are closely interlinked and that the more one takes a dynamic perspective of the impact of MNE activity, the less useful it is to consider each competitive-related variable separately.

The conditions of demand

Porter argues that the *structure* of domestic demand may affect the competitiveness of firms in the international market by providing an impetus for domestic firms to produce high quality, well designed, reliable and differentiated goods, relative to those supplied by their foreign competitors. Assuming that such an emphasis on product consistency or differentiation, rather than on a cost-reducing strategy, is the most effective strategy for firms to pursue,[13] to what extent is MNE activity likely to affect, or be affected by, such demand conditions?

Consider first the likely interaction between local patterns of demand and *inward* investment. Here the impact of such investment is likely to depend on the pattern and quality of the existing demand, and how it compares with that of the investing nation and that of other countries in which the MNE produces. It is also likely to depend on the product strategy of the investing firms and the extent to which they perceive product quality and reliability, themselves, to be critical competitive advantages. Another relevant variable is the extent to which a country's citizens have been previously exposed to the products of the investing company (e.g. through exports), and/or how far the products have been produced for export markets by indigenous companies. Much will also rest on whether the FDI takes the form of an acquisition of, or merger with, an existing firm, or a greenfield venture. Finally, over time, the affect on demand quality will rest on the impact of FDI on other facets of the diamond, e.g. domestic rivalry and indigenous technological capability.

It is possible to conceive of a number of possible scenarios. Take, for example, the case of a foreign chocolate producer which acquires a domestic firm in the same line of business, with the aim of gaining access to the local market. Assume, next, that the acquired firm produces high quality chocolate, but that the acquiring firm's competitive advantage lies in producing standardized low cost chocolate. Assume, too, that the acquiring firm has chocolate producing facilities elsewhere in the world, and that it does not intend exporting from the country of the acquired firm. Then, in such cases – unless the

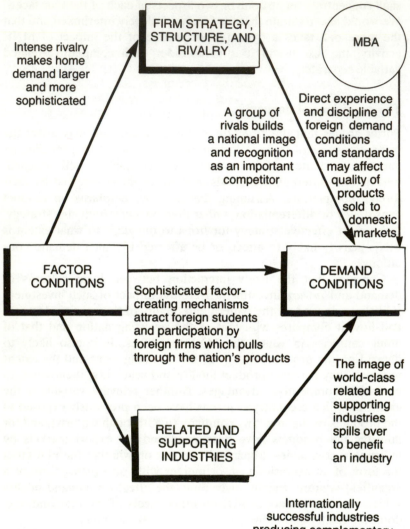

Figure 5.2 Influences on home demand conditions.

acquiring firm simply adds to the product range of the acquired firm – there could be a *lowering* of the standards of demand by the citizens of the host country.[14]

Consider next a scenario in which an investing firm perceives its main competitive advantage to be consistency of the quality of its color television sets. Assume that some impact on domestic consumer demand (via informing consumers about defect-free products and raising their purchasing standards) may have been made by the exports of the investing country, but that the presence of local production facilities increases this awareness. Then, given the other facets of the diamond, the upgrading of consumer expectations might force other firms to improve the quality, or lower the costs, of their products, which might, in turn, advance their competitiveness. This, in fact, is what appears to have happened as a result of Japanese direct investment in the European and US motor vehicles and consumer electronics industries. Chapter 7 presents further details.

Earlier, we suggested that the impact of inward investment on the diamond of competitive advantage may depend on the purposes of that investment. As far as the impact on *domestic* demand is concerned, this is clearly most likely to be felt where the intention of the investment is to service the domestic, and sometimes adjacent, markets, i.e. import substituting investment; although, whether or not this is the case depends, in part at least, on the extent to which the host government may influence the conditions of demand.[15]

Indirectly, demand conditions in the home country, including the influence of the host government over them (e.g. via the level and structure of direct and indirect taxation, their control over the quality of public goods and services, the harmonization and upgrading of technical standards, such as in the procurement of telecommunication systems, and the imposition of rigorous safety, health and environmental regulations) may influence the extent to which foreign firms are willing to invest in the host country, and hence their contribution to other parts of the diamond.

Consider next the way in which foreign activities of domestic MNEs affect, or may be affected by, the structure and content of domestic demand. Take the case of foreign investment by a company from a country in which either intermediate or final product consumers are relatively unsophisticated (perhaps because they are protected from foreign competition) operating in a country in which consumers are highly demanding. Assume, for the moment, that such an investment is possible because the investing companies have some kind of technological or marketing advantage over competitive firms in the recipient country. Then, insofar as consumer expectations and requirements in the foreign market affect the comparability, quality or cost of the product supplied to that market they may, in turn, influence the kinds of products sold in the domestic market. Alternatively, 'easy pickings' in an important foreign market could make a firm less aware of, or less willing to cater to, the more stringent demands of domestic consumers and, indeed, even lower the product quality and reliability of its locally produced output.

On the other hand, the ability of a firm to become an outward investor may be influenced by the extent to which domestic consumers have forced indigenous firms to provide more differentiated or higher quality products than those normally accepted by foreign consumers. A classic case is that of Japanese outward investment in the motor vehicles and consumer electronics sectors;[16] while, similarly, Japanese component suppliers faced with the rigorous demands of their industrial customers in these same sectors are in a better position to supply the latter's competitors in the international market.

So much for extremes and generalities. To what extent can one identify the conditions necessary for MNE activity to act as a vehicle for upgrading consumer demand?[17] We would suggest that the answer is comparatively simple. Consider first the demand conditions of the home country of the inward investor, or the host country of the outward investor, and compare these with those of the countries in which the inward or outward MNE already produces. Second, consider whether or not such knowledge about these conditions, and/or the impetus to create them, could be, or are, being achieved at lower cost, through alternative means. Third, consider whether or not consumers are likely to embrace such conditions. How sensitive are they, for example, to foreign purchasing customs and standards? Fourth, consider the *power* of consumers to influence the quality of products supplied by competitive firms. For example, how significant are they in relation to the purchases of similar products?

Finally, consumer awareness, or pressure for quality improvement, is not always a necessary (and rarely is it a sufficient) condition for the upgrading of consumer demand. Nor is it necessarily desirable if it results in a reduction of economic welfare in other directions.[18] One of the best examples which comes to mind is the quality of in-flight facilities provided by international airlines. Customers, irrespective of their nationality, applaud the quality of food and in-flight service offered by such airlines as Singapore, Thai, Cathay Pacific and Swiss Air, and almost unanimously believe that the caliber of the equivalent

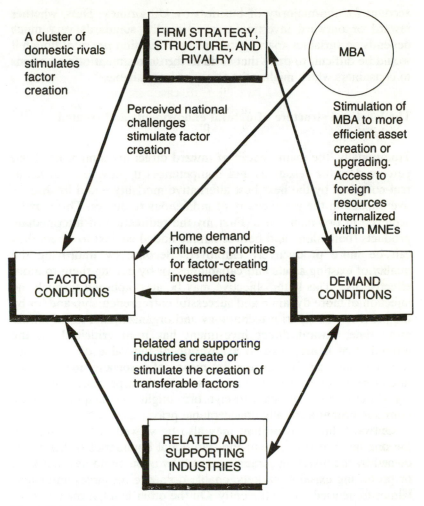

Figure 5.3 Influences on factor creation.

amenities provided by many US airlines is inferior. Why, then, it might be asked, don't US air travelers insist upon higher quality from their own airlines?

The answer seems to be twofold. First, the US airlines tend to compete on the basis of (indirect) price reductions, e.g. through generous frequent flyer mileage programs, which may appeal even to the most discerning business traveler. Second, there is no competition from the best foreign airlines on *domestic* US routes, which still account for the majority of business by US airlines. Thus, whether inward or outward investment raises quality standards very much depends on variables apart from consumer reaction *per se*, although it would be difficult to deny that such foreign investment offers options to consumers which might otherwise not be available.[19]

The level and structure of natural endowments and created capabilities

Traditionally, the main benefit of inward direct investment has been perceived as the resources and competences it provides – at lower real cost than by the next best alternative modality – and its distinctive impact on the productivity of indigenous resources. This may be achieved in two main ways. First, by the redirection of intermediate products (both along and between value added chains) to where they can be more productively employed. Second, by improving the quality of existing assets and capabilities, or by putting them to more effective use. This latter objective may be accomplished through the injection of more dynamic and successful entrepreneurship and/or by the provision of superior technology and organizational skills. At the same time, inward direct investment has been criticized on the grounds that it may lead to a lowering of the value of indigenous resources and capabilities, e.g. by means of a socially unacceptable rate of depletion of natural resources, or by the repatriation of assets, e.g. R&D facilities, which a foreign firm might have acquired from a domestic firm at a socially unacceptable price.

Outward direct investment may also be viewed in two ways. On the one hand, it may extend the traditional boundaries of the assets owned by the investing companies, and, by opening up new markets, or protecting existing markets, enable domestic resources and capabilities to be used more efficiently. On the other hand, it may transfer such resources and capabilities, notably finance capital and technology, which might have been deployed more productively in the domestic market.

Again, the balance of these costs and benefits, and the interaction between them, will depend on the motives for, and types of, MNE activity; the existing level, pattern and productivity of indigenous resources; and the economic environment in which the investment is made.[20] It will also rest on the alternatives to acquiring resources by FDI.[21] For example, throughout most of the post-war period, Japan has managed to obtain many of the benefits which inward investment might have provided by way of non-equity transfers of technology and human skills (including the conclusion of strategic alliances with foreign firms) and by importing knowledge intensive products. Smaller European countries like The Netherlands, Switzerland and Sweden could not have improved or retained their competitive positions without their companies producing much of their output outside their home countries. By contrast, some commentators (Gilpin, 1975, 1987) have argued that, by exporting advanced technology through outward direct investment, the US has eroded its competitive position, and reduced the capability of its own companies to maintain their innovating capabilities *vis-à-vis* their European and Japanese counterparts.[22]

The distinctive impact of MNEs on the international allocation of natural resources and created capabilities depends not only on ability and desire of such companies to internally transfer such assets between countries but also on the control exerted over the deployment of these and other intermediate products under their control. This is mainly reflected in the type of economic activity undertaken, which, in turn, will affect the kind and productivity of resources used, and the ability of the economy to adapt to changes in world supply and demand conditions. Moreover, insofar as foreign firms may effect both the sourcing of inputs and the destination of outputs, they may also have consequences for the stability of domestic resource deployment.

In examining the specific impact of FDI, it is important to distinguish between short and long run consequences. It is quite possible that in the short run, by producing more efficiently than its indigenous competitors, over a limited range of the value-added chain, a foreign firm may increase domestic output. However, if, in so doing, it competes out of existence a domestic firm that, taking the value added chain as a whole, has a higher domestic value added per resource used, this may lead to a less efficient use of resources and capabilities in the long run.

Such a consequence, however, might be acceptable to the host country if the actions of the foreign firm were in response to competitive market signals and the resources released could be redeployed more productively elsewhere in the economy. To this extent, it is important not to take a partial approach in examining the consequences of FDI. Let us give two examples. Take first a situation in which outward investment is directed either to activities which require resources and capabilities in which the investing country is comparatively disadvantaged, or is losing its comparative advantage, or where the purpose of the investment is to acquire resources and capabilities, which will add to the competitiveness of the existing assets of the investing company. Suppose, next, that, due to appropriate structural adjustment policies and the willingness of firms to reallocate resources, the resources released were taken over by foreign investors, who, by combining these with other foreign assets, e.g. entrepreneurship, technology, organizational capability, were able to use them more productively. Then, in such a case, MBA is likely both to increase and upgrade indigenous competences.

Consider now a second example. Assume that a foreign firm responds to import controls imposed by the host government, or takes defensive oligopolist reaction to produce goods which require resources, valued at international market prices, in which the home country has a comparative advantage. Suppose, too, that, to avoid unwelcome industrial or penal fiscal policies pursued by their own government, domestic firms choose to increase their foreign, rather than their home, investments. Then, in such cases, although overseas production might be a second or third best solution, the first best solution, in terms of domestic factor endowments, might be for the government to modify its macro-economic policies so that the prices of domestic inputs and outputs more accurately reflect their true opportunity cost.

Finally, the net effect on factor endowments and created capabilities of MNE activity is likely to rest on the price paid for the inward investment and the gains accruing from outward investment to the investing country. For example, a takeover of a domestic firm might reduce the competitiveness of the resources used by the acquired firm (although it may help to improve the competitiveness of those used by the acquiring firm). However, from the perspective of the host country, the takeover would be undesirable only if the agreed price was insufficient to compensate for these (possible) adverse affects. Here the distinction between the social and private price of an acquisition is of critical importance (Dunning and Steuer, 1969).

Similarly, the returns from outward investment should include not only the foreign income earned by the affiliate, but all the other benefits existing from its presence, e.g. the feedback of technological or managerial know-how and the increased market it makes possible for domestic resources. Various studies have shown that, in some sectors, and by some countries, MBA has made a significant contribution to the restructuring and upgrading of domestic resources.[23] Indeed, the foreign activities of Japanese MNCs have played an integral part in the restructuring and upgrading of the Japanese economy since the mid-1960s (Ozawa, 1989)

Domestic rivalry

Porter also argues that the extent and degree of competition between domestic rivals is an important variable affecting national competitiveness. In particular, he points to the larger number of firms competing with each other in Japan than in the US as a factor making for the higher industrial competitiveness of the former country.

The optimum structure of a market for competitive and innovatory stimulus has always been a matter for debate. Certainly, it would be erroneous to argue that a greater population of firms necessarily means more *effective* competition. The Canadian experience – and that of other countries with small markets – completely belies this. However, there can be little doubt that the number and type of competitors is an important variable affecting the strategic conduct of firms, and that some forms of market structure are more conducive to the promotion of short or long term competitiveness than others. Lawrence (1987), for example, views an optimum market structure as one which allows neither cut-throat or destructive competition on the one hand nor lethargy on the other, on the part of the constituent firms.[24]

The literature also suggests that MNEs are likely to impact on domestic market structure both by the resources, capabilities and/or markets they can provide and by the control exerted over these assets, and any others germane to their jurisdiction. In turn, these effects may impinge on the behavior of their competitors and the structure of the industry in which they operate.

Again, it may be helpful to illustrate from two extreme scenarios. The first is where a foreign firm takes over an existing producer and uses its global power to drive out local competitors. Furthermore, assume that this power is being used not to advance efficiency, but to promote a monopoly position. In such a case, it is likely that domestic rivalry will be adversely affected by such investment – although whether or not this lowers overall economic competitiveness will depend upon the other consequences of the takeover. The second scenario is where a foreign firm injects a new element of competition into a market supplied by a local monopolist, or where, as a result of an acquisition, it revitalizes an industry which might otherwise have perished because of insufficient or inappropriate competition.

A major drawback of most attempts to identify the optimum market structure of firms is that they tend to limit their attention to domestic or national markets. In a world in which the bulk of activity in many sectors is dominated by MNEs, this is unacceptable.

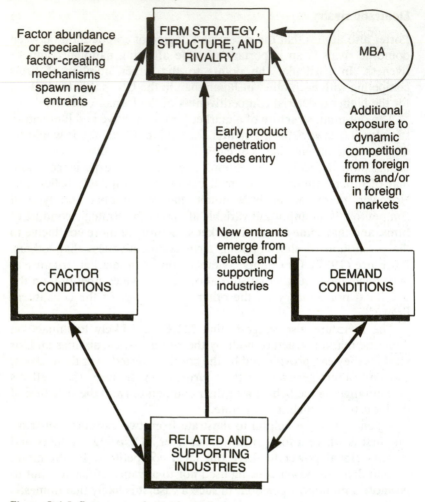

Figure 5.4 Influences on domestic rivalry.

Competition between the major pharmaceutical, consumer electronics, banking, oil, tire and motor vehicle companies is not mainly played out in national, but in world, markets. Michael Porter cites the greater number of Japanese firms in several industries as an illustration of competitive rivalry. Yet, at the time of Porter's research, the Japanese market was largely closed to foreign competition. Not only this: until recently, the majority of the output of Japanese companies was sold to domestic consumers.

The situation is very different in the case of some smaller advanced industrialized or industrializing countries, which are also well up in the competitiveness league table, notably Switzerland, Sweden, The Netherlands, Singapore and Hong Kong. We think it unlikely that the Chief Executives of Nestlé, Philips or SKF would accept that the competition they encounter is any the less intense than that faced by their Japanese or US equivalents. The difference is that the former is almost exclusively provided by foreign competitors. What is more important is that, as markets become globalized, and cross-border trading barriers are relaxed, the international dimension of interfirm rivalry is likely to increase.

Indeed, it is possible to go further and argue that a persuasive case can be made out that, in the right circumstances, rivalry by foreign firms might offer greater benefits than that between domestic firms. At the same time, domestic firms, which also produce outside their national boundaries, are, for the most part, likely to face tougher competition than those which supply only domestic markets – particularly where the latter markets are protected.

Our conclusion is, then, that there are consequences on domestic rivalry which are distinctive to MBA. We accept that, *a priori*, it may be difficult to predict whether or not, in the long run, these are likely to be beneficial or not. But, it is possible to argue that both inward and outward direct investment do have the potential for increasing healthy domestic rivalry, and hence improving this particular facet of the diamond of competitive advantage. Whether the potential is translated into reality depends on the existing domestic and international market structure, the type and form of FDI and its impact on the market structure,[25] and the role played by national governments in setting the appropriate signals for rivalry.

Agglomerative economies and the clustering of related industries

The presence of economies external to the firm but internal to a network or cluster of firms located in a particular geographical area is a familiar competitive advantage articulated by economists since the time of Alfred Marshall. The fact that clusters of related activities do exist and confer considerable benefits to the participating firms has been spelled out in various regional studies, notably those on the City of London (Dunning and Morgan, 1971), California's Silicon Valley (Scott and Angel, 1987), the location of government research establishments in south east England (Hall *et al.*, 1987), the Greater Grenoble area in France (Boisgontier and de Bernardy, 1986), several districts in Northern Italy (Malerba, 1990) and the Ibaragi

Prefecture in Japan.[26] Moreover, these studies suggest that the need for firms to draw on resources and capabilities, which have to be geographically concentrated to be efficiently supplied, is increasing.

The advantages of clusters, as described by Porter, is that firms benefit from a shared culture and learning experience, supply capabilities and local infrastructure, which gives them a competitive edge in both domestic and international markets.

Geographical clusters or networks of economic activity may take various forms. They may be between firms producing different products across value-added chains, or between firms producing similar products at different stages of the same chain. The related presence is assumed to benefit all firms within the cluster and, hence, protect or advance competitiveness.

In his book, Porter does not attempt to measure the significance of clusters as a facet of the diamond, nor whether or not this particular advantage has become more important with the passage of time. Nor does he give much attention to the conditions which make for successful clusters. Clearly, not all firms need to be part of a network of vertical or horizontal linkages. Moreover, not all linkages need to be in the same or similar locations.

Let us now consider the extent to which efficient clustering is likely to be affected by the MBA in either home or host countries. In what way does it respond to, or affect, the propensity of firms to cluster differently than that conducted by non-MNEs?

Perhaps the first point worth making is that the MNE (and, more especially, the large diversified MNE) is *par excellence* a network of interrelated activities. Indeed, one of its strengths derives from the external economies associated with particular types of activities, which it, as a coordinator of these activities, can capture. Corporate integration makes possible the economies of common governance. Sometimes, these economies are best exploited in the same location, and sometimes in different locations.

At the same time, there is some suggestion that MNEs may create their own clusters of foreign based activity. Indeed, Knickerbocker observed this as a phenomenon of MNE activity two decades ago (Knickerbocker, 1973), while, in the 1980s and 1990s, there is ample evidence that Japanese motor vehicle consumer electronics, rubber tire and chemical firms are pursuing a 'follow my leader' strategy in investing in Europe and the US. More than this, the presence of such firms is encouraging investment by Japanese component suppliers and subcontractors, and new intra-industry value chain networks are being established.

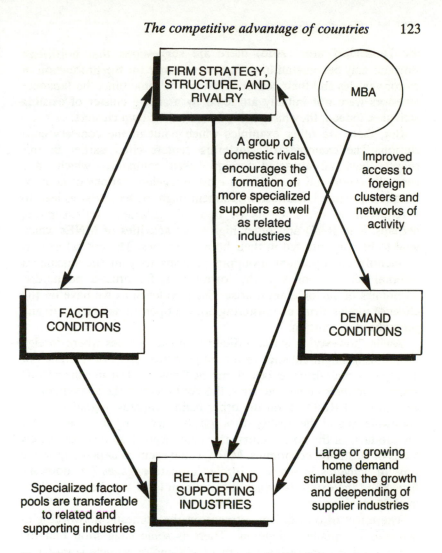

Figure 5.5 Influences on the development of related and supporting industries.

However, the data are inconclusive on the geographical distribution of these activities. Currently, 75 per cent of output of color television sets of Japanese affiliates produced in the UK are from factories located in South Wales. The Midlothian industrial conurbation in Scotland attracts two-thirds of all foreign owned firms producing semi-conductors in the UK. More than one-half of Japanese direct investment in German manufacturing industry is sited in the Dusseldorf area. And, there are suggestions that north-east England may become an important new center for the production of motor vehicles and their components. At the same time, the Japanese investors were not initially attracted by a strong cluster of existing activities; indeed, they have helped create their own clusters.

But, there are other examples which point to the contrary conclusion. The examples of clustering centers cited earlier in this chapter have all attracted foreign based companies which have generally reinforced the value of existing agglomerations of activity. On the other hand, outward investment might be expected to lead to a reduction in the intensity of domestic galaxies. An exception, perhaps, is in R&D and other high value activities of MNEs which tend to be concentrated in their home countries. The critical issue is to identify the optimum grouping of firms to gain the maximum external net economies at the lowest cost; for after a point, diseconomies of agglomeration arise. Such evidence as we have on the effect of foreign firms on clustering does not permit us to come to any generalized conclusion.

Again, however, it is not difficult to point to cases where foreign owned firms might enhance or inhibit particular types of clusters. For example, if such firms replace domestic firms and transfer their R&D activities to their home countries, this could reduce the agglomerative economies of R&D. If, on the other hand, affiliates upgraded factor endowments and the quality of output by increasing the demand for the products of the host country, this could lead to an increase in new kinds of clustering economies. Much would seem to depend upon the type of activities in which a foreign affiliate engages (cf. domestic firms) and the extent to which it buys from local suppliers or sells to local consumers.

The effect of outward investment on the domestic networking of activities is equally ambiguous. There is some suggestion that the Continental European investment of UK motor vehicle component firms was prompted by the better agglomerative economies offered by concentrations of industrial activity in the Ruhr Valley and in Belgium, and that this investment decreased the viability of the corresponding clusters in the UK (Cowling, 1986). At the same time, the competitiveness of the investing firms may well be improved by their investments in foreign clusters, and this may have other beneficial affects on the home economy.

MNEs, GOVERNMENTS AND COMPETITIVENESS

Although Porter addresses a whole chapter to the role of government as a shaper and monitor of economic activity, he has very little to say about the extent and way to which government policy is, itself, influenced by global economic forces, and, in particular, to those which are the result of the internationalization of production.

The interaction between MNEs, governments and competitiveness is a complex subject which is only now being addressed seriously by scholars.[27] Yet it is known to be extremely important, particularly in some developing and smaller developed economies. For the purpose of this chapter, however, we will confine our remarks to just two issues which we believe need to be incorporated into any analysis of the competitive advantages of nation states.

First, one of the distinguishing features of MNEs is their ability to shift value-added activities across national borders more easily than can uninational firms; indeed, this is a *sine qua non* for their existence. In the past, the spatial strategies of MNEs have been primarily based on the size of domestic markets and the relative competitiveness of national resources. In today's global economy, where international sourcing and markets are as, if not more, important as their domestic equivalents, the configuration of MNE activity (particularly within the Triad) is less dependent upon the availability and cost of unimproved natural resources, and more on the knowledge base and infrastructure facilities of economies in which they are producing or contemplating producing.

At the same time, governments can and do strongly influence the extent, quality and cost of these factors by their education, science and technology, industrial, trade, environmental, transport and communications and fiscal policies. Indeed, in a variety of ways, nation states are increasingly competing for resources and capabilities offered by MNEs.[28] The combination of the footloose nature of much modern industry (especially within integrated regions such as the EC) and the increasing significance of government influence on the transaction costs of such activity – and especially of high value activities in which MNEs tend to have a competitive advantage – is something which deserves the attention of scholars.

Second, MNEs can, themselves, influence government behavior, including that which directly impinges on the diamond of competitive advantage. In most industrial economies, MNEs are accounting for an increasing proportion of value-added activity. Egged on by the recent wave of cross-border acquisitions and mergers (A&Ms), such activity is also being concentrated in the largest 'x' per cent of firms. In their emphasis on wealth creating activities and competitiveness, governments are being forced to acknowledge the views of the leading wealth creators.

At the same time, such firms do not always (or solely) have their home country's interests at heart, as an increasing proportion of their sales and profits are earned outside their national boundaries (Dunning, 1993). So, governments may be prompted to take action which may affect the competitiveness of their location bound assets in a variety of ways, as described by Porter. In some instances, this can lead to more competitiveness and a synergy of goals between the long run interests of corporations and those of nation states; a good example is the initiative taken by some leading European MNEs to push forward the completion of the EC's internal market program. In others, the interest of MNEs may be best served (or perceived to be best served) by urging governments to adopt policies which, far from promoting dynamic competitiveness, may inhibit it by giving shelter to inefficient or non-innovatory firms.[29]

There can be little doubt that policy rivalry between nation states is a feature of the late twentieth century, and is likely to continue to be so for the foreseeable future. Up to now, most attention has been paid to the merits and demerits of strategic trade policy.[30] However, the real issue is one of competitive strategy, which embraces not only the facets of the diamond identified by Porter, but also the ability of firms to reallocate and upgrade their human and physical capabilities to the changing needs of the marketplace at minimum adjustment cost. In each of these areas, as Porter acknowledges, governments have a critical role to play both in setting the framework within which market forces and/or hierarchies can operate, and in counteracting any efforts, either by the participants of the market, or by other governments, to rig the workings of market to their own benefit.

However, in analyzing the behavior of particular national governments, an understanding both of the international forces affecting that behavior, and of the likely consequences of their actions on the goals of other governments is essential. In their role as instruments of the globalization of economic activity and as links between the strategic policies of the governments of the countries in which they operate, MNEs are likely to have a distinctive impact on the shaping of a whole range of government related actions which, directly or indirectly, affect the shape and quality of national diamonds of competitive advantage.

CONCLUSIONS

In answer to the question, 'Is foreign inward and outward direct investment likely to affect the diamond of competitive advantage?' our answer must surely be 'yes'. Multinationality does confer its own unique characteristics and bring about a distinctive impact on resource allocation and usage. Similarly, the evidence set out in this chapter suggests that the significance of this impact, particularly in the sectors in which the industrialized nations are seeking to promote their competitive advantages, is sufficiently noteworthy for the transnational business variable to be considered as a separate factor affecting the configuration of these advantages.

In answer to the question, 'Will foreign inward and outward investment improve the competitive advantage of host or home countries?' – the answer that is all too frequently (but justifiably) given by economists is 'it all depends'. The most (but this should not be belittled) an economist can do is first to set out the conditions under which, and the ways in which, domestic or foreign MNEs are likely to benefit national competitiveness (either in an industry or an economy) in the short and/or long run, and second to indicate what might be done (and at what cost) to optimize the impact of outward and inward investment (and associated activities, e.g. strategic alliances) on that competitiveness.

The interaction between the globalization of economic activity and national competitiveness provides a rich agenda for the scholar of the MNE. This chapter has sought to identify the ways in which national diamonds of competitive advantages are linked to each other by the operation of transnational enterprises. While Michael Porter provides a useful paradigm in identifying the main determinants of national competitiveness, his lack of attention to the ways in which such competitiveness may be affected by the ownership structure of firms and the way cross-border markets are organized weakens both the content and force of his thesis. But, the good news is that Porter has left the IB scholar plenty of interesting research to do![31]

Part III

Challenges to established patterns of MNE activity

Introduction

Nowhere are the global challenges to international business better shown than in the changing pattern of MNE activity and foreign direct investment since the early 1980s. The following chapters document, and examine the implications of, some of the main trends in the globalization of business activity over the last decade and speculate a little about the likely course of events for the rest of this century.

Chapter 6 discusses the emergence and growth of Japanese investment in both the US and Western Europe. Until the early 1980s, Japan's process of internationalization, elsewhere in the Triad, mainly took the form of exports. In 1982, while some 31.6 per cent of the global output of the largest US MNEs was accounted for by their foreign affiliates, the corresponding proportion for Japanese MNEs was only 5.5 per cent. By 1990, while the former figure had changed very little, the Japanese proportion had more than doubled and is rising rapidly, particularly in the US and the European Economic Community (EC). By March 31, 1991, these two areas accounted for three-fifths of the estimated world stock of Japanese FDI, compared with 35 per cent a decade earlier. Chapter 6 compares and contrasts the pattern of Japanese MNE activity in the EC with that in the US. While, in some respects, Europe is following one or two steps behind the US, both the kind of Japanese investment it is attracting, and the form it is taking, are rather different. Chapter 6 suggests that these differences can be explained by reference to the eclectic paradigm of MNE activity.

The eclectic paradigm is also used to trace the changing pattern of transatlantic direct investment since the early 1960s. Here the most noticeable changes have been first the revitalization of EC (and especially UK) MNE activity in the US, and second the restructuring of US direct investment in the EC consequent upon economic integration. Chapter 7 concludes by suggesting that the global challenges of the last decade, and the prospects of closer regional integration in Europe and North America, have led both US and European firms to engage in more transatlantic strategic asset acquiring direct investment, and strategic alliances.

The subject of strategic alliances – and particularly those concluded to protect or advance the technological assets of the participating parties – is the subject of Chapter 8. Most certainly, cross-border non-equity coalitions between firms producing on the same or on different value-added chains have been the fastest growing component of international business activity in the 1980s. Moreover, unlike the international contractual arrangements concluded in the 1960s and 1970s, most strategic business alliances (SBAs) are often a 'first best' organizational form, and part and parcel of a carefully orchestrated global strategy of MNEs. The reasons for this comparatively new form of business activity, and some of the essential conditions for their success, are set out in the chapter, which also describes the kind of industries and firms most likely to conclude SBAs.

The dramatic political changes which have occurred in Central and Eastern Europe pose new challenges to both the global economy and international business researchers. Already, there is a great deal of interest by Western, and, to a lesser extent, Far Eastern, firms in the opportunities which the privatization of markets in the Commonwealth of Independent States, and the erstwhile Communist countries to the West, are opening up. By July 1991, foreign firms had registered over 25,000 joint projects in Central and Eastern Europe. Chapter 9 both describes these projects, and then discusses three possible scenarios of the course which FDI might take in the 1990s. The conclusions it draws are moderately optimistic – at least for the latter part of the 1990s – if only the political fabric which is now being so painfully and delicately woven can hang together!

Chapter 10 turns to consider the industrial sector now attracting the most attention by MNEs. Over the last decade, the growth of FDI in services has consistently outstripped that in goods, and in many developed countries now accounts for over one-half of the total stock of inward investment. What explains the growth? Is it likely to continue? Does it hold good for all service sectors? Do we need new theories of FDIs to accommodate the service sector? Which countries are the leading exporters and importers of service MNEs? What does the increase in service FDI mean for manufacturing FDI? What, in particular, does the liberalization of service markets, e.g. banking, insurance and finance, mean to the way in which services are 'delivered' across national boundaries? These are just some of the questions addressed in Chapter 10.

The concluding chapter in this part examines the likely future pattern of MNE activity. It suggests that, barring a large scale war, and taking a reasonably optimistic outcome of GATT, and other international commercial negotiations for the rest of the decade, the 1990s offer tremendous opportunities for both large and small businesses in the global arena. These opportunities largely arise as a result of technological developments, moves towards closer economic interdependence among nations and the renaissance of the free market as an organizer and allocator of resources and capabilities. Insofar as MNEs, the main repositories of technology, and their value added activities are market driven, they are likely to play a critical role in both fashioning and responding to the global challenge of the 1990s. Chapter 11 speculates a little on some of the likely determinants of global business activity in the next decade and how this activity might be allocated among the major regions of the world.

6 Japanese MNEs in Europe and the US: some comparisons and contrasts

INTRODUCTION

Ten years ago, a comparison of the foreign direct investment (FDI) activities of Japanese multinational enterprises (MNEs) in the United States and Western Europe would have appeared somewhat misdirected, if not irrelevant. Japan's export success, rather than its foreign value-added activities, was a far more important measure of Japan's growing international competitiveness. Since the late 1980s, however, trade has taken a back seat to FDI as a key indicator of Japan's increasing involvement in the world economy. The rapidity with which this shift is occurring is remarkable, even as the context against which it is taking place is undergoing unprecedented change.

At the same time as Japanese firms are increasing their share of world international production, economic boundaries are being redrawn in Western Europe and North America to create regional rather than national markets, and entirely new market and production opportunities in Central and Eastern Europe are opening up. Taken together, the interaction between the increasingly outward orientation of Japanese industry and the changing shape of the world's marketplace is likely to have a profound impact on the location, organization and ownership of global economic activity.

While the proportion of production that large Japanese manufacturing firms perform overseas is still relatively low (somewhere between 8 per cent and 10 per cent in 1990), and considerably less than their European and US counterparts, their direct presence in the United States and (increasingly) in Europe is having a disproportionately large impact on the competitive profile of a number of key industries such as computers, cars and electronic components.

Although it is too early to predict the likely outcome of these trends, an analysis of recent developments raises a number of interesting questions and points to some possible answers. Will the competitive advantage of Japanese firms be modified now that they are increasingly exploiting these advantages from a foreign production base? To what extent will they be able to export their competitive advantages which owe much to the institutional, economic and cultural environment of their home country? How will their presence in Western Europe and North America affect the location specific advantages of these regions and the competitive advantages of indigenous firms? How do policy variables in general, and the European single market program in particular, affect the investment decisions of Japanese MNEs, and what is their impact, if any, on the locational advantage of the United States and the competitive advantages of its firms? Finally, what are the implications of increasing Japanese FDI for competition in regional markets where, in the foreseeable future, non-national champions will be in a position to determine the overall success or failure of a nation's industries?

A THEORETICAL DIGRESSION

The theoretical underpinning of this chapter is the developmental version of the eclectic paradigm of international production. The structure of this paradigm has been set out in detail elsewhere (Dunning, 1988, 1993) and will be only briefly summarized here.

At any given moment of time (time 't') the propensity of one country's firms to engage in value-added activities outside their national boundaries rests on three main factors. These are, first, their ability to serve particular foreign or domestic markets relative to that of their competitors of other nationalities. These competitive or ownership-specific (O) advantages are of two kinds. The first arise from the privileged possession of income generating assets (e.g. a patent, a superior production technique, exclusive access to raw materials or markets, etc.). The second stem from the superior ability of firms to take advantage of the economies of common governance of separate but related activities which might otherwise have been coordinated through external markets. Such advantages include the economies of scale and synergy, the spreading of geographical risk and the opportunities for cross-border price arbitraging.

The second factor influencing international production is the extent to which firms wish to create or acquire these advantages, or add value to them from a foreign versus a domestic production facility. These we shall refer to as the locational (L) advantages of countries. They depend on such variables as production and transport costs, the extent to which a product needs to be adapted for particular markets, and the costs of organizing cross-border, compared with domestic, multiproduct activities.

Third, overseas production will depend upon the extent to which firms choose to organize their O advantages from a foreign or domestic location by making use of the external market, or whether the net production and transaction costs of doing so are lower when undertaken within internal hierarchies (within the firm). These advantages are called internalization (or I) advantages. They essentially reflect the degree to which markets fail to operate in a perfectly competitive way. Of the variables which are likely to cause firms to internalize markets, the likelihood and costs of a contractual default[1] and the inability of a contractor to capture the external economies of any transaction are perhaps the two most important.

Other things being equal, the greater the ownership advantages of firms of a particular country, the more it pays those firms to create, acquire or add value to those advantages from a foreign location, and the greater the incentive to internalize their markets for those advantages or the value-added activities arising from them, the higher will be the propensity to engage in outward direct investment.

One country's outward investment is another country's inward investment; and so, to explain the propensity of a country to attract foreign investment, its location-bound resources or markets must be relatively attractive to foreign MNEs. Furthermore, these MNEs must be able to service the markets in question at least as effectively, if not more effectively, than indigenous producers. Finally, there must be some degree of failure in intermediate product markets to make it more attractive for foreign firms to own and control production in the host economy rather than in another country.

Given the configuration of OLI advantages of firms from different countries, and assuming no change in either the value of these variables or the strategy of the investing firms, and assuming no change in the response of other economic agents or of governments to the foreign production generated by these advantages, it is possible to determine the amount and distribution of MNE activity over some future period of time.

Of course, it is not quite as simple as that! For when a firm of one nationality invests in another country, it may impinge on the O advantages of indigenous firms and by influencing, for example, the productivity of the local labor force, the technological competence of suppliers or government policy towards inward investment, the host country's L advantages may be affected as well. Moreover, in addition to being influenced by the extent and pattern of interfirm transaction costs, these, in turn, may be influenced by the changing L advantages of countries. Finally, the efficiency with which a firm internalizes cross-border markets, e.g. through acquisitions and mergers, may, itself, affect its own O advantages, as the ability to organize transactions efficiently by hierarchical governance is a competitive advantage in its own right.

Over and above the dynamic interdependence between the OLI variables, and the wider economic and political environment of which they are part,[2] there is the question of how individual firms and/or Governments may respond to an existing OLI configuration. The fact that firms may pursue different economic strategies when faced with the same configuration of variables suggests that an explanation of these strategies must be incorporated into the paradigm.[3]

Let us now see how far the OLI paradigm can help to explain the level and structure of Japanese investment in US and European manufacturing industries, and the changes which may have occurred over the last decade or so. In particular, we might consider three sets of hypotheses. The first is that as

1   the O advantages of Japanese firms have increased
2   the advantages of producing from a European or US base (relative from a Japanese or another Far Eastern base) have become more pronounced, and
3   Japanese firms perceive that they can better organize the creation or acquisition of their O advantages or add value to them within their existing hierarchies, than increase Japanese owned value-added activities in European and US industry.

The second hypothesis is that since the OLI configuration facing Japanese firms which invest in the US is likely to be different from the one which confronts Japanese firms in Europe, both the level and the structure of their production in the two regions will differ. The third hypothesis stems from the differences between, on the one hand, the OLI advantages enjoyed by Japanese firms which have invested in Europe and/or the US and, on the other, the OLI advantages of domestic firms in these regions. Because of these differences between Japanese and local firms, it is likely that there will also be differences in the dynamic impact of cross-border transactions on the *future* OLI configurations of Japanese and US firms located in the US on the one hand, and Japanese and European firms located in Europe on the other. Indeed, the dynamic impact on the location bound advantages of the US and Europe are likely to be different.

Much has already been written about the changing nature of the O advantages of Japanese firms (Dunning and Cantwell, 1990; Porter, 1990), and of the increasing L advantages of Europe due to the single market program (Baldwin, 1989). The purpose of this contribution is first to describe some recent changes in the composition and structure of Japanese FDI, and second to analyze the extent to which such data uphold the proposition that Japanese subsidiaries in those regions are now exporting the competitive advantages of their parent companies, which were originally specific to their country of origin, and which, in many cases, contributed to their initial trade successes.

We would suggest that exporting these advantages is likely to have two consequences. First the competitiveness of Japanese MNEs might, itself, change as the firms are faced with a different set of locational endowments with which to combine their O advantages. Second, the direct presence of Japanese MNEs will affect the competitive behavior of local rivals, thus undermining or enhancing their own O advantages.

The outcome of the shifting distribution of O advantages among Japanese and home country firms will depend on a number of factors – including those described by Michael Porter in his analysis of the competitive advantages of nations (Porter, 1990). We shall also see, in the present context, that the trade and FDI policies adopted by the Japanese authorities has been of critical importance. Such policies have substantially influenced the pattern of Japanese MNE activity in terms of *where* and *in which* sectors it is made, *how* (through joint ventures, wholly-owned subsidiaries, or M&A) it is made, *in what measure* (degree of value-added performed by the foreign operation) it is made, and *when* it is made.

Thus, investments by Japanese MNEs in the United States and Europe will not just have an impact upon competition between Japanese and host country multinationals, but, through the channels of host country policies (L advantages), the shifting patterns of competition of their domestic firms (O advantages) and the relative benefits of organizing those advantags through the market *vis-à-vis* internal hierarchies, may also impact upon the global positioning of competition between MNEs from Europe and the United States for global positions, not only in each other's markets but also, increasingly, in that of Japan.

THE ROLE OF FOREIGN DIRECT INVESTMENT BY JAPAN PRIOR TO THE 1980S: A BRIEF OVERVIEW

It is important to note that Japanese outward foreign direct investment (FDI) in manufacturing has traditionally been a response to, rather than a factor determining, Japanese economic development. At the risk of oversimplifying, the years between 1945 and the early 1980s might be summarized as one in which output for which Japan had a comparative advantage was exported to hard-currency markets in order to pay for a strategic restructuring of economic activity towards sectors in which Japan was developing a comparative advantage, i.e. sectors which represented (or were perceived to represent) the high-growth opportunities which would power *future* industrial development (Ozawa, 1989b).

A buoyant export sector was essential to such a strategy, as was a proper set of macro-economic conditions in which industries could shift into ever higher value-, knowledge- and capital-intensive sectors. In this process of systematic upgrading, outward FDI has served as an outlet to relieve the pressures which, inevitably, build up in such a system: viz. rising wages and labor shortages;[4] an appreciating currency which weakened the competitive position of domestic exporters; the maturation of industries and technologies; and trade frictions with leading partners whose own goods, if let in freely as imports, would cause serious disruptions to the system. Given these circumstances, Japanese FDI policy was expressly guided by the government's overall strategic goals for domestic industrial restructuring (Ozawa, 1989a).

In the late 1960s and early 1970s, for instance, outward FDI was encouraged in light manufacturing sectors (textiles, toys) – former export 'stars' which were rendered uncompetitive by the increasing predominance of heavy industries (steel, chemicals, shipbuilding). Most of this labor-intensive FDI was made by small and medium sized Japanese companies and was directed to Asian developing countries, which, in the early 1990s, are export power-houses in their own right (Ozawa, 1989b)! Subsequently, outbound investment was aimed at securing access to natural resources (oil, minerals, etc.) required to fuel the growth of heavy domestic industries. Finally, the continuation of the upgrading process (and failure to attain sustainable O advantages in materials- and energy-intensive industries) demanded a shift up the value-added chain into higher knowledge and technology intensive activities.

It was at this stage, which occurred in the late 1970s and early

1980s, that Japanese MNE activity was guided to developed host countries to sustain or enlarge the markets for the exports of firms whose O advantages had by then reached rough parity with their Western counterparts (Ozawa, 1989c). In other words, because of changing location advantages of a European or United States location, and the much improved O advantages of Japanese firms, the latter showed an increasing preference in the late 1980s to exploit those advantages by foreign production. This was particularly true for Japan's burgeoning car and consumer electronics industries, whose highly competitive products (low cost, high quality and market oriented) were beginning to capture alarmingly high market shares in the United States and Europe.

In other words, industrial rationalization and restructuring mainly took place in Japan, with outward manufacturing FDI geared towards maintaining or advancing markets for Japanese exports (in developed countries) and relocating uncompetitive activities (in developing countries). But, relative to their United States and European counterparts, Japanese MNEs still possessed relatively weak O advantages in the innovation of many new technologies. This meant that industrial upgrading in Japan required a continual inflow of technology from abroad. Given this, a second important function of FDI was to act as a channel to absorb technologies developed in the West (Ozawa, 1989b). However, unlike West Germany, Japan preferred to acquire such technology through means other than direct investment (e.g. licensing, reverse engineering, etc.). Once fed back to the parent, such technologies could be adapted and applied to the production of goods which were then exported to – and often came to dominate – the very markets which gave them their technological inception in the first place, viz. Europe and the United States.

Thus, until the mid-1980s at least, manufacturing direct investment into and out of Japan was an important adjunct to, rather than a central facet of, Japanese industrial development. That trade was still the mechanism driving the machine is illustrated by the fact that as late as 1985 Japanese owned firms exported ten times the value of goods to Europe and the United States than their subsidiaries produced in those regions. What follows is a closer look at how these patterns have changed, and current indications that a fundamental shift in the role of outward Japanese FDI is now occurring, such that the very system of exporting → domestic upgrading → exporting which it has long supported is likely to be profoundly altered and, possibly, disrupted altogether.

1980–1984: KEY FDI STRATEGIES IN EUROPE AND THE UNITED STATES: COMPARISONS AND CONTRASTS

Defending current and future export markets

The above overview suggests that, up to and including the early 1980s, the FDI strategies of Japanese companies in the United States and Europe could be broadly classified as falling into two categories: viz. *defensive market oriented* and *offensive supply oriented.*

1 Defensive market-seeking investment

The primary purpose of these investments was to establish operations in Europe and the US to protect existing export markets, either in response to actual or potential trade barriers, or to counter the moves of competitors which threatened to disrupt domestic operations.

Since a defensive export-substituting FDI strategy is aimed at maintaining existing market share, these investments are likely to be concentrated in sectors in which Japanese firms already have strong O advantages, sustained and supported by strong L advantages to production in Japan. In the early 1980s, such firms were to be found mainly in the car and electrical and electronic equipment industries. The typical mode of this kind of foreign investment was the establishment of greenfield plants which performed relatively low levels of value-added activities. Since the O advantages already existed and were located in Japan, there was little incentive to conclude joint ventures and even less to acquire existing assets. At worst these operations were 'screwdriver' factories; at best, they were branch plants which replicated the output of the parent company, dependent on the latter for management decision making and control, inputs, and full product and process specifications.

2 Offensive, supply oriented investment

The second type of MNE strategy is targeted at gaining access to the information and technology needed to upgrade and rationalize *domestic* operations, and to advance a global competitive strategy. Such foreign production differs from the traditional conception of rationalized investment, in which MNEs relocate discrete value-adding activities to maximize operational efficiency by reaping the benefits of common governance over linked, but geographically dispersed, activities. In the Japanese case of offensive strategic FDI, some form of international rationalization is taking place, but the high value activities, e.g. design, research and product development, organization, sourcing and marketing strategy, and financial control are generally retained in Japan. The role of the foreign affiliate is to aid in the continual upgrading and rationalization of the parent company's operations by feeding it new information about markets, products and technologies. Such investments differ from the first type in that they are aimed at acquiring *new* O advantages rather than exploiting existing ones, and so will often be in sectors in which firms in the countries receiving the FDI possess O advantages which are superior to those possessed by the investing firm.

The evidence suggests that the majority of Japanese MNE activity in the United States and Europe in the early 1980s were of the first type, viz. defensive market-seeking investment. When Japanese MNEs were recently asked to rank their motives for investments in Europe and the United States, the most frequently cited answer was access to markets with technology acquisition and/or information sharing as the second most important reason, though given far less weight than the first (MITI, 1990). Furthermore, it is likely that a majority of market-seeking investments were of the defensive type, undertaken to avoid restrictions to Japan's exports. Such frictions, beginning in the 1970s, set off a wave of Japanese investments in its major export markets in the early 1980s. Figure 6.1 gives some illustrations of the direct relationship between the instigation of protective measures against Japanese exports to Europe and subsequent Japanese MNE activity in Europe.

Table 6.1 shows the remarkable increase in the absolute level of manufacturing FDI in this period, along with the stronger L advantages of the United States compared to Europe. Cumulative in-flows of investment increased by 88 per cent in the United States and by 9 per cent in Europe above the cumulated flows of *the previous 30 years combined.* The share of the United States in total Japanese FDI rose from one-quarter in the 1951–1980 period to nearly one-third in 1981–1984.

Table 6.2 shows the rapidly changing sectoral composition of Japanese manufacturing FDI in the United States and Europe in 1981–1984, and reveals the strong Japanese O advantages in the car and electric/electronic machinery sectors prevailing at the time. In the United States, the Japanese investment stake in the motor vehicle industry grew to nearly one-quarter of all manufacturing investment by the early 1980s; while that of the electrical equipment sector maintained its position as the dominant sector, accounting for about

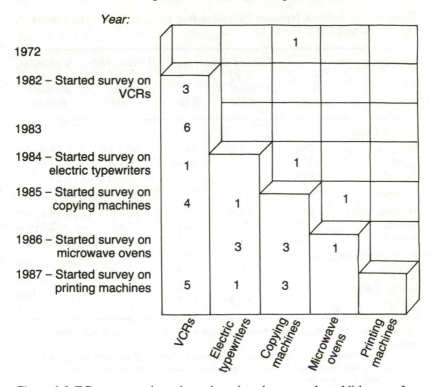

Figure 6.1 EC surveys to investigate dumping charges and establishment of
Japanese factories in Europe (numbers in bars show factories established that
year).
Source: Industrial Bank of Japan, 1989.

one-third of all manufacturing. In Europe, the share of both sectors
increased rapidly, such that by 1984 the structure, if not the overall
level, of Japanese manufacturing FDI was beginning to resemble that
in the United States.

It is also worth noting from Table 6.2 that in the United States, the
level of FDI in wholesale and retail trade (essentially import ducts for
Japanese products) fell, both in absolute and relative terms, in the
early 1980s, while in Europe, such investments increased, both in
absolute terms and as a percentage share of total FDI. This would
seem to suggest that Europe was, in the beginning of the 1980s, at an
earlier stage of absorbing Japanese FDI than was the United States.
Protecting existing export markets was clearly a concern, but direct
investment in European production facilities was not the primary

Table 6.1 Cumulative Japanese FDI stock in the United States and Europe 1951–1980 and 1981–1984

	$ mn	1951–1980 % of total FDI	$ mn	1981–1984 % of total FDI	% change from previous period
United States					
Manufacturing	2056	23.2	3870	35.1	88.2
Services	6273	70.7	7091	64.4	13.0
Total:*	8878	100.0	11015	100.0	24.1
Europe					
Manufacturing	844	18.9	921	20.0	9.1
Services	3501	78.3	3412	74.1	(2.6)
Total:*	4472	100.0	4601	100.0	2.9
Per cent of total Japanese FDI		*1951– 1980*	*1981– 1984*		
United States		24.3	31.5		
Europe		12.3	13.2		

*Includes investment in overseas branch offices which are not included in sectoral breakdown.
Note: Cumulative FDI stock calculated as the sum of yearly flows over the period. Does not include reinvested earning. Dollar figures are in current US dollars.
Source: Ministry of Finance.

response, as it was in the United States. Instead, new Japanese MNE activity in Europe mainly took the form of export distribution outlets. The reasons behind this difference essentially reduce to the different L advantages of the United States and Europe at that time. We shall return to these differences later in the chapter.

The data point to signs that the United States, as an industrialized host country to Japanese FDI, has played the role of the 'leader' with Europe following behind, such that the level and structure of the former, e.g. with respect to motives and modes of organization, would later be replicated, albeit on a smaller scale, in the latter. In other words, not only was there a series of stages of internationalization which Japan as a *home* country of MNE activity passed through but that, at the same time, developed *host* countries were mirroring this process by passing through a series of their own stages related to inward FDI. If this was so, then the key difference between Japanese FDI in the United States and Europe, in the early 1980s, was one not so much of structure, strategy or even of amount, but merely of the timing with which the investments were made.

Location advantages in the United States and Europe

Before comparing the L advantages of the United States and Europe in the period up to 1984, it is important to note that, while the two regions differ from each other in many ways, from a global perspective they shared many similarities. Both were important export markets of Japan, and both had started to clamp down on Japanese imports in the mid-1970s. Hence, the underlying motives for Japanese investments in the two locations were fundamentally the same, viz. primarily market-seeking, export-substituting FDI, with little or no rationalized (efficiency-seeking and/or cost-reducing) investments, the latter being concentrated in low cost Asian countries.

From a demand perspective, the two markets, while admittedly different in their size and rates of growth, were also structurally comparable. Indeed, it was mainly in the area of production economics where the greatest variances were to be found, although even these reflected not structural, qualitative differences, but rather different regulatory environments.

Looked at from a viewpoint of the Japanese investors seeking to evolve a transnational strategy, then, the two regions were very similar. The United States and Europe represented overseas concentrations of wealth and technology which were the necessary 'pull' factors in the upgrading of domestic Japanese economic activity.

Having said this, however, the data clearly indicate that the United States did have a far stronger attraction for Japanese FDI than did Western Europe up to and during the early 1980s. For example, the ratio of the cumulative Japanese direct investment flows directed to the United States compared to that in Europe (including non-EC Europe) rose from 2.4 to 4.2 in manufacturing and 1.9 to 2.4 for all sectors between 1951–1980 and 1981–1984. The reasons mainly reflect the larger size and growth of the US market for products in which Japanese companies had O-specific advantages, coupled with the combination of lax inward investment and tight trade-protectionist policies. This policy configuration, reversed in Europe, helped tip the balance of choice facing Japanese MNEs, to engage in FDI in the United States but to continue to export to Europe (Dunning and Cantwell, 1990). Put another way, the absence of restrictions on foreign-owned production – both in manufacturing and in services (banking, finance, insurance and trade-related activities) – meant that

Table 6.2 Sectoral composition of Japanese FDI stock in manufacturing and selected services in the United States and Europe 1951–1980 and 1981–1984

	United States			Europe		
	1951–1980 $ mn	1981–1984 $ mn	% change	1951–1980 $ mn	1981–1984 $ mn	% change
Elec. machinery	653	1073	64.4	128	224	75.0
% of manuf. FDI	31.7	27.7	15.2	24.3		
Transport equip.	87	880	906.0	61	240	293.4
% of manuf. FDI	4.3	22.7		7.2	26.1	
Steel and metals	304	507	66.8	157	68	(56.7)
% of manuf. FDI	14.8	13.1		18.6	7.4	
Chemicals	241	349	45.1	104	97	(6.7)
% of manuf. FDI	11.7	9.0		12.3	10.5	
General machinery	210	310	47.7	119	70	(41.2)
% of manuf. FDI	10.2	8.0		14.1	7.6	
Food, bev. tobacco	184	250	35.7	42	19	(54.8)
% of manuf. FDI	8.9	6.4		5.0	2.1	

Other*	378	503	233	203	32.9	(12.9)
% of manuf. FDI	18.4	13.0	27.6	22.0		
Total manuf.	2057	3870	844	921	88.2	9.1
% of total FDI	23.2	35.1	18.9	20.0		
Distributive trade	3325	3082	817	1260	(7.3)	54.2
% of total FDI	37.5	28.0	18.3	27.4		
Finance and insurance	931	1664	822	1920	78.6	133.6
% of total FDI	10.5	15.1	18.4	41.7		
Other*						
% of service FDI						
Total services	6274	7091	3501	3410	13.0	(2.6)
% of total FDI	70.7	64.4	78.3	74.1		
Total	8878	11015	4472	4601	24.1	(2.9)

* Other manufacturing includes: textiles, lumber and wood pulp, precision machinery, rubber, glass, other. Other services includes: agriculture/forestry, fishery, mining, construction, hotels and entertainment, transportation services, real estate businesses, other.

Note: Cumulative FDI stock calculated as the sum of yearly flows over the period. Does not include reinvested earning. Dollar figures are in current US dollars.

Source: Ministry of Finance.

Japanese firms could internalize the markets for their O advantages more easily in the United States, while arms-length transactions remained the norm in Europe.

More importantly, Europe at that period was a collection of fragmented, relatively protected national markets, the size and growth of which were considerably smaller than that of the United States. The fragmentation of the European economy meant that not only were economies of scale difficult to achieve along the value chain, but that economies of scope were constrained in a marketplace which was a patchwork of differing technical, safety and fiscal standards. These production constraints were compounded by prohibitively high cross-border transaction costs, due in part to administrative delays at customs borders (Cecchini, 1988). Finally, real wages in most European countries were uncompetitive with those in the United States, a crucial consideration for Japanese companies whose O advantages depended on maintaining lower price/quality ratios than their local competitors. These factors, coupled with the much larger sunk investment already in the United States, made that country a more attractive location for Japanese market-seeking investment in the first part of the 1980s.

Additionally, though less important at this stage, Europe's L advantages in innovatory activities, though strong, were inferior to those of the United States, particularly in the sectors in which Japan was seeking to establish a global presence. In particular, the United States possessed much stronger L advantages for information- and technology-seeking. Finally, a lower cost of entry favored the United States over Europe for all types of FDI, given cumulated experience gained through previous investments, and a more relaxed policy environment towards the acquisition of corporate assets through takeovers.

Summary and conclusions: why the trade-sustaining investments of the early 1980s were unsustainable after 1985

The early 1980s, then, was a period in which the principal aim of Japanese MNE activity in the United States and Europe was to protect the competitive advantages of Japanese made products. This was particularly true in what were then Japan's premier export sectors, viz. cars and electronic goods. That more investment was directed to the United States than to Europe was a reflection of the former's more pronounced L advantages, and the fact that because of differing regulatory environments, Japanese firms could internalize the market for their O advantages more easily in the United States than they could in Europe.

By the end of the 1980s, this picture of Japanese foreign production was no longer appropriate. The change was triggered by a series of developments which occurred roughly between 1985 and 1987, and forced a different FDI strategy on the part of Japan's leading MNEs, away from a trade-replacing function and towards a new phase of advancing global competitive strength. In place of defensive strategies, Japanese firms have increasingly had to adopt offensive strategies in their attempt to secure and advance their foreign markets. Such strategies have been largely driven by the need of Japanese firms to transform themselves from exporters to 'insiders' in the major markets of the world, and to keep in touch with the latest technological and organizational developments, while benefiting from economies of cross-border arbitraging and the gathering and disseminating of information.

This shift from defensive to offensive investment strategies implies a fundamental change in the traditional post-war system of exporting → domestic upgrading → exporting practiced in Japan. In the move to become successful insiders, Japanese MNEs had to internationalize the upgrading process, with the inevitable result that FDI gradually replaced trade as the mechanism driving the machine.

1985–1988: TRANSFERRING EXISTING O ADVANTAGES TO FOREIGN TERRITORIES

Variables triggering the change

Several factors contributed to the demise of a defensive market-seeking FDI strategy by Japanese MNEs in Europe and the United States. Among the first and most important occurred in 1985, when the Plaza Agreement revalued the yen against the dollar. This undermined Japan's ability to export low cost manufactured products. In an effort to retain their export markets, Japanese producers moved into higher value market sectors which, at that stage in Japan's industrial development, were mainly those producing technology and knowledge intensive goods. In many of these sectors, which included pharmaceuticals and speciality chemicals, advanced micro-chips, software and next-generation computers, US firms still maintained substantial O advantages *vis-à-vis* their Japanese counterparts. Mirroring the rise in price in Japanese exports was a cheapening of the price of assets denominated in US currency. Together, these factors combined to raise the attractiveness of the L advantages of the United States, particularly in knowledge intensive sectors.

In other words, the strong yen encouraged Japanese firms to create, or acquire, *new* O advantages, as there was now a rapidly expiring time limit on how long firms could defend and exploit their existing advantages. This was compounded by the fact that Western competitors, particularly in the US, were beginning to emulate some of the O advantages of Japanese MNEs, e.g. the consistency of their product quality and flexible production methods. The implication was that offensive information-seeking FDI was becoming a more attractive strategy than it had been in previous years. At a firm level, that meant it was desirable to internationalize innovatory activities and to enter alliances with partners offering synergistic cutting-edge technologies to feed the current wave of upgrading. At the same time, upgrading existing overseas investments became a more important strategic goal. If more value-added in production had to be located abroad due to the rising yen, then those activities had to be supported and sustained with complementary coordinating and control functions, including marketing, product development, and forward and backward linkages in the local economy.

Such an approach as this was a novel one for Japanese MNEs. Moreover, by the late 1980s, local rivals, particularly in the United States, had adopted cost and product strategies to meet the Japanese challenge. In a survey taken in the late 1980s, 75 per cent of the Japanese car affiliates in the US ranked 'increasing competition' as the main problem they expected to encounter; the corresponding percentage for a similar group of firms in the EC was 86 per cent (MITI, 1990). The appreciation of the yen, then, necessitated a radical reappraisal of the goals and structure of Japanese MNE activity, and of the home country's global market position, won through trade in the late 1970s and defensive foreign production in the 1980s, if it was to be sustained or advanced in the 1990s.

Not only the goals, but also the mode of international involvement had to change, as the risks of building greenfield facilities sharply increased. In the world car industry and related sectors, for example, there was serious threat of overproduction by the late 1980s, caused in part by new Japanese outward investment. The 1986–1987 recession in the computer industry and the build up of worldwide capacity in semi-conductors were also reasons why adding to the current stock of productive assets was not a wise choice. In contrast to the preceding years, acquisitions, joint ventures, strategic alliances, and increasing value-added in existing operations were becoming more desirable options than greenfield investments. Indeed, a 1988 survey by the Yamaichi Securities Company found that Japanese take-overs of foreign firms quintupled from 44 in 1984 to 228 in 1987, with 33 and 120 of those involving US companies (*Tokyo Business Today*, 1989). In the fiscal year 1988–1989, no less than 40 per cent of the value of new Japanese direct investment in the EC was by way of acquisition or merger (Kirkland, 1990).

Another important factor which undermined the earlier strategies was the decision to create a single, European market by the end of 1992. The boost that this gave to Europe's L advantages was substantial, and inward FDI from all countries increased following the announcement of the program in 1985. The profit opportunities in Europe were too important to ignore; not only were EC-based firms offered a once-and-for-all cut in costs through the removal of non-tariff barriers; they would also be given a larger market to operate in, in which income growth was estimated to rise by up to 20 per cent (Baldwin, 1989). The dynamic gains from the push of industrial rationalization and the pull of growing demand suggested that European industry was poised for a period of sustained growth and good profits, with the winning companies being those which possessed O advantages best able to benefit from the new configuration of L and I advantages being shaped in the region.

At the same time, firms located outside the EC were in danger of being locked out of this pot of gold. Japanese companies, in particular, were viewed as threats to the success of the new integrated Europe. Indeed, one of the central aims of Europe in 1992 was to help European MNEs break out of the economic sclerosis which had plagued them in preceding decades, so that they might compete against Japanese firms in sectors such as telecommunications and office equipment. Intraregional conflicts over local content and rules of origin, which are still being waged over Japanese products (copiers, VCRs, cars), portended future import barriers. The high degree of uncertainty facing Japanese firms over the future of the EC's trade stance with the rest of the world, coupled with the enormous potential rewards of market unification, meant that Japanese MNEs had to shift gears and switch their mode of supplying the EC market from exports to local production, and that they had to do so with some alacrity.

The nature of the changes: same sectors, different structures

There was also an accumulation of new investment in the mechanical engineering industry. This latter trend repeated itself in Europe, where there was also growth in the share of new investment going to the electrical and electronic sector. Transport equipment maintained its relative position, but, towards the end of the period, began to increase sharply. Also noteworthy in Europe was the plunge in the share accounted for by the wholesale and retail trading sector, mirroring a similar decline which occurred in the United States of the preceding period.

If, at first glance, it appears that Japanese firms were abandoning, in a relative sense, the car sector in the United States, upon closer examination of the data the contrary was occurring. Rather than moving out of this sector, the Japanese owned segment of the United States automobile industry had, by this stage, reached the point were clusters of supporting firms – which are at the heart of Japanese O advantages in manufacturing – were springing up to support the initial Japanese investments. In other words, there were signs that the Japanese automobile industry was beginning to 'export' its O advantages (if not its cars) to the United States in response to the rising yen and increasing competition.

Japanese O advantages in automobiles: a brief case study

Before examining the data in more detail, it is worth digressing briefly to remind ourselves of some key facets of the O advantages of Japanese firms identified in Chapter 2. We described there how innovations in the organization of work and production, such as just-in-time inventory systems and multiskilled, multitask labor, were as important factors behind the Japanese competitive edge in producing high quality goods at low cost as any technical prowess or access to low cost labor. By perfecting the art of flexible specialization, where clusters of firms are able to specialize in activities which can be regrouped and reconfigured to respond to rapid market changes at minimum cost, Japanese car manufacturers created a powerful competitive weapon with which to attack the American giants. At the time of the Japanese export onslaught in the 1970s, the latter were locked into mass-production methods that made market-induced changes, such as a shift to smaller cars, prohibitively expensive. Rigid divisions of labor and Fordist industrial relations also denied them the productivity gains of Japanese work practices such as job rotation and worker-teams.

Table 6.3 Sectoral composition of Japanese FDI stock in manufacturing and selected services in the United States and Europe 1985–1988

	United States $ mn	% increase from 1981–1984	Europe $ mn	% increase from 1981–1984
Elec. machinery	4141	286.0	909	305.8
% of manuf. FDI	25.0		29.4	
Transport equip.	1725	96.0	612	155.0
% of manuf. FDI	10.4		19.8	
Steel and metals	1637	222.9	103	51.5
% of manuf. FDI	9.9		3.3	
Chemicals	1715	390.7	393	305.2
% of manuf. FDI	10.4		12.7	
General machinery	2069	567.7	437	524.3
% of manuf. FDI	12.5		14.1	
Food, bev, tob	466	86.9	110	478.9
% of manuf. FDI	2.8		3.6	
Other	4802	855.5	528	160.1
% of manuf. FDI	29.0		17.1	
Total manufact.	16555	327.8	3092	235.7
% of total FDI	31.9		14.7	
Distributive trades	4942	60.3	1878	49.0
% of total FDI	9.5		8.9	
Finance and insur.	9358	462.4	12111	530.8
% of total FDI	18.0		57.4	
Other				
% of service FDI				
Total services	34831	391.2	17187	404.0
% of total FDI	67.0		81.5	
Total	51965	371.8	21091	358.4

Source: Ministry of Finance.

At the heart of the Japanese system is the relationship between the motor car manufacturer and the cluster of its suppliers – sometimes known as Toyotaism.[5] Not only does the former generally own a portion of the latter's firm, but the component suppliers and sub-contractors are put under enormous pressures to reach ever-higher levels of quality within stringent cost constraints. This very consider-able bargaining power of manufacturers means that suppliers have little choice but to meet the required specifications, and to reach the

desired levels of efficiency. Suppliers are also encouraged to participate in design and development functions, and deliver whole production systems, not just individual components. The relationship is a
close – even a filial – one. It is based on cooperation, trust, mutual
forbearance and a constant interchange of information and ideas. In
this respect, it is very different from supplier–manufacturer relationships traditionally found in the United States and Europe, where
manufacturers generally minimize the price of their components
through competitive bidding. Without this relationship, and its
emphasis on total quality at low cost, it is doubtful that the Japanese
car manufacturers could have achieved their astonishing export
successes of the late 1970s and early 1980s.

The implication of the above analysis is that – unlike many
American MNEs which still have O advantages in strong brand names
or the common governance of a range of related activities or superior
technology – the markets for the O advantages of Japanese firms are
not easily internalized in an overseas location. Part of the reason for
this is that it is initially more difficult to transfer any intra- or interfirm organizational structures than it is to transfer production or
marketing techniques across national boundaries (Kogut and
Parkinson, 1993). And, as Porter points out (Porter, 1990), nowhere
are the elements underlying the comparative advantages of a country,
which help to create and sustain the competitive advantages of its
own firms, more closely linked to one another than in Japan, where
they function as an organic and holistic system.

While such a situation is ideal for a country building up its
competitive advantage through exports, as Japan had done until
recently, difficulties may arise when such a country's firms are
compelled to replicate their successes internationally (or internalize the
markets for their O advantages through FDI) in different organizational
cultures. In this scenario, the main challenge is to move *the entire
system* to the target market. The risks inherent in such a move are
high, since the firm's original O advantages and the conditions which
make for their internal use are bound to change once transplanted to
foreign soil, as indeed are the O advantages of the host country's
firms, which are now given an opportunity to compete – and
cooperate – with their overseas rivals on their home ground!

Moving Japanese O and I advantages to the foreign marketplace

The data available for the second half of the 1980s suggest that, as
the internationalization of Japan's O and I advantages accelerated, so

did the character of Japanese FDI in the United States and Europe shift from being defensive and market-seeking to being aggressive and efficiency-seeking or strategic asset-acquiring. Increasing attention would now be directed to creating a global competitive advantage by ensuring that all value-added operations, both at home and abroad, were geared to this end. In some cases, this meant that the Japanese system of organizing production had to be transferred to a foreign culture.

One indication of the increasing cross-border internalization of the market for Japanese O advantages is given by comparative data on licensing and royalty fees between Japan, the United Kingdom and the United States. By measuring the ratio of fees paid by overseas affiliated firms to those paid by overseas non-affiliated firms, one can obtain some idea of the importance of FDI versus arms-length licensing transactions as a mode for transferring technology. Over the 1980s, the proportion of affiliated to non-affiliated royalty and license fees that were paid from the United States back to Japan rose from 0.4 in 1980 to 2.9 in 1989 (US Department of Commerce, 1990). In the UK, the ratio also rose, although it remained significantly lower than in the United States, reaching 0.44 in 1987 from 0.22 in 1981 (*UK Central Statistical Office*).

This indicates that internalizing the market for O advantages had become more important to Japanese MNEs than the licensing of technology to unrelated firms, at least in the United States. In other words, knowledge transferred to overseas locations was increasingly flowing from the supplying company in Japan to the overseas affiliate, instead of between two independent foreign producers. One possible explanation for this is that in the United States, Japanese MNEs were increasingly investing in sectors where it was strategically important for the owners of O advantages to control the *use* of those advantages. Such is the case in high technology sectors or those in which the way value-adding activities are organized is itself a source of O advantages. As firms move into such sectors, the propensity to internalize their O advantages through FDI will rise. Furthermore, as companies pursue more global strategies, and more closely integrate their domestic and foreign value added authorities, so does the need to control these activities rise. The evidence presented below indicates that that, indeed, was a feature of Japanese investments in the United States in the latter 1980s, and that there were signs that a similar trend was also beginning to emerge in Europe.

The growing internalization of the market for Japanese O advantages in the United States has mainly occurred in the car sector, in which, as discussed above, O advantages are often based on close interfirm relationships and a highly coordinated organization of production among a network of firms. There are indications that these O advantages were transferred by Japanese MNEs to the United States in the late 1980s. One of the most compelling is the fact that, in the 1984–1988 period, the average size of a Japanese direct investment in the car sector fell by 28 per cent (from $17 million to $12 million) while, as shown in Table 6.3, the amount invested in this sector rose by nearly 100 per cent. These data suggest that Japanese owned components and parts suppliers were investing in the United States to supply Japanese car manufacturers. Indeed, it has been estimated that, by the end of the 1980s, about 300 such plants had been set up in the United States (*Financial Times*, 1990).

A further indication of the localization of Japanese car FDI in the United States is the fact that investment in related industries grew rapidly over the period; much of the jump in the 'other manufacturing' category was due to the acquisition of Firestone Tire and Rubber by Bridgestone in 1988 for yen 333.7 bn. The other industry which recorded a strong gain – general machinery – also contains many sectors which are directly linked to car manufacturing. Two other large industries, steel and electrical equipment, are also strongly dependent on the car sector for their prosperity, the former directly as an upstream supplier, the latter indirectly through products and innovations which are adapted into car subsystems.

As for the necessity to shift overseas the Japanese system of organizing production, surveys indicate that, in response to policy pressures to increase local content, Japanese manufacturers tend to prefer to locate and foster locally-based subcontractors rather than create their own internal capacity (JETRO, 1988). This reaction is consistent with the need of such companies to protect one of their main O specific advantages, e.g. the flexible specialization of production. It is interesting to note the form that this development is taking; it appears that Japanese companies are not just utilizing more locally-based suppliers and subcontractors, but are replicating the close interfirm relationships which they enjoy in Japan.

Table 6.4 shows the breakdown of inputs and revenues of Japanese affiliates in the United States and the European Community, for all manufacturing affiliates and for those in the motor vehicles and electrical and electronic equipment industries. It reveals that the local content (i.e. the per cent of inputs locally procured) varies considerably between the sectors identified, though, generally, more stringent

Table 6.4 Structure of Japanese manufacturing and automobile subsidiaries, United States and Europe 1987

	All manufacturing		Transport equipment		Electric/electronic equipment	
	US	EC	US	EC	US	EC
Percentage of total inputs from[1]						
Local sources	32	46	35	61	17	31
of which:						
Intragroup[2]	(30)	(43)	(68)	(0)	(92)	(79)
Japanese imports	62	51	35	37	79	55
of which:						
Intragroup	(71)	(87)	(74)	(56)	(71)	(89)
3rd-country imports[3]	5	3	30	1	5	14
of which:						
Intragroup	(43)	(33)	0	(52)	(84)	(26)
Total inputs	100	100	100	100	100	100
of which:						
Intragroup	(56)	(65)	(49)	(21)	(75)	(77)
Local intragroup	(10)	(20)	(24)	(0)	(15)	(25)
Percentage of total revenues from						
Local sales	93	96	82	81	98	90
of which:						
Intragroup	(3)	0	(49)	(0)	(1)	(29)
Sales to Japan	3	1	11	0.1	1	2
of which:						
Intragroup	(78)	0	(97)	(100)	(97)	(100)
3rd-country exports	4	3	8	19	1	9
of which:						
Intragroup	(21)	0	(100)	(10)	(67)	(53)
Total revenues:	100	100	100	100	100	100
of which:						
Intragroup	(6)	0	(58)	(2)	(21)	(33)
Local intragroup	(3)	0	(40)	0	(1)	(26)

[1] All percentages calculated from yen values.
[2] Intragroup transactions are between different affiliates, not necessarily majority owned, of the same parent. Numbers in parentheses are the percentage of intragroup transactions within that category of inputs (or revenues).
[3] Third countries in Europe include other European countries.
Source: MITI.

local content policies tend to be followed. But, despite the fact that, in 1987, more than half of Japanese affiliates were still being imported from Japan, overseas affiliates had begun to establish backward linkages in the local economy. Furthermore, of their total local procurement in manufacturing, between a third and 40 per cent were sourced *from other affiliates of the same parent* of the United States and the EC, respectively. Thus, as backward linkages were established, they were also internalized, so as to protect the parent firm's O advantages in technology and in organizing production.

By contrast, the forward linkages of Japanese subsidiaries in their overseas locations are generally much smaller.[6] Partly, at least, this reflects the fact that in assembly-based production (i.e. trade-supporting branch plants) outputs are finished goods shipped directly to distributors, which are not generally owned by the manufacturer.

The comparative degree of vertical integration of Japanese investments in two key sectors is revealing; Japanese companies in the car industry appear to have established backwards and forwards linkages in their United States operations, but none in the EC, while in the electrical and electronic equipment industry, backward linkages have been established in both locations while forward linkages are much stronger in the EC.

One possible explanation for the difference in the comparative structure in the Japanese electrical and electronics sector in the US and the EC is that Japanese companies have made further inroads into acquiring the assets of European downstream companies – e.g. of computer and peripherals manufacturers – than they have in the United States. This is understandable, given that Japanese manufacturers enjoy relatively stronger O advantages *vis-à-vis* European computer firms than they do *vis-à-vis* United States firms, which still lead the world in the industry's most important market segments. The extent of backward linkages of Japanese subsidiaries in the EC, on the other hand, lags behind that of their United States counterparts. This, perhaps, reflects the fact that fewer Japanese components subcontractors had invested in the EC than in the US at this time, and that, in this industry, 54 per cent of firms polled in the EC in 1987 listed 'procurement of local components' as the key manufacturing constraint, versus a response rate to this question of 32 per cent for all manufacturers (JETRO, 1988).

In cars, the strong backward and forward linkages in the United States and their complete absence in the EC points to the more mature phase of Japanese FDI in the former location. By 1990, most Japanese car companies were well on their way to replicating the networks of their domestic interfirm linkages in the United States.

If the patterns of the past continue, then Europe should follow the lead set by the United States. This would imply that Europe should witness a further build-up of Japanese clusters of supporting sub-contractors (and service firms) around established Japanese car manufacturers, particularly as the latter respond to political pressures to increase local content levels.

One example of this likely trend is the acquisition of a UK radiator manufacturer by a leading supplier to Toyota in Japan (Nippondenso) to supply Toyota's nearby production plant (Kirkland, 1990). This kind of development is likely to increase competitive pressure on European owned car firms, already in a vulnerable position due to their low productivity levels relative to Japanese manufacturers. And it is likely that similar patterns will emerge in other sectors where the Japanese have strong production advantages, once the major Japanese players have firmly established themselves on European soil. Ironically, by forcing Japan to lessen her dependence on exports because of undue competitive pressures on local industry, European and US producers are likely to face a new wave of competitive pressures, this time within their own borders, from locally-based, highly productive networks of Japanese owned manufacturers, suppliers and service providers.

1989 AND BEYOND: CREATING NEW O ADVANTAGES AS REGIONAL INSIDERS

1988–1989: Europe takes the lead

Data about Japanese FDI in 1989 and 1990 point to the astonishingly rapid growth of Europe's L advantages as a production base, for both manufacturing and service industry. Indeed, an increasing number of Japanese MNEs now regard the EC as offering more investment opportunities than the United States. In a survey taken in September 1987, only 3.2 per cent of the firms polled listed the EC as the most important location for foreign value-added activities; by September 1989, 12.1 per cent cited it as their most important region. At the same time, the number of firms citing North America as the most important region for their investment dropped from 53.4 per cent to 43.1 per cent over the same period (Industrial Bank of Japan, 1989).

The data in Table 6.5 dramatically illustrate this trend. Between 1988 and 1989, the value of Japanese manufacturing FDI flows into the United States increased by only 1 per cent; in Europe they

Table 6.5 Composition of Japanese FDI in the US and Europe 1950–1989

| | $mn 1989 | Per cent of total FDI | | | | Per cent increase | | |
		1950–1980	1981–1984	1985–1988	1989	1950–1980 to 1981–1984	1981–1984 to 1985–1988	1988 to 1989
United States								
Manufacturing	8959	23.2	35.1	31.9	27.4	88.2	327.8	1.4
Services	23377	70.7	64.4	67.0	71.5	13.0	391.2	82.4
Total:*	32657	100.0	100.0	100.0	100.0	24.1	371.8	50.5
Europe								
Manufacturing	3090	18.9	20.0	14.7	20.9	9.1	235.7	99.6
Services	11438	78.3	74.1	81.5	77.4	(2.6)	404.0	56.6
Total:*	14777					2.9	358.4	62.1
Per cent of worldwide FDI								
United States		24.3	31.5	45.2	48.2			
Europe		12.2	13.2	18.3	21.9			

*Includes branch offices which are not shown in sectoral breakdown.
Source: Ministry of Finance.

doubled. On the level of corporate buy-outs as well, European firms are becoming more important targets for Japanese investors. A recent survey found that in the first half of 1990, Europe accounted for one-quarter of all Japanese acquisitions, up from 13 per cent in 1986, while the share of acquisitions made in the United States fell from 62 per cent to 54 per cent over the same period. It seems likely that the numbers, if not the total value, of acquisitions in the two locations will converge in the near future (*Japan Economic Journal*, 1990). At the level of the firm, 1989 was the first year in which Sony's sales of consumer electronics were higher in Europe than they were in the United States (Kirkland, 1990).

The 1992 program of the European Community is, to a large extent, responsible for the new wave of Japanese investment into Europe. The single market presents both opportunities (new and larger markets, buoyant demand) and threats (barriers to the import of non-EC goods) to firms from non-EC countries, making FDI in the region a strategic imperative to assure market access. Japanese MNEs are responding to the new L advantages being created by EC 1992 by injecting fresh capital into knowledge and technology intensive sectors. To the extent that European industry is strong enough to withstand this new competition, as well as the degree to which Japanese firms transfer high value (i.e. innovatory) activities to their foreign subsidiaries, this trend will contribute to the current restructuring and upgrading of European industry, and the resulting emergence of new world-class technology centers in the EC (Dunning and Cantwell, 1990). And by contributing to the increased rate of technological progress and stimulating local competition in the EC, Japanese investment may not only improve the L advantages of that region, but will, in turn, contribute to the slippage in the competitiveness of the United States in what had traditionally been the former's unchallenged domain, viz. technology intensive manufacturing capability.

Exploiting the L advantages of regional markets

In addition to the shift towards Europe, and the EC in particular, as a key strategic location for Japanese multinationals, another facet of Japanese MNE activity that is likely to change in the 1990s is the organization of their cross-border production operations. Increasingly, such organization is likely to reflect the character and needs of regional, rather than national, markets, including that of integrated production and distribution systems.

The data already point to a trend towards the regional organization of Japanese industry in North America and Europe. Japanese investment flows into Canada more than doubled following the passage of the US–Canada Free Trade Agreement. In Europe, the rapid increase of Japanese investment flows into Spain ($501 million in 1989, up 211 per cent from the year before) and West Germany ($1,083 million in 1989, a 165 per cent increase from 1988) also testifies to the changing geographical patterns of Japanese FDI in response to the new configuration of L advantages in the region. In the United Kingdom, historically the largest recipient of Japanese FDI, new investment increased by only 35 per cent in the 1988–1989 period.

A 1987 survey of 709 Japanese manufacturers in Europe revealed that the most frequently quoted response (164) to the unification of the EC was to 'Europeanize' operations through increasing local procurement and the localization of management. At that time, a large number (126) planned to grant more autonomy and responsibility to their EC operations, and indicated that they intended to 'establish an executive office to supervise our business operations in Europe including, but not limited to, manufacturing, production, financing and R&D' (JETRO, 1990). And while Japanese multinationals have been generally reluctant to venture into the unknown territories in Central and Eastern Europe, it is likely that joint ventures between large Japanese conglomerates (Matsushita, Mitsubishi) with West German firms (Siemens, Daimler Benz) will allow several of them to ride into the Central and Eastern European market on the backs of their more experienced partners.[7]

Such moves all point to the increased L and I advantages brought about by the newly integrated European markets. These stem from the new opportunities for fresh economies of scale and scope; the efficiency-enhancing effects of organizing cross-border activities so as to exploit the different L advantages of member countries in the region; and the increasing rate of technical innovation which is expected to follow from regional integration, derived from the dynamic impact of income growth and the static impact of a larger market against which a firm can amortize its technology investments. Japanese producers are rapidly increasing their overseas investments, particularly in Europe, in order to exploit these new opportunities. Not only do they possess strong O advantages in key industries, but they also benefit – as latecomers – from being able to integrate regional operations from the outset, without the costs associated with the reorganization of pre-existing assets (costs which many established US MNEs in the EC must face). Moreover, the integration of the production and organizational capabilities of Japanese firms in the Europe of the 1990s will, in turn, further enhance the L advantages of host countries within the regional markets.

Exploiting the O advantages of local firms

It has been shown that Japanese firms exhibit a propensity to internalize the market for their O advantages in their foreign subsidiaries as they increase local content levels by extending to those locations the interfirm networks which had formerly been specific to the home country. Other indicators also point to the rising strategic importance of Japanese FDI in both the United States and Europe. These include the rising levels of R&D performed by subsidiaries;[8] the setting up of overseas design facilities that help shift responsibility for product development from the parent to the affiliate; the increased numbers of Europeans and Americans in key managerial positions; and an overall rise in the managerial autonomy of overseas affiliates (JETRO, 1988, 1990).

In other words, the organizational structure of Japanese affiliates of a decade or so ago is being abandoned as their parent companies evolve a transnational strategy towards their foreign operations.[9] Partnerships and acquisitions of local firms in both the United States and Europe have become key elements of the organizational restructuring now taking place. Through strategic acquisitions, Japanese MNEs are gaining access to firms that capture L advantages which are unique to the target country, and, in so doing, are creating new O advantages which would be otherwise unattainable through trade or even a greenfield FDI.

By acquiring Columbia Pictures in 1989, for instance, Sony gained access to a broad spectrum of cultural-specific distribution channels for its manufactured goods; Fujitsu's newly-won control of ICL in the United Kingdom places it in a position to participate in the European R&D consortia, e.g. ESPRIT, EUREKA, which have been off-limits to Japanese companies and are, indeed, intended to develop technologies that will help the Europeans compete against Japanese multinationals.

Japanese investments in luxury branded consumer goods in Europe provide an opportunity to enter specialty niches which are intimately bound to the local culture. They are increasing investments – mainly via mergers and acquisitions – in industries where Japanese O advantages are inferior to local ones (e.g. processed foods, pharmaceuticals and chemicals in Europe, and household products, biotechnology and computers in the United States). In short, Japanese MNEs are strategically positioning themselves to acquire or create *new* O advantages which will complement their existing competitive strengths and power their future growth. Offensive moves such as these are likely to accelerate, as part of the strategic imperative to become 'insiders' in the major markets of the Triad. By adopting pluralistic modes of market entry, Japanese firms are exploiting differences in cross-border market failure both in the intermediate and final goods markets. It would seem that these new forms of international involvement by Japanese firms have, in part at least, replaced domestic upgrading as the primary weapon with which to prepare for future competitive bids in global markets.

Conclusions – the later 1990s: rising O advantages of Japanese MNEs, falling L advantages of Japan?

The story of Japanese FDI in the United States and Europe is one of remarkable strategic dexterity in response to the rapidly changing OLI configuration facing Japanese firms in the last two decades or more. In moving swiftly from exporting to defensive FDI strategies in both the United States and Europe in the late 1970s and early 1980s, Japanese MNEs are managing to maintain their O advantages in increasingly competitive markets.

The question that remains to be answered at this point is whether, and for how long, the evolution of Japanese FDI from defensive to offensive strategies can continue. Can Japan continue to upgrade her industrial infrastructure if many of the necessary instruments of that upgrading (specialized R&D assets, technical and managerial personnel, interfirm supplier networks) are geographically dispersed outside Japan?

Moreover, are the economic and cultural conditions, policies and institutions which helped Japanese firms build up its O advantages in the last 30 years likely to continue in the future?[10] To what extent, too, is it likely that Japanese MNEs will sustain their traditional O advantages in organizing production in countries where the social, political and legal structures and interfirm relationships are so radically different from those in Japan? Will the transaction costs associated with transferring these advantages to the US and European environments be prohibitive? How long will it be before the moves of host country rivals to 'copy' Japanese production methods succeed in eroding key Japanese O advantages? All these questions lead ultimately to the issue of the degree to which Japan can maintain her extraordinary economic performance, if and when FDI replaces trade as the engine of industrial restructuring and upgrading.

Numerous factors will determine the answer to these questions. Among the most important are the trade policies adopted by the newly integrated regional markets in Europe and North America and the gradual opening up of the Japanese economy to inward direct investment. Throughout most of the 1980s, in terms of structure and organization, Japanese direct investment in Europe lagged behind the United States, but current trends indicate that in the post-1992 era, Europe could surpass the United States in its strategic importance to Japanese MNEs. What is clear is that there has been a radical change in the nature of the 'Japanese challenge'; through the mechanism of FDI in Europe and the United States, the challenge has intensified, while at the same time it has become less Japanese.

7 Transatlantic foreign direct investment and the European Economic Community[1]

INTRODUCTION

This chapter addresses the question 'How far and in what way has European economic integration, and more specifically, the formation of the European Economic Community (EC) in 1958 and the prospects of completion of the internal market in 1992 (EC 1992) affected the level and pattern of transatlantic value-added activities?' For the purpose of this chapter, we define such activities as production owned and controlled by US owned firms in the EC and of EC owned firms in the US.

The chapter first presents a brief summary of the predictions of the eclectic paradigm of international production[2] of the consequences of economic integration for cross-border value-added activities into and out of the integrated area. The second and main part of the chapter reviews the extent and pattern of transatlantic production (TP) since the early 1950s.

In particular it considers four main periods:

1 The pre-EC years: 1950–1957
2 The EC prior to UK membership: 1958–1972
3 The maturing of the EC: 1973–1985
4 The pre-1992 years and the accession of Portugal and Spain to the EC: 1986–1989

Without engaging in any econometric analysis, the chapter tries to assess the role of the EC Mark I integration (the removal of tariff barriers) and some of the first effects of EC Mark II integration (the removal of non-tariff barriers) on the extent and form of TP.

THE THEORY OF ECONOMIC INTEGRATION AND INTERNATIONAL PRODUCTION

As outlined in the previous chapter, the eclectic paradigm of inter-national production (Dunning, 1988, 1993), asserts that firms will engage in value activities outside their national boundaries whenever they possess, or wish to acquire, assets of value to maintaining or advancing their global competitive position, and when they find it in their best interests to create or add value to these assets in a foreign location. The paradigm further avers that the configuration of the competitive and locational advantages facing firms will vary accord-ing to the countries (or regions), industries (or sectors of economic activity) or firms being considered, and indeed over time, and that any operational theory of foreign production will have to take these into account. Among the firm specific variables of some im-portance is the business strategy pursued by firms in response to the competitive advantages and locational opportunities facing them.[3]

In this chapter, our interest will be primarily directed to the way in which economic integration has affected the competitive advantages of US and EC owned firms; the locational advantages of the US and the EC as a production base; and the efficiency of transatlantic markets compared with US and European owned hierarchies as a mode of organizing the interaction between these two sets of advan-tages.

The primary affect of economic integration is to harmonize the conditions of production and lower the costs of trade between countries. This gives rise to a series of trade *creation* and *diversion* effects which, in turn, have consequences for the level, structure and location of investment and production. For example, in so far as integration helps lower the costs of production and reduces cross-border transport costs, or raises the level of consumer demand, it may encourage intraregional product and process specialization, make possible further economies of scale, and enable multiproduct firms to exploit fresh economies of scope. By improving the production or transactional efficiency of firms located in the integrated region, it may improve the competitiveness of these firms in global markets.

On the other hand, the received theory of integration (Robson, 1993) has little to say about its effect on the *ownership* of firms producing in the integrated area, or on the foreign activities by firms from the integrated area. To what extent, for example, might any diversion of production from the US to the EC mean a change of both the ownership and location of economic activity, or simply the latter? What determines whether the advantages of European economic integration show themselves in the better ability and willingness of EC firms to set up or expand production units in the US?

First, a general point: TP exists because of transatlantic market imperfections. Earlier in this book, we distinguished between two kinds of imperfection. The first are structural distortions, and the second are those which arise through endemic or intrinsic market failure. Ownership specific structural distortions may allow firms monopolistic advantages over others (e.g. with respect to access to markets or raw materials) and enable them to better penetrate or control foreign markets. Location specific distortions arise mainly from Government intervention; they include import quotas, tariffs and a variety of non-tariff barriers, such as border related controls, discriminatory procurement practices, technical standards, market entry barriers, incentives or disincentives to outward or inward investment, and so on. Although these distortions primarily affect the *where* of production in as much as some firms are better able to circumvent or take advantage of them, they may affect the ownership of production as well.

The second kind of market failure reflects the transactional costs of organizing activity. It suggests that, except where they are faced with perfectly competitive markets, firms may find it more profitable to coordinate separate but related value-adding activities under their own governance or ownership rather than to sell or acquire the output of one value activity to or from another firm. In other words, they perceive the net transactional benefits (i.e. transactional benefits less transactional costs) of hierarchies are greater than those offered by markets.[4] The transaction costs of markets have been extensively discussed in the literature.[5] Essentially, these reduce to the costs of uncertainty, and include those of bounded rationality, opportunism and moral hazard, adverse selection, and of monitoring. The transaction benefits of hierarchies (which, again, are obtainable only where market failure exists) include the capturing of the economies of interdependent activities, the opportunities to engage in price discrimination, and the exploitation of cross-border product and process specialization.

Economic integration affects the balance between hierarchical costs and market imperfections in two ways. First, by removing tariffs and/or non-tariff barriers, it reduces location specific structural distortions. Second, by opening up competition it may also help to reduce ownership structural distortions. This would suggest that TP may be a defensive reaction on the part of firms to get behind tariffs which have cut off their exports.

On the other hand, economic integration may lead to a lowering of hierarchical transaction costs and better enable firms to exploit transactional benefits, which the market cannot provide or provide as efficiently. By lowering intraregional transfer costs, it may aid horizontal and vertical specialization. Where, because of market failure, such cross-border speculation is better undertaken by firms under the same ownership, integration may lead to an increase in both intraregional and foreign direct investment.

Similarly, integration, by raising demand and lowering the production costs in the region (compared with outside the region), may encourage foreign firms to replace their exports to the region by producing inside it. By the same token, it could reduce outward production by firms in the region as the region has become a more attractive base for production.

Integration may also have discriminatory effects upon the ownership specific advantages of domestic and foreign firms. Again, predictions are not straightforward. One hypothesis is that firms from large integrated economies are able to build up economies of scale and scope which help finance innovatory activities, and that competition between firms is also greater within an integrated area. They may also help foster closer and more fruitful cooperation between firms and their suppliers. In as much as foreign subsidiaries from countries outside the region possess these advantages but those within the region do not, the latter may be expected to gain more from integration than the former. And, it is perhaps worth noting that the lineage of Europe 1992 may be traced to two business men, Weisse Dekker of Philips and Pehr Gyllenhammer of Volvo, both of whom believed that the only way European industry could hope to match the competitiveness of the Japanese and Americans was for the EC to become a truly single market (Franko, 1989)! An alternative hypothesis to the one just set out is that because foreign owned firms may already possess advantages relative to local firms, the former will be in a position to exploit any new gains from integration at a lower marginal cost than the latter. This, however, depends on the transferability of these advantages from a home to a foreign location (see Chapter 6). Clearly the impact on ownership advantages will differ between sectors, countries and firms, but, overall, the results are indeterminate on the impact on both outward and inward investment.

To summarize, regional economic integration is likely to affect the competitive advantages and the location of production of both foreign investors (or potential investors) and EC owned firms. As far as the former group of firms (and particularly TP) is concerned, depending on the level of the external tariff on non-tariff barriers, the locational effects are likely to favor the substitution of exports for local production; but within the integrated area, they will encourage more plant and process specialization, particularly in sectors where economies of scale are important. These benefits, and those arising from geographical diversification and the economies of scope are, together with the absence of trade barriers, likely to allow firms further to exploit the gains of common governance. These, in turn, will add to the advantages of EC owned firms which might be expected to rise if the penalties of tariff barriers affected them more seriously than foreign firms.

Outward investment might be expected to fall as the EC becomes a more attractive place for production. On the other hand, the improved competitive capability of EC owned firms will assist their penetration of foreign markets. In addition, to maintain or further advance their competitiveness, these latter firms might wish to invest in, or conclude strategic alliances with, US or Japanese firms at the 'cutting edge' of sectoral achievement.

THE EVIDENCE

The situation prior to 1957

In the 1950s, the US was at the peak of its technological hegemony. The competitive advantages of her firms in most activities were second to none. Yet, high real wage costs and the shortage of dollars compelled US firms to manufacture many of these products abroad, especially in Europe and some of the developing countries. In 1950, when the first post-war Census of Overseas Assets was carried out by the US Department of Commerce, the countries, which were later to be the six founder members of the EC, accounted for 5.4 per cent of the total foreign direct investment stake, and 8.3 per cent of that in manufacturing industry, by US companies. The rest of Europe accounted for a further 9.3 per cent and 16.1 per cent respectively, of which the UK alone was responsible for 7.2 per cent and 14.1 per cent. Throughout the 1950s, the situation remained much the same. Indeed, even in 1957, the UK, which had not been as badly devastated by the war as had much of Continental Europe, and was especially attractive to US investors because of their familiarity with its business customs, language, and access to Commonwealth markets (apart from Canada) had accounted for more than one-half (56.7 per cent) of the combined sales of US manufacturing affiliates in the EC and UK. In that year the ratio between the sales of US affiliates in the EC and the exports of manufacturers from the US to the EC was 2.04 (US Department of Commerce, 1959).

By contrast, European owned firms had few competitive advantages to sell in US markets; and what they had, they found it profitable to exploit through exports. Most of the US assets of European investors were sequestrated or sold to pay for the war, and by 1959 when the first US census on foreign direct investment in the US was taken, the stock of EC direct investment in the US was only 61.4 per cent of that of US direct investment in the EC.[6]

Data on the flow of US foreign direct investment show some interesting changes in the period immediately before the EC was initiated. As revealed in Table 7.1, the share of the increase in the total foreign direct investment stake of US companies directed to the EC (6)[7] rose from 6.5 per cent between 1950 and 1954 to 8.6 per cent between 1954 and 1957. US based surveys undertaken around this time revealed that US firms were stepping up their investments in the Community in anticipation of the benefits likely to accrue to firms producing within the Community, and, no less important, to avoid the costs likely to be incurred by those remaining outside (Edwards, 1964; Balassa, 1966)[8]

The formative years of the EC: 1957–1971

An increasing pace of US investment in the EC

The following facts may be highlighted from the US Department of Commerce data.

1   Table 7.1 reveals that the growth of the US capital stake in the EC rose sharply between 1957 and 1972. The EC share of new US investment over the period was 21.1 per cent compared with its share of the capital stake of 6.6 per cent in 1957. In other words, had the share of the total foreign investment stake by US companies in the EC in 1972 been that in 1957, that investment stake would have been 69 per cent less. At the same time, the share of other Western European (mostly E.F.T.A.) investment by US companies also rose substantially to 18.2 per cent from 9.7 per cent. *These data would suggest it was the attractions of Europe, rather than the EC per se, that was the main cause of the growth of US direct investment in the EC in the 1960s.* Nevertheless, the share of US investment directed to the UK as a proportion of UK plus EC investment fell to 38.6 per cent in 1972 from

Table 7.1 US direct investment stake in the EC and UK 1950–1990

	EC[1]				UK			
	$ mn	% of[2] total	% increase[3]	% of GDP[4]	$ mn	% of[2] total	% increase[3]	% of GDP[4]
1950	637	5.4		na	847	7.2		na
1954	1016	5.8	12.4	1.21	1263	7.2	10.5	2.53
1957	1680	6.6	19.6	1.22	1974	7.8	16.1	3.20
1959	2208	7.4	14.7	1.35	2477	8.3	12.1	3.67
1965	6304	12.7	15.8	2.18	5123	10.4	13.1	5.16
1972	15339	17.1	18.8	2.51	9638	10.7	9.5	6.09
1972	25653	28.5		3.22	9638	10.7		6.09
1977	49150	33.7	13.9	3.29	16709	11.4	11.7	6.67
1982	71522	34.5	8.4	3.26	27373	13.2	11.0	5.64
1985	81170	35.3	0.4	3.52	33024	14.3	6.7	7.36
1985	81380	35.3		3.48	33024	14.3		7.36
1986	95629	36.8	17.5	2.97	35389	13.6	7.2	6.39
1987	119428	38.0	24.9	3.01	44512	14.2	25.8	6.66
1987	123999	39.5		2.89	44512	14.2		6.15
1988	131115	39.0	5.7	2.77	49459	14.7	11.1	7.37
1989	149975	40.5	14.4	3.16	59827	16.2	21.0	6.84
1990	172940	41.0	15.3	2.97	64983	15.4	8.6	

[1] In this and the following Tables, data for 1950–1972 refers to EC (6), that for 1972–1985 EC (9), that for 1986–1988 EC (10) and that for 1988–1989 EC (12).
[2] Of the total foreign capital stake of US firms.
[3] Annual average.
[4] Gross domestic product.
Source: US Department of Commerce (v.d.) Benchmark Surveys of US Overseas Assets and Survey of Current Business.

54.0 per cent in 1957. It seems, then, that by remaining outside of the EC, the UK had become less attractive to US investors, although part of the explanation also rests with the slower rates of economic growth in the UK over these years.

2 At least part of the growth of US investment in the EC is reflected by the substitution of exports from the US for total production by US owned subsidiaries. Table 7.2 shows that, in 1957, for example, the manufacturing output of US subsidiaries in the EC was 67.1 per cent of that of both manufacturing exports from the US to the EC and local production by US subsidiaries. By 1966, in spite of the liberalization of dollar imports, this percentage had increased to 78.0 per cent and by 1972 to 84.2 per cent. Moreover, a substantial proportion of this increase in exports was directly due to the operations of US firms in Europe. For example, of the total exports of those US firms with affiliates in the EC in 1966, 90 per cent were bought by these affiliates, which accounted for about 40 per cent of all US manufacturing exports. Put another way round, if the EC local production[9] to local production plus exports ratio had remained as it was in 1957, then the US direct investment stake in the EC in 1972 would have been about one-fifth less than it actually was.

Table 7.2 Sales of US manufacturing subsidiaries in the EC and exports from the US to the EC 1957–1989

	(1) Sales $ mn	*(2)* Exports $ mn	*(3)* Total $ mn	*(4)* % of (1) to (3)	*(5)* Ratio of (1) to (2)
1957	2525	1240	3765	67.1	2.04
1962	5770	2097	7867	73.3	2.75
1967	12220	3442	15662	78.0	3.55
1972	35143	6584	41727	84.2	5.34
1972	51623	8974	60587	85.2	5.75
1977	95359	19471	114830	83.0	4.89
1982	132196	33621	165817	79.7	3.93
1985	138249	34417	172666	80.1	4.01
1986	211199	37954	249153	84.7	5.56
1987	221351	43784	292897	85.1	5.69
1988	260556	58364	319008	81.7	4.47
1989	280083	68364	348548	80.4	4.09

Source: As for Table 7.1, and UN Commodity Trade Statistics.

3   The growth of the output of US manufacturing affiliates in the EC outpaced that of their local competitors. Similarly, as Table 7.1 shows, the accumulated US capital stake in the EC rose faster than the EC's gross domestic product (GDP). This suggests that part of the effect of the formation of the EC may have been to increase the ownership advantages of US relative to EC owned firms. In 1957, the share of the sales of US manufacturing affiliates to the gross national product (GNP) of EC countries was 1.8 per cent. By 1967 this proportion had more than doubled to 3.7 per cent, and by 1972 it had increased further to 5.8 per cent. The relative significance of US firms in the UK economy also increased in these years, but the rise was not so impressive; thus there would seem to have been an EC specific effect on the ownership advantages of US affiliates. The respective proportions of the US sales to UK GNP were 3.2 per cent in 1957, 5.4 per cent in 1967 and 6.1 per cent in 1972.[10]

4   There is some suggestion that the fastest rates of growth, relative both to that in other geographical areas outside the EC and to other industrial sectors in the EC, occurred in those sectors in which economic integration might have been expected to have had the most pronounced affect, viz. those in which the opportunities for exploiting the economies of specialization and common governance are the greatest. Foremost among these are the chemicals and pharmaceutical sectors, where the increase in sales of US affiliates in the EC between 1957 and 1972 was 225.6 per cent, double the rate of growth of sales of US affiliates in that sector in the rest of the world, and 86 per cent higher than the increase in the sales of US affiliates for other sectors in the EC.

These data then suggest that, in the first 15 years of its existence, US investment in the EC rose faster than it might have done in the absence of economic integration. They further confirm that part of this increase was due to the improvement in the ownership advantages of US firms, and another, but probably lesser, part to the increased attractions of the EC as a location for production. What the data are not able to show, however, is the specific impact of regional integration (as opposed to other factors affecting the growth of the EC in bringing about these changes). As we have said, much of Continental Europe was still in the 'catching up' stage after the Second World War; and, undoubtedly, part – and if the data for the rest of Europe are anything to go by, probably at least one-half – of the growth of the GNP would have occurred in any case. Those attempts which have been made to isolate regional integration as a factor influencing US investment generally agree that this variable has been swamped by others, and in particular the actual and anticipated economic growth (Balassa, 1966; Krause, 1968). Moreover, even accepting the extremely close correlation between growth of real output per head and individual European countries and that of US investment in these countries (Dunning, 1970), it is probable that at least part of this faster growth is itself due to regional integration.

Some recovery of EC investment in the US

Between 1959 and 1972, the value of the investment stake by EC companies in the US increased from $1.35 billion to $4.03 billion (or 191.9 per cent), while that of other Western European nations rose from $0.84 billion to $2.07 billion (or 146.4 per cent). Over this same period, the EC's share of all inward investment in the US rose from 20.5 per cent to 27.1 per cent. At the same time, in 1972, the ratio between the US direct investment in the EC and the EC direct investment stake in the US was considerably higher (3.81) than it was in 1959 (1.64). Further details are set out in Tables 7.3 and 7.4.[11]

No data are available on the sales of EC owned subsidiaries in the US. However, Table 7.3 shows that the total direct investment stake of EC companies as a proportion of US GNP rose very slightly from 0.28 per cent in 1959 to 0.34 per cent in 1972. This suggests that the competitive position of (at least some) EC owned firms in the US improved over this period.

To what extent did EC firms prefer to exploit any competitive advantages they had in supplying the US markets from exports rather than by foreign direct investment? Relating data on (an estimate for) the sales of EC manufacturing subsidiaries in the US[12] to these sales plus exports of manufactured goods from the EC to the US, we see this proportion rose from 31.7 per cent in 1959 to 58.3 per cent in 1972. These percentages suggest that the relative locational advantages of supplying goods made by EC firms from a US location increased substantially over this period.

In summary, there is only limited evidence that the formation of the EC improved the relative competitive advantage of EC owned firms (*vis-à-vis* US owned firms) during the first years of its existence; and any improvement which did occur would seem to have been exploited more by production by EC subsidiaries in the US than by direct exports from the EC. On balance, the data strongly support the

Table 7.3 EC and UK direct investment stake in the US 1950–1990

	EC				UK			
	$ mn	% increase[1]	% of total	% of GDP[2]	$ mn	% increase[1]	% of total[2]	% of GDP[3]
1950	712[4]		21.0	na	1168		34.4	na
1957	na		na	na	1881	8.7	32.9	0.24
1959	1350	10.0[5]	20.5	0.28	2167	7.3	32.8	0.44
1965	1975	6.6	22.5	0.29	2852	4.8	32.4	0.24
1972	4030	10.8	27.1	0.34	4987	8.4	33.5	0.42
1972	9156		61.1	0.78	4987	8.4	33.5	0.42
1977	19301	17.3	58.1	1.01	6397	5.4	18.5	0.29
1982	73962	30.3	59.3	2.37	28447	35.4	22.8	0.91
1985	107105	13.2	58.0	2.70	43555	15.3	23.6	0.91
1986	126853		57.6	3.03	55935	28.4	25.4	1.33
1987	160619	26.6	61.0	3.69	75719	35.4	28.7	1.90
1988	188342	17.3	59.8	3.92	95698	26.4	30.4	1.99
1989	216132	14.8	57.8	4.19	105511	10.3	28.3	2.04
1990	229913	6.4	56.9	4.17	108055	2.4	26.8	1.96

[1] Annual average.
[2] Of the total foreign stake of EC or UK firms.
[3] Gross domestic product.
[4] Europe minus UK and Switzerland.
[5] Annual average 1950–1959.
Source: As for Table 7.1.

Table 7.4 Balance between US investment stake in the EC or UK and EC or UK investment stake in the US 1959–1990

| | US investment in | | Manufacturing investment in US by | |
	EC *$ mn*	*UK* *$ mn*	*EC* *$ mn*	*UK* *$ mn*
1959	1.64	1.14	2.82	2.31
1965	3.19	1.80	5.05	3.94
1972	3.81	1.93	4.98	3.36
1972	2.80	1.93	4.29	3.36
1977	2.44	2.61	3.89	3.61
1980	1.64	2.02	2.34	2.26
1981	1.25	1.63	1.56	1.72
1982	0.97	0.96	1.21	1.24
1983	0.85	0.86	1.09	1.18
1984	0.72	0.74	1.04	1.08
1985	0.76	0.76	1.12	1.09
1986	0.75	0.63	1.07	0.81
1987	0.74	0.59	0.98	0.58
1988	0.70	0.52	0.81	0.47
1989	0.69	0.57	0.68	0.37
1990	0.75	0.60	0.74	0.39

Source: As for Table 7.1.

continued economic and technological strength of US owned firms, both in their home countries and in Europe, especially in the high technology sectors (Dunning, 1988).

New members join a maturing Community: 1973–1985

Inward investment to the Community

In January 1973, the UK, along with Ireland and Denmark, acceded to the EC. Already prior to this date the rate of US direct investment directed to these three countries began to increase, although the pace of growth did not reach its peak until the early 1970s. However, for the period 1972 to 1985, the investment stake by US companies in the UK rose marginally faster than that in the rest of the EC, with the result that, by 1985, the UK share of the EC capital stake of US companies had risen to 40.7 per cent (from 37.6 per cent). However, the share of the EC sales of manufactured goods accounted for by the UK fell sharply to 13.1 per cent in 1985 from 29.4 per cent in 1972.

All the indices of the growing involvement by US firms in the EC identified in the previous section continued to apply until 1985, albeit with decreasing force. Indeed, in the early 1980s there was some retrenchment of US MNE activity in the EC. For example, between 1980 and 1984, the investment stake accounted for EC (9) actually fell from $80.4 billion to $69.2 billion or by 13.9 per cent. However, for the period as a whole, the growth of the US capital stake in the Community between 1972 and 1985 was 216.4 per cent compared with 132.1 per cent in the rest of the world. Excluding US investment in the UK, which recorded a rate of growth of 242.6 per cent, the growth of investment in the rest of the EC was 200.6 per cent.

Between 1972 and 1985, the manufacturing exports of US based firms to the EC rose faster than the sales of US manufacturing affiliates in the EC. In 1985, 80.1 per cent of EC sales of manufactured goods made by US owned firms were produced in EC subsidiaries compared with 84.2 per cent in 1972. Moreover, the proportion of US exports shipped to their manufacturing affiliates in the EC fell from around two-fifths to one-quarter over the same period. The share of the accumulated US direct investment stake in the EC also rose from 3.22 per cent in 1982 to 3.52 per cent. These data primarily reflect the relatively faster rates of economic growth in the EC compared with the US, and the strengthening of most European currencies *vis-à-vis* the US dollar.[13]

However, perhaps more interesting than the continued growth of US investment in the EC was its changing character. Earlier, we suggested that one of the advantages of integration was that it helped reduce the hierarchical governance of cross-border activities and encouraged product or process specialization and cross-border trade. Perhaps the best index we have of this is the growth of intrafirm trade of US subsidiaries within the EC. Unfortunately, the nearest comparable data we have is the proportion of exports of EC subsidiaries to countries other than the US. According to the US Department of Commerce, in 1985 these exports amounted to $86 billion, some 52.1 per cent of all the sales of the subsidiaries. Of this former figure, $48 billion or 56.1 per cent were to other affiliates. This compares with an equivalent figure of 31.2 per cent for non-EC US affiliates. This suggests that not only was some US investment in the EC likely to be of the rationalized or cost reducing kind, but that the proportion of such investment was higher in the EC than in other countries or regions of the world. The proportion of intrafirm exports by EC affiliates (to other than the US) has changed little since 1977 when it was 57.0 per cent.

Another measure of the extent to which US owned firms were internalizing their transatlantic markets for technology and management skills is provided by data on royalties and management fees received by US firms from European based firms. It may be reasonably hypothesized that, *ceteris paribus*, where the net hierarchical costs of organizing the cross-border use of technology and management skills are less than those of the market, the ratio between the royalties and fees received from affiliates of US firms to those received from non-affiliated companies will rise.[14] Earlier we suggested that European integration might be expected to lower the costs (or increase the benefits) of common governance of US subsidiaries in the integrated area. Table 7.5 suggests that between 1972 and 1985 the ratio of internal to external payments of royalties and fees has increased as far as transactions between the US and European based firms is concerned, but not as far as the rest of the world is concerned. Can one then, at least, cautiously conclude that the EC has had some effect on the organization of transatlantic flows of intermediate services?

During the period, the share of the US investment stake in the EC (9) as a percentage of the GNP of the EC continued to rise. In 1985 the percentage was 3.5 per cent, compared to 3.2 per cent in 1972. The rise appears to have been largely concentrated in the earlier part of the period. These data confirm that US firms continued to demonstrate superior ownership advantages over their European competitors and/or were concentrated in the faster growing industries in the 1970s. However, there is some suggestion that, during these years, the presence of such firms was beginning to spur the productivity of their European competitors. Research on the export performance of US subsidiaries of EC firms suggests that the share of US based firms of total EC exports in high and medium research intensive sectors increased from 11.2 per cent in 1965 to 14.4 per cent in 1975, but dropped back slightly to 13.5 per cent in 1982 (Dunning, 1988).

The fact that the response of US firms to regional integration has not been evenly spread across industrial sectors should prove no surprise to the student of the multinational enterprise. On the whole, as the theory would predict, the greatest impact seems to have been made in sectors supplying high technology products, those which benefit from scale economies and those in which the opportunities for product or process specialization are the most pronounced. At the

Table 7.5 Ratio between royalties and fees received from and paid to affiliated firms in the EC and US to those received from and paid to non-affiliated firms 1970–1990

	Received by US firms from			Paid by US firms to		
	EC	UK	All countries	EC	UK	All countries
1970	2.34	3.72	3.13	0.04	0.50	0.93
1972	3.12	5.05	3.63	0.11	0.32	1.00
1972	3.71	5.05	3.63	0.20	0.32	1.00
1977	4.77	7.16	3.93	0.41	0.30	1.30
1982	5.85	7.17	3.56	0.98	0.48	0.14[1]
1985	4.51	4.01	2.43	1.26	0.93	1.23
1986	5.93	5.51	2.94	1.14	1.29	1.31
1987	7.86	8.70	3.17	1.81	2.68	1.72
1988	7.89	9.12	3.32	1.50	1.51	0.89
1989	7.16	5.93	3.24	1.52	1.91	1.57
1990	7.24	5.71	3.44	1.66	2.14	1.58

[1] This figure is exceptionally low because of some negative flows of internal transactions between US firms and their foreign affiliates in the rest of the world.
Source: US Department of Commerce (v.d.) Survey of Current Business.

same time, rising European incomes have led to a noticeable increase in the sales of differentiated consumer goods (including many food products) with a high income elasticity of demand. It is these sectors in which US firms, partly because of their established competitive advantages and partly because they had already established manufacturing operations in several EC countries, were in a better position to exploit the economies of common governance.

To summarize: the maturing of the EC and the UK's accession led to some restructuring of US MNE activity in the EC. In the 1970s, it was the UK's turn to witness a speeding up of inward investment from the US, though all countries of the Community attracted a rising share of such investment, albeit at a reduced pace. During this period, and particularly in the 1980s, there were some signs that the competitiveness of the European economy and of European firms was beginning to pick up. At the same time, the rising value of some European currencies relative to the US dollar was beginning to make the EC a less attractive site for production. During part of the period, too, the world was in recession, profits of US affiliates in the EC fell, and US companies found it prudent to retrench some of their foreign (including European) assets. We have seen that between 1981 and 1984 the accumulated investment stake in the EC actually fell by one-fifth. This was partly accounted for by a fall in profitability from 17.5 per cent in the years 1978 to 1980 to 15.2 per cent in the years 1981–1984, and partly by a repatriation in assets.[15] Sales of US subsidiaries also remained fairly stagnant in these years, although the share of total EC sales accounted for by US affiliates continued to rise, albeit at a reduced pace.

However, the main feature of the period was the growth of intra-firm transactions in the EC made possible by reduced hierarchical transaction costs. Strategies by companies such as Ford, IBM, 3M, International Harvester, Honeywell, etc. to rationalize their EC subsidiaries were now starting to bear fruit; and the result was that such firms continued to outpace their European competitors who appeared less willing or able to exploit the economies of common governance.

A new EC thrust into the US by EC firms

In some respects, even more remarkable than the growth of US direct investment in the EC in the years 1972–1985, was the resurgence of EC direct investment in the US Table 7.4 shows that between 1972 and 1982 the ratio of the US direct investment stake in the EC (9) to the EC investment stake in the US fell from 2.80 to 0.97. Indeed in that year, for the first time since before the First World War, the countries comprising the EC had more invested in the US than the other way around; and by 1985 the ratio of outward to inward US investment had fallen to 0.76. Throughout the period, the UK remained the leading EC investor in the US, although its share of the total EC investment fell from 54.5 per cent in 1972 to 40.7 per cent in 1985.

The rapid rise in investment meant that EC investors dramatically increased their stake in the US economy between 1972 and 1985. Table 7.3 shows that the percentage of the accumulated stock of direct investment by the EC (9) in the US to the US's GDP increased from 0.8 per cent in 1972 to 2.4 per cent in 1982 and 2.7 per cent in 1985, while the manufacturing sales of EC affiliates in the US rose at twice the rate of the sales of indigenous US firms. Both EC exports to the US and local production by EC subsidiaries rose, with the latter rising slightly more rapidly than that of the former.[16]

These data suggest that the competitive or ownership advantages of EC firms improved in the 1970s and first half of the 1980s, as did the competitive advantages of the US economy in exploiting these advantages. It is true that at least part of this investment was motivated by the need to acquire US advanced technology, to promote scale or scope economies, or more generally to gain competitive strength *vis-à-vis* other US or Japanese companies. The number of acquisitions and mergers of US companies by EC firms more than doubled between 1984 and 1988; and in the three years ending in 1988, the takeover value was at least $80 billion. This was the beginning of the era of global enterprise. European companies, having recovered their market share of the domestic market, were now faced with competitive pressures. *In the late 1980s their EC investment in the US was partly a reflection of the economic vitality of the investing countries, and partly a deliberate strategy by European multinational firms to protect or advance their global competitive positions.*

Table 7.5 shows that, until the late 1970s, EC based companies obtained most of their US royalties and fees from unattached firms. But then followed a sharp increase in intrafirm payments, such that by 1985, internal and external transactions of intermediate services were more or less balanced. At the same time, the table also reveals, the ratio between the respective variables is totally different from that in the case of royalties and fees received by US from EC firms. Since intrafirm transactions are most likely to predominate in advanced technology sectors and those subject to economies of scale and scope, these data are themselves instructive on the character of transatlantic production.

In the 1980s, the industrial structure of EC investment in the US began to look very similar to that of US investment in the EC; though there remain some important differences. To explore these differences in any detail would take us outside the scope of this chapter. We have introduced the question of EC investment in the US because we believe this is part and parcel of European industrial recovery, and reflects the growing ownership advantages of EC firms and the need to exploit these advantages from a US production facility.

Towards 1992

A resurgence of interest by US investors in the EC

The last five years for which data are available – viz. 1986 to 1990 – have shown a marked increase in US direct investment in all EC countries. Plans for capital expenditure by US foreign affiliates in 1991 and 1992 released by the US Department of Commerce (Mataloni, 1990) show that the EC is expected to account for nearly one-half of foreign plant and equipment expenditure by US firms compared with 38.8 per cent in 1985, 24.2 per cent in 1972 and 7.9 per cent in 1957. EC sales of manufacturing affiliates in 1988 showed a 88.5 per cent increase over their 1985 sales; this compares with a corresponding *increase* in the rest of world sales of 30.7 per cent. The value of acquisition and mergers (A&Ms) of European firms by US companies between 1988 and 1990 was more than three times that of the previous three years (Walter, 1992).

Numerous surveys by accounting firms, business consultants, banks and market research analysts all point to the expectations of US firms about the effects of completion of the internal market as having a distinctive impact on the level and direction of US direct investment abroad.

It is worth noting that, although this increased investment has been spread throughout all industrial sectors, the greatest increase between 1985 and 1988 has occurred in those which economists have suggested were most likely to be affected by the 1992 provisions. For example, compared to an increase in sales of all EC subsidiaries of 56.2 per cent, those of pharmaceutical affiliates rose by 81.0 per cent, those of motor vehicles by 130.5 per cent, those of finance (except banking) by 176.2 per cent, and those of business services by 141.5

per cent. Moreover, the growth of EC subsidiary sales of these goods and services during this period compares with only a marginal *increase* of sales in developing countries of 4.1 per cent. Other data on transatlantic A&M's and strategic alliances suggest that the propensity for US firms to conclude collaborative arrangements with European companies is particularly noticeable in those sectors most likely to be affected by EC 92 (Walter, 1992).

To what extent is the resurgence of interest by US investors consistent with the predictions of received theory? The main affect of Mark 2 EC integration is likely to be first, a reduction in cross-border transaction costs; second, a reduction in production costs, brought about by the harmonization of technical standards and fiscal duties; and third, an increase in demand brought about by rising incomes. Less well analyzed has been the likely effect of the completion of the internal market on the amount, character and consequence of acquisitions and mergers and/or strategic alliances between both EC and non-EC firms of different nationalities and between EC firms. All of these developments, however, point to a further specialization of economic activity, and to additional economies of geographical diversification and cross-border networking.

Again, it cannot be without significance that between 1985 and 1988 the fastest growing component of the sales of EC affiliates of US owned firms were sales to other non-US (mainly other EC based) affiliates. These rose by 93.8 per cent compared, for example, with local sales of 47.4 per cent.[17] But, most remarkable of all was the increase in the sales of services by EC based US affiliates to affiliates in other countries (mostly elsewhere in the EC) than the US. These rose by 177.9 per cent between 1985 and 1988, with the sharpest increase (of sevenfold) being recorded by the US affiliates in The Netherlands.

But what of the role of US investors compared with that of their indigenous counterparts? Table 7.1 shows that the percentage of the US investment stake to the GDP of the EC actually fell from 3.5 per cent in 1985 to 3.2 per cent in 1989. However, this fall partly reflected the 35 per cent depreciation of the US dollar. At a constant $ value the share of the US direct investment stake would have risen to 4.0 per cent. The only information available on the industrial structure of this increased involvement by US MNEs concerns the export share of their affiliates. These suggest that in the high and medium technology sectors they have showed sharp increases. However, since, as we have suggested, part of these represent intra-EC trade between affiliates, it follows that the import ratio of such affiliates may also have risen. It is difficult, then, to conclude much about the implication for the competitive advantages of US compared with EC owned companies.

The same difficulty arises in analyzing the sourcing of the output of US firms. While between 1985 and 1988, the growth of manufacturing output of US affiliates was greater than that of exports of manufactured products from the US to the EC, part, at least, of these sales represented intrafirm, intra-EC, exports. At the same time, as pointed out earlier, a sizeable part of the exports from the US to Europe are sold directly to US affiliates and included the latter's sales. So, both sets of statistics may exaggerate the true picture.

Nevertheless, the data generally point to a continued reorientation of the location of output supplied by American owned firms from the US to the EC. Indeed, it might be argued that as the EC becomes wealthier and enlarged it is becoming a self-contained unit in the supply of American based goods. In 1989 the value of US manufacturing exports to the EC, which were not directed to the affiliates of US firms, were $52.0 billion or 18.6 per cent of the total sales of these same affiliates.

To what extent have the comparative locational advantages of producing in the EC and the US shifted since the mid-1980s? Table 7.2 shows that in 1986 and 1987 an overwhelming proportion (91.5 per cent) of the increase of sales of US MNE to EC consumers were accounted for by their subsidiaries in the EC. In 1988, exports from the US rose rather more than the sale of EC subsidiaries. These changes in the modality of servicing the EC market reflect partly movements in extra rates, and partly fluctuations in the earnings and reinvested policies of US subsidiaries in the EC.

Finally, Table 7.5 suggests that there has been a greater tendency among both US companies exporting technological and managerial expertise to the EC, and EC firms exporting such intermediate products to the US, to do so via internalized transactions rather than by use of the open market. These data strongly suggest that the transatlantic exchange of intermediate products is increasingly geared towards supporting rationalized and strategic assets acquiring FDI, the purpose of which is primarily to exploit the economies of common governance.

More EC investment in the US

The second half of the 1980s saw a continued rapid growth of EC investment into the US. Indeed, between 1985 and 1990 the value of *new* investment of $123 billion was more than the total investment stake at that former date. As revealed in Table 7.4, in 1990 the ratio of the US capital stake in the EC to that of the EC stake in the US had fallen to 0.75. UK firms had nearly twice the amount invested in the US than did US firms have invested in the UK, whereas only ten years earlier the reverse situation applied.[18] The sharp rise in the accumulated EC investment stake in the US, relative to the US GDP (as set out in Table 7.1), also suggests that the competitive advantages of EC firms were improving relative to US firms, or that the former were engaging in strategic asset acquiring investment in the US.

Table 7.6 makes some interesting comparisons between the industrial structure of the sales of US affiliates in the EC and that of EC affiliates[19] in the US in 1977 and 1988. The final column A/B for each year gives the ratio between the two sets of sales. Around an average of 1.50, the table shows that, in 1988, the US firms had a revealed comparative advantage over EC firms in sectors such as drugs, other chemicals, machinery, transportation equipment, rubber and plastic products and instruments, and business services, while EC firms record their best performance in real estate services, retail trade, printing and publishing, finance and insurance, primary metals, lumber and furniture and (rather surprisingly, although the data are greatly influenced by the contribution of Philips of Eindhoven) in electrical machinery and electronics products. With the exception of some chemical sectors, rubber products and wholesale trade, between 1977 and 1988 the sales of EC subsidiaries in the US have grown faster than the sales of US subsidiaries in the EC in 17 of the 21 sectors for which data are available, with the greatest improvement in the A/B ratios being in the service and high technology manufacturing sectors.

CONCLUSIONS

The data set out in this chapter have traced the changing transatlantic direct position of EC and US owned firms over the past 30 years. Using the framework of the eclectic paradigm, the chapter has identified some of the changes in the competitive configuration and locational opportunities facing both groups of firms, and how this has affected the amount, structure and balance of transatlantic production.

The chapter has also attempted to explore the likely impact of economic integration since 1957 on the competitive advantages of

Table 7.6 Sales of US affiliates in the EC and EC affiliates in the US 1977 and 1988

	1977			1988		
	A	*B*	*A/B*	*A*	*B*	*A/B*
Petroleum	*54.7[1]*	*19.7[1]*	*2.78*	*80.3[1]*	*53.6[1]*	*1.50*
Manufacturing	*95.4*	*31.3*	*3.05*	*260.6*	*154.1*	*1.69*
Food and kindred products	10.0[1]	4.6[1]	2.17	31.0[1]	22.3[1]	1.39
Chemicals and allied products	17.1	12.7	1.35	54.4	40.5	1.34
Industrial chemicals	7.7	10.3	0.75	23.9	25.5	0.94
Drugs	4.2[1]	1.8	2.33	15.1	4.3	3.51
Soaps, cleaners	3.3	1.5	2.20	9.2	7.5	1.23
Agricultural chemicals	0.4[1]	1.3[1]	0.31	0.7	NSA	—
Others	2.0[1]	0.2[1]	10.00	5.5	3.2[2]	1.72
Primary and fabricated metals	5.7	3.5	1.63	11.7[1]	14.9[1]	0.79
Primary	2.1[1]	2.9[1]	0.73	2.8	5.1	0.55
Fabricated	4.0[1]	0.8[1]	5.00	8.9[1]	8.9[1]	1.00
Machinery	27.5	6.2	4.44	69.2	35.7	1.94
Machinery except electrical	20.0[1]	3.0[1]	6.67	55.2	14.2	3.89
Electric and electronic	10.3[1]	3.7[1]	2.78	13.9	21.6	0.64
Transportation equipment	21.1[1]	NSA	—	50.7	6.7	7.57
Textile products and apparel	1.5	0.7	2.14	2.1	2.0	1.05
Lumber and furniture	0.3[1]	0.1[1]	3.00	0.4	NSA	—
Paper and allied products	1.3	NSA	—	6.3	5.1	1.24
Printing and publishing	0.8[1]	0.5[1]	1.60	2.1	6.5	0.32
Rubber and plastic products	2.1	0.7	3.00	9.1[1]	1.4[1,4]	6.5
Stone, clay and glass products	1.7	1.9[1]	—	3.6[1]	13.1[1]	0.28
Instruments and related products	4.4	0.7	6.29	15.6	4.1	3.81
Other	1.3[1]	0.8[1]	1.63	2.2[1]	8.3[1]	0.27
Services	*42.2[3]*	*48.1*	*0.88*	*144.0*	*194.9*	*0.74*
Wholesale trade	29.0	35.6	0.82	102.4	99.3	1.03
Retail trade	4.9	6.2	0.79	5.8	36.0	0.16

Table 7.6 continued

	1977			1988		
	A	B	A/B	A	B	A/B
Finance (except banking)	0.7	0.9	0.78	9.4[1]	13.6[1]	0.69
Insurance	1.2	3.3	0.36	6.0[1]	27.5[1]	0.22
Real estate	0.1	0.4	0.08	NSA	3.2	—
Construction	1.7[1]	0.5[1]	3.40	2.7	4.6	0.59
Communications[3]	0.5	0.4	1.25	NSA	3.9[1]	—
All industries	*183.9*	*99.0*	*1.86*	*456.0*	*397.6*	*1.15*

[1] Europe (not EC).
[2] Including agricultural chemicals (or in the case of A estimate for agricultural chemicals).
[3] Including public utilities.
[4] Not including rubber products.
A = Sales of US majority non-bank affiliates in the EC.
B = Sales of European or EC majority non-bank affiliates in the US.
Source: As for Table 7.1.

EC and US owned firms and on the comparative advantages of the EC and the US as locations for the value-added activity of both EC and US owned firms.

The main conclusions of the chapter are that the initial effect of the formation of the EC was to improve the competitive position of US owned firms rather more than EC owned firms, and that these competitive advantages were increasingly exploited from an EC location and by the US companies themselves. Gradually, however, both regional integration and the competitive stimuli of the US direct investment has led to an improvement of the ownership advantages of European companies, which, by the late 1970s, were increasingly penetrating the US market through direct investment.

The challenges of 1992 have led to a revitalization of US direct investment in the EC, while these same challenges and prospects, together with the wider imperatives of technological advances and the globalization of production and markets, have encouraged an explosion of A&Ms and other forms of EC (and especially UK) direct investment in the US. Increasingly, it would seem that TP is taking the form of a restructuring of the leading US and European companies in a variety of strategic alliances; with both groups of firms building up their core assets on both sides of the Atlantic, while shedding, or disinternalizing, their peripheral assets.

Moreover, part, at least, of transatlantic investment in the latter 1980s was to protect or advance the global competitive position of the investing companies – particularly *vis-à-vis* the increasing internationalization of Japanese corporations. Though it is difficult to trace all these activities directly to Europe 1992 almost certainly the likely happenings in Europe over the next decade, not to mention the Japanese response to these happenings, are causing US and EC owned MNEs to realign and restructure their TP in a way which could keep researchers such as ourselves in full employment for at least the foreseeable future. Certainly, both the fear of 'Fortress Europe', and the market prospects offered by the completion of the internal market, has encouraged US firms to increase their physical presence inside the EC at a faster rate than their exports to the Community. While there is a good deal of evidence to suggest that US MNEs are rationalizing their European value-added acti-vities, there is much less reason to suppose that they are pursuing an integrated transatlantic production strategy. However, since an increasing proportion of such production is the outcome of A&M activity, this situation may change in the 1990s.

The future of the balance between the participation of US MNEs in the EC and EC MNEs in the US is uncertain. Much will rest on the relative competitive strategies of the two groups of firms in a unified Europe, and the competitiveness of the US and European economies. The opening up of Central and Eastern Europe has added a new dimension to an already rapidly changing transatlantic scenario.[20] The extent, too, to which integration in Europe and North America will induce complementary trading ties between the two regional blocs, or lead to structurally distorting rivalries, will also be an important determinant of the future of transatlantic investment relationships. In its turn, the trading and industrial strategies pursued by the US Federal government and the European Commission may rest on how each perceives its economic relationships with Japanese firms and the Japanese government is likely to develop.[21]

8 Technology-based cross-border alliances

INTRODUCTION

Firms, particularly multinational enterprises (MNEs), are increasingly engaging in a network of cross-border business relationships. These relationships are sometimes with competitors, sometimes with suppliers, and sometimes with customers. The form of these relationships ranges along a spectrum from outright ownership to the most informal agreement between the transacting parties, for one or other, or both, to undertake certain kinds of value-added activities. One of the main characteristics of these cross-border networks is the creation, diffusion and commercialization of technological innovations.

The transnationalization of R&D activities by MNEs is comparatively new, but, in the early 1990s, is proceeding at a rapid rate. Many Japanese MNEs undertaking innovatory activities in their foreign affiliates have sent thousands of engineers to be trained at European and American universities and have set up R&D laboratories in Europe (e.g. Sharp, Sony and Nissan in England and Hitachi in Ireland) and in the United States (NEC in Princeton and Kobe Steel and Fujitsu in Silicon Valley, etc.). European and American companies have also established innovatory centers overseas. For example, in 1991, TI opened a basic research laboratory in Japan as Dow, Corning, IBM, DuPont and W. R. Grace had already done. Kodak, Dow Chemical, Pfizer and Digital Equipment are already doing applied research in their Japanese laboratories (Moffatt, 1991). Philips, ICI and Hoescht are among the European MNEs which have research laboratories in the United States and Japan as well as elsewhere in Europe and in some developing countries. And, in 1990, a Canadian MNE – Northern Telecom – transferred part of its domestic R&D facilities to the Southern USA.

Some of these international R&D operations are realized through cooperative agreements. Over the past decade, the organizational structure of several technology intensive industrial sectors has been transformed by a wave of joint ventures (JVs) and strategic alliances. Many of these involve large MNEs working together on difference continents. By cooperating with foreign partners, firms may benefit from the sharing of risks and the pooling of assets, based on their respective O specific advantages, and on the competitive advantages of the nations in which they operate.

Cross-border strategic alliances, which differ from traditional interfirm coalitions in as much as they are concluded to advance the global strategy of the participating firms, have increased dramatically in the past few years (Clarke and Brennan, 1988). For example, in 1982, cooperative agreements concluded between US and foreign firms outnumbered the number of fully owned foreign subsidiaries by a factor of at least four to one (Contractor and Lorange, 1988). In the later 1980s, US firms formed well over 2000 agreements with European corporations. A McKinsey study reveals that the number of US international JVs established annually increased sixfold from 1976 to 1987 (Hladik and Linden, 1989). In the EC as well, the number of cooperative agreements also rose markedly. Some details are set out in Table 8.1.

Tables 8.2 and 8.3 reveal that interfirm agreements have tended to be concentrated in high technology industries (micro-electronics, aeronautics, new materials, biotechnologies) and in industrial sectors which are using robotic manufacturing techniques, e.g. car sector. Thus, for example, over half of the firms in the fields of biotechnology and machine vision are engaged in strategic alliances (Hull and Slowinski, 1987), and most of these agreements are R&D related.

The data bases also suggest that it is generally large corporations which seem the most inclined to favor strategic alliances. The world's leading MNEs are operating through an intricate global web of formal or informal coalitions, most of which are in the advanced industrial countries. These developments induce the formation of oligopolistic galaxies with the major world producers at the hub of the galaxies. In the words of a report published in 1986:

> In the case of agreements between large firms in 'world markets' or global industries, the arrangements must be set in the context of the mutual recognition and interdependence of decisions on the part of firms, which characterize concentrated industries in which oligopoly prevails.
>
> (OECD, 1986: 3)

Table 8.1 Evolution of cooperative agreements established annually
1974–1989

	(a)	(b)	(c)	(d)	(e)	(f)	(g)
1974			37				169[1]
1975	3		14				
1976	7		16			31	
1977	7		15				
1978	7	2	14				
1979	13	1	27				317[2]
1980	22	4	34	85		94	
1981	28	22	40	169			
1982	23	19	35	197			
1983	39	16		292	46		
1984	66	42		346	69		1504[3]
1985				487	82		
1986				438	81		
1987					90	180	
1988					111		
1989					129		2629[4]

Sources
(a) Jacquemin *et al.* (1986): data on 212 cooperative agreements formed between 1978 and 1984 by at least one EC firm.
(b) Haklisch (1986): Cooperative agreements formed by the world's 41 major semi-conductor producers.
(c) Hladik (1985): US international JVs created in high income countries between 1974 and 1982.
(d) Cainarca *et al.* (1989): Arpa data base on 2014 agreements formed between 1980 and 1986 in the information technologies sectors (semi-conductors, computers and telecommunications).
(e) Commission's Reports on the EC's competition policy. See, for example, Commission des Communautés Européennes, 1989.
(f) Hladik and Linden (1989): McKinsey Studies on US international JVs created in 1976, 1980 and 1987.
(g) Hagedoorn and Schakenraad (1990): Cati data base on 9,000 agreements formed until July 1989.
[1]Before 1974, [2]1975–1979, [3]1980–1984, [4]1985–1989.

At the same time, smaller companies are becoming more involved in strategic alliances, particularly with their larger customers. According to the ARPA – an Italian data base – asymmetrical agreements between large and small enterprises in the later 1980s were growing faster than those between large firms (Cainarca, Colombo and Mariotti, 1988). For example, in the computer sector, IBM is collaborating with Microsoft to exploit its growing expertise in software for desk-top computers. In the biotechnologies sector, Hoffmann LaRoche has established links with the smaller and more entrepre-

Table 8.2 Distribution per sectors of US international JVs created in 1980 and in 1987

Sector	1980 %	1987 %	R&D JVs 1987 %
Transport equipment	10	12	14
Computers	3	8	14
Semi-conductor and optical disks	8	8	18
Other electric and electronic equipment	4	7	4
Pharmaceutical products	3	7	21
Other chemicals	19	21	14
Instruments	7	7	11
Others	46	30	4

Source: Hladik and Linden, 1989.

Table 8.3 Distribution per sector of US JVs in the EC* 1984–1989

Sector	Number	%
Food and beverages	30	6.10
Chemicals, rubber, glass and ceramics	101	20.50
Electric and electronic equipment	102	20.70
Instruments, machines	60	12.15
Information technology equipment	20	4.05
Metal products and manufacturing	48	9.75
Transport equipment	27	5.45
Wood, furniture, paper	34	6.90
Extractive industries	15	3.05
Textile, leather, shoes	7	1.40
Construction materials	27	5.45
Others	22	4.45
Total	493	100.00

*JVs among firms: (a) from the same member state; (b) from more than one member state; (c) from member states and outside states but with a significant effect on the EC market.
Source: Commission des Communautés Européennes, 1990: 332.

neurial non-Swiss firms such as Genetech, Immunex/Ajimoto, Centocor, Cal Bio, Amgen, Cetus and Synergen (*Business Week*, 1990). Alliances between small- and medium-sized enterprises are particularly frequent in the EC, where these activities are actively promoted by the Commission.

The causes, mechanisms and consequences of strategic business alliances (SBAs) are still uncertain, since most cases are very recent. In this chapter, attention will be given to these topics in order to evaluate the importance of R&D related alliances in the general context of the internationalization of innovatory activities. The chapter is divided into four parts. The first presents a theoretical approach of the determinants of the R&D strategic alliances; the second deals with management related issues; the third studies the mechanisms of R&D cooperative agreements; and the fourth offers some explanatory reflections on their likely consequences for the corporations and countries involved.

THE ANALYTICAL FRAMEWORK OF DETERMINANTS OF SBAs AND SOME EMPIRICAL EVIDENCE

Kogut (1988) suggests that the motives for SBAs fall into three main groups, viz. the enhancement of market power, the evasion of small number bargaining, and the transference of organizational knowledge. A cost/benefit analysis of cooperative agreements may help to understand *when, where, why* and *which types of* firms cooperate. According to the main studies on strategic alliances, interfirm agreements are intended to provide the following advantages:

1 sharing of the large investments needed for specific activities such as in R&D;
2 acceleration of return on investment through a more rapid diffusion of the firm's assets;
3 spreading of risks;
4 enhanced efficiency through economies of scale, specialization and/or scope;
5 coopting the competition.

At the same time, SBAs often involve substantial set up and monitoring transaction costs. Those costs include the possibility that one's partners may behave in a way detrimental to one's own interests, and – and this is particularly important where one's partner is also a major rival – that he may improve his overall competitive position relative to one's own.

A no less relevant question is why other organization forms fail to achieve the same results as alliances in a more cost-effective way. Contractor and Lorange (1988) present a comparison in terms of costs and benefits in order to answer this question. But, one of the problems that remains unsolved is why, and under what conditions, cross-border SBAs are likely to offer a more efficient organizational form than other modes, such as an FDI integration or a market transaction.

Economic theories of games, oligopoly, international production, competitive strategies, each help us to understand why firms prefer to cooperate rather than pursue a go-it-alone strategy or a spot-market relation.

Game theory

There are two branches of game theory which respectively analyze the determinants and likely outcome of (a) non-cooperative (or forced) and (b) cooperative or voluntary agreements. The theory of non-cooperative games may help to explain under what conditions cooperation is likely to emerge and survive in a world of egoists without central authority. Analysis of the prisoner's dilemma (Shubik, 1970) and specific developments of this dilemma, such as the study of the tit for tat strategy (Axelrod, 1984), show that a non-cooperative agreement is possible when: (a) the game is repeated indefinitely; (b) the interests of the players are not in total conflict; and (c) the future is important, relative to the present. Non-cooperative games theory further postulates that the prospective partners must have mutual needs and be willing to share the risks to reach a common objective and that both reciprocity and retaliation play an important role in the relationship (Lewis, 1990).

By contrast, cooperative games theory studies the negotiation tactics among the partners who have to decide the partition of the cooperative payoff. Under the development of model negotiation for two-person games (Nash, 1950, 1953) and n-person games (Von Neumann and Morgenstern, 1947) it is possible to understand the conflicting interests among allies, particularly in the objectives sought from interfirm coalitions. The theory suggests that the interface between transaction costs (including negotiation costs) and the cooperative payoff is likely to vary according to the relative power of the partners (which is itself conditioned by the relative position when the firms do not choose to cooperate); the maximum cooperative payoff available to each partner (Kalai and Smorondinsky, 1975); the likely costs of the agreement relative, for example, to its duration (Rubinstein, 1982, 1985); the risk aversion of each partner to accept a non-cooperative solution (Zenther, 1930); and that these variables will also determine the conditions under which cooperation is likely to be achieved. Studies of the characteristic function, the Shapley value and the bargaining set are also useful in understanding the emergence of inter- and intrafirm networks of rival and cooperative interests (Shapley, 1953; Aumann and Maschler, 1964). Thanks to this kind of approach, it is possible to evaluate complex situations and several kind of agreements which, while strengthening the competitive position of all partners relative to outsiders, will weaken the position of some partners *vis-à-vis* the others.

However, neither non-cooperative games (non-communicability and unenforceable agreements) nor cooperative games (communicability, enforceable agreements) theories are able fully to encompass the complex problem of SBAs, which occur in situations in which rival behavior coexists simultaneously with cooperative behavior – in other words, where companies join forces in some areas, and pursue go-it-alone strategies in others. To overcome these deficiencies, models, such as *almost non-cooperative* games (Harsanyi, 1977) and *almost cooperative* games (Gugler, 1991) have been developed. Such models help both to evaluate SBAs in the context of the competitive incentives among allies and the competitive rivalry within industrial sectors (Kogut, 1988), and to provide a taxonomy of the transaction costs and of the cooperative benefits (synergistic surpluses) related to the adhesion to specific coalitions, according to the parameters developed in the non-cooperative games theory, such as the discount parameter and the aversion for risk (Buckley and Casson, 1988) This approach also shows that a cooperative agreement is a continually evolving bargain among the partners, and that a long-term view is necessary for any collaboration to survive and flourish in a non-zero sum game situation.

Transaction cost theory

Transaction cost theory has also been widely applied to explaining the growth of SBAs.[1] According to Coase (1937), a firm will expand its output up to the point where the costs of organizing an extra transaction becomes equal to the costs of acquiring this transaction on the open market. This dichotomy between the market and the hierarchies, as transactional modalities, has been criticized because it fails to take account of the fact that firms sometimes cooperate rather than compete with each other. For example, according to Richardson (1972), networks of cooperation and association exist because firms need to coordinate complementary but dissimilar activities. Likewise, Teece (1986) introduces the notions of specific and co-specific assets, both of which, he argues, are necessary to commercialize an innovation. In some cases, SBAs are the best way to benefit from these co-assets. Thus, the comparison of transaction and control costs is a possible way to understand why firms wish to cooperate with each other. For example, Kogut writes,

> In summary, the critical dimension of a joint venture is its resolution of high levels of uncertainty over the behavior of the contracting parties when the assets of one or both parties are specialized to the transaction and the hazards of joint cooperation are outweighed by the higher production or acquisition costs of 100 percent ownership.

(Kogut, 1988: 321)

Applying these ideas to R&D alliances, it is possible to argue that firms opt for these in order to eliminate the control costs of an in-house development, or those involved in a merger or an acquisition (such costs include rigid structures – which inhibit the flexibility of R&D, capability, strategy, development orientation, etc. – high capital costs and resource risks), and to avoid the costs involved in a pure market transaction such as those arising from moral hazard and adverse selection (Jacquemin, 1988).

The theory of international production

The above analysis, however, does not, by itself, explain why firms choose to cooperate with *foreign* based partners. The theory of international production argues that to invest abroad, firms must find it more profitable, or strategically worthwhile, to engage in foreign rather than domestic production. Similarly, cross-border SBAs may be presumed to offer *additional* advantages to those provided by their intracountry counterparts. Models developed by Hirsch (1976), Agmon and Hirsch (1979), Rugman (1981) and Buckley and Davies (1979) are among the many developed by economists to evaluate the costs of supplying foreign markets by different organizational routes. The theory of transaction costs provides a good framework (a) to compare FDI with non-equity forms of international business arrangements (Teece, 1981, 1986; Hill and Kim, 1988), (b) to analyze 'scale' and 'linked' equity JVs (Hennart, 1988), (c) to study firms' horizontal and collaborative JVs (Beamish and Banks, 1987), and (d) to explain vertical integration and collaborative agreements (Anderson and Gatignon, 1986).

At the same time, it is questionable whether purely economic theories can adequately explain why firms cooperate and why they collaborate on an international level. Buckley, for example, argues despite listing of these costs and classification (information costs, bargaining costs, enforcement costs, governance costs), nowhere do we find estimates of such costs. How significant are they in relation to transport costs, production costs, marketing distribution costs? Casual empiricism suggest that they are very high, and there are some wild estimates of the proportion of transaction costs in GDP. However, estimates are essential if we are to move beyond heuristic models to concrete predictions about market configuration.

(Buckley, 1988: 184)

Thus, many costs associated with the organizational forms compared are underestimated, as shown in a study on the transaction cost approach to the make-or-buy decisions in the car sector (Walker and Weber, 1984). Furthermore, as observed by Contractor (1989), transaction cost minimization does not necessarily result in strategic optimization in the long run, nor does profit maximization in the short run. The static orientation of most of the transaction costs theoretical developments may explain this deficiency. Thus, as noted by Teece (1985), transaction-cost economics must be married to organizational decision theory if the dynamics of channel selection are to be properly appreciated and understood.

The comparative models of choice of an organizational mode and the theory of transaction costs may be completed by reference to the eclectic paradigm of MNE activity which embraces the main vehicles of trans-border business involvement, including SBAs, and suggests the determinants likely to influence the modality actually chosen. Since the paradigm has been fully explained elsewhere in this volume, we shall content ourselves with the observation that its dynamic version (see Chapter 3) offers a powerful conceptual framework for analyzing the different types of organizational forms for each activity along a firm's value-added chain, considered in relation both to its other activities, and to its overall strategic position. Figure 8.1 presents a simple model, showing the contribution of the OLI parameters as explanatory tools of strategic alliances, particularly in the R&D field. The figure helps identify the major factors which help to explain the emergence and the growth of SBAs in the 1980s, according to the OLI configuration of the participating firms. In fact, new developments such as globalization of business, the development of cross-border organizational networks, and the emergence of core technologies (or technological systems) affect the way to create, maintain and improve the O advantages and, consequently, the L and

TECHNOLOGICAL INNOVATION

- Emergence of new technologies
- High investments
- High risks
- Rapidity of innovations
- Rent of returns' period reduced

CONVERGENCE OF TECHNOLOGIES

- Mastering simultaneously several technologies
- New borders of industrial activities
- New structure of the markets

ADVANTAGES

OWNERSHIP

- Rapidity of new O advantages' development
- Rapidity of existing O advantages' exploitation
- Higher flexibility
- O advantages based on the combination of complementary but non-similar assets
- O advantages based on the supply of a complete range of systemic and compatible products
- O advantages based on products with a dominant standard

LOCATION

- Access to complementary assets based on the nations' competitive advantages, originated in the partners' home countries
- Access to the main worlds' markets for the inputs and outputs when a go-it-alone solution is not possible because of the high capacities needed to exploit them alone

INTERNALIZATION

- Sharing the costs and spreading the risks in high uncertainty situations
- Transaction costs less important because of the technological diffusion rapidity
- Benefit from scales economies
- The launching of projects with high sunk costs
- New oligopolistic reactions to replace traditional oligopolistics strategies which are inadequate because of the concentration, instability and asymmetry of oligopolies

GLOBALIZATION

- Concentration, asymmetrical and unstable oligopoly
- World's products adapted to local demand
- Systems product
- Products based on world's accepted standards

Figure 8.1 The value of strategic alliances.

I parameters. This approach takes into account some recent theoretical insights of such scholars as Hill, Hwang and Kim (1990), who seek to identify the choice of entry modes by firms into foreign markets in terms of (a) strategic related, (b) environmentally related and (c) transaction related variables.

The analysis of structural and transactional market failures, emphasized by both the internalization and eclectic paradigms, is also useful in analyzing the determinants of cooperation in specific sectors. Shan (1990) considers cooperative agreements to be the product of a double failure of the market. The first is the transactional difficulties in transferring the services of specialized assets. The second embraces the interfirm relational costs of the internalizing of both production and transactional functions. Nevertheless, an important role is also played by structural market failures such as entry barriers and government intervention and those affected by recent changes in the world economy. An overview of three of these exogenous factors insofar as they have specifically affected the conclusion of R&D alliances are now briefly examined. The three factors are technological innovation, technological convergence and the globalization of markets.

Technological innovation

The development and emergence of new technologies (defined as an industry paradigm shift) can trigger changes in existing market structures (*International Management*, 1984). As underlined many years ago by Vernon (1966) competitive threat and/or profit opportunities are the main forces behind oligopolistic response by competitor, and offer new profit opportunities. Consequently, they are likely to be an important influence in the choice of competitive strategies.

The development of the new technologies and materials of the 1990s is being characterized by more intensive competition in innovatory activities, *inter alia* to achieve a first mover advantage. But, once an innovation is made, the innovator needs to commercialize it quickly because of the erosion of its monopoly position (shorter product life-cycles, diffusion of technology, new innovations, etc.) and the need to promote common standards. In this context, SBAs may help accelerate the marketing process and safeguard the rent of the innovating companies ties).

Along with the uncertainty attached to the successful commercialization of innovations, the development and production costs of such commercialization and escalating are huge. Examples include an estimated £2 billion for the development of a new global car and £500 million for a new mainframe computer (Clarke and Brennan, 1988). Designing and manufacturing the new four-megabit RAM is reported to have cost $2 billion, double that of the previous generation of computers. Yet, current (1992) world market for all types of RAMs is probably worth less than $15 billion in annual sales.[2] In the electronics sector, the top 100 US-based publicly-held companies spent $18.2 billion on R&D in 1988, a 15.7 per cent increase from the $15.7 billion logged in 1987 (*Electronic Business*, 1989). Even the largest MNEs cannot muster all the financial resources and take the risks inherent in such huge R&D investments. In 1991, a *Financial Times* survey indicated that even if the three main European chip-makers – Philips, Siemens and SGS-Thomson Group – had each increased their share of the world market in 1990, they would still not have generated the returns needed to fund the huge R&D investments necessary to remain competitive against the American or Japanese challenge (*Financial Times*, 1991).

Convergence of technologies

Innovation increasingly depends on combining incremental technological advances across a wide range of disciplines. The interdependence between different kinds of product and process technologies is one of the major features of the early 1990s. This convergence may be observed both within and between technological clusters. Firms are increasingly having to master different, but complementary, technologies, with the result that R&D expenditures are increased. The new core technologies are applicable to different sectors and branches. Hence, new opportunities for SBAs arise. For example, Olivetti (computers) and AT&T (telecommunications) concluded a variety of agreements between 1984 and 1990 in order to match some of their O specific resources. AT&T is also collaborating with IBM for the development of network systems. The increasing use of opto-electronics in telecommunications requires the major producing firms to master know-how and technologies in the field of optical fibres. Corning Glass, a leading firm in this field, for example, is now at the center of an international alliance network. Ciba Geigy (chemicals) is cooperating with the American firm Olin in R&D materials used for high performance semi-conductors.

The modern robotics industry also requires the integration of a multitude of different kinds of technologies (Van Tulder and Junne, 1988). Firms have to acquire various knowledge and, thus, make large investments in R&D in order to maintain their global competitive positions. As noted by the ECE/UNCTC Joint Unit on TNCs (1987), the main robot producers have been driven to achieve economies of scale through collaborative agreements.

Globalization

One of the main forces behind SBAs is the need to compete internationally. As underlined by Fortune (1989: 70) 'for many major companies, going global is a matter of survival, and it means radically changing the way they work'. Economic globalization both changes the spatial dimension of MNEs and creates a need for more flexible production and marketing systems, and new forms of organization.

Firms trying to position themselves as global players face several problems, such as the cost of building a simultaneous presence in several product areas and foreign markets. For example, the limited size of the UK market, and the problems Apricot encountered in selling its hardware abroad, prompted the company to conclude SBAs with several foreign partners who could provide market access and access to technology, which Apricot felt unable to develop on its own.

Globalization of markets mainly takes place within a market structure, which is characterized by high concentration, instability and asymmetry. These oligopolistic features induce a variety of actions and reactions by the participants. For example, in the case of market concentration, SBAs may be viewed as a new kind of follow-my-leader strategy, in situations where the costs of hierarchical entry into a new market are perceived to be too high (Knickerbocker, 1973). Asymmetry may involve collaborative strategies such as technology leveraging, and the protection of market positions. Oligopolistic instability may also induce interfirm cooperation to meet the challenges of new competition; the major collaborative programs launched in the EC or in the US are also aimed at competing against Asian producers.

Global markets may further be characterized by the convergence of consumer needs and preferences. As noted by Ohmae,

> for a firm with a good grasp of the shared needs of 630 million people and the courage to launch a product in the Triad market, it is essential to have networks that can deliver a newly developed product nearly simultaneously to scores of different points on the

globe. (....) Presently, the most pragmatic and productive method of expanding a product's market is the formation of a consortia alliance.

(Ohmae, 1989: 86–87)

The emergence of product-systems is another feature of a global market, which may also lead to more SBAs. For example, in 1991, Silicon Graphic signed two R&D agreements – one with Microsoft and the other with the computer producer Compaq. These deals have helped create a powerful technological core in the computer industry, because they have linked together three leaders, one in software, the second in exploitation systems and the third in computers.

The promotion of worldwide standards is another factor to be considered. European firms like Philips are cooperating for the promotion of a European standard for European High-Definition Television (HDTV). In May 1990, Philips and Thomson-CSF signed an agreement which involved joint R&D on integrated circuits, flat screens, liquid crystal displays and broadcasting equipment; this agreement was specifically aimed at initiating new standards (*New York Times*, 1990). In 1991, AT&T and IBM also signed an agreement to make their competing systems compatible.

The completion of the European internal market is also likely and the path towards the globalization of value-added activities. For example, it will no longer be necessary for a firm to be located in every EC country to avoid non-tariff barriers and for non-EC firms; to be outside the Single Market will be perceived as a strong O specific disadvantage; while harmonization of regulations and the introduction of new legal structures are also likely to modify the internalization parameters. Confronted with the new conditions of the Single Market, firms are currently reconsidering their corporate strategies to create or sustain their competitive advantages. SBAs are certainly one of the means by which to exploit the new opportunities and challenges – including those of penetrating world markets – which follow from the removal of barriers in the EC (Buigues and Jacquemin, 1989).

R&D strategic alliances have, then, to be studied in the context of firm-specific technology strategies designed to exploit, develop and maintain the sum of the company's knowledge and abilities. Globalization of the market creates a need for restructuring, which involves interfirm links. The rising costs and uncertainty of R&D call for the sharing and pooling of risks. Convergence of technologies drives firms to seek speedy access to know-how and capabilities and markets they do not possess. All these factors pose a limit to hierarchical growth. They require new parameters to the explanations of the limits on a firm's expansion suggested in the literature (e.g. Penrose, 1958, 1980; Chandler, 1962). They necessitate venturing into external markets through SBAs both to acquire and exploit O specific advantages which require co-assets in which the firms are disadvantaged.

MANAGING STRATEGIC ALLIANCES

SBAs may provide unique opportunities to share the assets and capabilities of a wide network of partners, including customers, suppliers, competitors, distributors, universities, etc. But, cooperative agreements are not risk-free. Perlmutter and Heenan (1986: 142), for example, found that in a number of US-Japanese alliances, 'Japanese colleagues took advantage of valuable US technology and marketing know-how only to discard their American partners'. Reich and Mankin (1986) asserted that, while the Japanese partners of American firms tended to retain the higher value-added activities in Japan, and gain important project engineering and production process skills from their US partners, the latter benefitted from some design and quality control procedures that could, in any case, have been obtained from other sources more cheaply! History has shown that cultural differences, lack of agreement about the objectives of the partnership, and/or of the right managerial handling of it, poor communications and opportunism among partners have been among the frequent causes of failure of collaborative arrangements. By cooperating, a firm may have access to some information at a lower price than it would otherwise have to pay, and it may use this knowledge to compete with its partner. Such risks are higher in R&D alliances. For example, Daimler, which is collaborating with General Electric (GE), also concluded an alliance – through its MTU subsidiary – in 1990, with UTC's Pratt and Whitney division. GE alleged that this act broke its agreement with MTU to cooperate in the development of the next generation of high-thrust engines. It also asserted that it had provided MTU with business and technological information, which could help a competitor develop an alternative to the GE90 engine. But, Pratt and Whitney argued that the agreement with MTU was a logical extension of the close collaboration which the two firms had enjoyed over many years.

This kind of conflict is not unusual, and it seems to be becoming increasingly frequent with the development of interorganizational networks. Firms may cooperate with other firms' partners in one network, while competing with them in other networks. For example, in 1974, Snecma (France) signed an agreement with GE (US) to produce a new type of engine, while UTC's Pratt and Whitney division held 10 per cent of the Snecma stock. Aeritalia (Boeing's partner) and Aerospatiale (Airbus industries' member) are also cooperating in the development, production and marketing of the commercial aircraft ATR; while Boeing's Japanese partners (for the production of the 767) have other alliances with Boeing's main US competitors, viz. McDonnell Douglas.

The case of GE–Daimler is an example of the kind of conflict which may occur between partners to a technologically based SBA. In his study of a group of collaborative ventures, involving US and non-US firms, Mowery (1989) concluded that the way in which technological development was managed by the partner firms was critical to their success or failure.

In order to minimize the risk of their unique technological advantages being used by their partners to their own determinant, firms have adopted various protective devices, five of which we will now briefly describe.

Restrictive and exclusivity clauses

According to Lewis (1990), one useful tactic, adopted by some partner firms, is to agree to limit undesired market entry by a partner, an alliance, or product of the alliance. In 1986, Texas Instrument concluded an agreement with Hitachi to develop a 16-megabit dynamic RAM chip. The agreement catalogued precisely the intellectual property that belonged to each company. It was also agreed that whatever technological advances stemmed from the agreement would be jointly owned, but would not be shared with outsiders without the express permission of each partner (Kraar, 1989). To give another example, in January 1990, Siemens signed an agreement with IBM jointly to develop a chip capable of storing 64 million bits of information. One clause of this agreement prohibited either firm from cooperating with any Japanese company in memory chip development.

In some cases, of course, such restrictions run counter to national or regional, e.g. EC anti-trust, provisions. Lewis quotes the interesting example of General Electric and Rolls Royce, who formed an alliance to produce a pair of each other's jet engines. Each firm also obtained privileged access to the other's markets. The deal came apart when Rolls modified one of its engines to compete with the GE engine they shared. Beyond that point, further cooperation became impossible as Rolls would have had access to sensitive GE sales information. While there was some feeling within GE that Rolls was obliged *not* to compete with GE, there was no denying that Rolls had been given a sales opportunity that created a strong incentive to move on its own. Anti-trust constraints had precluded a formal agreement on this.

Limitations placed on technology transfer

Information is always pooled when firms cooperate. Yet, as noted by Hamel, Doz and Prahalad (1989), companies must carefully select the skills and technologies they pass on to their partners, and should develop safeguards against unintended informal transfers of information. Firms may also be tempted to minimize the transfer of technology to avoid a disclosure of their core competences. This may be done, for example, by sharing only the *results* of applying the product or process technology. In the case of the consortium International Aero Engines (which includes Pratt and Whitney, Rolls Royce, Fiat, MTU, Ishigawajima-Harima Heavy Industries, Kawasaki Heavy Industries and Mitsubishi Heavy Industries), Pratt and Whitney and Rolls Royce minimized the contribution of their own cutting-edge technology by designing the engine in modular form, and by assigning the development of different modules to different partners. At the same time, the partners must be cautious that the efforts taken to prevent any undesirable disclosure of information do not work against their own interests.

The division of control and responsibilities in collaborative ventures

The division of control and responsibility is also an important issue which needs to be resolved prior to the commencement of any SBA. The partners must also find an organizational solution to combat the uncertainties in their relationship. Some legal forms may provide one or other of the partners with more administrative control than others. Thus, collaborating firms may choose legal forms through which (a) the partners are more able to exercise significant control over the other's relevant activities, and (b) 'free riding' behavior could be avoided, and the alliance is stabilized through the creation of mutual hostage positions, whereby all the parties stand to lose if the agreement is breached. Each kind of organizational mode implies a different level of jurisdiction, which has to be jointly optimized, depending on the level of commitment and the dissemination of risk.

Efficient alliance planning

Firms entering into alliances will wish to be clear about the terms of the agreement, and to be able to monitor its consequences. In planning an alliance, each partner needs to form an unambiguous picture of the agreement's implications (in terms of rights and duties) for each partner, and to use this as a guide for partner choice and alliance design (Geringer, 1988, 1991). The clarity of goals is vital. According to Lynch (1990), ambiguous goals, fuzzy directions and uncoordinated activities are the primary causes of failure in cooperative ventures.

No issue of concern to either party should be taken on trust that can reasonably be formalized. At the same time trust and forbearance are critical ingredients of any successful alliance if conflicts of interest to do with the use of the participating firms' core competences are to be avoided.

But, while it may be easier to cooperate when partners' non-competitive interests are far apart, this does not mean that collaboration among competitors is necessarily an undesirable strategy. Alliances between rivals still may be worthwhile for each partner. But, the conditions to succeed, as underlined by the games theory, have to be respected.

Selection of alliances based on trust, commitment and compatibility

This selection could be a successful way to avoid insurmountable conflicts of interest among the partners. As quotes the words of one Chief Executive Officer:

> You've got to be sure you're working with earnest and ethical people who aren't trying to undermine your company. Usually, a partner will have access to your trade secrets. He might attempt to complete a few projects, learn what you do, then exclude you from a future deal.

(Geringer, 1988: 61)

Firms may also be more cautious of their potential partners' stability. This issue is also important to bolster trust and commitment. For example, the President of a Japanese company complained about its

American partner, which had gone through three ownership changes over the preceding decade: 'we never know who we are dealing with' (Lewis, 1990: 250). Daimler's purchase of MTU may also have contributed to the destabilization of the MTU's collaborative ventures. As suggested by the games theory, successful cooperation develops only with efforts over time.

THE MECHANISMS OF R&D ALLIANCES: A NETWORK APPROACH

The various kinds of alliances

The literature identifies several different kinds of cooperative ventures. These include formal and informal alliances; vertical, horizontal and conglomerative links; equity and non-equity agreements; production R&D, marketing, supply or multiple agreements; national, regional or trans-national alliances (Buckley, 1993).

R&D alliances may be classified under four main headings. These are:

1 University-located alliances which involve more than one industrial firm. The Semi-conductor Research Corporation (Sematech) in the US falls into this category.
2 Private strategic alliances negotiated and organized without the intervention of government.
3 Interfirm agreements organized through intergovernmental agreements (e.g. European Spatial Agency, Airbus).
4 National or international collaborative programs such as ESPRIT in the EC, EUREKA in Europe, ICOT in Japan, Alvey in the United Kingdom, etc.

As seen previously, R&D strategic alliances may involve the exchange and pooling of existing technologies or the development of new technologies. For example, Hitachi is selling TI the secrets of how to stack semi-conductors on a single silicon chip, in exchange for TI's expertise in software. In 1990, Siemens and IBM concluded a joint venture to develop a new generation of micro-chips, while AT&T and Tandem Computers agreed jointly to develop and market computer systems which combine Tandem's 'fault tolerant' designs and AT&Ts Unix operating system software. Under the terms of another alliance, concluded in 1990 between AT&T and NEC, the American company has the right to market, design and produce chips licensed by NEC and, in return, the Japanese firm will receive computer-aided design tools that AT&T has developed. In the computer software sector, Wordperfect and Lotus have been working together since 1988 to develop a common interface for the next generation of their products. In the aeronautics sector, Rolls-Royce (United Kingdom) and Snecma (France) signed a new cooperation agreement in 1989 to jointly develop a new generation supersonic engine.[3]

However, in the majority of R&D related agreements, technology is transferred in exchange for 'something else', such as access to new markets or human capabilities. Coalitions involving the use of corporate venture capital (CVC) are frequent in some industrial sectors, such as biotechnology. As noted by Mariotti and Ricotta.

> for a large company, CVC is an additional investment and in some cases, it is particularly well suited to take advantage of the continuous flow of new technologies produced by small and medium-sized companies. Through the CVC, a company can appraise its interest in a business in formation in 'real time'. It is the flexible financial activities of the small innovative units, which remain completely autonomous.
>
> (Mariotti and Ricotta, 1986: 39)

In other cases, each partner contributes a different kind of value-added activity. For example, in 1990, AT&T and Mitsubishi signed an agreement covering technology sharing, worldwide marketing and manufacturing of static random access memory (SRAM) chips. The agreement gives the right to AT&T to manufacture and market SRAM chips designed by its Japanese partner, including current and future generations of products. In April 1991, Toshiba and GE announced a wide-ranging alliance for the joint development and marketing of home appliances, and the establishment of two joint ventures. One of Toshiba's stated objectives was to minimize the adverse affects of any trade restrictions which might result from a possible surge in US protectionism and anti-Japanese sentiments.

Some R&D agreements, which are initially concentrated on the sharing of technological assets and capabilities, have been progressively extended to the manufacturing and/or marketing stages of production. In 1990, for example, British Aerospace (UK) and Aerospatiale (France) agreed to undertake a five year feasibility study on a supersonic commercial airplane to replace the Concorde. The decision on whether to launch a $10 billion production program is to be made in 1995 on the basis of the results of the study. An investigation concerning the strategies of 750 US electronics firms, undertaken in

1990, pointed to a probable increase in the manufacturing and technology agreements in the years up to 1995, while marketing alliances were expected to decline. Some details are set out in Table 8.4.

R&D agreements have also been formed as part of governmental collaborative programs. For example, more than 300 companies are involved in the ESPRIT program launched in 1984 by the European Commission. Around 1,600 firms (99 per cent of which are European) participate in some 300 EUREKA projects. Previously closed to foreign subsidiaries, national and intergovernmental collaborative programs are becoming increasingly open to them. For example, AT&T and IBM participate in some EC programs through their affiliates established in Europe. In Japan, foreign owned companies have been invited to participate in a $195 million governmental project to develop jet engines for supersonic passenger aircraft.

Small- and medium-sized companies are also involved in several collaborative programs. For example, firms employing up to 500 people participated in 49 per cent of the first round of the BRITE program and in 60 per cent of the second round. Nevertheless, it is estimated that EC programs represent only 4 per cent of the private and public R&D investments in Europe (Kuentz, 1990).

The dynamics of networks

Firms are often involved both in private and in public cooperative ventures within complex networks, which, like consortia, may have the potential to affect entire industries.

Table 8.4 Major types of agreements formed by 750 US electronics firms in 1990 and expected for 1990–1995 (percentage of total respondent)

Types of agreements	1990 (A)	1990–1995 (B)	% expected change
Marketing agreements	67	61	−9
Providing technology licensing	45	54	+20
Research contracts	38	43	+13
Receiving technology licensing	36	43	+19
Receiving equity	34	42	+24
Manufacturing agreements	33	44	+33
Providing equity	14	28	+100

Source: *Electronic Business*, 1990.

In these networks, R&D links involve far reaching relations based on the co-existence of cooperative and competitive interests. Such linkages have to be studied within the general context of interfirm networks, which are both stable and changing; and where the business transactions among firms generally take place within the framework of established relationships (Johanson and Mattson, 1987). While these networks portray the interaction of the participants, they also identify the situations within which the interactions take place. Thus, their study normally embraces the social environment as well as the intra- and interorganizational interactions (Porter and Fuller, 1986).

Alliance networks seem to be a powerful tool to study the motivation, structure, mechanisms and effects of interfirm agreements. According to Cook and Emerson (1978), a network may be defined as a 'set of two or more connected exchange relations'. Interfirm networks are articulated by a time-structure, a power-structure, an interest-structure and a capacity-structure. The capacity-structure determines the synergistic surplus which results from the alliances' connections inside the network (Kamman and Strijker, 1989). As shown in games theory, the individual cooperative payoff depends on several factors, including the 'status quo' position (which means the player's 'payoff' when he doesn't cooperate). In fact, the resources controlled by the participating firms are generally the basis for acting and interaction in a network (Axelsson, 1987).

Industrial markets are, in fact, complex systems of formal and informal relationships between economic, political and social agents. Alliance networks represent a particular pattern of interorganization transactions. As observed by Engwall and Johanson (1989), every relationship formed between firms within a network offers a potential conflict over the distribution of economic rent, and the course of the future development of the network. At the same time, there are powerful forces making for collaborative commitment and mutual forbearance.

Several kinds of industrial networks may be identified. These include intrafirm networks, non-cooperative interfirm networks and cooperative interfirm networks. The relative importance of each kind of network depends on the country-, industry- and firm-specific circumstances. For example, more than half of Corning Glass's profits are from its 23 joint ventures. In 1988, 60 per cent of Aerospatiale's sales came from cooperative ventures in which it was involved. According to a survey undertaken in the mid-1980s, Japanese firms obtain 5 per cent of their supplies through non-cooperative transactions, 40 per cent from their internal networks, and about 55 per cent from cooperative networks. By contrast, only 6 per cent of supplies of US firms come from alliance networks in the United States (Hull, Slowinski, Wharton and Azumi, 1988).

In many industrial sectors (aeronautic, telecommunications, computers, semi-conductors, etc.), it is possible to identify hierarchical or heterarchical galaxies, with a pivotal group of firms being surrounded by satellite partners. For example, as illustrated in Figure

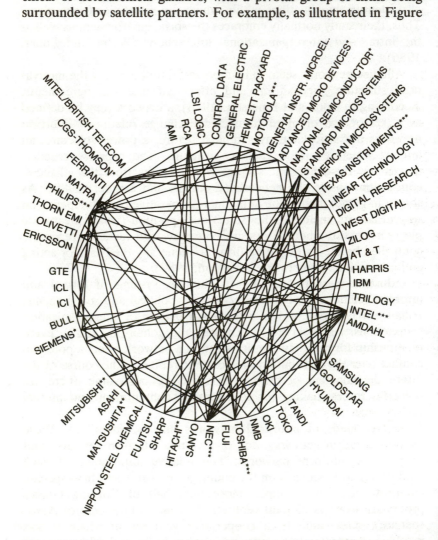

Figure 8.2 Alliance networks in the semi-conductor industry 1990.
Source: Gugler, 1991.

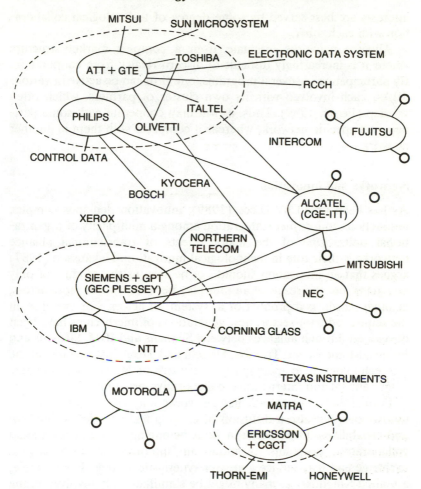

Figure 8.3 Interfirm clusters and networks in the telecommunication industry.
Source: Gugler, 1991.

8.2, the major world producers of semi-conductors have a focal position in a complex web of alliances. At the same time, new coalitions may induce new market structures. Figure 8.3 shows that, at the end of the 1980s, the market for international telecommunications equipment is dominated by a limited number of closely linked interfirm clusters. These companies are joined around systemic technological clusters and/or technological trajectories. The result is an emerging web of international oligopolists who perceive that their individual interests are best served by some degree of technological collaboration with each other.

Alliance networks originate from a complex market structure where it is increasingly difficult to discern rivalry from cooperation. By participating in several programs, one firm can be active in various SBAs, each involved with its own cluster of partners, which often overlap (Ferné, 1989). Thus, a firm may cooperate with some partners in a specific network, whereas it competes with them in another network.

Networks and innovation

As has been noted by Teece (1989), innovation demands complex interactions and *de facto* integration among a multiplicity of organizational units. One of the major effects of transnational alliance networks is their role in technological innovation. Hakansson (1987) argues that an innovation should not be seen as the product of only one actor, but the result of an interplay between two or more actors, in other words as a product of a 'system' of actors. For example, in the semi-conductor sector, new generations of micro-chips have been developed through alliances between Siemens and IBM, Siemens and Philips, Motorola and Toshiba, Hitachi and Texas Instruments. In the bio-technology field, perhaps the majority of innovations originate from national and international collaborative programs.

Formal and informal alliance networks may create not only new innovations, but also a diffusion of existing technologies, know-how and capabilities. Links between firms belonging to different national collaborative programs promote an internetwork technological exchange and may induce a greater synergistic surplus. For example, a United Kingdom company might be simultaneously involved in the national Alvey Program, the European EUREKA, ESPRIT or RACE Programs and the US SDI Program (e.g. IBM [Sematech] cooperates with Siemens [ESPRIT, RACE, JESSI, Megaproject]; Philips [ESPRIT, RACE, EUREKA, Megaproject] with Toshiba [VLSI, ICOT] with Texas Instrument [Sematech]; [VLSI, ICOT] with Texas Instrument [Sematech]; etc.).

Nevertheless, interfirm agreements do not always induce new innovations or major technological transfers. In fact, there are some risks of this type of collaboration, the purpose of which is to delay or frustrate new innovations or to slow down the rate of technology diffusion (Hawk, 1988). Furthermore, technology transfers among partners may be limited because the firms do not wish to reveal too much of their cutting edge technologies to potential competitors. For example, in the aeronautics sector, in several cooperative agreements, transfers of technology are minimized by assigning the development of different modules to different participants (Mowery, 1989). As a result, it took several years to negotiate how technology would be transferred between General Dynamics (US) and Mitsubishi on the FSX fighter plane, in order to minimize technology transfer from the US to Japan. In Japan, companies taking part in national R&D programs have been known to keep information about their own technologies in sealed envelopes, to be opened only in case of disagreement over the allocation of the results (Ferné, 1989).

In some cases, alliance clauses prevent technological diffusion from the partners to other firms. We have already cited the case of Siemens and IBM, who are cooperating in the development of a new generation of chips, who have signed a clause which prohibits either company from cooperating with any Japanese firm in memory chip development. Thus, competition among interfirm networks may preserve innovative competition and prevent collusive restraint of technological innovation and diffusion. Nevertheless, networks' potential anti-competitive effects may be significant and need to be closely monitored by the authorities.

SOME REFLECTIONS ON THE EFFICIENCY OF R&D ALLIANCES

Clearly, technological alliances have implications for the competitiveness of both firms and nations. Unfortunately, it is difficult to measure the impact of alliances, in terms, for example, of additional output or profits generated by joint R&D activities. What is the share of R&D jointly realized, as compared with all R&D activities? What is the importance of cross-border technological alliances in the globalization of technological activities? What is the role of technical cooperation in new innovations? To what extent can one attribute any success of the commercialization of a particular innovation to its particular organizational structure? What is the contribution of each partner to the assets and competences exchanged and/or shared? What share in the local innovation realized through strategic alliances do foreign firms have? Where exactly are some R&D joint activities accomplished?

According to the data available, it is difficult to answer these questions. Nevertheless, as we have already mentioned, it is possible to glean some hints from specific cases. For example, new generations of semi-conductors have been developed through alliances among the major world producers. The European HDTV standards may compete with the Japanese standard, thanks to collaborative ventures, particularly in the EUREKA framework. Without the Airbus Industries, which involve technical as well as production and marketing cooperation, it would have been difficult for the countries involved to maintain a nationally based commercial aircraft industry.

Some years ago, Hawkins (1982) observed that technological cooperation may be both positive or negative for global industrial productivity, and be both good and bad from a national viewpoint. He went on to suggest that much will depend on the conditions of the individual case, and on the perspective taken as the reference against which goodness or badness is judged.

The rising popularity of SBAs has not occurred without a measure of skepticism. Some scholars refer to the disappointing history of cooperative ventures in the past, and point out the organizational problems which have arisen because of the incompatibility of goals and differing 'corporate cultures' of the partners (Drucker, 1989). Furthermore, some consortia, particularly in the US (e.g. Sematech, Semi-conductor Research Corp. [SRC] and Micro-electronics and Computer Technology Corp. [MCC]) have been a major disappointment to their supporters. Some R&D consortia among competitors seem to have failed because of a lack of confidence among partners. In the US, opponents of government involvement assert that Federal programs, far from encouraging innovation, may have stifled entrepreneurial efforts. In Europe some critics argue that the EC programs are spread among too many projects and/or too many firms to be efficient.

In the past, *The Economist* has been particularly scathing about government support for commercial R&D consortia. In an article published on February 3, 1990, it argued that such consortia would

> neither improve education nor reduce the interest-rate-boosting federal budget deficit. Instead of encouraging the heartening trends in R&D, consortia refill the troughs of big-company lobbyists.

> (*The Economist*, 1990: 66)

Yet, there is evidence to suggest that cooperative projects seem to have succeeded. One example is the VLST program in Japan which has played an important role in helping Japanese companies to overtake US competitors in semi-conductor memory technology and production. Another is the EUREKA project for the development of an international standard or HDTV, which may well help European producers to head off the threat of Japanese domination. In some cases, government projects may also stimulate R&D; according to the EC Commission, thanks partly to collaborative programs, the European information technology industry doubled in the past four years.

Furthermore, it seems that the major criticisms of national consortia concern more the political management and organization than the concept of R&D collaboration. The possible pitfalls of some governments' projects could also be attributed to the firms themselves. Some companies, for example, choose to collaborate only on the technologies that are not essential to the competitiveness of the goods they produce. Sometimes, firms participate in projects only to keep an eye on competitors. Therefore, the cooperative goals are insufficiently determined, and the partners fail to achieve a successful commercialization of the technologies jointly developed, e.g. Porter, 1990.

Some business analysts have stressed the potential anti-competitive effects of cooperative agreements, and advise governments to restrict some kind of alliances, such as horizontal agreements. To others, strategic alliances fill a real need to share costs that are beyond the scope of many firms. In the words of Davidson

> anti-trust policies that were appropriate in a domestic economy with few linkages to the international system can be self-destructive in an internationally competitive environment.
>
> (Davidson, 1988: 20)

Confronting this debate, governments adopt 'reason rules' in their anti-trust regulations. Cooperative agreements are generally tolerated whenever it can be shown that they offer enough economic benefit to compensate for any possible anti-competitive effects. In fact, as we have seen, R&D alliances are less concerned with anti-trust considerations than production and/or commercialization agreements, simply because they are less likely to give rise to monopolistic behavior among the participants. Viewed from a national perspective, R&D collaboration may also induce higher productivity, avoid a duplication of research investment, reduce structural overcapacity, and improve the competitiveness of indigenous MNEs.

The socially beneficial effects of R&D strategic alliances obviously depend upon the industry-, market- and firm-specific characteristics. For example, as noted by Jacquemin (1988), R&D alliances are most likely to have positive effects in markets where a high rate of R&D

sharing or between-member spill-over is feasible. Jacquemin's analysis is based on the kind of technological market failures which might occur in the absence of complete appropriation of returns.

Technological alliances seem to involve higher positive effects in the basic research field. In fact, it is usually hard to make profit from basic research. For example, it is reported that neither AT&T's introduction of the transistor nor IBM's Nobel prize-winning discovery of higher-temperature super-conductors seems to have revitalized their competitive positions (*The Economist*, 1990). Thus, private and public collaborative projects in basic research may promote innovations which otherwise wouldn't have been developed. For example, AT&T has joined with its rival IBM to support a long-term research project into super-conductivity, at the Massachusetts Institute of Technology.

But, there are circumstances in which R&D agreements do involve high economic or strategic social costs. Where, for example, collusive behavior stifles future innovation, restricts the diffusion or dissemination of technology, or creates additional barriers to the entry of competitors, it might reduce the social product. It may also result in a strategically unacceptable technology drain from the home country. In the information technology sector, for example, thanks to licenses conceded by Sun, Hewlett-Packard and MIPS to Japanese partners, Fujitsu, NEC, Sony, Toshiba and Hitachi are now able to build RISC-based work-stations (*Business Week*, 1989). It is not surprising then that some economists and business analysts oppose such alliances. In the Boeing–Japanese joint venture, for example, it has been argued that Boeing will lose its technological competitive advantage and help the Japanese firms to acquire the know-how to develop and produce airplanes. In the US, the FSX Fighter case (already mentioned earlier in this chapter) also underlines the risk of a technological drain. The source of the debate was the project of the coproduction with Japan (Mitsubishi as the prime contractor) of a new tactical fighter plane, based on the American F-16 produced by General Dynamics. Critics of this coalition feared it would lead to an erosion of American technology and add to the ability of Japan to launch a civilian aerospace program that would directly compete with the American firms (Inman and Burton, 1990).

The probable impact of technological strategic alliances on the competitiveness of both firms and countries is, indeed, difficult to predict. However, it may safely be concluded that such alliances play an important role in both the ownership and location of innovatory activities. The potential impact of R&D joint activities may be appreciated from a private and a public point of view. It constitutes a new factor in the bargaining game between firms and governments, particularly when the private interests related to SBAs oppose the social, economic and political goals of governments.

CONCLUSIONS

Within a web of strategic alliances, companies perceive that they gain valuable technological synergism and risk-reducing benefits.

This chapter has attempted to provide a broad overview of the major developments related to strategic alliances, particularly in the R&D fields. It has also tried to indicate the probable impact of technological cooperative agreements from a private and a social viewpoint. Obviously, such an overview cannot be conclusive or comprehensive, if for no other reason than that the reality it tries to analyze is complex, dynamic and not depicted enough with a statistical basis. Despite this caveat, we believe our analysis has demonstrated four main things:

1. that international inflows and outflows of technologies organized through SBAs vary between sectors, countries and firms;
2. that SBAs have to be understood not only as a substitute for FDI, but also as a complementary organizational form, necessary to create, maintain and enhance the technological and O specific advantages of the firms and the specific advantages of countries;
3. R&D cooperative ventures are part of complex intra- and inter-organizational networks in which technologies are created, exchanged and improved upon on an international basis; and
4. that strategic alliances have to be integrated in the major economic theories and to be analyzed both within the framework of the internationalization of firms' activities, and of the intra-/interfirm exchanges as well as intra-/interindustrial exchanges.

9 The prospects for foreign direct investment in Central and Eastern Europe[1]

INTRODUCTION

Much has already been said, written and speculated about the subject of foreign direct investment (FDI) in Central and Eastern Europe.[2] Almost daily, we read about a new joint equity venture being set up in Eastern Germany, Russia, Poland or Hungary; or of a strategic alliance being concluded between a Central European and Western or Japanese firm; and, scarcely less frequently, about the efforts of one or other of the East European governments to revamp its foreign investment rules and regulations, or to offer new tax concessions to make its country more attractive to foreign investors.

SOME FACTS AND FIGURES

Yet substantive and reliable data on the full extent of the participation by foreign firms in East European countries, or even the flows of investment into these countries, is hard to come by. Moreover, what data we do have are rarely comparable across countries or industrial sectors. This, in a way, should come as no surprise, as for so long, because of the absence of any proper financial or accounting procedures in Central and Eastern Europe, most domestically produced economic statistics are of dubious value.

Perhaps the best, and certainly the most publicized, data we have concern the number of joint ventures involving foreign (by which we mean non-East European) registered firms. As shown in Table 9.1, these reveal a rapid growth of the *intentions* of foreign firms to invest in Eastern Europe. At the beginning of 1988, 165 ventures involving foreign partners had been established. A year later, this figure had risen to 562, by March 1990 to 3,595, by December 1990 to 14,640 and by July 1991 to 25,845. More particularly, in the first half of

Table 9.1 Joint ventures registered in Central and Eastern Europe 1988–1991

	Investment stake July 1, 1991 (estimated billion)	Population mid-1989 (million)	Jan. 1 1988	Jan. 1 1989	Jan. 1 1990	Jan. 1 1991	July 1 1991
Soviet Union	$3.2	288.0	23	191	1275	2905	3700
Hungary	$1.1	10.6	102	270	1000	5695	9100
Poland	$0.4	37.9	13	55	918	2800	4350
Czechoslovakia	$0.4	15.6	7	16	60	1600	3700
Bulgaria	n/a	9.0	15	25	30	140	800
Romania	$0.2	23.2	5	5	5	1500	4195
Total	$4–5	384.3	165	562	3288	14640	25845

Source: ECE Data Bank on East–West Joint Ventures.

1991, there was a dramatic increase in new joint ventures registered in Romania and Belgium.

However, as yet, only a small percentage – probably about 10 per cent – of these ventures, are currently operational. The great majority of registered ventures – particularly in high technology sectors in the former USSR – have come to naught. We do, however, know that, as of mid-1991, the highest proportion of joint venture start ups had occurred in Poland and Hungary and in the service rather than the manufacturing sector.[3]

The table also shows that the rate of growth of joint ventures is currently concentrated in three countries, viz. the former Soviet Union, Hungary and Poland. In the Soviet Union, where the growth potential of a large market is the main attraction, the estimated foreign capital invested in July 1991 was $3.2 billion – an amount about the same as the stock of inward investment in Sweden, Nigeria or Singapore. In Hungary, which is, perhaps, furthest along the road towards a market economy, it was $1.1 billion, about the same as the FDI stock in Pakistan, Uruguay or Cameroon; whereas, in Poland, where in spite of a larger population and longer experience with joint venture capital,[4] the less stable political and social regime has limited inward direct investment to around $340 million.

Who are the major foreign players in Eastern Europe? According to the ECE data bank on East–West Joint Ventures, of the 1721 joint ventures reported as having been established in Czechoslovakia, Hungary and Poland in the early 1990s,[5] 533, or 31.1 per cent, involved Western German partners, 308, or 17.8 per cent, other EC partners, 304, or 17.7 per cent, Austrian partners, and 98, or 5.7 per cent, US partners. As Table 9.2 shows, the distribution of foreign investors in the former USSR is rather more dispersed, although, in October 1990, Western European firms still accounted for 60.8 per cent of the 1884 joint ventures which had then been registered, and US or Canadian firms for 14.0 per cent.

There is some evidence to suggest that physical distance and cultural affinities are important determinants in the choice of foreign partners. Thus Austrian firms are the leading investors (by number of joint ventures) in Hungary, while Swiss firms are unusually active in Czechoslovakia, and US and Finnish foreign investors in the former USSR. There is also some intra-Central and East European FDI. For example, in 1990, the erstwhile CMEA countries accounted for 9.8 per cent of the registered foreign investment projects in Czechoslovakia and 7.7 per cent of those in the former USSR. There has also been a considerable upsurge of interest shown by developing country

Table 9.2 Registered or operational foreign investment projects in selected countries in Central and Eastern Europe by origin of foreign partner

	Czechoslovakia* (Mar. 1991)	Hungary* (Jan. 1990)	Poland† (Jan. 1990)	USSR† (Oct. 1990)
Western Europe	88.6	77.8	81.2	60.8
(of which EC)	(39.5)	(34.5)	(60.3)	(34.2)
North America	1.8	7.0	8.4	13.4
(of which US)	(1.8)	(6.5)	(6.1)	(11.4)
Japan	0.0	0.3	0.1	1.8
CMEA Economies	5.2	NSA	1.5	7.7
Developing countries	1.3	1.5	2.0	9.9
Unclassified or multiparty	3.1	13.4	6.8	6.4
Totals	100.0	100.0	100.0	100.0
Total number of projects	228	582	911	1884

*Registered.
†Operational.
Source: ECE Data Bank on East–West Joint Ventures.

investors in the larger East European countries. By October 1990, there were 116 joint ventures, involving developing country partners, registered in the former USSR, of which 28 were Indian and 24 Chinese.

Finally, according to Ozawa (1992), as of the end of 1990, Japanese firms had concluded only 48 joint ventures with Central or Eastern European firms, 33 of which were within the former Soviet Union.[6]

Which sectors tend to attract the most inward investment? An analysis of the sectoral distribution on the investment intentions by foreign firms, set out in Table 9.3, reveals some noticeable differences. Within manufacturing industry, which is currently attracting the most interest of Western capitalists in the former Soviet Union and Poland, the former country seems to offer the best prospects in most branches of the mechanical engineering sector (and especially in office equipment and computers), whereas in Poland, the favoured sectors include food processing, clothing and wood products. In Hungary, business services, trade and transport undertakings account for 33 per cent of all approved applications by inward direct investment. In the former Soviet Union, fast food chains and construction and business services (including computer related activities) attract the largest share of operational investments. In Poland, construction, trade and hotels, and in Czechoslovakia, trade and business activities stand out as the service sectors with the largest number of joint ventures. Although some Central and East European countries have extensive mining and other natural resources, apart from some oil and agri-chemicals investments in the former USSR, there has been very little foreign participation in these sectors.

Of the more noteworthy individual investments (or investment intentions) by MNEs in Central and Eastern Europe, mention might be made of several investments by MNEs, e.g. Siemens (Germany), Alcatel (France), ABB (Sweden/Switzerland) and General Electric (USA), in the telecommunications and energy sectors; a $3 billion capital stake by Volkswagen in the Skoda car plant in Czechoslovakia; a $1.5 billion investment by the same company in a new production facility in East Germany to produce the Golf and Polo range of cars; a $200 million investment by General Motors in a railway carriage and machine factory in Hungary; a $150 million participation by General Electric in Tungsram, East Europe's leading light bulb manufacturer; Suzuki and Itoh's 40 per cent stake in a $10 billion venture to manufacture cars in Hungary; Gillette's joint venture in the former Soviet Union to produce razor blades; ASEA Brown

Table 9.3 Sectoral registered or operational distribution of joint ventures in selected Central and Eastern Europe involving foreign parties

	Czechoslovakia*	Hungary*	Poland†	USSR†
Primary activities	3.9	1.5	4.3	2.0
Agriculture, forestry and fishing	3.5	1.5	4.0	1.8
Other	0.4	—	0.3	0.2
Secondary activities	32.0	46.0	74.6	49.6
Technology intensive[1]	15.7	19.3	19.0	23.0
Other	16.3	26.7	55.6	26.6
Tertiary activities	64.1	52.5	21.1	48.4
Trade	19.7	15.8	3.2	3.3
Hotels and restaurants	2.1	0.9	3.2	6.8
Business related activities	19.7	20.6	5.2	21.5
Infrastructure[2]	14.4	13.2	7.6	11.6
Other	8.2	2.0	1.9	5.4
Totals	100.0	100.0	100.0	100.0
Total number of projects	228	582	911	1884

* Registered.
† Operational.
[1] Defined as chemicals, engineering and precision instruments, motor vehicles and rubber and plastics.
[2] Transport and communications includes construction, education, health, social work and sewerage disposal.
Source: ECE Data Bank on East–West Joint Ventures.

Boveri's acquisition of a majority stake in a leading Polish turbine and generating producer; and MacDonald's multimillion dollar stake in a chain of fast food restaurants in the former Soviet Union, East Germany and Hungary. Many leading Western accounting and management consultancy MNEs have also set up offices in the former Soviet Union, Hungary and Poland.[7] In addition, there are several instances of MNEs – especially from Japan and the US – forging alliances with Austrian or German firms from the Western *Länder*, to penetrate Central and Eastern markets.[8]

Most foreign owned joint ventures are set up either to serve the domestic market of the host country or to serve foreign (and mostly other European) countries with goods and services which require resources and capabilities in which that country is comparatively well endowed (or is expected to be endowed). It is the prospect of Hungary, Poland and Czechoslovakia – not to mention the Eastern lander of Germany – syphoning away manufacturing activity which might otherwise have been created in their territories that is causing some Southern European and Far Eastern countries some concern. There have been several well published cases of both Japanese and Western manufacturers switching the location of their new investments from the Iberian peninsula and Greece to Central and Eastern Europe[9] in order to take advantage of lower wage and transport costs,[10] and, in some sectors, a well trained and skilled labor force.

As might be expected, the relative importance of foreign owned enterprises in most Central and East European economies is still extremely small. In Poland, it is estimated that in 1989 they accounted for only 1.9 per cent of all enterprises, 3.1 per cent of exports and 1.6 per cent of all employment. In other East European countries it was considerably less, although Hungarian statistics suggest that in some manufacturing sectors foreign joint ventures now account for 25 per cent or more of the country's exports. However, when one recalls that, prior to 1987, the joint venture was not permissible at all in the then Soviet Union, the opening up of the economy to both international trade and investment has been quite remarkable.

THE PROSPECTS FOR MORE MNE ACTIVITY

So much for a thumbnail sketch of the present state of foreign direct investment in Central and Eastern Europe. What now of the prospects for the future?

Most commentators agree that, taking a long-run perspective, the economies of Central and Eastern Europe offer a tremendous challenge and opportunity to foreign direct investors. Yet, at the end of 1990, the countries comprising this area which had a combined population of over 400 million received about the same amount of investment as did Ireland and Norway, each of which had a population of less than 5 million. Even industrial market oriented countries, with the same average income per head as the most prosperous of the East European economies, attracted 40 times more investment per head of population.

Assuming just a doubling of living standards and a completion of the major privatization schemes planned by the major East European economies by the year 2000,[11] it would not be unreasonable to expect foreign and intra-Eastern European investment to rise from its 1990 figure of $2–3 billion to around $100 billion – or about two-fifths of its current level in Western Europe.

These, however, are just orders of magnitude of what *could* be achieved. The human capabilities and natural resources of most Central and East European countries are impressive. What is lacking is the right institutional structure, managerial expertise, access to foreign markets, entrepreneurial and work culture, organizational capabilities and monetary incentives to efficiently utilize and upgrade these resources and capabilities.

While foreign MNEs are uniquely able to supply many of the necessary ingredients for economic growth, a reshaping of attitudes to work and wealth creation, the redesigning of the way economic activity is organized and the supporting legal framework, especially with respect to property rights and contracts, the costs of establishing and running a market system, and the introduction of macro-economic policies which encourage domestic savings, but accept the discipline of currency convertibility and an open trading system, are too substantial for individual companies – and, sometimes, for individual countries – to bear. These are the *real* costs of restructuring the economies of Central and Eastern Europe; and, at least some progress on this front must be made, *and be seen to be made*, prior to any substantial commitment of direct investment funds by foreign MNEs.

ALTERNATIVE MODELS OF DEVELOPMENT

What, then, is the most likely course or path of development in East Europe?

Let us consider three possible models or scenarios – accepting that the pattern and pace of restructuring is likely to vary, for example, between Hungary and Albania, or between Czechoslovakia and Bulgaria or between Romania and Poland. The first is the *developing country* model. This hypothesises that, curently, the economies of the erstwhile Communist countries may be likened to those of the industrializing developing countries, and that just as these, notably Brazil, Mexico, Korea, Thailand, Taiwan and Singapore, have moved along a particular development path or trajectory – from attracting little to attracting substantial inflows of foreign capital – so, as they develop, Central and East European countries will do the same. The model also seems appropriate insofar as the new regimes are in a similar position to many in the Third World in that the organizational and institutional capacity for capitalist development are currently inadequate and frequently distorted (Radice, 1991).

While at first sight this seems an attractive scenario, the assumptions on which it is based are questionable. World Bank statistics suggest that, in the mid-1980s, the population of most East European economies (Albania is the main exception) were considerably better educated, medically cared for, and housed, than even the most prosperous developing countries (Singapore and Hong Kong are exceptions). They also consumed more energy, and their R&D expenditure as a percentage of gross national product even approaches that of some Western economies.[12] On the other hand, the industrial performance of these countries, and their commercial, transportation and communications infrastructure were generally no better than that of many middle income developing countries, and considerably inferior to that of the fastest growing newly industrialized countries; and, the proportion of the gross national product absorbed by central Government was two to three times that of the developing countries of the same income levels. Table 9.4 sets out some details of health and educational standards of a group of eight central and East European countries, including Yugoslavia.

The second model is to compare the present situation of East European economies with that of West Germany and Japan after the last World War. Let us call this the reconstruction model. This model has intuitive appeal in that it might be supposed that the resource potential of the larger East European countries is comparable to that of the two most war-devastated countries, but that to exploit these resources requires a fund of technological, organizational and management capabilities no less than that demanded by Japan and Germany in 1945. At the same time, this model fails to take account of the enormous institutional impedimenta and the extent of the

Table 9.4 Education and health facilities in East European countries in the mid- or late 1980s

	GNP Per capita (1989) $	EDUCATION Primary	Secondary (% of population in appropriate age group)	Tertiary	HEALTH Population per physician	Daily calorie supply	Infant mortality (per 1000 of births)	Life expectancy
East European countries								
USSR	na	106	na	na	270	3399	25	67
Hungary	2590	97	70	15	310	3569	16	70
Poland	1790	101	80	18	490	3336	16	72
Romania	na	97	80	10	570	3373	24	70
Czechoslovakia	3450	96	na	na	280	3448	13	67
Bulgaria	2325	103	na	na	280	3642	14	72
Albania	na	100	na	na	na	2713	24	72
Yugoslavia	2920	95	80	19	550	3289	25	72
Developing countries								
Upper- to middle-income countries	3150	101	54	20	1220	3117	42	68
Middle-income countries	2040	101	67	17	2190	2846	52	66

na = not available.
Source: World Bank, 1991.

political and attitudinal and cultural changes required by most Central and Eastern European nations *before* private enterprise (which, after all, was stifled for only a decade or so in both Japan and Germany) is prepared to undertake the entrepreneurship, investment – including investment in R&D and manpower training – for economic restructuring and growth.

The third model is one which combines the more appropriate ingredients of the *developing country* and *reconstruction model* but also takes account of the macro- and micro-organizational and attitudinal changes necessary for economic progress. This might be called the *systemic model* – the word 'systemic' being chosen because it suggests that the willingness and ability of foreign (or, for that matter, domestic) investors rests mainly on the speed and extent to which East European economies can reorganize both their economic and legal systems, and the ethos of their people towards entrepreneurship and wealth creating activities.

The three scenarios predict a different role for FDI. For example, depending on whether Central and East European governments adopt a German or Japanese strategy towards inward investment – and we think the former is much more likely – the *reconstruction* model points to the most speedy and widespread involvement of foreign owned firms. The likely contribution of inward direct investment in the *developing country* model will depend on the momentum and pattern of economic development, how this integrates into the world economy, and the kind of foreign participation it is likely to induce. Like the first scenario, the extent of foreign investment predicted by the *systemic* model depends on the nature of the systemic changes required and the rate and efficiency with which they are introduced; but the model does suggest a much slower initial participation of foreign firms due to the substantial establishment and learning costs they might have to incur in setting up production units and in marketing their products.

Because of the current differences in the economic development, political systems and institutional frameworks of the individual Central and East European countries, it is likely that each country will follow a somewhat different path of integrating itself into the world economy. The Eastern *Länder* of Germany are, in fact, already following the course of the reconstruction model, with Hungary and Czechoslovakia two or three steps behind. By contrast, Albania, Romania and Bulgaria are more likely to fit into the developing country model. But much will depend on the speed and extent to which each country proceeds with its privatization process; the extent to which governments are able to rid themselves of their centralized and bureaucratic control, and instead become more mission oriented and supportive of an emerging private sector to help produce the wealth required in the most cost effective manner;[13] and how far it is able to stimulate both the entrepreneurial ethos of its people, and the upgrading of the expectations of industrial and domestic consumers for better produced and superior quality products.

In any event, the role of FDI is likely to fluctuate according both to the form and stage of economic development. This idea has been explored by the author in other publications (Dunning, 1988, 1993), and was taken up briefly in Chapter 3.[14] In two recently published papers, Teretumo Ozawa (1991b, 1992) has suggested that, in her economic development, Japan passed through four stages of industrial restructuring. The first was in the 1950s and was marked by the production and exports of labor intensive, and fairly low skill products. As Japanese wage rates rose, and her human and technological capacity became more sophisticated, her comparative advantage shifted into scale intensive, non-differentiated products, e.g. heavy chemicals, steel, ship building, etc. The third phase, which lasted from the mid-1960s to the early 1980s, was that in which Japan made considerable inroads into the international markets for mass production durable goods, e.g. motor vehicles and consumer electronics. The fourth stage, in which the Japanese economy is now entering, is that in which production and exports are highly innovatory and skill intensive or, as Ozawa puts it, are Schumpeterian type products. Depending on the policies of host governments, inward FDI may play an important role in fashioning each of these development phases; but outward direct investment is not likely to materialize to any major extent until Stages 3 and 4 are reached.

The application of the Japanese model to the development and restructuring of the Eastern European economies and the role which MNEs might play in the process, will depend very much on location specific assets which the individual countries can accumulate, and the policies pursued by their governments to advance their 'diamond of competitive advantages'.

As to the existing technological assets, some hints may be gained from an examination of the kind of patents, registered by the world's leading enterprises, in the US, which they attribute to their innovatory activities in Eastern Europe. In an exercise conducted over the period 1969 to 1986, John Cantwell (1990) identified the industrial sectors in which the Warsaw pact countries recorded an above average share of registered patents. The chemical (excluding pharmaceutical) and mechanical engineering sectors both stood out, with both high research intensive and labour intensive sectors recording well below the average share of patents. Of the foreign firms which carried out the most technological activity in Eastern Europe, those of West European – and especially of German – origin scored the highest, those of US and Japanese origin were well behind in second and third places.

THE ROLE OF MNEs

What then of the likely role of MNEs in this restructuring process? In the mid-1980s, the authors of some 12 country profiles concluded that inbound and outbound MNE activity had a generally beneficial affect on trade, productivity and economic restructuring (Dunning, 1985). It may, then, be reasonably expected that the opening of Central and Eastern Europe to market forces will, by encouraging inward direct investment, markedly improve the economic lot of its citizens. If the experience of most countries in Western Europe and the more market oriented developing countries is anything to go by, then foreign technology, management expertise and the access to foreign markets can, providing the conditions are right, play a critical role in Central and Eastern European economic development.[15]

At the same time, we would contend that such a role is likely to be different to that experienced by Western European countries in the past, or developing countries today in at least three ways. First, the form of foreign participation is likely to be more pluralistic. It may well be that, as in Western Europe, the 100 per cent owned affiliate firms will eventually become the dominant form of participation by foreign firms. But, we would also expect a multitude of collaborative agreements, subcontracting and networking arrangements, crossing many different lines of economic activity, both along and between value chains, to be concluded. An example of such pluralism is shown in the car industry where Volkswagen and Fiat are both substantially involved in a number of Central and East European economies but in very different ways.

Second, we would anticipate that at least the larger MNEs will respond to the challenges and opportunities of Eastern Europe in terms of its likely impact on their *global* marketing and production strategies. This is what is already largely happening in Western Europe and, to some extent, in the US and Canada as well. If current trends are anything to go by, Western and Japanese MNEs are unlikely to treat their East European affiliates as stand alone ventures, but will view them as part and parcel of a Pan-European or even an international network of activities. This would suggest that, from the start, the managerial strategies and organizational systems of European joint ventures, will, insofar as they are endorsed by the local partners, be locked into those currently pursued by the foreign firms. Western European firms, in particular, look forward to new and enlarged markets for their products, over which they may spread the escalating costs of R&D and marketing, and, by so doing, enable them to compete more effectively with Japanese and US MNEs. In some sectors, in which there is currently surplus production capacity in the Western world, both US and European firms are hoping that increased demand opportunities, especially in the former Soviet Union, Poland and East Germany, will help absorb some of this slack.

Third, there is every suggestion that, to some extent at least, the international community, and especially the EC, has an enormous stake in the success of the political and economic restructuring of the erstwhile Communist bloc countries. By such means as direct grants, aid or loans; by the encouragement of private direct investment, e.g. by tax incentives and investment insurance schemes; by the provision of information about production and marketing conditions, laws and regulations in different East European countries; by action taken to improve economic transparency and promote a better understanding by Western investors of the business environment in Eastern Europe (e.g. the PHARE programme); by assisting the education and training of East European technicians, scientists, accountants, and the like; by the encouragement of industrial cooperation agreements between EC and East European firms; by technical advice on the appropriate macro-economic and structural adjustment policies for East European governments to pursue, individual Western governments, the European Commission, the EBRD[16] and various international agencies such as the World Bank are likely to exert even more critical influence on the shape of an enlarged Europe in the 1990s, than did (US) Marshall aid and similar schemes play in the design of Western Europe in the 1950s.[17]

Certainly there is no shortage of ideas for the kind of multilateral aid programme which might be given to Central and East European countries. One particularly interesting suggestion, called the Strasbourg Plan for Central and Eastern Europe, was put forward in 1991 by Michael Palmer, former Director General of the European Parliament (Palmer, 1991). Palmer argued that an aid package of around $16.7 billion a year is needed from the advanced industrial nations if economic restructuring in the seven Central and East European countries (including the former GDR) is to be completed in the next two decades or so. This equates with between 0.1 per cent and 0.5 per cent of the GDPs of the leading Triad countries in 1990.

However, as a *quid pro quo* for such financial aid, it is proposed that each of the recipient governments should work out an overall plan for economic growth, and within the plan, a shopping list of priorities. The governments should then launch a joint appeal to the international community. It is envisaged that priority should be given to radical improvement in transport and communication networks, a rapid reduction of environmental pollution, establishing an efficient market system, and encouraging currency stabilization and balance of payments support. As with the earlier Marshall plan, the basic goal would be to establish the necessary conditions for private investment, including FDI, to be profitably undertaken.

We do not need to identify, in any detail, the ingredients of these necessary conditions. Suffice to assert that both the productive and institutional infrastructure of most Central and East European countries is two or even three generations behind that of Western Europe. In a recently published assessment of the market building strategies in Hungary, Poland and Czechoslovakia, the OECD concluded that the only real progress that had been made was in the area of restoring property rights to private owners, removing some market imperfections, e.g. consumer subsidies, and trade flow distortions, and increasing investment in education and labor skills.[18] But such are the prizes offered to foreign firms by their resources and markets, and to Western democratic governments by the prospects of a free and thriving market of 400 million inhabitants, that the incentive to overcome the huge barriers to restructuring is very great indeed. To this extent, we believe that a parallel can legitimately be drawn between the US interest in the economic and political recovery of West Germany and Japan, and that of the OECD nations, in the future of Central and Eastern Europe.

Again, at the risk of generalizing, we would submit that the extent and pace at which East European economies will become fully integrated with the rest of Europe will largely depend on the outcome of three factors. The first is the ability of governments efficiently to promote restructuring *and* to convince their own people that, in spite of additional economic hardships they will inevitably have to endure, there is light at the end of the tunnel, and the democratization of markets will release a treasure of talents and entrepreneurship. The second is the likely future course of the economy of the Commonwealth of Independent States (CIS). The potential market of this economy is three times greater than the rest of Eastern Europe combined. If the CIS flourishes, this is likely to create demand for products from the more advanced Central and East European economies, and hence, encourage further foreign investment into them. The third determinant is the extent to which the necessary finance capital for long term development can be found in a global economy in which the claims for international savings are so much greater than the supply. At the end of the day, capital constraints could well limit the pace and pattern of the economic regeneration of Eastern Europe.

We conclude this section with a review of two recent surveys of the opinions of business executives about the investment opportunities offered by different countries in Eastern Europe. The first is that conducted by *Financial Executive* and published in its September/ October 1990 issue. The Eastern *Länder* of Germany were perceived to offer the most attractive business environment to foreign investors, while Hungary was thought to afford the best indigenous assets for undertaking business. Some further details are set out in Table 9.5. The erstwhile Yugoslavia (which was included in the survey) and Czechoslovakia were ranked third or fourth – although, interestingly, Yugoslavia was believed to have the best history of entrepreneurship, yet the worst but one record of speed or stability in economic reform. Currently, Romania and Bulgaria would not appear to be serious contenders for inward direct investment.

In another field study conducted by three US business school analysts in August 1990 (Mikhail, Nandola and Prasad, 1990), and based upon questionnaires completed by a sample of 79 US business executives, it was found that of some eight possible modalities for exploiting East European markets, joint ventures with US minority equity interest was listed as the fifth most likely, following exporting from a West European subsidiary (ranked first); exporting from the US; licensing, bartering and countertrade. Joint ventures with a US majority interest was ranked seventh after management contracts; while the least likely form of entry was thought to be the wholly owned subsidiary.

Concerning the perceived ability of East European countries to adapt to the changes required of them if they were to attract more investment, the respondents considered the progress made by East Germany the most significant, followed by that of Poland, Czechoslovakia and Hungary. Of the seven categories of change identified, the most progress had been made with political reform and the host country attitude towards foreign direct investment, and the least

Table 9.5 Indicators of attractiveness to foreign direct investors

(a) Business Environment

	Standing with Western Banks	Speed/stability of economic reform	Reliability of infrastructure	Extent of currency convertibility	Extent of profit repatriation	Extent of government bureaucracy	Average score
East Germany	1	1	4	1	1	2	1.8
Hungary	4	2	2	2	2	1	2.2
Czechoslovakia	2	3	1	4	4	3	2.8
Yugoslavia	6	7	3	3	3	4	4.3
Poland	7	5	5	5	4	5	5.2
Bulgaria	3	6	7	6	7	7	5.8
Soviet Union	5	5	6	6	6	8	6.1
Romania	8	8	8	6	8	6	7.3

(b) Business Asset attractiveness

	Existence of export-oriented business	History of entrepreneurship	Average score
Hungary	1	2	1.5
East Germany	2	3	2.5
Yugoslavia	4	1	2.5
Czechoslovakia	3	3	3
Poland	5	5	5
Soviet Union	6	6	6
Bulgaria	7	7	7
Romania	8	8	8

Source: Financial Executive Sept./Oct. 1990.

progress in the upgrading of infrastructure. Finally, it was the opinion of the US executive that West German MNEs from Germany were likely to be the most likely future investors in Eastern Europe, with those from the USA and Japan following some way behind.

CONCLUSIONS

The resources and markets of Central and Eastern Europe offer huge and exciting challenges to Western and Japanese firms, and to fledgling indigenous entrepreneurs. These opportunities are likely to be exploited in a variety of ways, notably through trade, joint ventures and strategic alliances between Central and East European and foreign firms. Because of their O specific advantages and their operating presence in many different countries, MNEs are ideal vehicles for spearheading industrial restructuring. Through their ability to transfer technology and management skills; through their introduction of up to date industrial practices and quality control techniques; through their example and their spill-over effects on local entrepreneurship, suppliers and competitors; and through their network of international linkages – with both large and small firms – they can provide much of the competences and initiatives for economic growth.

However, such FDI will occur only if it advances the global strategies of companies. In a scenario of increasing shortages of capital but widening opportunities for growth, this places considerable burdens on the authorities of East European economies to offer the most favorable environment for value-added activities – be these to produce goods and services for the domestic or international market. This is *not* simply a question of liberalization of investment policies or of offering foreign investors generous fiscal incentives. Equally, if not more important, it is for governments both to create and sustain an economic and social environment in which both domestic and foreign firms can compete effectively, and to foster right attitudes by labor and management alike towards productivity improvements and competing in a global environment. While, as we have said, MNEs can supply some of these initiatives, particularly insofar as they can link the recipient countries into the world economy, at the end of the day, it is the responsibility of governments as custodians of the welfare of their citizens to set the commercial, institutional and attitudinal framework in which private enterprise can both flourish and provide the much needed engine for economic development.

While the long term future for FDI in Central and East Europe is highly promising, the next decade or so are likely to be particularly taxing times for both foreign investors and the governments of host countries. The current recession, the collapse of intraregional trade, brought about *inter alia* by the worsening economic situation in the CIS, and the Middle East crisis, have each added to the already daunting restructuring problems facing most of Central and Eastern Europe. Indeed, economists are agreed that, economically speaking, things must get worse before they can get better. In addition, uncertainties about legal instability, ownership restrictions, currency inconvertibility and supply constraints, and the absence of the required legal accounting and financial infrastructure are causing Western firms to reappraise the optimistic scenario on which they had earlier based their investment intentions. In the words of Carl McMillan (1991), 'The initial euphoria and the favorable business climate it engendered has now begun to wear off. The new mood is reinforced by greater awareness of the practical difficulties posed by investment in the area.'

These are sensible words. At the same time, it would be unfortunate if the pendulum of business attitudes and expectations should swing too much towards the pessimistic. One very recent encouraging sign is the commitment of the Heads of governments of the seven leading industrial nations to assist the former Soviet Union in its efforts to move away from a command-dominated to a market-oriented economic system.[19] Should this commitment be translated into action, the medium term future of FDI in Central and Eastern Europe is, indeed, a promising one.

Examples of recent FDI in Central and Eastern Europe

Year	Investor	Host country	Industry	Investment
(1) US investment				
1988	Occidental	Russia	Petroleum	$6b
	Guardian Glass	Hungary	Glass	$207m
	McDonald's	Russia	Foods	$50m
1989	General Electric	Hungary	Lighting	$270m
1990	General Motors	Eastern Germany	Automobiles	$680m
	General Motors	Hungary	Automobiles	$200m
	Phibro	Russia	Energy	$100m
	Ford Motor	Hungary	Automobiles	$150m
	Gillette	Russia	Consumer goods	$50m
	Tambrands	Russia	Consumer goods	$11m
	Pizza Hut	Russia	Foods	$10m
1991	Sara Lee	Hungary	Foods	$108m
	US West	Czechoslovakia	Telecom	$80m
	General Motors	Hungary	Automobiles	$59m
	Coca-Cola	Poland	Foods	$50m
	General Electric	Hungary	Lighting	$47m
	Procter and Gamble	Czechoslovakia	Consumer goods	$20m
1992	Cheveron	Kazakhstan	Petroleum	$10b
	Coca-Cola	Eastern Germany	Foods	$450m
	Philip Morris	Czechoslovakia	Consumer goods	$413m
	AT&T	Kazakhstan	Telecom	$200m
	Newmont Mining	Usbekistan	Minerals	$75m
	Dow Chemicals	Czechoslovakia	Chemicals	$25m
	Coca-Cola	Russia	Foods	$12m

Appendix continued

Year	Investor	Host country	Industry	Investment
(2) EC investment				
1990	Fiat Autos	Russia	Automobiles	$4.16b
	Volkswagen	Eastern Germany	Automobiles	$3.15b
	Daimler-Benz	Eastern Germany	Automobiles	$1.08b
	Lufthansa	Russia	Airports	$441m
	Bertelsmann	Eastern Germany	Telecom	$225m
	Dresdner	Eastern Germany	Banking	$222m
	BASF	Eastern Germany	Chemicals	$200m
	Pilkington	Poland	Glass	$140m
	Sanofi	Hungary	Pharmaceuticals	$80m
	Volkswagen	Yugoslavia	Automobiles	$60m
	Italtel	Russia	Telecom	$30m
	Telfos	Hungary	Rail Manufacturing	$12m
1991	Volkswagen	Czechoslovakia	Automobiles	$6.63b
	CBC	Czechoslovakia	Tourism	$175m
	Linde	Czechoslovakia	Gas	$106m
	Siemens	Czechoslovakia	Electronics	$55m
	Thomson	Poland	Electronics	$34m
1992	Fiat Autos	Poland	Automobiles	$2b
	Elf Aquitaine	Kazakhstan	Petroleum	$600m
	Fiat Autos	Poland	Automobiles	$550m
	Daimler-Benz	Czechoslovakia	Automobiles	$209m
	Thomson	Poland	Electronics	$100m

(3) EFTA investment

Year	Company	Country	Sector	Amount
1990	Prinzhorn	Hungary	Paper	$140m
	Agrana	Hungary	Foods	$60m
1991	Electrolux	Hungary	Consumer goods	$83m
	Hamburger	Hungary	Packaging	$82m
	Nestlé	Hungary	Foods	$65m
1992	ABB	Poland	Power	$10m

(4) Japanese investment in Eastern and Central Europe

Year	Company	Country	Sector	Amount
1990	Suzuki	Hungary	Automobiles	$235m
1991	Mei/Nissei Opto	Eastern Germany	Electronics	$50m
	Glaverbel	Czechoslovakia	Glass	$48m

Developing country investment

Year	Company	Country	Sector	Amount
1990	Hyundai	Russia	Petrochemicals	$2.5b
	Oberoi	Hungary	Travel	$80m
	Goldstar	Russia	Electronics	$33m

Source: Data bank of Professor T. Gladwin, Stern School of Business, New York University.

10 The globalization of service activities

INTRODUCTION

In recent years, students of the MNE have been criticized for paying insufficient attention to the determinants and impact of the foreign owned output of services. In one sense, this is a strange criticism as many of the O specific advantages of MNEs identified by scholars relate to their ability to create and internalize cross-border markets for intangible products, notably entrepreneurship, technology, management and marketing skills, and organizational capabilities. Indeed, Mark Casson (1987) has defined an MNE as a firm which internalizes international markets for intermediate products, and, as like as not, these products are likely to take the form of services.

But, what the critics have in mind perhaps, is that scholars have given too much emphasis to the role of MNEs as producers of *final* products. Such a focus, so they argue, is misplaced as, for some years now, the value of the output of foreign owned services has been as great as, and in some cases greater than, the output of foreign owned goods. Moreover, services are currently the fastest increasing component of MNE activity both in developed and developing countries.

But, is it true that there has been a relative neglect in studies on the determinants of foreign production in services? First it should be emphasized that some 85 per cent of all international direct investment in services is in two groups of services – viz. trade related activities, and banking and finance (UNCTC, 1988). As regards the former group, two points should be made. First, most trade-related FDI is a means towards an end, rather than an end in itself. The goal is to create or acquire markets for the export of goods and services of the investing company, or to assist it in acquiring imports on the most favorable terms. Second, viewed from a dynamic perspective, some trade related investment represents a stage in the internationalizing process of the firm, which might be followed by foreign production of the goods being traded. Such an internationalization process has been studied in some detail by scholars,[1] although only a few have considered conditions in which a firm should choose to undertake its own sales and marketing activities, or its import merchandising, rather than using foreign agents to perform these tasks. Of all kinds of trade-related investments, however, perhaps the most extensive are those of the Japanese Soga Shosha and Korean Chaebol companies.

By contrast, there have been numerous studies of the internationalization of banking and financial services. These include some which have specifically sought to explain the extent, pattern, and ownership structure of international production. These include those of Grubel (1977, 1989), Gray and Gray (1981), UNCTC (1981), Yannopoulos (1983), Cho (1985), Casson (1989), Gray (1990), Campayne (1990) and Sagari (1992).

Even outside the two main sectors, there have been a wide variety of studies on the internationalization of services. These include those on the international construction and design engineering industry (Rimmer, 1988; Seymour, 1987; Enderwick, 1989; UNCTC, 1989); the hotel industry (Dunning and McQueen, 1981); multinational news agencies (Boyd-Barrett, 1989); the advertising industry (UNCTC, 1979, Terpstra and Yu, 1988); the accounting industry (Daniels, Thrift and Leyshon, 1989), and trans-border information data flows (UNCTC, 1984; Roche, 1992). Again, some of these have been directed to theorizing about the determinants of foreign production. And, as we have already indicated, the export of managerial skills, information and organizational techniques is one of the main forms of intrafirm cross-border trade.

Nevertheless, it remains true, that a lacunae exists in the repertoire of the IB scholar seeking to explain the growth of FDI in services. There has, for example, been no substantive work on the internationalization of management and business consultancy, education and medical services, motion pictures, legal services, and transportation services, and much less than might be expected on FDI in the telecommunications and computer software sectors.

This brings us to a second reason for the apparent neglect of services. That is that many services are, in fact, supplied by goods producing firms. It is, indeed, very important to distinguish between specialized *service MNEs* and *MNEs that produce services*. According to the UNCTC (1988), in 1982, about one-half of all foreign service affiliates of US origin were owned by industrial companies. In that same year, 55 per cent of US direct investments in banking and finance, and 82 per cent of those in wholesale trading were undertaken by companies whose main activity was the production of *goods*. Since the production of services by these companies is usually considered to be a secondary activity to the production of goods, it is possible that they have not gained the attention that they might have done had these same services been supplied by specialist service firms. No less relevant is the fact that goods producing firms may produce their own intermediary services. Since these are not generally sold to external purchasers, but, instead, are embodied in tangible goods, such activities, e.g. design and engineering, advertising, market research and transportation services, are grossly underestimated in both company and national accounts.[2] Later, in this chapter, we shall consider some of the implications for the theory of international production of the increasing service intensity of goods producing firms.[3]

Third, the data suggest that the degree of internationalization of services is generally less than that of goods. Again, trade is an exception. Some relevant data drawn from a variety of sources, but first published by the UNCTC (1988) are set out in Table 10.1. Here we come closer to the possible reason for relative neglect of services, which we shall examine in more detail in the next section.

DIFFERENCES BETWEEN MNE ACTIVITY IN GOODS AND SERVICES

We would like to emphasize six distinctive characteristics of MNE activity in services. First, some goods producing investments largely reflect the international distribution of natural resources. Since a lot of oil, minerals and agricultural products are to be found only in certain parts of the globe, it follows that the ratio of foreign to total production for firms located in, at least, some countries will be high. With a few notable exceptions, e.g. tourism, the geographical distribution of services is less geographically concentrated.[4]

Second, some goods producing industries are truly international by nature. In today's technological and economic environment, the leading goods producing firms in such sectors as oil, cars, pharmaceuticals, tires, computers, and consumer electronics can only sustain or advance global competitiveness by selling and producing in the major markets of the world.[5] The growth of intra-industry, trade and cross-border FDI over the last 20 years testifies to this phenomenon. However, there has not been the same imperative to internationalize the production of many services.[6] Most service firms do not need global markets to be competitive. The exceptions are precisely in those sectors in which the proportion of global output accounted for by foreign production is highest, noticeably in finance and investment banking, some kinds of consultancy, up-market hotels and advertising.

Third, and related to the second factor, is the growth of the international division of labor in goods which the MNE has, itself, helped advance. Perhaps the best example is the restructuring of inward (and especially US) direct investment which has taken place in the European Economic Community (EC) since its establishment in 1957 (Cantwell, 1992). The elimination of all intra-EC tariff barriers has enabled foreign owned firms to engage in product and process specialization in particular countries in the EC, and to supply other European markets from there. The result, as described in Chapter 7, has been a quite remarkable upsurge in intrafirm intra-EC trade.

Such intrafirm specialization has not occurred to the same extent in the services sector. This is partly because of the limited possibility for trade in some services, and partly because the non-tariff barriers within the EC have impeded both trade and investment in services much more than they have in goods. Hence, the amount of rationalized global or regional investment is much smaller in the service sector than in the manufacturing sector, and, in consequence, so is the foreign production ratio of service firms.

Fourth, we observe that there are several differences between the kind of O specific advantages likely to be enjoyed by service MNEs as compared with their goods producing counterparts. The extent to which these firms enjoy or can acquire these advantages clearly depends on the characteristics of the economic activity in which a firm is engaged and/or those related to the possession of scarce idiosyncratic resources and technology, or those which arise from the geographical dispersion of assets or engaging in cross-border arbitrating tend to be less pronounced. While these advantages are visible in some kinds of financial activities, information intensive services, advertising, and international airlines, they are much less apparent in tourism, hotels, fast food chains, car rental, health services, road and rail transport, education and consultancy, and a whole range of personal services. Generally, however, it would be our contention that, for the moment at least, the competitive advantages of specialized service MNEs, arising from their multinationality, *per se* are likely to be less than in the case of goods producing MNEs.

Fifth, while some service activities by MNEs *precede* that of goods activities abroad, they are often likely to be financed by loans or

Table 10.1 Degree of transnationalization of US non-bank transnational corporations 1984[1]

Industry	Share of foreign affiliates in			Number of	
	Sales	Assets	Employment	TNCs	Foreign affiliates
All industries	26.2	19.7	25.9	2088	16892
Manufacturing	27.3	24.4	30.3	1221	11075
Petroleum	41.7	34.2	31.1	77	1644
Other industries	25.3	21.7	39.7	24	98
Services	16.6	11.3	16.9	673	3943
Finance, insurance, real estate[2]	12.0	9.7	27.9	127	999
Finance	16.3	13.2	14.6	34	227
Insurance	10.2	7.3	24.8	77	733
Trading	18.0	14.7	16.5	217	904
Wholesale	24.8	23.6	21.6	165	685
Retail	11.6	10.7	15.6	52	219
Transportation, communications, public utilities	6.5	7.1	10.7	83	437
Construction	23.6	22.5	16.3	33	173

Business and other services	11.6	12.7	10.9	158	758
Hotel	7.6	11.1	6.5	8	67
Advertising	20.3	24.2	29.4	22	179
Motion pictures	20.0	13.9	11.5	9	79
Engineering, etc.	23.9	20.5	15.3	23	72
Management consulting and public relations	14.2	15.4	15.6	18	43
Equipment rental (excluding autos and computers)	3.2	3.8	8.1	7	7
Computer and data-processing services	10.3	11.9	8.9	13	37
Health	3.1	7.4	4.4	9	26
Accounting	–	5.3	–	6	31
Other	10.6	11.6	12.3	49	238
Petroleum-related services	28.7	20.5	25.6	55	663

[1] Measured by the share of foreign affiliates in total TNC activities.
[2] Including holdings, excluding non-business entities.
Source: UNCTC, 1988.

grants from international banks, development agencies or govern-ments, rather than by direct investment from corporations. Examples include transportation and communication networks and some social infrastructure, e.g. housing, hospitals, public utilities and schools. Exceptions include some pre-production commercial activities by goods producing MNEs, e.g. R&D, employee training, construction and consultant engineering and some infrastructure activities neces-sary for the operation of efficient markets, which firms are, them-selves, prepared to finance (e.g. some kinds of education, housing and health care activities). In addition, as we have already mentioned, many trade related investments by MNEs precede investment in goods.

Nevertheless, a sizeable proportion of FDI in services *follows*, rather than *leads*, investment in goods. These support activities such as business and professional services, finance and insurance, as well as consumer services which have a high income elasticity of demand, e.g. insurance, leisure and travel related services and speciality retailing. Also, the service component of goods producing activities by foreign affiliates tends to increase as the local content of the sales generated by them rises.[7]

Sixth, and lastly, there is the question of the appropriability of assets as a measure of the internationalization of services. Clearly, this is not the case for airlines – unless the temporary presence of aircraft in different parts of the world is, itself, counted as a foreign invest-ment. More to the point, many services are not capital intensive, and their contribution to the value-added process is better measured by their sales, net output or employment. The difference this makes is well illustrated by the data set out in Table 10.1, and also by the more general statistic that the share of GNP accounted for services in most countries has risen much less dramatically since the mid-1970s than that of employment (World Bank, 1990).

We now turn to consider some of the implications of these facts for the theory of foreign production in services.

THE THEORY OF FOREIGN PRODUCTION IN SERVICES

Introduction

Why should one need a special theory of foreign production[8] in services? Does one, in fact, need a special theory?

These questions can be responded to at two levels. The first is, does one need a different general paradigm than that (or those) advanced to explain initially the foreign value-added activities production in goods? The second is, does one need a different set of specific theories to explain the foreign production of particular kinds of services, or groups of services, compared with those put forward to explain the foreign production of particular kinds of goods?

General paradigms

The literature identifies four reasons why firms should wish to engage in foreign based value-added activity. The first is to acquire inputs for further processing activities in other parts of the investing firm's operation, or for export to external markets. Examples of supply oriented or resource based service investment are tourism, car rentals, resort based hotels, some construction, news agencies and relating services, film making and entertainment. Almost by definition, cross-border transport services also fit into this category.

The second motive for FDI is to supply a foreign market with goods and services more beneficially than by alternative routes, e.g. by exports. Such investment may be initiated as a *defensive* response to protectionism by importing countries or to the actions of competitors, or as an *aggressive* strategy to relocate existing production to where it is likely to be more profitable in the future, or to steal a march on competitors. The customization of products to local sourcing capabilities or market needs and after-sales maintenance is another motive for market based investment. Examples of such activity MNE in the services sector include most business and professional services, commercial banking, insurance, telecommunications, some educational services, restaurants and telecommunications.

The third kind of foreign direct investment grows out of the first two. It is *sequential* rather than *initial* investment in that it builds upon and/or restructures an existing portfolio of foreign assets. It represents an international division of labor of the production of MNEs so as to maximize the benefits of differences in factor endowments (both natural and acquired), to exploit the economies of specialization and scope, and to minimize environmental volatility (Kogut, 1985). The most noticeable manifestation of MNEs practicing a 'rationalized', rather than a 'resource based' or 'market seeking' investment strategy is the extent and pattern of cross-border trade within their own networks.[9]

Earlier in this chapter we suggested that since the degree of multi-nationalization in the service sector was less than that in the goods sector, it was only to be expected that rationalized investment would be less. Another reason is that, until recently, many services could not easily be traded. Exceptions included those services which were transferred across boundaries by people, e.g. educational and medical services, management consultancy and business services incorporated in tradable goods, e.g. engineering designs on computer printouts, chemical formulae, information technology, work materials, advertising material on film or diskette, etc. Recent advances in the computerization of service related production and in telecommunications have dramatically changed this situation. Today, the global integration of a wide range of banking, financial services, insurance and information providing and disseminating activities is widespread, while in some sectors, e.g. engineering, construction management and some kinds of market research, there is an increasing tendency for the affiliates in one country to be delegated responsibility for supplying a particular group of services either to a regional or global market.

The fourth type of MNE activity is different from the other three in that it is primarily motivated to *acquire* assets or some kind of competitive advantage rather than to exploit the use of an existing competitive advantage. Such activity, which is normally initiated by way of an acquisition, merger or strategic alliance, is undertaken in the expectancy that the complementarity between the asset acquired and those already owned by the purchasing firm will protect or improve its *overall* competitive position in a particular market or in a group of markets.

Such fragmentary data as are available suggest that A&Ms among accounting firms, banks, finance and security analysts (and, particularly those involving Japanese firms) do appear to have some of the characteristics of asset-acquiring manufacturing investments. At the same time, there have been substantial cross-border purchases of service firms by manufacturing firms to gain access to final or intermediate distribution channels and marketing outlets. Examples include the purchase of Columbia Records (one of the leading purchasers of video equipment and compact discs) by the Sony Corporation. Joint ventures and strategic alliances between firms to produce intermediate services or to achieve risk spreading or other economies of integration are also rising (Contractor and Lorange, 1988). In some technology and marketing sectors, the major *fixed* cost of production is increasingly *service* rather than *goods* based. Examples include the bio-technology and the semi-conductor industries. But, in almost all goods producing sectors, the proportion of service intensive inputs and of 'created' factor endowments is rising, and rising fast. This, then, might suggest that not only is the current round of A&Ms related as much to the rationalization of the production of intermediate services as to that of the final products produced, but that new investment by information or capital intensive service firms might be increasingly prompted by the desire to acquire, protect or advance a competitive position.

In the course of the last 20 or so years, two core paradigms of international business have evolved. The first is the internalization paradigm, which, as Chapter 4 has explained, is essentially concerned with explaining why MNEs exist in the first place, and what explains their growth *qua* MNEs. The proponents of this approach[10] essentially view the MNE as a particular form of multi-activity firm, and direct their attention to identifying the particular advantages which such firms may have over uni-activity firms, *which specifically arise from the internalization of cross-border markets.*

There have been several applications of the internalization paradigm to the service sector. Examples include Mark Casson's analysis of the banking and information services sectors (Casson, 1989, 1990), and that of Peter Buckley on tourism (Buckley, 1987). Each offers a persuasive explanation of *why* MNEs engage in FDI rather than in some other form of international involvement, e.g. licensing to produce a service in a foreign country, with intermediate products supplied by the investing firm. Moreover, in the case of some kinds of investment, e.g. sequential investments offering strong economies of common governance and those made to acquire strategic assets, the gains anticipated from internalizing foreign markets may provide a sufficient O advantage for the initial investment.[11]

At the same time, as Chapter 5 has already suggested, the internalization paradigm cannot provide a complete framework for explaining the totality of foreign value-added activities undertaken by MNEs. This is simply because it chooses to regard as exogenous variables those competitive advantages of MNEs which have nothing to do with the internalization of cross-border intermediate products. These advantages (which may or may not be time limited) essentially embrace the ability of a firm to supply consumers efficiently with the products they require independently of *where* it locates its plants or *whether or not* the cross-border markets for products exported from the home country are internalized or not.

Take, for example, the case of a Swiss corporation which has found an effective and affordable cure for AIDs, where the R&D leading to the discovery of the vaccine was undertaken in Switzerland. The successful discovery of this new drug (which, itself, may reflect the past ability of the innovating company to organize its R&D activities efficiently), obviously gives the company a substantial competitive advantage over its competitors.

Let us now suppose the corporation wishes to sell its drug to US consumers. Exactly how is it going to do it? One way is to produce the drug from start to finish in its Swiss factory and to export the final product to the US. Another is to export the know-how on how to produce the drug to a US owned company for it to manufacture. A third is for itself to acquire or set up a factory in the US or to increase the output of either its or someone else's factory in the US. Suppose it opts for the third alternative. The value-added in the US by the Swiss subsidiary is foreign production. What explains the amount of this value-added? The internalization economist would assert that without the incentive to internalize the market for the drug technology and to locate production in the US, no foreign investment would take place. But, no less true is the fact that if the Swiss firm had not discovered the drug in the first place, no foreign production would have been possible.

The eclectic paradigm of international production seeks to over-come this particular problem. While accepting the basic concept of internalization, the propensity of firms to produce outside their boundaries reflects three things. The first is their capability to profit-ably produce saleable goods and services to intermediate or final consumers, *vis-à-vis* their competitors or potential competition. The second is the extent to which it is profitable to combine these advan-tages with factor endowments in a foreign country, rather than under-take further value-adding activities from domestic plants for export or as an alternative to import. The third is that the firm possessing the capabilities may find it profitable to add value to these assets, rather than to sell the right to do so to other firms.

The eclectic paradigm is, perhaps, the dominant paradigm of international production. It is different from the internalization paradigm in as much as, in the former the ownership advantages (apart from those arising from internalization of cross-border market) are assumed to be a determinant of foreign production, while in the internalization model, they are regarded as exogenous variables.[12]

It is further accepted that the configuration of OLI advantages will vary according to *industry-*, *country-* (or region-) and *firm-*specific characteristics. Included in these latter characteristics are a group of idiosyncratic variables, including firm-specific differences in strategic behavior. Applying the paradigm to the services sector, the lower propensity of the hotel industry to engage in foreign direct investment relative to the advertising industry (see Table 10.1) is hypothesized to be because MNEs have fewer unique competitive advantages *vis-à-vis* domestic firms, *or* because hotel firms believe that they better appropriate the rent on these assets by way of using the external market than can advertising firms, *or* because, relative to hotel firms, the value-added activities of advertising firms are better undertaken from a home rather than a foreign production base. It is more likely, however, to be a combination of all three factors.

Since the eclectic paradigm was first put forward in 1976, there has been a number of modifications to it.[13] In particular, it (and, similarly, the internalization paradigm) has been subject to two main criticisms both of which have been the subject of previous chapters.[14] First, it is claimed that both offer only a snapshot view of the MNE or international production, or, at best, compare the propensity of firms and/or countries to be international direct investors at different time periods. There is, so it is alleged, no dynamic theory of MNE activity. Second, it is argued that neither paradigm satisfactorily takes account of the strategic response of firms as an independent variable affecting the scale or scope of foreign value-added activities. In other words, couched in a neoclassical framework, and working on the assumption of profit maximization and very limited uncertainty, it is implicitly assumed that two or more firms faced with an identical OLI configuration would react (as far as their foreign value activities are concerned) in the same way.

We know, of course, that this is not the case. GM does not have the same strategy towards its European manufacturing operations as Ford. Sony is a much more internationally involved company than is Sanyo. The geographical portfolio of the major US oil companies is very different. Each of the European chemical MNEs choose to pursue very varied innovatory strategies. The sourcing strategies of Japanese color TV companies is very different to that of their European or American counterparts. The degree of multinationalization by the three leading UK pharmaceutical companies[15] varies from 20 per cent to 60 per cent. In the services sector, there is no homogeneity of competitive strategies or of modes of servicing global markets among, for example, the big accounting, advertising, money management, engineering and architectural consultancy, and hotel MNEs. Is this lack of homogeneity a reflection of idiosyncratic behavior on the part of decision takers, or is it a genuine difference of opinion about, for example, the probability of certain events occurring in the future or the likely consequence of certain actions taken by the company on its competitors' behavior? Whatever it is, somehow or another any paradigm of international production of services must take these firm-specific differences into account.

Chapter 4 has already suggested that one way this might be done is to incorporate strategic behavior as dynamic add-on variable to the OLI determinants of MNE activity. Thus, we argued, the amount of international production undertaken by a firm in time t could be regarded as a function of the OLI configuration facing that firm at that time, together with the strategic response of the firm to past OLI configurations and any changes in the value of the OLI variables and the strategy of the firm between the past and present time. Similarly, international production at a future point of time (t + 1) can be considered as a function of the OLI configuration at time t, any changes in the strategy of the firm, given that configuration, and any changes in the OLI configuration, together with the effect which these, in turn, have on strategy, between that time and time t + 1.

It is not the purpose of the present chapter to review the literature on strategic management. Suffice to point out that it covers a spectrum of scholarly effort ranging from quite esoteric models on contestable markets and game theory developed by some economists to a variety of taxonomic classifications of the strategies of firms, put forward by some business analysts.

In between these extremes, economists such as Caves, Porter and Spence (1980), Buckley (1990), Casson (1987, 1990), Teece (1984) and Kay (1991), and business analysts such as Chandler (1962, 1971), Kogut and Kulatilaha (1988), Bartlett and Ghoshal (1989) have attempted to identify and/or evaluate the significance of strategic related variables as factors influencing not just the decisions of firms to adopt hierarchical structures rather than seeking a market solution to reduce transactions and/or production costs, but also the *form* of organizational structure which optimizes decision taking. Similarly, marketing scholars have given some attention to the role of strategic related variables in determining the modes of entry into particular markets; while the main thrust of business analysts has been to evaluate not only why certain kinds of firms build up and/or sustain certain kinds of competitive advantages, or why they choose one particular strategy towards, e.g. product development, product diversity, manufacturing, purchasing, marketing, R&D, etc., rather than another, but also the factors determining the strategic postures adopted by firms.

Out of all this research, a sense of a generic or core strategy is beginning to emerge; but, as yet, it tends to be confined to particular functional areas of the firm (e.g. product development or marketing policy). Examples include Porter's cost reducing and product differentiation strategy (Porter, 1980) and Douglas and Rhee's five kinds of marketing strategy (Douglas and Rhee, 1989).

Two exceptions might be noted. The first is the distinction made by Mintzberg (1978) between *intended* and *realized* strategy. Whether they accept it or not, all firms *do* have a strategy (even if that strategy is no strategy!). When firms review their achievements and performances over the past year, for example *vis-à-vis* that of their competitors, and there is some dissatisfaction with that performance, the usual course of action is to try to do something different, in other words, change strategy. The *incremental* effect of such a change can often be monitored more easily than that of the strategy as a whole. In our model set out in Chapter 4 a change in strategy, given the OLI configuration facing firms, will occur because a previous intended strategy has not been fully realized.

The second exception is to do with internationalization strategy *per se*, and here distinct progress has been made from the time of Howard Perlmutter's classic article on the evolution of the organizational structure of MNEs in 1969 (Perlmutter, 1969) to the recent work of Bartlett and Ghoshal (1989) and Hedlund (1993) on the changing organizational perceptions and needs of corporations as they become more globally integrated in their markets and production. But, even in these cases, there has been no real attempt to formulate any general behavioral or strategically related model of the MNE or international production. Perhaps, indeed, such a model is a contradiction in terms, for it would seem that the more generic is the subject to be explained, the wider the strategic options become, and the greater the difficulty of identifying the most significant strategy related variables.

The possible responses are numerous and varied. We will mention just three. The first is to construct a framework of variables which embrace all strategic options, and then to consider, for each main type of international production, the particular options most likely to influence decision taking specific to those kinds of production. The second is to reclassify types of international behavior by the commonalty of strategic response. This latter response is consistent with the concept of strategic groups (McGee and Thomas, 1986).

The third possible response is to relate sources of OLI advantages to particular strategic objectives. Ghoshal, for example, has identified three main types of competitive advantages enjoyed by firms, including those associated with the location of their production,[16] to three strategic objectives, viz. achieving efficiency in current operations, managing risks and innovation learning and adaptation (Ghoshal, 1987). Presumably, it would be possible to produce a rather different kind of matrix by plotting those strategic choices which specifically relate to the different stages of the internationalization of production or to the different motives for international production.

We have introduced the strategic dimension into our analysis of the determinants of international production mainly because, with the growing plurality of forms of globalization – and especially the explosive growth of cross-border collaborative alliances – strategic decision taking has become an increasingly important component of competitive success. It is also an area which seems to have escaped the attention of most scholars interested in the globalization of services. Compared with the large volume of publications on the global strategy of goods producing companies, there has been very little research done on the strategy of service MNEs. Most work on the determinants of the internationalization of services has so far been undertaken by economists, geographers and scholars interested in services *per se*, rather than by business analysts interested in the behavior of firms.

More recently, however, some attention has been given to the application of overseas market entry strategies to the services sector (Sharma and Johanson, 1987; Erramilli and Rao, 1990). Erramilli and Rao, for example, suggest that it is possible to relate the foreign entry mode of firms (graded by the degree of resource commitment involved) to the motives for entry, and these, in turn, to different kinds of service firms. In particular, the authors distinguish between *Client Following* (CF) and *Market Seeking* (MS) entry strategies. (Both of these, it should be noted, are variants of a market seeking investment strategy identified earlier.)

The first of these strategies is self evident. Service firms go abroad to service their clients who have preceded them abroad. Sometimes service firms follow their clients in their organizational strategies. Thus, while many professional service firms initially followed their clients (mostly goods producing companies) to the countries in which they set up their factories, today it is the ability of such firms to offer global services which appeals to their clients, who, themselves, are global corporations. The second strategy of service firms is to enter foreign markets to supply new foreign (or foreign and domestic) clients.

These two strategies can then be related to different types of MNE service firms. One possible grouping is by the kind of service provided, another is the ease at which the production of a service can be separated from its consumption (Hirsch, 1988). Table 10.2 reproduces the table compiled by Erramilli and Rao, who then go on to theorize that, compared to MS strategies, CF strategies are more likely to be associated with 100 per cent equity ownership than a joint venture or some form of non-contractual form of involvement, and that firms pursuing MS strategies are more prone to conclude cooperative alliances than those adopting CF strategies.

The hypotheses were tested separately for coupled (soft service) and decoupled (hard service) firms and controlled for country-specific affects.[17] The first hypothesis held well across the board for soft service firms, but not for hard service firms. Part of the reason for this may be differences in the factors influencing entry models of the two groups of firms. As regards the second hypothesis, firms pursuing an MS strategy showed a far greater inclination to team up with external entities than did firms opting a CF strategy.

We have cited this study not because its methodology is particularly unique or because its conclusions are especially exciting, but as an example of the way in which strategy related variables might be incorporated into economic explanations of international production.

For the most part, however, the application of strategic management to the services sector remains at a rudimentary stage. One example of the kind of thinking now going on is contained in a series of articles published by the *Sloan Management Review* on the impact of new service technologies on organizational strategies. Quinn and Pacquette (1990), for example, argued that there is no conflict

Table 10.2 Examples of entry strategies associated with two types of service firms

	Soft-service firms	*Hard-service firms*
Client following	An advertising agency sets up office abroad to serve a domestic client's foreign subsidiary.	A software company provides software support to the foreign subsidiary of a domestic client.
Market seeking	A fast-food chain appoints a franchisee in a foreign market to serve the local customers there.	An architectural design firm sells blueprints to foreign customers.

Source: Erramilli and Rao, 1990.

between a low cost and differentiated product strategy to achieve maximum value from service technology, and that, in any event, greater focus should be given to the ways in which firms respond to the demands of new technologies, e.g. the innovatory, production and marketing strategies. In a companion article, Quinn, Doorley and Pacquette (1990), gave some examples of the way in which new service-intensive technologies might impact on management strategies and organizational structures.[18]

We now return to the main theme of this chapter. In a study prepared for the UNCTC in the late 1980s (Dunning, 1989) an attempt was made to identify the main *economic* variables which might determine the international production in services. It also tried to pinpoint those OLI variables likely to be particularly significant in explaining the activities of MNEs (TNCs) in the service, and to review some of the more significant changes in the OLI configuration affecting these activities over the last decade.

The following section briefly summarizes (and, where appropriate, develops further) the main conclusions of our earlier study.

THE OLI ADVANTAGES OF SERVICE-BASED FIRMS SUPPLYING SERVICES IN INTERNATIONAL MARKETS

Ownership advantages of firms

We might identify five competitive or O specific advantages which are particularly relevant in the case of service firms. These are:

1   *Quality consistency, reputation and product differentiation.* Examples include customer specific or collectively idiosyncratic services, e.g. personal, business and professional services, entertainment and car repair services, airlines and shipping cruises. Often these services are associated with the ability of the selling firm to create and sustain a successful brand image, e.g. American Express and Visa (credit cards), Saatchi and Saatchi (advertising agencies), Royal Viking Lines (up-market cruises) etc., and/or to build up a personal reputation with a client, e.g. legal, or accounting and management consultancy services.[19]

2   *Economies of scope.* Examples include most large multiple retail establishments, investment analysts, travel agents, insurance companies and business consultants.

3   *Economies of scale and specialization.* Examples include airlines (e.g. use of 747s and DC10s), cruise shipping (the latest cruise

ships average 50,000–60,000 tons), reinsurance, health and education establishments and industrial cleaning.

4 *Access to, control of and ability to effectively process and disseminate information.* Examples include stockbroking, foreign exchange and securities dealing, commodity broking, various data-providing processing and service bureaux, e.g. Extel and Reuters and data transmission networks (e.g. TYMET). Here, the ability of firms to provide these and similar kinds of services is often complementary to their capability to supply complementary equipment and physical goods, and the knowledge of how to produce and disseminate data. Even if the provision or transmission of information is, itself, a service, its outlets depend upon the simultaneous use or part-use of equipment and physical facilities which might be owned or leased.

5 *Favored access to inputs and/or markets.* The need to gain access to inputs and to sustain or preserve a competitive advantage is particularly noticeable in information intensive industries. Examples include executive search companies, consultant engineers, investment banks, insurance firms, airlines and shipping companies, each of which tend to cluster their offices in the same location. Because of their size and reputation, some firms may have a better access to quality inputs than their competitors. Examples include Ivy League Universities or Medical Schools, the more prestigious advertising and public relations companies and the top accounting and legal institutions.

As regards access to their customers, we have already suggested that some service firms initially venture abroad to serve the foreign subsidiaries of their domestic clients. Mention should also be made of the competitive advantages of the East Asian general trading companies, which stem from the global span and close networking of their activities, their immense bargaining power, their unsurpassed experience and knowledge of international market conditions, their control of wholesale outlets for the products they buy and sell, and their ability to reduce foreign exchange risks and environmental turbulence by diversifying their trading portfolios (Ozawa, 1987).

The trading companies are, indeed, an example *par excellence* of the sequential advantages of the multinational service company which tend to be correlated with the degree of multinationalization (Kogut, 1983). Such benefits are also likely to be a feature of foreign exchange dealers, investment banks and cross-border information gathering and processing firms, e.g. Reuters.

Several other of the O specific advantages described (especially (1) and (3) above) may have little or nothing to do with the fact that a firm is an international producer; at the same time, both may be enhanced by the globalization of production.

Locational advantages of countries

Many of the factors affecting the location of goods producing activities help explain the location of services. There are, however, two variables of particular significance in the siting of the production of services.

1   The first is the extent to which the service is tradeable – either in its own right or when it is embodied in goods or people. Many services are, in fact, location bound, i.e. immovable across space. Examples include public utility services, warehousing, wholesaling and retailing services, most forms of public administration and social and community related services, and personal services which require a face to face contact between buyers and sellers. Such services can be provided to consumers either by a foreign firm via inward direct investment or by an indigenous firm under license to the foreign producer. By contrast, the tradeability of other services essentially rests on the availability and cost of the right kind of transportation facilities by which the services can be imported or exported. Technical advances, in the form of the computerization of a wide variety of cross-border telecommunication facilities, have dramatically increased the speed at which knowledge and information can be transmitted across the world; and have proved especially important in the case of business and financial services.

2   The second factor, especially relevant to the location of services, is the regulatory environment of host countries. In general, countries have adopted more controls on trade and investment in services than in goods (UNCTC, 1988). In the past, entry or performance requirements have been widespread in the provision of business services and in the operation of financial and commodity markets. Country-specific laws and regulations tend to govern entry into many professions while price fixing and/or market sharing is common – and often upheld by governments – e.g. in the air transport, education and training, and public utility sectors. Though there has been some movement towards the privatization and deregulation of markets, non-tariff barriers

(NTBs) continue to be a major factor influencing the mode by which markets are serviced by foreign owned firms (Enderwick, 1989). This is why Europe 1992 is likely to be particularly significant for the location of production by service MNEs, and of goods producing MNEs which are highly service intensive, e.g. pharmaceutical and telecommunication companies.[20]

More generally, the specific variables affecting the siting of service activities by MNEs will depend upon the type of services being provided. The distribution and location bound natural resources, including scenery, climate and topography, largely determine the siting of tourist activity. Geography also partly explains Singapore's strength in ship repair facilities and London's pre-eminence as a financial and trading center. The ability of the Philippines and Turkey (and, at one time, South Korea) to supply construction services to the Middle East rests on their possession of a plentiful supply of cheap, well motivated and transportable *unskilled* or semi-skilled labor force.

The location of most import substitution and rationalized service investment is motivated by very different considerations, including the size of the local market and the cost of skilled labor. The role of government may also be important, particularly in the provision, and/or ensuring the supply of adequate transport and communication facilities, of labor training and mobility, and of business and financial services.[21] Other work by the present author and a colleague has shown that *transaction cost* related factors (which might best be described as the costs of doing business effectively) are likely to be more important in influencing the choice of location of business related services within a broad region (e.g. in the European Economic Community) than are the costs of actually producing the services in any particular country (Dunning and Norman, 1987).

Table 10.3 sets out an illustration of the importance of some of the locational factors identified by 83 large MNEs with branch or regional offices in the UK in the mid-1980s. The numbers represent averages of the ranking given by firms on a scale of 1 to 5, with 5 being the most important.

The specific advantages offered by countries, both as home and host to service based MNEs, are likely to vary according to their ESP[22] characteristics and the configuration of their diamonds of competitive advantage. The need for customerization or adaptation of services supplied by MNEs to the needs of domestic purchasers is likely to be the greatest in host countries with different cultures,

Table 10.3 Importance of factors influencing the location of an office in the United Kingdom, mid-1980s[1] (percentage of respondents)

Factor	Engineering consultancy B	Engineering consultancy R	Management and business consultancy[2] B	Related business services[2] B	Computer and information technology B	Computer and information technology R	Trade and finance B	Trade and finance R	Total B	Total R
Proximity to										
Clients	3.0	2.8	4.0	3.9	3.0	3.4	3.3	2.5	3.5	2.5
Corporate headquarters	1.1	0.0	0.2	0.6	0.0	1.0	0.7	2.5	0.8	0.9
Other European affiliates	0.3	0.8	0.4	1.1	1.0	2.0	0.7	2.0	1.0	2.1
Offices of companies supplying similar services	1.4	2.8	1.0	1.9	0.5	0.9	2.1	1.5	1.2	1.2
Specialist services[3]	3.0	1.0	1.6	1.3	0.8	1.7	2.9	3.0	1.9	1.8
Government departments	1.3	0.3	1.2	0.6	0.0	0.7	1.1	0.8	1.1	0.8
Market size and prospects	2.6	3.5	3.2	4.0	2.8	3.3	2.9	2.5	3.2	3.1
Transport and communications										
Airport	3.0	3.8	2.6	2.3	2.5	3.7	2.3	3.9	2.6	3.5
Road or rail links	2.0	2.3	2.0	1.1	3.0	1.6	1.3	2.0	2.1	2.4
Postal services	1.4	2.8	1.8	1.3	1.8	2.1	1.3	2.0	1.8	2.4
Telephone and telex quality	1.7	3.0	2.6	1.6	2.0	3.0	3.4	3.8	2.3	3.0
Telecommunication costs	1.7	2.8	1.4	1.0	1.8	2.3	2.5	2.3	1.8	2.5
Travelling costs of executives	2.9	1.8	1.2	1.0	1.8	1.7	2.0	1.5	1.9	2.0
Manpower availability or quality										
Expatriate[4]	2.6	3.5	2.6	2.3	1.0	1.7	2.3	2.8	2.3	2.4
Local executive or managerial	1.4	1.8	2.8	1.7	3.3	3.1	2.0	1.8	2.1	2.6

Local professional or technical	3.0	3.0	1.8	2.0	3.3	3.4	2.4	2.3	2.4	2.9
Local secretarial or clerical	1.6	2.8	2.6	1.0	2.0	2.1	2.3	2.8	2.0	2.4
Manpower productivity	1.7	3.3	1.6	1.3	3.0	1.9	1.6	2.8	1.8	2.5
Industrial relations	1.3	2.0	0.2	1.0	1.8	1.6	1.3	1.5	1.3	2.2
Hiring, training rules, restrictions	1.6	1.8	0.8	0.9	2.0	2.9	1.9	2.8	1.4	2.7
Manpower costs										
Expatriate	1.4	2.3	1.0	0.7	1.3	0.9	1.7	2.0	2.5	1.9
Local executive or managerial	1.4	2.5	1.8	1.3	2.8	1.7	1.1	2.3	1.7	2.2
Local professional or technical	2.7	3.3	1.4	1.6	2.5	2.0	1.3	2.0	1.9	2.3
Local secretarial or clerical	1.6	2.0	1.4	1.1	2.0	1.7	1.4	2.5	1.6	2.1
Fringe benefits[5]	1.3	2.8	0.8	1.1	1.8	1.1	1.1	2.0	1.4	2.1
Dismissal costs[6]	1.6	2.5	0.2	1.1	1.8	1.3	1.4	1.8	1.3	2.0
Language, social and cultural factors										
Language	3.1	2.5	3.8	2.7	3.3	4.0	1.9	4.0	3.0	3.4
Local environment or image	2.7	2.8	1.6	2.3	1.8	1.9	2.1	4.0	2.4	2.5
Living conditions for expatriates[7]	1.6	2.8	1.2	2.1	1.3	1.6	1.4	2.8	1.6	2.3
Business framework										
General framework[8]	2.9	2.5	2.6	2.4	2.0	2.3	2.6	3.8	2.6	3.0
Level of personal taxation	1.4	2.3	1.4	1.9	1.3	1.7	1.3	2.5	1.4	2.1
Level of corporate taxation	1.0	2.0	1.8	1.7	1.3	2.1	1.3	2.5	1.5	2.2
Availability of government incentives[9]	1.0	0.8	0.8	0.7	0.8	1.7	1.0	1.3	1.0	1.6
Attitudes of government to foreign companies	2.1	3.0	2.4	1.6	2.8	2.0	2.0	2.3	2.1	2.6
Attitudes of customers and business community to foreign companies	2.0	2.5	2.2	1.9	2.3	2.0	2.3	2.5	2.2	2.3

Table 10.3 continued

Factor	Engineering consultancy		Management and business consultancy[2]	Related business services[2]	Computer and information technology		Trade and finance		Total	
	B	R	B	B	B	R	B	R	B	R
Trading freedom										
Controls on capital, imports dividend remittances, etc.	1.4	2.0	1.6	1.4	2.8	2.4	2.3	3.0	2.0	2.5
Tariff or other import controls	0.7	1.0	0.0	0.0	1.8	2.1	0.7	1.8	0.7	1.8
Non-tariff barriers[10]	1.1	0.8	1.2	0.4	1.8	1.7	0.9	2.0	1.1	1.7
Availability and cost of accommodation										
Availability of right premises	2.9	3.3	2.2	1.1	2.5	2.3	2.9	2.5	2.5	2.9
Cost of right premises to rent, etc.	2.3	3.3	2.0	1.1	3.0	2.0	2.4	1.5	2.2	2.6

B = Branch offices; R = Regional offices.

1 Data provided by 83 respondents (0 = not at all important; 4 = very important).
2 Too few respondents for analysis of regional data.
3 Legal, financial, consultancy, etc.
4 Work permits, readiness to work in this location.
5 Including social security payments.
6 Redundancy and severance pay.
7 Housing, entertainment, health care, education.
8 General legal and commercial framework availability, quality of financial and consultancy services.
9 Grants, tax allowances, etc.
10 Government regulations, procurement policies favouring local production rather than imports.

Source: Dunning and Norman, 1987.

tastes, living habits and industrial needs than those of the investing countries. Developing countries are unlikely to display the demand or supply conditions necessary to attract high-income consumer or sophisticated producer service activities.

To give some examples, the opportunities for tourist-related TNC activities fluctuate considerably between countries or territories. The United States, United Kingdom and France generate an above average proportion of MNE hotel chains than other developed countries. MNEs from the US would appear to have a competitive advantage in the supply of health care, market research, education, fast-food restaurants, advertising, computer software accounting and management consulting services; those from Japan, in general trading; those from the UK in commodity broking, professional and entertainment-related services; those from the France, Republic of Korea, Turkey and the Philippines in construction services; those from Switzerland in reinsurance; those from Greece and Liberia in shipping services; those from India and the US in motion-picture production; those from China, India and Japan in ethnic restaurants; and those from Singapore and Hong Kong in airlines, financial services and trade.

While an above average proportion of MNE activity in finance and investment banking, insurance business, and professional services (indeed most industrial services apart from the supply of technology) tends to be between developed market economies, the services of tourism, building and construction, and trade and distribution are relatively more concentrated in developing countries. Finally, as we already mentioned, the attitudes and policies of governments of host countries towards trade and investment in services are highly country-specific.

Table 10.4 sets out Michael Porter's estimates of the comparative advantage of different countries in supplying a range of services (Porter, 1990). Porter further argues that these advantages have less to do with the cost and availability of created technological capabilities and human competences, and cost of natural factor endowments, and more to do with the characteristics of domestic demand, the presence of complementary and supporting industries,[23] and the extent and form of domestic rivalry among indigenous service firms. Surrounding and influencing these variables is the role of government, particularly in stimulating entrepreneurship and innovation upgrading human capital, and in the helping to provide the infrastructure and complementary assets necessary to insure the competitiveness of service sectors in international markets. This catalogue of

Table 10.4 Estimated patterns of national competitive advantage in international service industries

Industry	Denmark	Germany	Italy	Japan	Korea	Singapore	Sweden	Switzerland	UK	US
Food										
Fast food										XX
Food service/vending										X
Retailing										
Convenience stores									X	
Specialty stores			X						XX	
Education and training										
Secondary and university education		X						X	X	XX
Graduate education										XX
Corporate training										XX
Leisure										
Entertainment									X	XX
Auctioneering									XX	XX
Medical										
Health care services								X	X	XX
Hospital management										XX
Travel related[1]										
Hotels				X				X	X	XX
Car rentals										XX
Airlines		X				X		X	X	X
General business										
Accounting									X	XX
Legal services									X	XX

Industry						
Advertising				X		XX	XX
Public relations		X				X	X
Management consulting	X		X		X	X	XX
Engineering/architectural[2]			X			X	XX
Construction			X			X	X
Construction research							X
Design services		XX					XX
Temporary help	X					X	XX
Industrial laundry/apparel supply	X						
Industrial cleaning (facilities, tools, equipment)					X	x	X
Security services					X	x	X
Building maintenance services	X				X	x	X
Equipment maintenance and repair					X		
Wages support and management						XX	XX
Trading				X		XX	XX
Financial							
Credit card						XX	XX
Consumer finances						XX	XX
Credit reporting						XX	XX
Merchant/investment banking				X		x	XX
Commercial banking						XX	XX
Leasing		XX				x	XX
Money management		XX		X		XX	XX
Reinsurance				X		X	XX

Table 10.4 continued

Industry	Denmark	Germany	Italy	Japan	Korea	Singapore	Sweden	Switzerland	UK	US
Information										
Information processing										XX
Custom software[3]									X	XX
Information/data									X	XX
Transport										
Air cargo										X
Airport terminal		X						X	X	
Shipping	X	X		X				X		
Port services						X	X			
Ship repair						X				
Logistics management								X		
Service stations									X	X

XX = leading position.
X = position.
1 Excludes tourism attracted to a nation.
2 National positions in engineering tend to be in different types of projects.
3 France also had a significant position in custom software.
Source: Porter, 1990.

variables broadly corresponds to those which help to make both for the competitiveness of the MNEs or potential MNEs of a particular country, and for an attractive location for value-added activities by foreign based service MNEs.

The internalization advantages of firms

As a broad generalization, the transaction costs of using the market, compared with the hierarchical route of exchanging intermediate services, are likely to be higher than in the case of goods. The reasons are sixfold:

1 Most services contain a larger element of customer tailoring than do goods, and they are more idiosyncratic.
2 Since there is generally a greater human element in their production, their quality is likely to vary much more than that of goods (e.g. one can process chemicals or attach electronic components to a printed circuit board almost entirely by automation, but the pure service element attached to the dental consultation, a university seminar, a restaurant meal, or a shipping cruise may vary on each occasion).
3 Until very recently, at least, a major proportion of the information provided and the certain knowledge and experience connected with interpreting and evaluating the information was tacit and non-codifiable.
4 Due to (3) above, and the fact that information or knowledge related to service activities may be inexpensive to replicate, the possibility of abuse or dissipation of that knowledge is a real threat to the firm possessing it.
5 Since markets for many services are highly segmented, the opportunities for price discrimination, which can be best exploited by hierarchies, are considerable.
6 The control of some service activities may be perceived to be a crucial element in the success of non-service producing companies. For example, some shipping lines may be owned by manufacturers to ensure delivery of goods on time, while the prosperity of large retail outlets may be dependent upon the expertise and goodwill of their buyers of foreign goods.

Together with the fact that many services are impossible or difficult to trade over space, the above reasons explain both the presence and the rapid growth of MNE activity in this sector. As suggested earlier, both people and firms tend to spend more on services as incomes rise, while technology, information, business, professional and financial services, software facilities and repair and maintenance services are becoming an increasingly important component in the value-adding process of a wide range of goods. Some non-service firms are becoming increasingly involved in service activities (examples include large petroleum MNEs diversifying into banking, and computer hardware companies into the provision of software);[24] and new specialized service companies are being set up as the provision of some services becomes more complex. All of these trends are making for an intensification of international activity in its varied forms.

Some recent changes in the organizational strategies of MNEs

There have been forces making for both more FDI and cross-border collaborative alliances in services over the past decade or so. Foremost among the former has been the deregulation of national markets and the liberalization of policies towards trade and inward MNE activity. Up to now this has most noticeably occurred in the airline, financial, insurance and telecommunication sectors; but, no less important, it has also impinged on the location and organization of some service intensive goods sectors, e.g. health care products.[25]

The second factor has been the dramatic developments in the technology and management of information collection, handling and storage (for example, system integration services, facilities management, remote computing services) and of data transmission (for example, satellite and optic cables). By reducing the cost of co-ordinating decision making across national boundaries, these technological advances have tended to increase the scope for, and advantages of, centralized control (Sauvant, 1986). This can be seen in such service industries as engineering and project control (through the increased use of computer-aided design and graphic systems) and in banking, insurance, airline reservation systems and hotel room bookings. Some excellent examples of the ways in which this is being achieved are given by Feketekuty and Hauser (1985).

At the same time, service firms have been increasingly prompted to conclude cross-border joint ventures or collaborative non-equity arrangements. Four main reasons may be cited. The first is the increasing specialization among suppliers of finance capital, information and people-related services (e.g. employment agencies). When considered alongside the maturation of some kinds of intermediate services and the increasing ability of sellers to exercise control over their proprietary rights without ownership over them, firms in such diverse industries as hotels, telecommunications and international construction are increasingly opting for technical service agreements, management contracts or franchises as an organizational mode to maximize the returns on their competitive advantages, while minimizing their resource commitments. Second, as economic development proceeds, the necessary indigenous infrastructure required by foreign MNEs in the service sector to conclude service related joint ventures or strategic alliances improves as well.

The third reason is that the assets required to provide some services – and particularly those which are data intensive – are either too costly or require different skills and technology which no one firm can hope to fully possess. Because of this, there is an increasing tendency for the more information or technology intensive firms to merge, or collaborate, on particular projects. Some examples are given in UNCTC (1988), Porter (1986) and Contractor and Lorange (1988). About 17 per cent of some 839 agreements concluded between 1975 and 1986 were in the telecommunications sector (Hergert and Morris, 1988). Cross-border acquisitions and mergers have been particularly marked in the insurance and advertising sectors (UNCTC, 1988). Examples of consortia of firms include the setting up of the Society for Worldwide Inter-bank Financial Telecommunication (SWIFT) in 1973 as in international clearing system for the banking sector and the development of various public data networks. Another is the formation of SC International, an alliance of accounting firms of various nationalities based in London. Such cooperative arrangements help their participants to reduce risks while capturing the advantages of joint information and technological synergies.

The fourth reason (and this is the same as the second reason making more direct investment) is the reduction in cross-border market failure brought about by improved communication facilities. The hypothesis here is that this could ease the possibility of non-equity arrangements for specific projects, even though improved data flows could encourage more equity involvement by large and diversified TNCs pursuing global strategies.

Some illustrations

To conclude this section, Table 10.5 gives some illustrations of the kind to OLI variables likely to determine the extent and form of international production in a number of business-related service sectors.

Table 10.5 Illustrations of ownership, location and internationalization advantages relevant to the activities of transnational corporations i
selected service industries

Industry	Ownership (competitive advantages)	Location (configuration advantages)	Internalization (coordinating advantages)	Foreign presence index* (United States data)	Organizational form
Accounting/ auditing	Access to transnational clients	On-the-spot contact with clients	Limited interfirm linkages	High (92 per cent) Little intrafirm trade	Mostly partnerships or individual proprietorships
	Experience of standards required Brand image of leading accounting firms	Accounting tends to be culture-sensitive Adaptation to local reporting standards and procedures Oligopolistic interaction	Quality control over (international) standards Government insistence on local participation		Overseas subsidiaries loosely organized, little centralized control Few joint ventures
Advertising	Favored access to markets (subsidiaries of clients in home markets) Creative ability; image and philosophy Goodwill Full range of services Some economies of coordination Financial strength	On-the-spot contact with clients Adaptation to local tastes, languages Need to be close to mass media Import restrictions on foreign commercials	Quality control over advertising copy Need for local input National regulations Globalization of advertising-intensive products To reduce transaction costs with foreign agencies	High (85 per cent) Some intrafirm trade	Mainly 100 per cent; some joint ventures; limited non-equity arrangements

Commercial banking/ financial services	Access to transnational clients, foreigners abroad Professional expertise Access to international capital and financial markets Economies of size and scope Intrinsic value of reserve currencies Control over trans-border data/communication networks	Person-to-person contact required Government regulations High-value activities often centralized Lower costs of foreign operations Psychic distance	Quality control Economies of scope Economies of coordinating capital flows Importance of international arbitraging	High (virtually 100 per cent) Some intrafirm trade in information and finance capital	Mostly branches or subsidiaries, some agencies Some joint ventures, notably, where governments insist Some consortia
Computer software/ data processing	Linked to computer hardware Highly technology- or information-intensive Economies of scope Government support	Location of high skills and agglomerative economies often favors home country Government incentives to encourage offshore data entry	Idiosyncratic knowhow; need for protection against dissipation Quality control Coordinating gains		
Engineering, architecture, surveying services	Experience in home and other foreign markets Economies of size and specialization Economies of scope/ co-ordination	Customization to local tastes and needs Need for on-the-spot contact with customers and related producers	Joint ventures to gain local experience and expertise Quality control Knowledge often very idiosyncratic and tacit	Fairly high (75 per cent) Substantial intrafirm trade (in technology and management skills)	Mixture, but often professional partnerships Some licensing

Table 10.5 continued

Industry	Ownership (competitive advantages)	Location (configuration advantages)	Internalization (coordinating advantages)	Foreign presence index* (United States data)	Organizational form
Information services: data transmission	Highly capital- and human skill-intensive Sometimes tied to provision of hardware Considerable economies of scope and scale Quality of end product/services provided	Varies according to type of information being sold and transmission facilities between countries Where people-based clients may visit home country or firms supplying services in client's countries News agencies are location-bound, i.e. where the news is	In case of core assets, need for protection from dissipation Quality control Substantial gains from internalizing markets, to capture externalities of information transactions Cognitive market failure, asymmetry of knowledge	Balanced (50 per cent) Some intrafirm	Mixture, but 100 per cent where market failure pronounced
Insurance	Reputation of insurer; image (Lloyd's of London) Economies of scale and scope and, sometimes, specialized expertise (e.g. marine insurance) Access to transnational clients	Need to be in close touch with insured (e.g. life insurance) and related services (shipping finance) Oligopolistic strategies among large insurers Governments prohibit direct imports; regulatory provisions Economies of concentration (or reinsurance)	Economies of portfolio risk spreading Tacit knowledge Need for sharing or large-scale risks (reinsurance syndication) Government requirements for local equity participation	High (78 per cent) Some intrafirm trade	Mixture; strongly influenced by governments, types of insurance and companies

Investment banking (brokerage)	Reputation and professional skills (an 'experience' service) Substantial capital base Knowledge of and interaction with international capital markets Financial innovations	Need to be close to clients Need to be close to international capital/finance markets, and main competitors Availability of skilled labor	Complex and organic character of services provided Protection against exchange/political risks Need to pursue global investment strategy Quality control	High (84 per cent) A lot of intrafirm trade in form of control/coordination from headquarters	Mainly via 100 per cent subsidiaries
Legal services	Access to transnational clients and knowledge of their particular needs Experience and reputation	Need for face-to-face contact with clients Foreign customers may purchase services in home country Need to interact with other local services Restrictions on use of foreign barristers in courts Extent of local infrastructure	Many transactions are highly idiosyncratic and customer-specific Quality control Need for understanding of local customers and legal procedures	Low (2 per cent) (mainly because trade in legal services is people-embodied)	Some overseas partnerships, but often services are provided via movement of people (clients to home country lawyers or vice versa)
Management, consultants and public relations	Access to market Reputation, image, experience Economies of specialization, in particular, levels of expertise etc., skills, countries	Close contact with client; the provision is usually highly customer-specific TNC clients might deal with headquarters Mobility of personnel	Quality control, fear of underperformance by licensee Knowledge sometimes very confidential and usually idiosyncratic Personnel coordinating advantages	Balanced (55 per cent) Some intrafirm trade headquarters often coordinates assignments	Mostly partnerships or 100 per cent subsidiaries A lot of movement of people

Table 10.5 continued

Industry	Ownership (competitive advantages)	Location (configuration advantages)	Internalization (coordinating advantages)	Foreign presence index* (United States data)	Organizational form
Medical services	Experience with advanced/specialized medicine; high-quality hospitalization Modern management practices Supportive role of government	Usually consumers travel to place of production, but also to some foreign owned hospitals or medical facilities	Quality control	Favors exports (39 per cent) Little intrafirm trade	A people-oriented sector; overseas operations, mainly 100 per cent owned subsidiaries
Telecommunications	Knowledge-intensive Technology, capital-scale economies (e.g. ability to operate an international communications network) Government support	Government regulation of trade and production Sometimes location-bound (telephone communications)	Large costs often require consortia of firms Quality of goods part of service often needs hierarchical control (e.g. by companies like AT&T); otherwise service usually provided on leasing basis, or exported	Balanced (50 per cent) Some intrafirm trade	Mixture, but a good deal of leasing

*The percentage in brackets represents the proportion of sales of United States exports plus sales of foreign affiliates to United States exports plus sales of United States foreign affiliates to United States exports plus sales of foreign affiliates, as reported by United States, Office of Technology Assessment (1986), *Trade in Services: Exports and Foreign Reserves*, Washington, DC: Government Printing Office.

Source: Dunning, 1989.

To these OLI variables it would be desirable to add a set of strategic related variable(s), the purpose of which would be to identify the major kinds of behavioral response which firms might be expected to adopt to the OLI variables within each of the sectors.

As already indicated, very little work has been done on this subject by business analysts. However, a reading of some of the literature on particular service sectors suggests that the main areas of strategic choice are in the areas of (a) innovation, e.g. is the firm a leader or a follower; and if the former, what form does the innovation take?, (b) product quality and range, e.g. is the firm aiming for high quality and/ or diversified services or does it prefer to specialize in a limited range of differentiated or standardized services?, (c) markets to be targeted, e.g. niche or general markets, foreign or domestic and, if the former, which foreign markets, and (d) the extent to which a firm chooses to produce both goods and services, or to be a specialist service producer.

Technological events of the 1980s suggest that service firms are becoming more specialized in their final outputs, but are also engaging in strategic businss alliances with other service firms and goods producers along a particular value-added chain. In other words, they are repackaging their portfolio of activities. The larger service companies are also becoming increasingly international-ized. This is especially so in those sectors where globalization brings its own competitive advantages. Perhaps the most obvious examples are investment banking and finance and currency, accounting, advertising and management consultancy, reinsurance, hotels,[26] car rentals, and arbitrage related operations, where all the major players are large MNEs, many of which have extensive webs of foreign affiliates and cooperative arrangements with foreign firms. We have also suggested that an increasing number of cross-border service investments – particularly within the Triad – are being made to acquire or sustain competitive advantages. Examples include some recent A&Ms in the accounting, advertising and hotel sectors, and alliances in the airline, construction and the telecommunication sectors.

Finally, we would emphasize the growing interdependence between the services and goods sectors. Not only is the service intensity of the production of goods rising, but the cost and quality of external services bought by both goods and service producing firms are becoming an increasingly important determinant of the competi-tiveness of such firms. Moreover, the linkages between service and goods producing activities are becoming more complex. The locational decisions of manufacturing MNEs are frequently strongly influenced by the quality of transport, telecommunication and educational services. The competitive advantages of firms supplying durable consumer goods are becoming increasingly dependent on the extent to which the goods require after-sales maintenance and repair and the likely cost of such services.

Because of these and other interdependencies, it makes little sense to try to develop a new paradigm to explain the transnationality of the services sector. At the same time, the growing service intensity of FDI and cross-border collaborative alliances is inevitably requiring some modifications to the existing explanations of this phenomenon. This is simply because the OLI configuration facing service producing firms, and possible strategic responses to that configuration, is likely to be different to that facing goods producing firms, as indeed it is likely to vary between particular service producing sectors.

PARTIAL THEORIES AND FDI IN SERVICES

Introduction

We have suggested that, to explain particular kinds of international production in services, more specific explanations than those offered by either the internalization or eclectic paradigm may be in order. Alternatively, it is possible that groups of different kinds of service activities have common features, which may be explained by a one or a small number of variables.

The literature reveals that in service sectors, there may be very different motivations for foreign production in goods producing sectors.[27] We have also asserted that the growth of existing foreign value activities in services might require a different set of explanations than that of initial decision to invest abroad. To conclude this chapter, we briefly review some of the specific or partial theories which were initially put forward to explain FDI in the goods sector, and consider their applicability to explaining service related MNE activity.

The product cycle theory

The product cycle theory, originally propounded by Vernon (Vernon, 1966), purported to explain why particular competitive advantages possessed by MNEs or potential MNEs originated in one country rather than another, and how these advantages tended to be exploited first by domestic production for the home market, then by exports and finally by FDI. The theory was essentially put forward to explain US direct investment in import substituting manufacturing activities in countries which were a step or more behind the US in living standards and economic structure. It was also largely confined to identifying the O specific advantages of firms which supplied particular products, or engaged in particular production processes, and had little to say about the advantages of common governance or of transnationality *per se*. It was, therefore, more useful in explaining the entry of MNEs into certain foreign countries than the subsequent growth of such firms.

We would suggest that the product cycle theory is helpful in pinpointing some of the reasons for the early foreign involvement of some service MNEs in such areas as commercial banking, advertising, market research, public relations, management consultancy, insurance, industrial laundering, design services, hotels and fast food, whose initial competitive advantages strongly reflected the economic and cultural environment of their home countries, and which set up foreign producing facilities after having first serviced the domestic market. However, in cases where services – particularly consumer services – are location bound, the theory adds little to the reasons for the entry of foreign firms into these sectors.

The theory is also useful in explaining the initial destination of FDI, and the kind of customer served by it, by reference to the similarities between the economies of the capital-exporting and the capital-importing countries. At the same time, it sheds little light on the extent to which non-service MNEs might wish to engage in service activities, or why some service MNEs are, themselves, diversified. Neither does it help explain the growth of two way (i.e. inward and outward investment) in such service industries as banking, hotels, air transport and business services.

The core-asset theories

Following Hymer's (1976) theory of FDI, which purported to explain the territorial expansion of a firm in terms of its exclusive or privileged possession of intangible assets, which, it perceived, could best be utilized in a foreign country, several writers have tried to identify *which* O specific rights were the most significant in determining the ability of MNEs to compete in foreign markets. To Johnson (Johnson, 1970) and Magee (Magee, 1977), the critical asset was technology or knowledge; to Caves (Caves, 1974), in the consumer goods sector at least, it was the ability of firms to differentiate their products by quality or variety, and to create a distinctive brand image or trademark. As in Vernon's theory, the ownership of these advantages, though specific to particular enterprises, was thought to reflect the resource endowments and/or markets of the home countries of the investing firms. Both theories were largely applied to explaining the share of foreign affiliates (and mainly US affiliates) of the output of different *manufacturing* sectors in particular countries, and both were upheld to a point (UNCTC, 1988; Dunning, 1988).

These theories also have some relevance to explaining the role of foreign service companies in some market-seeking sectors and, unlike the product cycle theory, in some resource-based industries. The proposition is that the share of local production of foreign affiliates is likely to be greatest in technology on information-intensive service sectors, and in those in which the importance of the firm's reputation (in this case, by attaching its own name to the services it supplies, rather than that of a particular product) is regarded as a major selling point by customers. Examples in the first case include US investment in the European software, advertising, industrial laundering, accounting and business consultancy industries and, in the second, US and European investment in top quality tourist hotels in the Caribbean or business hotels in Europe and South-East Asia.

However, these theories pay little attention to the locational decisions of MNEs or the 'where' of FDI, and they underestimate the importance of the organizational mechanism by which the competitive advantages are exploited. Neither do they explain why the extent of MNE activity in a particular sector varies between individual MNEs, or why, in spite of their technological advantages or ability to differentiate products, some firms fail to become successful MNEs. For these reasons, they are only of a limited use in explaining the growth of MNEs in globally oriented and integrated service industries.

Strategy related the theories

The first systematic attempt to examine the strategy of MNEs was that of Knickerbocker (1973).[28] Knickerbocker hypothesized that MNE activity would tend to be concentrated in industries characterized by high seller concentration, and that firms in those industries will engage in 'follow my leader' tactics in the timing of their foreign investments, to protect or advance their global competitive positions. Widespread evidence in support of this thesis is to be found in the investment patterns of MNEs in the oil, motor vehicle, pharmaceutical, semi-conductor, consumer electronics and rubber-tire industries.

In general, it might be supposed that this thesis is less relevant to explaining MNE activity in services since the market structure of most service sectors is less oligopolistic (UNCTC, 1988; Dunning, 1993). But, increasingly the Knickerbocker thesis and the related exchange-of-threat hypothesis (Flowers, 1976; Graham, 1978) are gaining credence in such industries as airlines, international banking, hotels (at least in major business conurbations), car-rental, life and marine insurance, credit card, money management, industrial leasing, accounting, market research, advertising, architectural and consultant engineering, and particularly insofar as they help explain the nationality and location of FDI. It is also more successful than the theories previously discussed in analyzing particular FDI decisions of MNEs as part of an integrated international strategy.

However, strategy related theories are less comfortable in dealing with the different modalities of foreign involvement, and with the growing diversification of service companies outside their main areas of activity. Neither can they explain changes in the market share of the leading MNEs, nor the emergence of new MNEs in the service sector (for example, the entry of the Japanese in banking and securities management). In short, they may be usefully applied to explaining some of the strategies of MNEs in service sectors, but they cannot explain either the origin of competitive advantages of MNEs, nor the reasons for much of the changing locational pattern of MNE service activity in recent years.

The risk diversification hypothesis

The idea put forward by Rugman (1979), following a classic article by Grubel (1968), that firms seek to diversify their direct investment portfolio among countries to avoid or minimize risks appears less relevant in explaining MNE activity in services as, for the most part, such activity is not capital intensive. Exceptions might include risks underwritten by the foreign affiliates of insurance companies and the international debt profiles of the large transnational banks. Those hotels which purchase the properties they manage in foreign countries might also be expected to relate new asset portfolios to their existing portfolios. Similarly, engineering and construction companies may not wish to tie up too much of their working capital in projects located in the same country or group of countries. As Rugman himself accepts, however, this approach to understanding MNE activity can be well encompassed in a more general theory of international production, particularly in his view, in the internalization paradigm (Rugman, 1981).

The Aliber thesis

Aliber's (Aliber, 1970, 1971) interest in foreign direct investment theory is not why firms produce abroad, but why they pay for their foreign assets in their domestic currencies. This he explains in terms of the ability of firms from countries with strong currencies to raise capital more cheaply abroad than can those from countries with weak currencies, and the different rates at which the two groups of firms capitalize their expected income streams. Aliber further argues that disequilibrium in the foreign exchange market allows firms to make foreign exchange gains through the purchase or sales of assets in an undervalued or overvalued currency.

Since the Aliber thesis is likely to be of most relevance in explaining MNE investment in capital-intensive sectors, it has little applicability for much of service based FDI. However, since some service industries, such as telecommunications, real estate (including hotels) and most transportation services, are highly capital-intensive, it is in those industries, and in others where an acquisition of existing assets is perceived the best modality of entry into foreign markets, that the Aliber thesis might be of some validity. An analysis of the timing of the acquisition of US service companies (noticeably in retailing, hotels and insurance) by UK MNEs in the last 10 years lends partial support to the idea that such FDI will occur when the pound sterling is strong relative to the dollar, and when the price of US stocks is low relative to their replacement costs. But, so far, there has been no systematic testing of the Aliber hypothesis. Thus, the extent to which it is a powerful explanation of at least some kind of service investment by MNEs remains unknown.

The Kojima thesis

Kojima, in a number of contributions (for example, Kojima, 1978, 1982, 1990) argues that countries should undertake outward direct investment in industries which employ resources in which they are comparatively disadvantaged (or becoming less advantaged), while encouraging inward direct investment in those industries which require resources in which it is comparatively advantaged (or becoming less disadvantaged). To that extent, Kojima's theory is a normative rather than a positive one.

Since there is only a limited amount of service investment by

Japanese companies outside trade, finance and tourism, it is not really possible to test the applicability of Kojima's thesis to this sector.[29] But, since exports and FDI are not really alternative modes of foreign involvement in many service industries and, in others, service activities support trade and investment by non-service companies, one must doubt the relevance of the Kojima approach.

However, it is clear that, while some service investments, like manufacturing investments, do seek to take account of differences in natural resource endowments between countries (for example, in trade, tourism, shipping, construction, some kinds of insurance, professional and personal services), others (for example, investment banking, reinsurance and information-intensive services) follow the pattern of their manufacturing counterparts, which aim more to exploit the benefits of common governance and economies of scale across national boundaries than the differential costs of factor endowments. It is in those industries in which intra*firm* trade is greatest and where the Kojima theory is at its weakest. And it is inadequate because Kojima down-plays the importance of the organization of cross-border transactions as an explanation of MNE activity and particularly the transition of such activity from being ethno- or geo-centric to being poly-centric in its governance.

Kogut's sequential theory

Bruce Kogut (Kogut, 1983, 1987; Kogut and Kulatilaha, 1988) has suggested that established MNEs tend to be influenced by different variables in their international production decisions than *de novo* foreign investors. While the latter are likely to behave in a way predicted by the product cycle or core assets theories (the exception is where firms engage in cross-border investment to acquire a competitive advantage), the former are more likely to look for OLI advantages resulting from multinationality *per se*. Kogut describes these as those to do with reducing or spreading environmental volatility, capitalizing on differences in country-specific, created and acquired factor endowments and demand.

The Kogut hypothesis seems to hold up well in explaining the growth of investments of the more capital- or information-intensive sectors (notably financial services, reinsurance and certain types of consultancy); or those producing fairly standardized services, which can readily be adapted to meet local needs (e.g. hotels); and those whose logistical management needs to be integrated at a regional or global level (e.g. airlines).

CONCLUSIONS

While the partial theories of FDI and international production may be relevant to explaining some kinds of service activity by MNEs, we believe that only a generalized paradigm, such as that outlined in an earlier section of this chapter, can provide an adequate analytical framework for examining all kinds of MNE service activities. In particular the chapter has sought to show how the eclectic paradigm might be used to identify and evaluate the main O specific advantages of firms providing services, the way in which those advantages might best be used to advance the strategic goals of MNEs, and the reasons why, at least for some, value-added activities, necessary to create, or to utilize, those advantages are best undertaken in a foreign location.

The chapter has also identified some of the reasons for the growth of international production in services over the last two decades and, in particular, why FDI has been the preferred route for organizing cross-border activities involving services. Special attention has been addressed to the increasing need of firms, both in service and non-service sectors, to integrate their domestic activities with services obtained from, or sold to, foreign countries. Some emphasis has also been given to the fact that, over recent years, both demand and supply-led forces have intensified the advantages of common governance for providing a variety of services. Moreover, new opportunities for industrial and geographical diversification have created their own locational and ownership advantages which have strengthened the position of MNEs in an increasing number of service industries. That trend is likely to continue throughout the 1990s, assuming that governments do not impose substantial new restrictions on trade and investment in services and service-related activities.

Finally, we would suggest three possible directions for further research on the theory of MNE service related activity. The first is on the interaction between the production of services and that of goods, and the implication of such interaction for the configuration and coordination of value-added activities. The second relates to the strategies of service producing firms. The third is to identify and evaluate the competitive advantages of countries in service producing activities, and the ways in which governments, directly or indirectly, may help their own firms to improve their international competitive position and to attract more service-type investment by foreign companies to their shores.

11 International direct investment patterns in the 1990s

INTRODUCTION

We begin this chapter on an optimistic note. This last decade of the twentieth century promises to offer more opportunities and challenges for cross-border direct investments and cooperative ventures than any of the others which preceded it. Indeed, the 1990s may well see the maturing of the global economy, the emergence of which began in the 1960s, faltered in the 1970s, and was resuscitated in the 1980s.

At the very heart of our optimism lies the renaissance of the international market economy, and the positive role which both multinational enterprises (MNEs) and national governments can play in facilitating and using this tried and tested mechanism to create sustainable and balanced economic development, and in a way which is both humanly acceptable, culturally sensitive and environmentally friendly.

Our optimism is, however, qualified and guarded. There are several clouds on the global political-economic horizon. Three, in particular may be identified. First, the recent conflict and current unrest in the Middle East and parts of Central and Eastern Europe forcibly reminds us how fragile and volatile our progress towards international accord is, and that how, in spite of man's ability to devise new ways of creating and sustaining material prosperity, differences in political systems, values and ideologies can so easily tear our modern economic fabric to shreds.

Second, less dramatic, but of no less long-term economic significance, is the danger that the world may become divided into a number of regional fortresses or trading blocs and that national protectionism, so damaging to the world economy in the 1920s and 1930s will be replaced by regional protectionism in the 1990s. In

particular, the doubtful future of the current round of GATT negotiations could well set up the stage for a round of beggar my neighbor
trade restrictions reminiscent of the inter-war years. But this time the
potential damage to the globalization of production by MNEs could
be even more devastating.

Third, we have considerable reservations on both the ability or
willingness of governments and wealth-creating institutions to wisely
handle the kind of freedom and power which the unfettered market
economy offers. One Cambridge economist (Eastwell, 1982) has
written 'the market is an excellent servant, but a ruthless master'. The
nineteenth and twentieth centuries were replete with examples of the
market dominating, rather than being dominated by, the majority of
mankind; and there was a perfectly natural reaction – particularly by
those most adversely affected by its imperfections – for it to be
controlled or replaced by (what was perceived to be) a more bene-
volent and equitable system of organizing the world's resources and
capabilities. But one man's gain is often another's loss; and if the
losers happen also to be the wealth creators, in the end, no one is
better off – although to be sure, misery is more equally shared! Now
the market mechanism has been given a powerful new lease of life.
One can only but hope that some of the lessons of the past have been
learned; and we can recognize that, in our modern, economically
interdependent, technologically complex and environmentally sensitive world, national governments *do* have a *critical* role to play –
albeit a very different one from that perceived by earlier socialist
regimes in the way in which markets are organized and wealth is
created and distributed. Even one of the arch-priests of the free
enterprise system – The World Bank – has written in the World
Development Report of 1991, 'governments and markets should pull
together to create and sustain a "market friendly" strategy for development'.

But before considering some of these issues in more detail, let us
recite some of the emerging trends in international direct investment
and MNE activity.

THE CURRENT STATE OF FOREIGN DIRECT INVESTMENT (FDI) AND MNE ACTIVITY

A report prepared by the UNCTC in 1992 estimated the world stock
of FDI to have reached $1.7 trillion by the end of 1990 (UNCTC,
1992b). Since 1983, direct investment outflows have increased at the
unprecedented compound annual rate of 29 per cent a year, three

times faster than that of the growth of exports (at 9.4 per cent) and four times that of the growth of world output (7.8 per cent) (UNCTC, 1991a).

There can be no question that MNEs are not only assuming an increasingly important and pluralistic role in the global economy, but that, in the early 1990s, they are one of the principal engines of its growth and development (UNCTC, 1992b). Such an engine is fuelled not just by the cross-border transfer of finance capital, technology and management capabilities, but also by the way in which MNEs, by their hierarchical control, and product marketing and sourcing strategies, influence economic integration and the international division of labor, and by their entrepreneurship, provide an impetus for the efficient restructuring of national economies. For example, MNEs not only account for 80 per cent of the private R&D expenditure in the world; they are also directly or indirectly responsible for about the same proportion of world trade.

Table 11.1 sets out some data on the growth and geographical composition of the stock of outward direct investment. Two things are particularly worthy of note. These are, first, the growing importance of FDI in relation to the gross domestic product (GDP) and gross fixed capital formation (GFCF) of almost all capital exporting countries, and particularly that of Germany, Japan and the UK. The data also suggest that foreign-based MNE activities are now less subject to cyclical fluctuations than they used to be.[1] The second is the widening participation of source countries. Most dramatically, the share of the world's international direct capital stake accounted for by the US fell from 50.4 per cent in 1967 to 25.9 per cent in 1990; while the combined contribution of Germany and Japan rose from 4.0 per cent to 21.6 per cent. International Monetary Fund data on investment flows since that date confirm these trends. They suggest that Japan has now assumed the role of the world's leading outward direct investor, followed by the UK and the US,[2] and that MNEs from developing countries are now accounting for about 5 per cent of all new FDI (compared with only 1 per cent in the early 1980s).

Table 11.2 sets out the geographical distribution of the FDI stake by recipient countries. It should be noted that, for a variety of statistical reporting reasons, the figures on the stocks of outward and inward investments are not the same. We would make just four observations. First, paralleling the date of Table 11.1, FDI has become a more important ingredient of GDP of most recipient countries over the past three decades. Second, in spite of the shift of interest by outward investors away from developing towards developed

Table 11.1 Stocks of outward FDI, by major home country and regions 1967–1990 (billions of US dollars)

Countries/regions	1967			1973			1980			1990		
	Value	% of total	% of GDP	Value	% of total	% of GDP	Value	% of total	% of GDP	Value	% of total	% of GDP
Developed market economies	109.3	97.3	4.8	205.0	97.1	5.1	503.6	97.2	6.2	1593.0	95.7	9.8
United States	56.6	50.4	7.1	101.3	48.0	7.7	220.2	40.0	8.2	426.5	25.6	7.9
United Kingdom	15.8	14.1	14.5	27.5	13.0	9.1	79.2	14.8	15.2	244.8	14.7	25.1
Japan	1.5	1.3	0.9	10.3	4.9	2.5	19.6	6.6	3.4	201.4	12.1	6.8
Germany (FDR)	3.0	2.7	1.6	11.9	5.6	3.4	43.1	7.8	5.3	155.1	9.3	10.4
Switzerland	2.5	2.2	10.0	7.1	3.4	16.2	22.4	7.0	37.9	64.9	3.9	28.8
Netherlands	11.0	9.8	33.1	15.8	7.5	25.8	42.4	7.6	24.7	99.2	5.9	35.5
Canada	3.7	3.3	5.3	7.8	3.7	6.1	21.6	3.9	8.2	74.7	4.5	13.1
France	6.0	5.3	7.0	8.8	4.2	3.8	20.8	3.8	3.2	114.8	6.9	9.6
Italy	2.1	1.9	2.8	3.2	1.5	2.4	7.0	1.3	1.8	60.0	3.6	5.5
Sweden	1.7	1.5	5.7	3.0	1.4	6.1	7.2	1.3	5.8	50.7	3.0	22.2
Other*	5.4	4.8	0.8	20.0	9.5	1.7	15.4	3.2	1.9	78.3	4.8	4.3
Developing countries	3.0	2.7	0.6	6.1	2.9	0.6	13.3	2.8	0.7	51.2	3.1	1.2
Total	112.3	100.0	4.0	211.1	100.0	4.2	516.9	100.0	4.9	1644.2	100.0	8.0

*Australia, Austria, Belgium, Denmark, Finland, Greece, Ireland, New Zealand, Norway, Portugal, South Africa, Spain.
Sources: Rutter, 1992; UN, 1992c and 1993; Dunning and Cantwell, 1987; and World Bank (various editions).

countries – and this continued in 1991 and 1992 – the relative contribution of inward investment to GDP continues to be more significant in the case of developing countries. Other data suggest that, in 10 developing countries, such investment now accounts for more than 10 per cent of domestic gross capital formation, whereas, in the developed world, only in the UK, The Netherlands, Greece, Spain, Australia and Belgium is it more than 5 per cent.

Third, there has been a noticeable shift of interest by multinational investors within the Third World. East and South Asia and mainland China have been the main gainers, and Latin America, the Caribbean and most African countries the main losers. It is also an unfortunate fact that the share of new inward investment directed towards the poorest developing countries has fallen over the last decade.

A fourth observation on Table 11.2 is the emergence of the US as the leading recipient of foreign MNE activity. To repeat but one set of figures given in Chapter 7: in 1972, US firms had nearly three times as much invested in the 9-member countries of the EC than did EC firms have invested in the US; by 1990, EC firms had 25 per cent more invested in the US than American firms had invested in the EC. And this is in spite of the fact that, in preparation for Europe 1992, US firms (like their Japanese counterparts) have considerably stepped up their pace of new investment since the mid-1980s. Indeed, plans for capital expenditure by US foreign affiliates show that EC countries are expected to account for one-half of the total foreign plant and equipment expenditure of US firms in 1991 and 1992, compared with 38.5 per cent in 1985 and 24.2 per cent in 1972.

It is, however, the Japanese MNEs which are stepping up their investments in Europe at the most remarkable rate, although there is some suggestion that the pace of new investment, particularly in the banking and finance sector is decelerating. The stock of new investment approvals rose from $3.5 billion in 1985/6 to $14.8 billion in 1989/90 before falling back to $9.4 billion in 1991/2.[3] About one-fifth of all new Japanese outward investment is curently going to Europe, compared with less than 10 per cent in the mid-1980s. All the same, the US remains the most favored destination of Japanese MNEs, and over the five years concluding in March 1992, attracted between 40 and 50 per cent of all inward foreign investment.

These data, of course, tell us nothing about one of the most momentous developments of the last few years, viz. the opening up of Central and Eastern Europe to FDI. As described in Chapter 9, by the end of the second quarter of 1991, there were over 25,000

Table 11.2 Stocks of inward FDI, by major host countries and regions 1967–1990 (billions of US dollars)

Countries/regions	1967			1973			1980			1990		
	Value	% of total	% of GDP	Value	% of total	% of GDP	Value	% of total	% of GDP	Value	% of total	% of GDP
Developed market economies	73.2	69.4	3.2	153.7	74.0	3.8	394.1	78.0	4.7	1328.9	81.2	8.1
Western Europe	31.4	29.8	4.2	79.9	38.4	5.6	211.6	42.0	4.8	726.3	44.3	10.6
United Kingdom	7.9	7.5	7.2	24.1	11.6	13.9	63.0	12.5	12.0	205.6	12.5	21.2
Germany	3.6	3.4	1.9	13.1	6.3	3.8	47.9	9.5	5.8	132.5	8.1	8.9
Switzerland	2.1	2.0	8.4	4.3	2.1	9.8	14.3	2.8	14.1	43.4	2.6	19.3
United States	9.9	9.3	1.2	20.6	9.9	1.6	83.0	16.4	3.2	396.7	24.2	7.3
Other*	31.9	30.2	4.2	53.2	25.6	4.2	99.5	19.7	6.5	205.9	12.6	4.9
Japan	0.6	0.6	0.3	1.6	0.8	0.4	3.3	0.7	0.3	9.9	0.6	0.3
Developing countries	32.3	30.6	6.4	54.4	26.1	5.4	111.2	22.0	5.4	310.0	18.9	7.1
Africa	5.6	5.3	9.0	10.2	4.9	8.7	13.1	2.6	4.1	35.3	2.1	14.6
Asia	8.3	7.8	3.9	15.3	7.4	3.6	35.8	7.1	5.0	155.1	9.4	14.6
Latin America and the Caribbean	18.5	17.5	15.8	28.9	13.9	12.3	6.3	12.3	8.4	119.6	7.3	11.8
Total	105.5	100.0	3.8	208.1	100.0	4.1	505.3	100.0	4.7	1638.9	100.0	7.9

* Other developed – Australia, Canada, Japan, New Zealand, South Africa, Sub-saharan Africa, Algeria, Egypt, Tunisia, Morocco.
Sources: Rutter, 1992; UN, 1992c and 1993; Dunning and Cantwell, 1987; and World Bank (various editions).

registered joint ventures in this part of the world, with an estimated stock of nearly $9 billion. However, only about 10 per cent of these were active; it was reported in May 1991, for example, that just 140 of 1,500 joint ventures registered in the then Soviet Union had begun operations. As of mid-1991, in spite of the serious economic difficulties in most East European countries, there are signs of a considerable speeding up of new investment, especially in Hungary and Poland.[4] But in the foreseeable future, the most promising area of economic expansion is likely to be in the Eastern *Länder* of Germany; although since over nine-tenths of the 'outside' investment is likely to be undertaken by Western German firms, it will not be counted as FDI in the statistics.

Taking the data of Tables 11.1 and 11.2 together, one of the most remarkable features of the last decade has been the growing degree of internationalization of business and the extent to which countries are engaging in two-way investment. Within the Triad nations,[5] at least, patterns of the international production of firms are increasingly coming to resemble those of international trade. More and more, trade and foreign investment are complementing, rather than substituting for, each other. Increasingly, too, outward and inward investment are becoming more balanced. Of the leading industrial nations, only Japan has a large direct investment surplus with other countries. As of March 1990, the value of her cumulative foreign direct investments were 16 times those of investment by foreign MNEs in Japan. By contrast, at the end of 1990, the other five leading capital exporters – the US, UK, Germany, France and Italy – had, on average, only 20 per cent more invested abroad than they had invested in them.[6]

One final indicator of the globalization of economic activity is the fact that, on average, in 1989 the leading billion dollar industrial companies – that is, those with global sales of more than $1 billion, and which are believed to account for about four-fifths of all MNE activity – produced about one-third of their output from outside their home countries. This proportion also varied between countries. As might be expected, it was highest for MNEs from the smaller European countries, notably Belgium, Switzerland, The Netherlands and Sweden, and lowest for Japanese MNEs, where, with a few exceptions, less than 10 per cent of their world output was produced overseas. The fact that Japan is in an earlier stage of her internationalization strategy shows the great potential for Japanese MNE activity. To take just one example: of the goods and services produced by US owned firms and bought by UK consumers in 1990,

85 per cent were made by US subsidiaries in the UK, and the balance imported from the US. In the case of goods produced by Japanese firms and bought by UK consumers, these ratios were reversed, i.e. 15 per cent are manufactured by Japanese subsidiaries in the UK (or elsewhere in Europe) and the remainder were imported from Japan.

Once one gets away from FDI statistics, the data on the globalization of economic activity become very unsatisfactory. Only a dozen or so countries, for example, collect information on the foreign employment of their own MNEs, or on the employment of the foreign affiliates in their midst; and even fewer give any insight into the ownership structure of their firms. We do know, however, from US, Japanese and UK data, that the number of joint ventures has been expanding more rapidly than that of 100 per cent owned affiliates, and that small- and medium-size MNEs have recorded particularly impressive rates of growth. At the same time, as a percentage of the world-wide sales of MNEs, those accounted for by fully owned subsidiaries continue to rise. Partly, this reflects the corporate response to regional economic integration; partly, the fact that technological advances, particularly in areas like micro-electronics and biotechnology, are demanding a closer integration and coordination of value-added activities; and partly, the more relaxed attitude of many host governments to the non-residential ownership of their firms.

Closely allied to the expansion of joint ventures has been the rapid growth of cross-border non-equity cooperative alliances of one kind or another. Such alliances, though specific in purpose and limited, are no less a feature of globalization than is FDI. They number tens of thousands: they are most prevalent between large- and medium-size MNEs from the Triad; they tend to be concentrated in technologically advanced manufacturing- or information-intensive service sectors, and they are concluded both between firms engaged in similar activities and between firms producing at different stages of the same value-added chain. While the motives for alliances may vary, most are formed to capture the economies of scale or synergy, and to advance the competitive position of the participating firms (Gugler, 1991).

Why have cooperative agreements increased so rapidly in the last five or so years? Four reasons are commonly adduced. The first is the steeply escalating costs of R&D and the increasing rate of technological obsolescence; the second is the need of companies to share their core technologies in order to produce a new generation of products more speedily than can their competitors; the third is the intense competitive pressure to gain quick and efficient access to new and often unfamiliar markets; and the fourth is the need to sustain or advance a global competitive position in a turbulent and ever changing world economic environment.

Increasingly, as cross-border cooperative and competitive relationships are being intertwined, the boundaries of firms are becoming increasingly blurred; and the discrete and uni-dimensional transactional relationships between firms and their customers, suppliers and competitors are being replaced by multidimensional networks or systems of value-added activities. It is indeed the belief of many international business scholars, e.g. Ghoshal and Bartlett, Hedlund and Casson,[7] that the ability of firms to manage and organize a system of quite complex cross-border innovatory, production and transactional relations in one, both along and between value-added chains will become an increasingly important competitive advantage of MNEs in the 1990s and beyond.

This brings us to the question of the organization of MNE activity. Here – again mainly in response to technological advances (not least in information and communications technology) and the changing shape of the world economy – quite revolutionary changes are afoot. From being mainly a provider of resources and capabilities to its outlying affiliates, each of which operated more or less independently of each other, and then a coordinator of the way in which resources are used within a closely knit family of affiliates, the decision taking nexus of the MNE in the early 1990s has come to resemble the central nervous system of a much larger group of interdependent, but less formally governed, activities, the purpose of each of which is to advance the global competitive strategy of the organization into two. However, unlike the earlier mother–daughter relationship which existed between parent and subsidiary, the modern global corporation is better perceived as a heterarchy rather than a hierarchy. In the words of Bartlett, Doz and Hedlund (1990, p. 7) 'the organization of the genuinely global MNE is made up of a set of reciprocally interdependent and geographically dispersed centers, held together largely by shared strategies, norms and a multilateral channelling of experiences, information and resources'.

This new organizational form – which Hedlund and Rolander (1990) liken to a hologram – is having enormous implications for both the structure of MNE activities, and the way in which they impinge upon nation states. To discuss this further would take us beyond the scope of this chapter; suffice to underline the fact that purely statistical measures of MNE activity, e.g. sales, assets, employment, exports, etc., may well disguise qualitative contributions of MNEs, and how in the long run, their presence affects a particular country's economic well-being, and its relationships with the rest of the world. The whole question of the impact of inward direct investment on the upgrading of domestic technological capacity and human skills is, for example, intimately bound up with the global goals of the investing organization, and of how the MNE views the contribution of its foreign subsidiaries to the achievement of these goals.

In this compressed analysis of the recent trends in international direct investment, mention should also be made about the changing modality by which firms are engaging in their cross-border activity. Traditionally, the main form of investment entry has been the greenfield venture, and numerically, it still remains important today. However, the most dramatic development of the second half of the 1980s has been the growth of acquisition and mergers (A&Ms) as a means of entry into or expansion of MNE activity. This is particularly noticeable in the case of transatlantic investments, although, in the last two years, there have also been sizeable acquisitions of European by Japanese firms. We shall offer some reasons for this growth later in this chapter. For the moment, it is worth observing that, of the *new* capital outflows of MNEs, it is common for four-fifths to take the form of A&Ms.[8] In 1989 and 1990, even 40 per cent of the new investment by Japanese firms in the EC were of this form. By contrast, because of legal and institutional obstacles, there are very few permitted takeovers of Japanese firms by foreign investors.

Let us now summarize the main features of the recent movements and patterns in MNE activity.

1   It is assuming increasing importance in the employment, trade and output of most nation states and is taking on the role of both the leading engine of economic growth and the main chapter of the global market economy.

2   It is becoming more pluralistic in its origin, its geographical distribution, and its modality. In the last few years, FDI, as a form of international economic involvement, has been increasingly complemented by (and occasionally replaced by) a whole range of cooperative ventures. At the same time, the strategic acquisition of foreign assets and capabilities has become an increasingly important motive for the transnationalization of firms – and particularly among international oligopolists in high technology and capital-intensive sectors.

3   The cross-border organization of MNEs is becoming more

complex and interwoven. From being a federation of loosely knit and foreign production units designed primarily to serve the parent company with resources and manpower, or local markets with manufactured goods and services, the larger MNE is now increasingly assuming the role of an orchestrator of a variety of value-added activities within a cluster or network of cross-border internal and external relationships, each of which is intended to service its global strategic interests.

THE FUTURE PROSPECTS

Let us now turn to consider the prospects for MNE activity in the global economy of the 1990s.

Some assumptions about the future

To predict such a role in a world whose economic and political scenario is changing so rapidly, and often so unexpectedly, is a daunting task. However, without some assumptions about the course of future events – which only time will show are justifiable – it is impossible to make any progress at all.

Let us make three basic assumptions about the next decade or so – which, in a sense, are also forecasts! The first is that, while accepting that economic development in certain parts of the world, notably in East Asia and some Latin American countries, will proceed rapidly, the center of economic gravity will continue to rest with the Triad nations, whose interaction with each other, with neighboring territories and with the developing world will largely determine the future pace and direction of global economic progress.

The second assumption is that technological and organizational innovations will continue to shrink corporate and national boundaries, and yet, at the same time, force firms both to seek new markets, and to collaborate with each other in their value-added activities.

The third assumption is that the relationships between countries will continue to be dominated by the schizophrenic desire of governments to reap the benefits of economic interdependence while maintaining real political sovereignty. On balance, the world, as a whole, appears to be moving in the direction of a global village, but one in which national or regional cultures, ideologies and aspirations are likely to play a more decisive role.

Added to these three basic assumptions, two others might be offered which have especial implications for MNE activity. The first is that national governments in their policies towards both outward and inward MNE activity are likely to be increasingly influenced by the contribution of such activity to the competitiveness of the firms or industries, as all the signs are that the 1990s will be a decade of intense competition between countries for the world's supply of technological, financial and human resources. Second, we shall assume that some extra economic issues – notably the environment and national security – will play a more up-front role in the attitudes of both national governments and the international community towards MNE activity.

It is not difficult to identify the economic and political conditions under which international direct investment flourishes. Imagine the global economy as an extension of the individual nation state, and MNEs as an extension of national firms, then all the conditions for domestic economic success – strong markets, successful macro-economic policies, a climate for an adequate supply of domestic savings, entrepreneurship and innovation, a positive work ethic, effective interfirm rivalry and so on – apply in the international arena. However, we will focus on just seven of the factors likely to condition the growth pattern of international direct investment in the 1990s.

Factors likely to affect the future growth and pattern of MNE activity

Economic growth and stability

The first factor is the likely future world environment for economic growth. In the past, the growth of MNE activity has taken on a cyclical pattern. It flourished in the three decades prior to the First World War, in the 25 years after the end of the Second World War, and, since the mid-1980s, it appears to be entering a new golden age. Each of these eras was (and is) characterized by a prosperous world economy, important technological breakthroughs and a relatively free movement of assets, goods and people across national boundaries. By contrast, MNE activity stagnated (relatively speaking) in the restrictive economic and political climate of the inter-war years, and in what might be termed the confrontational, or anti-MNE, period of the 1970s.

While the golden age of the 1980s seems likely to continue into the 1990s – albeit, perhaps, at a more sedate pace – there are too many clouds on the international horizon to warrant making a direct comparison with the two earlier periods of MNE activity. For all its technological and organizational advances, the world is a much more uncertain and volatile place than it was. Indeed, because of the pace of change and the increasing ease at which people, ideas and money can move about, the opportunity for individuals or groups of individuals, who perceive their life styles and beliefs to be threatened by these events, to behave in an economically destructive way is greatly enhanced. In many ways, the world is much more on an economic knife edge than it used to be. It has the resources and capabilities to generate wealth as never before; but its cultural and institutional framework to implement the economic re-structuring demanded by technological change is often outdated or unyielding. Inappropriate macro-economic policies by the leading investing countries, e.g. with respect to budget and/or trade deficits, might critically affect the supply of savings available for foreign investment. In the last decade, we have already had hints of the fragility of the global financial system, while intraregional ideological or political wrangles, unless controlled, can embroil nations which, otherwise, are moving closer to détente.

Like all commercial entities, MNEs dislike uncertainties, although, where the long-term prospects are perceived sufficiently favorable, e.g. as in some parts of Central and Eastern Europe, they will embrace them. But as shown by the shifting geographical balance of the investment portfolios in the past 20 years, MNEs have generally increased their stake in the fastest growing markets, and the ones in which they believe the political and economic risks are the lowest. With a widening choice of investment outlets, they have eschewed countries like India, which, until recently, imposed unacceptable entry and performance requirements, and have focused their attention on countries or regions which are liberalizing or privatizing their markets, e.g. the EC, North America and Australia. Academic research has suggested that countries which follow market-oriented economic policies and which impose the fewest performance requirements on inward direct investors are those which have attracted the most additional US investment in the late 1970s and early 1980s (Contractor, 1990), and this is more than borne out by case studies of particular countries, e.g. Mexico and Chile.

The direction of growth: new technologies

Second, a no less important factor influencing MNE activity in the 1990s will be the nature of economic growth likely to occur. One reason for the increasing role of international investment in the world economy has been that the sectors in which MNEs *qua* MNEs have unique competitive advantages are those which have been increasing their share of world output. Examples include petroleum, motor vehicles, electronics, pharmaceutical, financial services, hotels and management consultancies. In the 1990s, these sectors are likely to be augmented or replaced by others. But perhaps more importantly, the classification of economic activity itself is likely to require modification as technologies become more generic and multipurpose. Indeed, two Dutch scholars, Van Tulder and Junne (1988) have suggested that the time has come to re-classify technologies in terms of the impact they make on their industrial consumers. For example, Van Tulder and Junne define core technologies as those which will (a) lead to many products, (b) have a strong impact on a wide range of production processes, (c) are applicable in many sectors, and (d) re-fashion the trajectory of economic progress. They identify two clusters of such core technologies of the 1990s – viz. the micro-electronics or information technology cluster and the biotechnology cluster. Around these clusters, new technology webs are being created – semi-conductors, robots, computers, telecommunications equipment, computer-aided design and manufacturing equipment in the micro-electronics cluster, and DNA technology, cell fusion, enzyme technology and bio-process technology in the biotechnology cluster.

Each of these galaxies of activity is linked to the other, and advances in one galaxy often become a precondition for progress in another. In turn, each cluster generates its own network of overlapping technologies, and is critically linked to the development of new materials. The result is a complex and changing configuration of technologies which firms are required to master if they are to sustain, let alone advance, their global competitive positions. While such mastery may offer valuable economies of technological scope, it also makes enormous financial and organizational demands. This is because the technologies we have described are costly to produce and to assimilate. They also require a modern and well integrated infrastructure of complementary assets. While the technologies are often environmentally friendly, and while they provide more flexibility in the production of goods and services, they also demand a sophisticated and diverse network of skills and competences – the sources of which are likely to be both industrially and geographically diversified.

All these features of technological progress underline the need for organizational systems which are either managed by large single firms or jointly and severally managed by consortia of firms linked by ownership or by cooperative agreements. In either event, the technological imperative would seem to point to a shift in the particular competitive advantages of the MNE, from those based on the intangible assets which it possesses and utilizes in different countries, to those which stem from its ability to identify, source and utilize a group of inter-dependent and internationally located technological inputs, which may then be used to produce a range of products. The extent of its product range will depend both on the efficiency of the MNE as an innovator and producer, and on how far it is able to exploit cross-border economies of scope and arbitrage, not only in R&D and production, but also in sales and marketing activities. The full implications of new marketing and distribution methods, arising from the micro-electronics and communications revolutions, is yet to be assessed, but in service-oriented sectors, e.g. banking, they are already well in evidence.

Kinds of value added activity

There is another quality related change in the activities of MNEs likely to arise in the 1990s, and that relates to the increasing internationalization of *higher value* production.[9] We have already referred to two past golden ages of MNE activity. In the first, FDI was essentially directed to the exploitation of natural resources, and was largely located in territories owned or managed by the investing countries. Most of the high value secondary processing of these resources, however, was carried out in the home countries. In the second, FDI was primarily undertaken to service local or adjacent foreign markets with goods and services which, in an earlier phase of their life cycle, had been supplied by the home countries. While in the more advanced host countries, there was some innovatory activity, for the most part, this was undertaken in the home countries.

The current phase of MNE expansion is very different from the other two. The most pronounced motive for FDI in the 1990s is not so much to acquire natural resources or to seek out local markets,[10] but to restructure or rationalize existing investments to capitalize on the benefits of global or regional economic integration, or to acquire additional technological, organizational or marketing assets to more effectively pursue, maintain or advance a global competitive position. These latter two motives for FDI imply a very different cross-border configuration of value-added activities than the first two. Moreover, while rationalized investment tends to lead to more specialized and complementary lines of value activity, the latter is encouraging large MNEs to establish a substantial R&D presence in each of the main innovating regions of the world. In some cases, this has led to the setting up of greenfield and self-contained R&D laboratories, notably in science and technology parks; and in others, it has meant the acquisition of foreign companies with innovatory facilities. Such a strategy is being pursued not only by first world MNEs but by those from the Third World, e.g. Taiwan, India and Korea, seeking to acquire an insight into the latest technological developments.

Hard and fast macro-data are scant on the geographical diffusion of innovatory activities by MNEs. We do know, however, from US figures, that R&D expenditure both by foreign firms in the US, and US firms abroad, is increasing faster than both the total sales of such companies and R&D undertaken by indigenous US firms. International patent statistics also demonstrate that the share of new innovations originating from the foreign subsidiaries of MNEs is rising,[11] while data on cross-border royalties and fees suggest that these are increasing relative to the foreign direct investment stake. Company data lend further support to the technology-diffusion hypothesis. The Japanese MNEs, in particular, are sensitive to criticism that their foreign operations are just bridgeheads to Japanese exporters of intermediate products, and, as a consequence, are accelerating the rate at which the local content of their sales in Europe and US is increased; meanwhile, several European MNEs – and particularly those from smaller nations – are now locating upwards of one-third of their R&D activities abroad. B.A.T., Philips of Eindhoven, Nestlé, SKF and Ciba Geigy are some examples.[12]

Service TNCs

It is not only manufacturing MNEs which are globalizing their value-added activities to sustain as well as to exploit their competitive advantages. The fastest rate of growth of FDI in the 1980s occurred in the services sectors, especially in trade and finance-related activities (UNCTC, 1991a). Over the period 1975–1989, the stock of US outward direct investment in the tertiary sector rose by 12.6 per cent per annum compared with 7.4 per cent in the secondary sector and 4.7 per cent in the primary sector. For Japan, the corresponding percentages were 26.5 per cent, 19.9 per cent and 10.0 per cent and for Germany, 14.0 per cent, 10.7 per cent and 7.6 per cent (UNCTC, 1991a). Table 11.3 shows that services now account for one-half or more of the new outflows of FDI of the leading capital-exporting countries. It is particularly high in the case of Japan, where there was

Table 11.3 Sectoral composition of the stock of outward foreign direct investment of major home countries (percentage share and compound annual growth rate)

Country	Period	Primary	Secondary	Tertiary	Total
			Sectors		
Canada					
Composition	1975	9	62	29	100
	1989	7	52	42	100
Growth rate	1975–1989	13	14	19	17
France[1]					
Composition	1975	22	38	40	100
	1989	13	40	47	100
Growth rate	1975–1989	23	28	29	27
Germany					
Composition	1975	5	48	47	100
	1989	3	42	56	100
Growth rate	1975–1989	7	10	13	22
Japan					
Composition	1975	28	32	40	100
	1989	7	26	67	100
Growth rate	1975–1989	10	20	27	22
The Netherlands					
Composition	1975	47	39	15	100
	1989	35	24	41	100
Growth rate	1975–1989	6	5	17	12
United Kingdom					
Composition	1975	31	43	26	100
	1989	27	34	39	100
Growth rate	1975–1989	13	11	23	15
United States[2]					
Composition	1975	26	45	29	100
	1989	8	44	47	100
Growth rate	1975–1989	0	8	12	12

1 Based on cumulative flows of direct investment from 1972.
2 The vertically integrated petroleum industry is included in the primary sector in 1975. In 1990, only the extractive portion of the industry is included in the primary sector, with processing included in the secondary sector and marketing and distribution in the tertiary sector.
Source: UN estimates, based on UN, 1992b and 1993.

a dramatic upsurge of new outward investment in financial and insurance activities in the 1980s. This was mainly due to the restrictions placed on Japanese domestic financial institutions in engaging in securitization and the need of these same banks to diversify their portfolio of assets to remain competitive in global markets. At the end of March 1990, the finance and insurance sector alone accounted for just under one-half of all Japanese investment in Europe which was then increasing at the rate of 35 per cent per year. Subsequently, the less favorable economic climate both in Japan and Europe has reduced the growth of new investment to about half that level.

More generally, while trade- and finance-related activities account for the bulk of outbound service investment by MNEs, it is also growing rapidly in many other areas, notably management and engineering consultancy, hotels and fast food chains, and construction and related activities. For at least three reasons, the 1990s will almost certainly see a further increase in service-related investment. First, services are accounting for a rising proportion of consumer spending. Second, the service intensity of manufactured goods (particularly in the core technology and information-intensive sectors earlier described) is increasing. Third, assuming an even modest success in the current GATT negotiations, the liberalization of cross-border (and particularly intra-EC markets) markets, coupled with the dramatic technological advances in telecommunication facilities, is likely to lead to a substantial rise in both service-based trade and investment.

It is, of course, one thing to forecast a change in the level or pattern of international economic activity, and quite another to argue that a rising proportion of activities will be concentrated in the hands of MNEs. In the services, as in other sectors, a pluralistic organizational ownership structure is likely to emerge. At the top tier, stand the MNEs – the population of which is likely to change over time. They will almost certainly continue to dominate the internationally oriented service sectors, e.g. airlines, insurance companies, accountancies and merchant banks, simply because technological and economic forces are continuing to favor firms which can exploit the benefits of arbitrage and risk diversification, scale economies, and the learning experiences from operating in different cultures. The second tier of firms are the medium to large, but predominantly nationally oriented, companies, which operate either in sectors supplying local markets, or are specialist but leading subcontractors to MNEs – i.e. they comprise the inner ring which surrounds the final group of firms. Often, the second tier of producers supplies goods or services under licence to, or engages in cooperative ventures with, foreign MNEs. The third tier is a heterogeneous group of small specialist firms, some of whom provide the seedbed for new innovations, and others are outer-ring subcontractors.

While it is difficult to predict the extent to which international investment might increase over the next decade, a good case may be made out that MNE-related activity – by which is meant all economic activity which is driven, or influenced, by firms which have major international interests – is likely to become more, and substantially more, important. While prudence demands some skepticism about the outcome of the spate of strategic alliances now being concluded, it does seem likely that cooperative ventures in one form or another will continue to flourish, and become more numerous and diverse in form. In brief, national objectives, technological progress and international political events will continue to generate the kind of resource governance needs, which MNEs, working with, rather than against, markets and working with, rather than against, national governments, are particularly well suited to provide.

FDI-led trade and integration

There is every sign that FDI will be both a major engine of growth in the 1990s, and also an increasingly important fashioner of economic integration and world trade. Not only is three-quarters of the world trade (outside that of China and Eastern Europe) in the hands of the MNEs, but between two-fifths and one-half of this amount is either internal to MNEs or between companies engaging in cross-border cooperative agreements of one kind or another. In the words of Julius (1990), 'International investment is both multiplying and deepening the trade and production linkages among national markets; in the same way as that international financial integration took place from the mid-1970s to the mid-1980s.' Such corporate led integration is likely to have enormous implications for national governments. In particular, it may be postulated that just as there are currently efforts to coordinate macro-economic policies among the group of leading industrial nations – so the 1990s will force a convergence of macro-organizational and structural adjustment policies among these same nations. At the same time, for reasons already suggested, it is likely there will be more rivalry between nation states – especially in Europe – for MNE activity as governments seek to deploy such activity to protect and advance their own competitive stakes in the global economy.

TNCs, the environment and cultural issues

The sixth, and perhaps the most difficult, issue to get to grips with concerns the interaction between MNE-related activity and – to use a phrase which is now coming into popular usage – 'environmentally and culturally friendly or sustainable economic development'. Along with many other actors, MNEs are likely to play a critical role in fashioning the quality of the future environment, and the health and safety of the world's population. This is chiefly because of their dominance as users of both renewable and non-renewable resources, and as innovators of new production methods and products,[13] which may or may not be environmentally friendly, and because of their ability to influence the cross-border dissemination of safety and health standards, especially for high hazard products and processes. In the past, MNEs, *qua* MNEs, have had a mixed record on their impact on sustainable development, but there can be no doubt that they possess the resources and capabilities, which, given the right signals by governments and the international community, could be harnessed to the benefit of the planet. There is also evidence that many of the larger international investors engaged in environmentally sensitive activity are becoming increasingly aware of their responsibilities as trail blazers in promoting environmentally friendly development, and that this need not necessarily be at the expense of their more commercially-oriented goals.

Along with their environmental impact, we also foresee the role of MNEs as influencers and arbitrators of corporate consumer culture sharply accelerating in the 1990s, especially as MNEs from the East and from Latin America begin to make investment inroads into First World countries. In the EC in particular, economic regionalism and cultural decentralization are proceeding hand in hand; and the success of the member states to balance the gains from these two (apparently) opposing forces will determine the long-term success and viability of the Community (Moller, 1991). As one of the main instruments for economic integration, the MNE is likely to be increasingly judged by its sensitivity to national cultural needs and aspirations, and the way in which it relates its product marketing and organizational strategies to these needs.

The geography of MNE activity

Seventh, and finally, this chapter takes a bird's eye view about the likely geography of MNE activity over the next decade.

First, we perceive that the geographical ownership of FDI will increasingly come to resemble that of trade in manufactured goods and services. If this is correct, the share of the US, as a major source of MNE activity, will continue to fall – and probably that of the UK as well. By contrast, that of the larger continental European countries will increase, as will that – and most markedly so – of Japan and the first generation of the Asian tigers via Hong Kong, Korea, Taiwan and Singapore. Mainland China is already making substantial investments elsewhere in Asia, and especially in Hong Kong and Taiwan. At the same time, the contribution of the leading investing nations may be expected to fluctuate according to the competitiveness of their firms and the strength of their domestic economies. Depending on their progress towards economic restructuring, their macro-policies, their debt-reducing capacities and the outcome of NAFTA, Mexico, and to a lesser extent, Brazil and Argentina, could joing other Third World countries as quite important outward investors. The more market-oriented policies of Sweden and her intended accession to the EC in 1995 is likely both to increase her outward investment, and to focus it more to her southern neighbors than in the past.

Second, the destination of FDI is very much likely to reflect the resources, capabilities and markets of the recipient nations, and the attitude of host governments towards their nation's role in the international economy, and how they perceive inward investment contributing to that role. Relating these variables to the assumptions we made earlier about the configuration of the world economy in the 1990s, let us pinpoint each of the main likely growth areas.

Central and Eastern Europe

Excluding the Eastern lander (i.e. district) of a unified Germany, which, in any case is likely to attract an overwhelming proportion of its new investment from the Western lander (some estimates for 1991 put this proportion as high as 95 per cent), most of the rest of Central and Eastern Europe, while certainly stepping up its capital imports in the early 1990s, is unlikely to attract really large sums of foreign investment until the mid-1990s. Economic recession, the Gulf War, uncertainty about the political and social outlook for the area, and the debilitating economic performance of the former Soviet Union are all contributing to the dampening of an earlier euphoria by foreign investors. All being well, however, and depending very much on the extent to which the West is prepared to assist the Commonwealth of

Independent States in its market liberalization and industrial restructuring programmes, the stock of inward direct investment could rise
to between $75 and $100 billion by the late 1990s, or between one-
quarter and one-half of its 1990 level in Western Europe.

Western Europe

EC 1992 has already proved a major boost to inward investment,
and, providing the targets of the European Commission are met, the
EC should continue to be an attractive venue for US and Japanese
MNE activity well into the 1990s. One suspects that the renewed
vigor of the Community, the reduction of intra-EC transaction costs,
and the perceived need of non-EC firms to be insiders in the single
market (partly for defensive and partly for aggressive reasons) will
also lead to a substantial increase in intra-EC investment and a
stepping up of cross-border production by other European, including
Scandinavian, investors.

North and Central America

The Canada–America Free Trade Agreement is stimulating – and the
North American Free Trade Agreement is likely to stimulate – more
intra-regional MNE activity. Both are also likely to lead to some
restructuring of non-American investment within the integrated
region. For example, one might expect more European or Japanese
companies set up plants in labor-intensive sectors in Mexico to supply
the US market.

Asia

India is the big uncertainty here, but, most certainly, it is the country
which offers enormous potential to foreign investors. The easing of
the regulations on inward investment announced in July 1991, which
included raising the equity limit for foreign investment in high priority
joint ventures to 51 per cent from 40 per cent, should go some way to
raising the flow of inward investment from a paltry $75m in 1990;
but much more needs to be done to inject a more market-oriented
and entrepreneurial culture if foreign MNEs are to have their sights
tempted away from the more lucrative and less risky markets of East
and South Asia. Here, the most rapid progress would seem likely to
be made by the second generation of Asian tigers – notably Thailand,
Indonesia, and, if only it would get its political problems sorted out,

the Philippines. For the first half of the 1990s, Thailand seems set to follow in the wake of Taiwan and South Korea, but because of its larger population and industrial base, and its oil revenue, Indonesia is, perhaps, the more promising long-term prospect for foreign investors. With the opening up of Vietnam to market forces, FDI in Indo China also looks set to increase in the next few years.

The outlook for FDI in the mainland of the People's Republic of China clearly rests on the future of the Chinese economic system and the burgeoning economic interaction between the Eastern seaboard, Taiwan and Hong Kong. While there is some reason for optimism about the future of intra-Chinese trade and investment, it is all too tempting to infer that the events in Central and Eastern Europe will soon be repeated in China. But even if this were to happen in the next two or three years, the disappointing performance of many of the earlier joint ventures would suggest that foreign firms will exercise considerable caution before committing large investments to a country whose resource base and infrastructure for a globally-oriented market-based economy is even more backward and culture specific than that of the former Soviet Union.

If the future is uncertain in India, and difficult to predict in mainland China, Japan is the great enigma of the East. Japan, with a current GNP per capita 15 per cent higher than that of Western Germany, attracts only one-eighth of the latter's inward FDI. Accepting all the problems of investing in Japan – many of which, according to established foreign firms, are considerably exaggerated – it is difficult to see how inward investment cannot expand, and expand markedly in the 1990s. US Department of Commerce data reveal that US MNEs report that they plan to increase their capital expenditures in Japan by a greater percentage amount in 1992 and 1993 than in any other major industrial area. As Japanese consumers become more accustomed to (hopefully) better quality Western goods, the FDI is likely to follow trade in the traditional product cycle fashion.

It is, however, the very unfamiliarity with the Japanese way of life and the lack of knowledge about the Japanese business culture, distribution practices and Government regulations that make Western MNEs reluctant to make resource commitments until they are doubly sure of their market prospects. But as the Japanese market grows and prospers, an increasing number of Western firms may find that the costs of *not* engaging in FDI will be more costly than they can bear. It is also reasonable to expect that some FDI will grow out of the collaborative alliances now being forged between Western and

Japanese firms. It does, however, seem improbable that, in the fore-seeable future, Japan will allow, or have the institutional machinery properly to deal with acquisitions and mergers involving foreign firms. This, indeed, may be the single most important factor in keeping down the scale of investment in Japan by Western MNEs.

The rest of the world

For the rest of the world, a patchy picture emerges. In South America, much rests on the macro-economic policies of the consti-tuent countries, the success of new schemes for economic integration (e.g. Mercosur) and the extent to which the impetus from NAFTA spreads southward. As the African continent struggles to find its economic soul, one might anticipate some increase in some kinds of FDI in countries like Kenya, Nigeria, Zimbabwe, particularly by Third World MNEs. However, for the most part, we would foresee a continued marginalization of sub-Saharan Africa as a recipient for MNE activity.[14] By the end of the 1990s, South Africa, too, may be attracting much more interest by foreign investors. More generally, investment flows seem likely to become more regionalized than in the past. Intra-Triad investment will almost certainly dominate the activi-ties of First World MNEs – although the European component will increasingly embrace parts of Central and Eastern Europe, and the American component, Mexico. But, within the developing world, the fastest growth in intra-regional FDI seems likely to occur in South and East Asia,[15] while on sub-Saharan Africa, Asian owned MNEs are establishing an increasingly significant foothold. The future of the Mediterranean and African countries seems less secure as Southern and Eastern European nations increasingly compete for the FDI which might otherwise have gone to them. Much will depend on whether or not these countries can embrace effective regional inte-gration schemes. Finally, firms from some smaller and resource-based developed countries like Israel, New Zealand and Norway appear to be stepping up their foreign-based activities.[16]

Scenarios for developing countries in the new global economy

This brief overview of the likely direction of MNE activity in the 1990s suggests that the world may be conveniently classified into nations whose economic strategy is intimately bound up with the globalization of production and markets, and those whose orientation is mainly directed to national or regional production and markets.

The indications are that, for the first group of countries, the economic prospects of the 1990s are good, and that MNEs are likely to play a critical role in affecting these prospects, both as providers of resources and capabilities, and in the way they are organized across national boundaries. But, what of the countries – and particularly the poorer developing countries – which are on the periphery or margin of the globalization process?

Consider two possible scenarios. The first is that nationally- or regionally-oriented developing nations will be increasingly drawn into the network of the globally-oriented nations, partly as suppliers of materials, and intermediate or final goods which require resources and capabilities in which they are comparatively well endowed, and partly as a result of the increased real incomes of the latter group of nations, part of which is likely to be spent on the former's products. Whether one takes an optimistic or pessimistic view of this scenario depends on how far one believes that the non-globalizing developing economies can upgrade the competitiveness of their resources and capabilities to meet the levels achieved by some of the industrializing globally-oriented economies, e.g. those in Southern and Eastern Europe, East Asia and Mexico. But, in any event, globalizing-led growth seems likely to be very unevenly spread among the nationally- or regionally-oriented economies.

The second scenario is that the main impetus for development of the peripheral economies will be endogenous to those economies. The critical question, here, is whether the prospects for growth, and the ability of countries to attract the foreign resources and capabilities which are necessary to fuel that growth, are sufficient to keep them out of the 'static development' trap, which is the ill fortune of many developing countries today. Here, much will surely rest on the macroeconomic and organizational strategies pursued by host governments, the extent to which the international community is prepared to assist the least developed economies to evolve such strategies (as seems likely to occur in the case of Eastern European economies), and how far the smaller developing countries, at least, can group together to foster some kind of regional free trade area.

However, even taking an optimistic view on all these counts, it is difficult to envisage the larger MNEs playing a major role in nationally- or regionally-oriented development in the 1990s, except, perhaps, in the more heavily populated developing countries. Far more promising – and this should be encouraged wherever possible – is the contribution which might be made by medium- and smaller-size MNEs, and particularly those countries either elsewhere in the region or others one or two steps up the ladder in development. In this connection, one might both hope and expect to see more South/South FDI in the 1990s, particularly within Asia, and between Asia and sub-Saharan Africa.[17]

CONCLUSIONS

We conclude this chapter by underlying two of its recurrent themes. The first is that the MNE is a continually evolving organizational phenomenon, and that the typical MNE of the early 1990s is very different from its counterpart of the 1960s, which, in turn, was very different from that of the early twentieth century. Our speculation about the MNE of the late 1990s is that it is likely to be the center of governance for a network of pluralistic organizational and operating units, each of which is systematically linked to the other as part of a regional and global heterarchy.

Second, all the various global scenarios we have painted rest on a mainly peaceful world, and one which acknowledges the benefits of economic interdependence and international commerce. Unfortunately, neither event is guaranteed. While the outlook for harmony among the major powers is as good as it has been for a century or more, trouble which could embroil the major powers – as, for example, is currently occurring in Yugoslavia and Czechoslovakia, and could so easily flair up in various parts of Middle East Asia or Latin America – is never far away. The world is truly a tinder box of ideological uncertainties and economic unrest.

The question of economic interdependence both within the developed world and between it and the developing world is also delicately balanced. Here, the outcome of the GATT negotiations could determine the future course of events for at least the next decade. If international direct investment is increasingly the engine of economic growth, and entrepreneurship, technology and human skills are the fuel which makes possible that growth, it is governments – both individually and collectively – which provide the signals, which, in the last resort, will determine the extent, speed, direction and quality of that growth. At the moment, the signals appear to be set to two yellows – rather than green – which suggests the track is clear ahead for a reasonable distance; yet further down the line, if the engine of growth proceeds too fast, or goes on the wrong track, be warned – the signal could be at stop.

Part IV

Challenges to national and regional government policies

Introduction

This final part touches upon the implications of the global challenge, and the role played by MNEs in fashioning and responding to that challenge, for governments in their role as custodians of the economic welfare of their citizens.

Chapter 12 examines the way in which the contribution of three main organizers of economic activity, viz. governments, firms (or hierarchies) and markets has changed over the last 100 years, and, no less important, of how the *form* of that involvement has changed. Chapter 13 takes up this theme in more detail and suggests a paradigmatic framework by which it is possible to assess the costs and benefits of these alternative organizational mechanisms. Essentially, it uses the concept of market failure – but extends this to identify and evaluate the strengths and weaknesses of hierarchies and governments as transactional modes. It suggests that within the framework of a market-oriented economy, hierarchies and governments each have an important market facilitating role to play. The balance of the governance of particular groups of transactions – together with the influence exerted over the behavior of the participants to these transactions – will depend according to the nature of the transactions and the relative stakes and bargaining strengths of the participants. For it is these variables that will ultimately determine the social, as well as the private, costs and benefits of the transactions.

Chapter 13 uses the market failure paradigm to trace the changing relationships between MNEs and governments over the past 20 years or so. It suggests that the kinds of market failure which governments and MNEs both focused on in the 1960s and 1970s, and accused each other of engineering or exploiting, were those associated with structural distortions of what might otherwise have been an improved market situation. Since these distortions usually led to MNEs gaining and governments losing, or vice versa, conflicts inevitably arose. In the later 1980s and 1990s, both governments and firms are beginning to realize that there is another kind of market failure, caused not by governments or firms (or even consumers – the often neglected party to an exchange) but by the inherent or endemic characteristics of the market itself. In such a situation, firms and/or governments might intervene to privately or socially 'internalize' markets to the benefit, not of one at the expense of the other, but to both. In such a case, it is in the interests of both governments and firms to cooperate with each other either to correct market failure or to help compensate against it.

Chapter 13 goes on to argue that the globalization of business activity is not only partly the result of endemic market failure, but that it itself can help overcome such failure, and that this may work to the benefit of the governments which are home and host to their activities.

Chapter 14 continues the theme of the previous two chapters by detailing the way in which the political economy of MNE activity has changed over the past two decades. In doing so, it pays especial attention to the instruments used by governments to influence such activity. It concludes that, whereas in the 1960s and 1970s, governments tried to influence the behavior of MNEs directly, e.g. by particular and specific policies addressed to them, in the 1990s, governments are placing more emphasis in getting their general macro-organizational strategies right, so that MNEs, in response to these strategies, may behave in a way acceptable to their citizens.

The final chapter traces some of the more specific policy changes which affect MNE activity, that are now occurring in the EC as a result of increased corporate and regional integration in that region. The chapter describes the changing organizational strategies of MNEs consequent upon technological change and the initiation of the EC, and then goes on to examine the implications of these strategic changes both for national governments and the EC commission. It concludes by suggesting that although many of the government related determinants of MNEs are being increasingly vested in the EC, in their attempts to use MNEs to promote the competitiveness of their own resources and capabilities in global markets, national governments are tending to adopt a more strategic posture in the framing of their domestic macro-organizational policies, and that this posture is sometimes in direct conflict to that pursued by their foreign competitors. The global challenge is, then, requiring a realignment, not only of the focus of interest and competitive strategy of firms, but of that of governments as well. The successful countries of the 1990s will surely be those which are best able to adapt their domestic economic policies, not only to meet the demands of that global challenge, but, partly at least, to fashion it to meet their own interests.

12 Governments, hierarchies and markets: towards a new balance?

INTRODUCTION

These are exciting and momentous times. There is a sense that our world, as we know it, is at a watershed in its evolution. The last decade has witnessed fundamental shifts in ideological and political trajectories, and new attitudes and initiatives towards social and environmental issues. The accelerating pace of technological change is encapsulating time and space, and is demanding a reappraisal of tried and tested economic systems and institutional structures. As the cross-border interchange of people, goods, assets, ideas and cultures becomes the norm, rather than the exception, so our planet is beginning to take on the characteristics of a global village.

Of all the events of the last decade, none has been more dramatic and, potentially, more far reaching that the political and economic reform of Europe. At the same time, the recent turbulence in Yugoslavia and the Middle East has forcibly reminded us how fragile and volatile progress towards international accord is, and how, in spite of man's ability to create and sustain material prosperity, differences in perceptions, values and ideologies can so easily tear our modern economic fabric to shreds.

Yet, underpinning and interweaving with these happenings has been a stream of technological advances. Such advances, unlike movements in political doctrines and economic systems, are largely irreversible. Barring natural catastophes or war, each generation adds to the stock of human knowledge and experience, and the physical capital of its predecessors. Much of the life style most of the world enjoys today was virtually unknown to our grandparents. Many of the products we regularly buy contain ingredients, or are manufactured by methods of production, unimagined, except on the pages of science fiction, less than half a century ago. Semi-conductors, robotics, satellite communications, high definition TV, optic fibres, micro-surgery and supersonic aircraft are just a few examples of the innovations of the last 30 or so years which have altered, and are continuing to alter, the very texture of our lives.

Such changes as we have just described have had a widespread repercussion on the way economic activity is organized and managed. Let us give just three examples.

The first relates to the increasing roundaboutness of the production process. Such roundaboutness may be measured by the ratio of the total value of circulating intermediate products to the value of final output within the production system. It simply reflects the growing vertical division of labor within or between firms, and the increased number of separate economic activities required to produce a given end product. The second example is the increasing significance of fixed or overhead costs as a component of the total costs of production. Direct labor and material costs, for example, now account for about one-half the proportion of total manufacturing costs of 50 years ago. By contrast, expenditure by firms on innovatory and all forms of production supporting and marketing activities have risen sharply.

The third example is the globalization of the market for many goods and services. Around 1850, probably 90 per cent of all goods and services produced by firms were made with labor, materials and components bought from suppliers located within a radius of 100 miles, and sold to buyers within the same distance. Successive reductions in transport and communications costs have spectacularly extended the reach of the market. Today, on average, in the industrialized world, more than one-half the output of corporations is produced or sold outside their countries of origin, whereas about the same proportion of the raw materials and intermediate products bought by corporations is imported, or produced abroad by their foreign affiliates.

In this chapter, we shall consider the changing character of the cross-border organization of production. We shall suggest that the nature of the governance of that production, at any given moment of time, is determined by the configuration of, and the interaction between, a triarchy of organizing mechanisms, viz. *governments, privately owned commercial hierarchies* and *markets.* We shall further argue that changes in the relative significance of the three modalities will reflect changes in the respective costs and benefits of each to perform the functions required of them.

To illustrate a little further, consider just four kinds of organizational arrangements. These are depicted as 1 to 4 in Figure 12.1. In a purely communist society, neither private hierarchies nor markets play any part in managing the allocation of resources: each is assumed to incur unacceptably high transaction costs (see 1). In a purely market economy, private buyers and sellers are the sole determinants of the level and composition of goods and services produced and traded. Governments play a minimal role, while firms engage in only a single value-added activity, the inputs for which and outputs of which are bought and sold in the market. In this scenario, the transaction costs of the market are assumed to be negligible, while those of hierarchies and governments are both assumed to be positive (see 2). In a hierarchical-market managed economy, economic activity is organized partly by markets, and partly by multiproduct firms which govern the use of intermediate products which might otherwise have been bought or sold in the market[1] (see 3). This

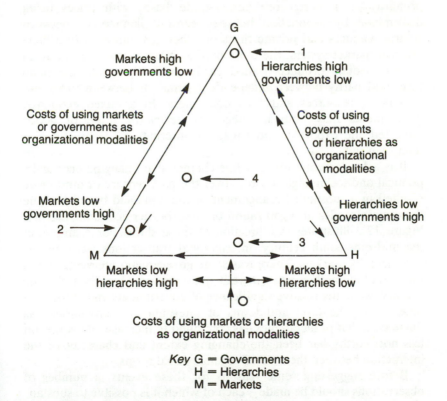

Figure 12.1 The triad of organizational mechanisms.

scenario suggests that different kinds of economic activity require sufficient modes of governance, and that the greater the market failure, the more likely its functions will be performed by and within hierarchies. In a mixed economy (see 4), governments, along with markets or hierarchies, may either directly engage in production and transactions; or they might indirectly influence the structure of resource allocation, which, otherwise would be decided by the other two members of the triad. Such a tripartite arrangement presupposes that governments perceive that, in the case of some activities at least, neither markets nor hierarchies, by themselves, can achieve socially optimum results, and hence some additional form of organization is required.

Consider, next, the way in which international value-added activities are organized. In a purely market-oriented economy, all trade will be conducted between independent economic agents at arms length prices. Trade between, or involving, communist countries will be primarily on a barter or counter-trade basis, with prices being determined by negotiation between central planners or between central planners and private firms or other governments. In a hierarchical-market system, the cross-border linkages will take the form of intermediate products traded partly internally within the same firm, and partly between independent firms, or between firms and owners or resources and final consumers. In a mixed economy, governments may both influence the terms of trade of goods imported and exported, and engage in international transactions in their own right.

It is a fundamental tenet of this chapter that changing economic, political and technological forces over the past century or more have resulted in a substantial realignment of the costs and benefits of the three main modes in organization of cross-border economic activity. Figure 12.2 illustrates the direction of these shifts. For example, in the mid-nineteenth century, international transactions were mainly organized by markets. There was some government intervention, but the role of hierarchies was generally quite limited. Over the following century, while the relative significance of governments and markets in determining the level and terms of international transactions has fluctuated, that of hierarchies has continued to increase. However, no less noteworthy has been the changing extent and character of the interaction between the triad of organizational forms.

Before suggesting some reasons for these events, a number of observations should be made – each of which it is possible to substantiate by empirical evidence.[2]

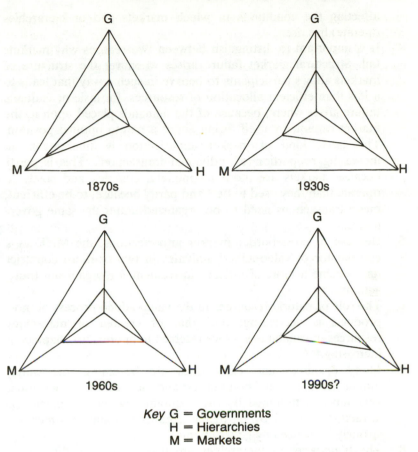

Figure 12.2 Changes in the configuration of the triad of organizational mechanisms.

1 Relative to the number of goods and services produced in the world economy, the number of separate and discrete economic activities required to produce and market these goods and services has increased. In other words, the transactional intensity of economic activity has risen.

2 An increasing proportion of these activities is conducted across national boundaries.

3 While the role of government in influencing the level and pattern of international transactions has varied over the years, in general, its *direct* intervention in the conduct of cross-border markets and hierarchies has declined, while its *indirect* intervention (i.e. in

affecting the conditions in which markets and/or hierarchies operate) has risen.

4   It is important to distinguish between two reasons why markets fail. Structural market failure arises whenever the structure of markets allows participants to behave in such a way that leads to a less than efficient allocation of resources. Intrinsic or endemic failure arises where, because of the demands placed upon it, the market cannot, by itself, bring about a pareto optimal position. This latter kind of market imperfection is inherent in an increasing proportion of individual transactions. This is partly because markets are more incomplete, complex and costly to operate than they used to be;[3] and partly because, to be efficient, many transactions need to be organized under the same governance.

5   Because of cross-border market imperfections, the MNE as a coordinator of value-added activities in two or more countries has become a more significant instrument for organizing transactions.

6   The role of natural resources in the value-added process of most products is decreasing; and that of created or man-made resources or capabilities, as we referred to in previous chapters, is increasing.[4]

7   Many resources and capabilities are becoming increasingly mobile across national boundaries; and the location of their use is very much determined by the economic, political and cultural attractions offered by particular countries, some of which are strongly influenced by governments.

8   The boundaries of hierarchies are becoming more difficult to delineate. Firms both cooperate and compete with each other. They are linked by webs of trust, tradition, commitment and contractual relationships as well as by ownership. Mutual tolerance, reciprocity and forbearance are features of networks. Increasingly, as Chapter 2 has explained, economic activity is taking the form of a system of incomplete hierarchies (or heterarchies) and markets, in which the interest of a single firm or market is determined by the success of the system or group of firms of which it is part.

These propositions, taken together, add up to a dramatically changing world scenario for international commercial transactions, and suggest a major shift in the relative costs and benefits of alternative organizational modes. Let us now illustrate these propositions with some historical reflections.

THE CHANGING PATTERNS OF ORGANIZATIONAL MODES

Mid-nineteenth to mid-twentieth century

For most of this era, international commerce largely took the form of trade in assets, goods and services between independent buyers and sellers. The market acted as the invisible hand or broker for such trade. At the start of the period, there were only a few MNEs, and these were mainly in the primary sector or were trade supporting. However, the end of the nineteenth century heralded a new generation of technological advances which extended the boundaries of markets and firms, and offered new opportunities for the cross-border division of labor. Not only this, they also made it possible – indeed desirable – for firms to own and control an increasing number of related activities in both their home and foreign countries.

Of course, such international corporate linkages did not begin at this point. They were forged between Hanseatic merchants and Italian banking dynasties in the fourteenth century, by the giant trading companies in the seventeenth and eighteenth centuries, and by the colonizing and land development companies of the sixteenth century onwards (Dunning, 1993). But, any widespread transnational investment, with all its attendant risks, had to wait until the advent of managerial capitalism and the limited liability of investors. At the same time, the costs of market failure, notably those associated with the protection of the reputation and property rights of sellers, and assuring uninterrupted deliveries of intermediate products (especially essential raw materials) to buyers, led to indirect cross-border linkages being replaced by direct linkages.

During these years, the role of governments in shaping international transactions was threefold. First, by their strategies towards the pattern, pace and organization of economic development, governments helped mold their own nation's position in the world. Second, by the use of import restrictions and, in the case of metropolitan governments, by the control of goods, resources and capabilities supplied to and by their foreign possessions, they affected the location of economic activity. Third, by a series of agreements and price regulatory and stabilization schemes, they influenced the terms at which many commodities were traded. Such intervention had mixed results. In some instances, e.g. in the United States, it prompted development; but in others, attempts to manage trade simply resulted in changing the form of economic linkages from those involving intrahierarchical trade in intermediate products.

At a global level, the period from 1850 to 1950 was marked by a shift in the world economic leadership from the UK to the US, and a series of technological and organizational advances which favored the growth of domestic and international hierarchies. Not only did the average size of firms increase, but so did the number of activities performed by them. Value-added chains were restructured, and, for the most part, lengthened. Firms began to diversify their range of end products. But the path of growth and development was rarely smooth or without risk; and to exploit or protect themselves against the less desirable consequences of markets, firms sought to replace them by other organizational forms. At the turn of the century, and in the inter-war years, industrial cartels, interlocking directorates and collaborative agreements abounded; and often, these arrangements were concluded between firms in different countries.

Mid-twentieth century to mid-1980s

The 40 years following the Second World War saw an acceleration of all forms of technological and organizational progress, which, together with a determined effort by industrialized countries to engineer and sustain a regime favorable to cross-border trade and investment, resulted in a rapid increase of all forms of international commerce. The MNE was a leading player in this internationalization process. As Chapter 11 has shown, by the mid-1980s, the ratio of the inward plus outward foreign direct investment stock to the gross national product of non-communist countries was double that of 1950; and trade conducted by or within MNEs was accounting for three-quarters of all trade. In 1990, of all forms of commercial trans-actions across national boundaries – apart from short term capital and financial flows – those undertaken within corporations, or between corporations engaged in collaborative ventures, probably accounted for more than one half; and this percentage was even greater in the case of transactions undertaken by economic agents domiciled in the leading industrialized countries.

There are various reasons for the impressive rise in international corporate transactions. In the first half of the post-war period, US – and later European – firms responded to the difficulty of selling their products to many foreign markets by setting up producing affiliates in these markets. Such investment decelerated in the 1970s and early 1980s. This reflected partly the slower rate of world economic growth, and partly the fact that some developing countries, dis-enchanted with their impact or behavior, expropriated the assets of many foreign subsidiaries, and generally took a more aggressive posture towards prospective investors. At the same time, the repercussions of the oil price hikes and a swing to the left of many governments led to more state intervention in markets, including cross-border markets. In an attempt to circumvent these, as well as to take advantage of the opening up of new markets, MNEs continued to expand their investments in some parts of the world, and to discover novel means of collaborating with foreign firms to satisfy the requirements of governments.

The last decade of the post-war period has been characterized by three interrelated features. The first is the emergence of Japan as the world's second most powerful industrial nation – a modern phoenix rising from the ashes of the last war. Her rise as an international direct investor, though not unexpected, because of her earlier trade successes, has been spectacular. Partly as a carefully conceived global strategy and partly forced by protectionist fears – as witnessed by her schizophrenic attitude to Europe 1992 – the value of Japan's stock of foreign direct investment rose from under $22.2 billion in March 1978 to $352.4 billion in March 1992.

The second factor has been the change in economic ideology and policies of nations across the globe. The renascence of faith in market forces and a renewed desire to participate more actively in the international division of labor has undoubtedly been stimulated by the failure of socialist regimes to provide either the political freedom or the economic performance which people believe they have the right to expect. However, no less germane has been the success of several Asian developing nations in penetrating US and Western European markets, and in demonstrating enviable improvements in their economic prosperity. Led by the US and the UK, the 1980s have seen a steady, yet accelerating, movement towards the privatization and deregulation of markets, a reduction in State interventionism and the opening up of many previously closed economies.

Alongside the restructuring of the organization of economic activity has come a re-ordering of national objectives. On the political agenda of most countries, social and distributive goals have been downgraded, while measures designed to promote the competitiveness and restructuring of domestic industry, and the protection of the environment, have been ungraded. Governments are being forced to reexamine the costs and benefits of their own involvement in economic activity; and there is a movement – although a slow one in some countries – towards exposing the activities of public authorities to the discipline of the market, and encouraging governments to be more customer mission and driven, more market and results oriented and more competitive and entrepreneurial (Osborne and Gaebler, 1992). The fear of Japanese competition has provided a powerful driving force for the new economic realism; but, equally pressing have been the demands of technological advances on the strategy of large and small corporations.

The escalating overhead costs of modern industry, together with increasingly rapid rates of obsolescence of products and production methods, have forced firms either to extend their market boundaries, or to share the risks and capital requirements of these activities. Hence, the growth of cross-border acquisition and mergers (A&Ms) and of strategic alliances in the later 1980s. Even Japanese firms, which, until very recently, had invested in the US and Western Europe predominantly by way of greenfield ventures, are not immune to this trend. Of all new Japanese investment in Western Europe in 1989 and 1992, nearly one-half took the form of A&Ms.

A combination of pro-market and, sometimes, pre-hierarchical, strategies pursued by governments, and the demands of modern technology, have also affected the organization of cross-border production. It has done so, first, by shifting the *raison d'être* of such activity to the uneven distribution of 'created', rather than 'natural' factor endowments (i.e. from resources to capabilities). Second, it has caused a reorganization of the cross-border transactions away from the external market towards hierarchies.[5] Third, the market and/or hierarchical facilitating role of governments has become more important as the complexity of, and uncertainties associated with, international markets have increased; while, contemporaneously, firms have found that global economic forces demand that they have a presence in these markets.

The current and likely future situation

As detailed in Chapter 11, the 1990s promise to be among the most challenging of the entire twentieth century. The configuration of the triad of organizing modes is likely to undergo further restructuring as, indeed, are the cross-border linkages between nation states and the rest of the world. While it is possible to envisage a variety of future scenarios, rarely has it been more difficult to predict the one most likely to occur. Perhaps, the most optimistic scenario one can imagine is the continuation of the democratization and economic interdependence of the world economy, and that technological advances, rising markets and sound macro-economic management in the leading industrial countries will generate a material propserity in which all nations will share.

The most pessimistic scenario – a global conflagration – is that such developments, or a modified version of them, will impose too big a strain on the existing international trading and financial system and on economic management, and this will lead to a new round of trade wars, a major financial crisis and world recession. Certainly, the current trading imbalances between the leading economic powers does little to inspire confidence that the huge reconstruction, development and innovatory programs planned for the 1990s can be accommodated without a considerable realignment of currencies and domestic economic policies. For, in spite of technological progress – and to some extent because of it – the competition for the creative use and exploitation of global resources and capabilities is almost certainly going to increase in the 1990s (Stopford, 1990).

But, however fascinating it may be, forecasting the future is not the main purpose of the chapter. Rather, it seeks to offer some general comments about the more important trends in the organization of international activity now beginning to emerge.[6]

1   Consider, first, multinational hierarchies. All the evidence points to the further pushing back of their territorial partners, and to a larger number of them initiating regional or global production and marketing strategies, particularly within the triad. The organizational forms of these strategies are likely to become more pluralistic as firms develop a more holistic approach to their trans-border operations. The boundaries of firms will become increasingly blurred as they forge new allegiances, and as their networking with other firms becomes multifocused. While it is probable that internalized cross-border bonding will increase, other less formal exchange relationships – of the Keiretsu variety – are likely to proliferate as firms interpenetrate each other's territories. More and more, the MNE will become an orchestrator of a set of geographically dispersed, but interdependent, assets. Some of these, which represent its core capabilities, it will wish to own; but others (which may be no less important to its commercial success) it will either jointly supply with other firms, or purchase from its global network of suppliers.

Another feature of the MNE of the 1990s is likely to be its continual state of metamorphosis. While the A&M boom of the 1980s may not continue, it seems likely that companies will continue to revamp their organizational structures and activities both along and between value-added chains. Disinternalization of some markets and increased intercorporate networking will go hand in hand with the integration of other markets and more centralized hierarchies. There are strong suggestions that, within the leading industrial countries at least, many MNEs will deepen their value sets and widen their value circles. An increasing proportion of their research and development is likely to be undertaken outside their home countries. As firms also see competitive advantage in localizing their products and, at least, some of the managerial functions, it could be that regional offices will take over many of the governing responsibilities currently exercised by head offices. The ability to transfer culture specific assets, or adapt these to the needs of particular host countries, is likely to become an even more important feature of successful MNEs. To reduce interfirm transaction costs, and to maximize on the benefits of shared assets and learning experiences, organizational systems of hierarchies are being gradually replaced – at least in some larger MNEs – by heterarchical control structures.

2   Next, consider the role of governments. We are currently in the midst of a wind of change towards the liberalization of markets, and a reduction of government interventionism in the production process. However, while accepting the dramatic changes now occurring in the economic management of the erstwhile communist countries, the role of government in affecting the organization and productivity of economic activity in market economies has, in no way, diminished. Several of the most market-oriented national administrations – and the UK and US might be included among these – have consistently pursued strategies and policies which have had a very fundamental impact upon the manner in which economic activity is managed. In a variety of ways, and to achieve many diverse objectives, governments are increasingly taking actions which, taken as a whole, have repercussions on the competitiveness of markets and hierarchies far in excess of anything that the kind of industrial policies practiced in the 1970s, and which are so much an anathema to right-wing policitians, ever achieved.

The fact is that governments do themselves a disservice by belittling their role as a promoter and sustainer of the efficient organization of hierarchies and markets. It is the consensus of many studies (e.g. Scott and Lodge, 1985; Wade, 1988; Porter, 1990) that national governments have played a critical role in influencing the success or failure of post-war industrial economies; and that it is not the countries with the least government involvement which have performed the best, but those which have worked most closely and efficiently with hierarchies and markets to promote the most efficient and cost-efficient allocation and upgrading of resources under their jurisdiction. These are also the same governments which acknowledge that, while they, as resource managers, must minimize their own transaction costs, markets and hierarchies *do* sometimes fail, and that a systemic and integrated approach is needed if economic activity is to be optimally organized.

It is difficult to imagine the significance of government as a shaper of economic activity diminishing in the 1990s: indeed, it is more likely to increase. Industrial competitiveness is becoming the number one item on the political agenda. But, the determinants of competitiveness rest on the ability of a country to provide the right economic and cultural environment for its firms to be innovatory and productive in world markets, and to attract the subsidiaries of foreign firms to its borders. By themselves, because of the unacceptably high transaction costs involved, neither markets nor hierarchies can fully, or optimally, achieve this task. Nor can they always meet the challenges of structural change in a socially different way.

3   Finally, what of the characteristics of markets? Despite the current fashion towards the deregulation and liberalization of markets, we suspect that the unaided efficiency of that particular exchange mechanism for most products (in the classical sense of the word) is likely to fall in the 1990s. This is partly because we foresee a greater supramarket control over the conditions of supply of a whole range of products, to reduce information asymmetries, harmonize technical and safety standards and advance environmental goals, and partly because the interdependence between, and the risks associated with, the markets for intermediate products seems likely to increase. We also think it probable that there will be a recasting of international supervisory or control mechanisms, e.g. GATT, to take account of the specific attributes of global production, and also to minimize the adverse effects of 'beggar my neighbor' strategic behavior on the part of national governments.[7] At the same time, developments in information and communications technology may well reduce the costs of organizing corporate networks, while a combination of the opportunities afforded by regional integration and the fear of regional protectionism is prompting firms to become insiders in both Western Europe and the US.

CONCLUSIONS

We conclude. It is our belief that in the 1990s, governments, commercial hierarchies and markets will more closely interact than ever before, and the way in which they interact – which is essentially the responsibility of governments – will determine the competitiveness of developed countries and the development path of the rest of the world. We foresee that largely unfettered markets will continue to determine the price and conditions of supply of unskilled labor, natural resources, primary commodities, many final goods and services and financial assets, but that networks of hierarchies will increasingly determine the pattern of transactions of intermediate products, including property rights. This is partly because of the idiosyncratic character of many of these products, and partly because interdependencies between the markets for many of them require collective governance to maximize the value of their usage. In this respect, providing that there is competition between hierarchies, and they are subject to the discipline of the market for the final products they produce, corporate groups may act as surrogates for markets. Indeed, by reducing both production and transaction costs, they may help final markets to operate more efficiently. Though they may replace individual markets, hierarchies should, nevertheless, be perceived as an integral part of the market system.[8]

Similarly, we believe that governments will increasingly use one of their main responsibilities to promote and fashion an economic system by which resources may be organized for efficiency and growth. All too frequently in the past, the actions of governments have appeared to be antisymbiotic or combative to those of both markets and hierarchies. In the early 1990s, the role of governments is increasingly being seen as complementary or symbiotic to that of markets and hierarchies. They are motivated to cooperate with firms because, in their desire to be competitive in a global economy, governments realize that firms are peculiarly well equipped to be wealth creators. At the same time, they acknowledge their responsibility to provide the legal, institutional and financial framework so that firms can fulfil this function efficiently and with the minimum transaction costs.

Governments are also coming to recognize that 'markets' themselves are not free goods. They have to be created and sustained, and this costs resources. Moreover, since, when they operate well, they do so to the benefit of the community, governments have an active responsibility to ensure that market failure is minimized. Nowhere is this responsibility better demonstrated than in the supply of long term finance to industry; and nowhere is there such a vivid contrast between the attitudes and policies of successive German and Japanese administrations on the one hand, and those of the UK and US on the other. We repeat: the question of whether or not governments should intervene in economic affairs is no longer a sensible one to ask. The key question is how should government intervene so as to promote the maximum economic welfare at minimum cost? So far as we are aware, this is not a question at the top of the agenda of most national governments.[9]

At an international level, it is likely that transactions in intermediate goods and services will account for a higher share of all forms of trade. It also seems probable that an increasing proportion of such trade will be conducted within MNEs or corporate groups. We foresee the nationality of a firm's ownership being increasingly irrelevant to the location of wealth creating activities, and to its impact on national economic welfare. And finally, it may be anticipated that the countries most likely to achieve economic success in the 1990s are those whose governments will adopt a systemic and holistic approach towards the triarchy of economic organization, and who will, in their efforts to achieve the configuration which is most cost effective and which best promotes the country's long term competitive advantage, fully take account of the growing globalization of business activity.

13 Governments and multinational enterprises: from confrontation to cooperation?

INTRODUCTION

There have been many studies of the ways in which governments[1] may directly affect the activities of multinational enterprises (MNEs). Few, however, have attempted to analyze the extent to which outward or inward direct investment – through its effects on the economies of investing or recipient countries – has led governments to modify their existing economic objectives and strategies, or, indeed, of the way in which governments, themselves, have sought to influence the level and pattern of MNE activity, as part of a package of policy instruments designed to advance a broader set of economic and/or social goals.

It is the purpose of this chapter to review the dynamics of the systemic interaction between government and foreign direct investment (FDI) over the past three decades or so, and to speculate a little on its likely direction in the foreseeable future. By systemic interaction, we mean the interface between the global strategies of MNEs designed to advance corporate profitability and growth, and the strategies of national governments designed to promote the economic and social welfare of their citizens.

There are three main tenets of the chapter. The first is that for most countries, and until very recently, the actions of governments to influence the value-added activities of MNEs have rarely been explicitly related to their wider economic management. This was primarily either because such activities were perceived to be relatively insignificant (e.g. in the case of the US), or because governments believed that they could absorb their consequences without making any adjustments to their existing economic policies (as in the case of several developing countries). A combination of the growing importance of MNE investment in, or by, the economies of most countries, and a realization (often brought about by hard experience) that, by integrating the use of foreign and domestic resources, FDI inevitably affects the outcome of national economic strategies, has considerably modified this viewpoint.

The second is that governments are being forced to look at the competitive advantages of the resources under their jurisdiction as a national economic objective in its own right, and it is here, particularly, that both inward and outward investment are likely to have an important impact. This change in emphasis has occurred for two reasons. The first is the convergence in the economic structure of the leading industrialized economies. Rather than trading different goods and services with each other, these countries are increasingly competing with each other in the supply of similar goods and services. Second, the liberalization of (some) cross-border markets and the increased mobility of resources, brought about by lower transportation and communication advances, has enabled companies to be more footloose in their locational choices, at least within particular regions of the world. While this has sometimes led to increasing competition for inward investment – within the European Economic Community (EC) the UK competes with Belgium and France, just as do Maryland, New Jersey, and California within the US – the formation of regional economic blocs, together with some interregional protectionism, has led several MNEs to seek a presence, and particularly an innovatory related presence, in each of these territories to protect or advance their global competitive postures.

Our third tenet is that the way in which governments are affecting the resource allocative decisions of MNEs is increasingly by actions taken to advance *other* economic or social goals, rather than by those directed specifically at these companies. Moreover, governments (whether deliberately or not) are increasingly affecting the behavior of MNEs through their impact on the *transaction* costs of organizing economic activity, rather than on the costs incurred and the revenue received from the direct *production* of goods and services. Since this is a critical tenet in our analysis and is little understood by politicians and administrators – at least in the West – we propose to explore its implications in more detail in the following section.

THE CONCEPT OF TRANSACTION COSTS

Let us define two kinds of costs incurred in the supply of goods and services, viz. production and transaction costs. We define production costs as those costs which have to be incurred to supply a given quantity of goods or services *in the absence of market failure in intermediate product and factor markets.* Essentially, these costs represent the opportunity costs of the resources used, i.e. the price paid for the inputs multiplied by the number of units of each used to produce a given output. In a perfectly competitive market, all firms are assumed both to optimize the combination of inputs needed to produce a given output,[2] and maximize the value-added from any given combination of inputs. In this situation, *private* transaction costs are assumed to be zero, i.e. the market *per se* is assumed to be a costless mechanism. However, to create and sustain complete or perfect markets, there may well be set-up and running costs which have to be borne by society as a whole. These include a legal system designed to ensure that the rights and responsibilities of buyers and sellers are protected, and an insurance industry, which is designed to spread risks of individual market transactors over a larger number of such transactors.

Now, let us assume some kind of market failure or imperfection is introduced. Such a failure may occur for two reasons. First it may be brought about by the anticompetitive behavior of participants in the market, or by governments intervening in the market to achieve objectives which the market is unable to achieve. This behavior gives rise to *structural market distortions.* Second, markets may fail because the demand or supply conditions underlying a particular transaction are such that the market cannot fulfil the tasks ideally required of it. We shall call this failure *endemic or intrinsic market failure.* Both kinds of market imperfections raise supply price over and above the opportunity cost of the resources used, i.e. they result in positive transaction costs.

Let us now give some illustrations. The literature identifies a variety of *structural market distortions,* but the common feature of each is that they confer some degree of monopoly power on the part of the sellers of factor or intermediate products.[3] The *origin* of this power might be a reduced number of sellers, or some barrier to market contestability, or the ability of the seller to differentiate his product from that of his competitors.[4] The *outcome* of this power may take various forms, including the charging of an above competitive price, a reduction or variability in the quality of output, irregularities in the supply of inputs, and increased negotiating costs over wages or working conditions. These imperfections show themselves sometimes *directly* to the supplying firm in the form of higher input costs, and sometimes *indirectly* through increases in transaction costs associated with the acquisition or utilization of factor services or intermediate products.

Endemic transaction costs stem from five main kinds of market failure. First, wherever there is uncertainty (i.e. uninsurable risk) associated with the supply of, or demand for, goods and services, a simple Pareto optimum condition can no longer exist. Uncertainty is an activity related transaction cost which, incidentally, may affect a firm's revenue as well as its cost expectations. These costs include the uncertainty over future prices or qualities of inputs, over future demand conditions, and over the behavior of competitors (Vernon, 1983).

Second, it is assumed that, in perfect markets, the effect of the transactions concluded are borne solely by the participants in the market. By itself, the market mechanism is not designed to cope with the consequences of a particular transaction to other economic entities, or to society at large, i.e. market externalities. Where such costs or benefits arise, it follows that societal costs and benefits of transactions may be different from those incurred or gained by the participants to the exchange.

Third, in perfect markets, it is assumed that all firms can reach their optimum (i.e. least average) production costs, where the elasticity of demand for the product being produced is still infinite. Such a situation makes implicit assumptions about the relation between the firm's production function and size of the market for the product it is supplying. However, in practice, the optimum size of output may not be reachable without it becoming sufficiently large to influence the market price.

Fourth, and related to the third condition, is that, in the case of some goods, the marginal cost of production is very low, or even zero, once the good is actually produced, but that the start-up or fixed costs are extremely high. This suggests that, *de facto*, the good takes on the characteristics of a public good.

Fifth, perfect markets are assumed to adjust easily, and without cost, to changes in the conditions of demand or supply for the good or service being transferred. However, in practice, there are many markets – notably the market for some kinds of labor and capital goods – in which rigidities of one kind or another inhibit the optimal operation of market forces, and sometimes, where there are externalities, of that of social efficiency as well.

The literature has classified the nature of transaction costs in various ways. Essentially, they arise from the *costs of organizing relationships over and above that which have to be incurred in a perfect market.* The costs may be both endogenous and exogenous to firms. They may be incurred in both static and dynamic markets.

Endogenous transaction costs embrace the *internal* coordinating costs of hierarchies, given the price and quality of intermediate products. Exogenous transaction costs arise from *external* (or market) transactions. Both kinds of costs may vary between *countries, sectors of activity* and *firms.* Both kinds of costs may reflect elements of both structural and endemic market failure.

The transaction costs will vary according to how economic activity, or changes in that activity, are organized, and the incentives and penalties facing firms, which will influence their ability and desire to minimize such costs. Much of the literature has concerned itself with the costs and benefits of using *markets* or *hierarchies* (either singly or as a group) as modes of transactions. While not disputing the legitimacy of this approach, it is no less appropriate to look at the costs and benefits of alternative ways of organizing value-added activities. For example, where one firm acquires another firm to benefit from the economies of scale or scope, although this is a market replacing activity, it also results in a different organization of production (viz. one firm produces what was previously produced by two firms). The question of how *production* is optimally organized is, then, no less relevant than the question of how best are *transactions* optimally organized.

We have suggested that transaction costs reflect the degree and form of market failure. A perfect market would cause production to be optimally organized. Production in imperfect markets may or may not be optimally organized depending upon the nature of the imperfections. *Structural* market distortions usually result in suboptimal resource allocation and higher transaction costs for at least some participants in the market. However, firms might respond to *endemic* market failure in a beneficial way by reorganizing production to lower transaction costs.

In practice, both markets and hierarchies – and, indeed, the private enterprise system itself – are constrained in their ability to minimize transaction and production costs by the political and institutional framework, and the economic and social milieu within which they operate. It is, however, important to distinguish between the kind of internalization by firms which is designed to advance or exploit power, and that intended to promote a more efficient allocation of resources (Teece, 1985).

So much for the reasons for endemic market failure, which might cause production and transaction costs to be higher than is socially desirable, and which might justify some kind of action by governments, on behalf of society, to try and reduce these costs. But, it is important to observe that this kind of intervention is very different from that required to remove or reduce structural market distortions, or from that in which the State itself believes that planning is a superior organizational mechanism to the market. The kind of interventionism to reduce transaction costs is essentially *pro-market* and *symbiotic* with the goals of firms. It is *cooperative* and *complementary* to the actions of the market rather than *combative* or *substitutable*. It is pro-active to promote competitiveness rather than reactive to curb anticompetitive behavior. It concerns itself with efficiency and structural adjustment rather than distributional questions. Far from forcing firms to behave contrary to their own interests, it helps them to improve their economic performance and to behave as they would if markets were perfect.

We believe that it is imperative that governments should better understand the reasons for, and effects of, the two forms of market imperfection just described, if for no other reason than that the kind of policy reactions to them is totally different. Rather than repeat or enlarge upon what has already been written, we have encapsulated, in Table 13.1, the main attributes of structural and endemic market failure, and the possible responses of governments to them. The reader may care to bear these attributes and responses in mind, as the argument of this chapter proceeds.

In this chapter, we shall be primarily concerned with the organization of resource allocation to achieve economic objectives. With the risk of oversimplifying a quite complicated issue, the theme of the chapter is that, over the past 30 years, the interaction between governments (and particularly governments in advanced industrial countries) and MNEs has changed from being primarily one of conflict arising from the perceived differences in the objectives of the two parties, to being one of cooperation to achieve mutually compatible or complementary goals. In the first case, governments intervened (and, of course, still do) to reduce the (perceived) structural distortions caused by MNEs in order to achieve their own economic objectives. To the MNEs, themselves, the frequent perception was that governments, by inappropriate interventionist policies, were more likely to exacerbate rather than cure market failure, and to inhibit rather than enhance the welfare creating effects of FDI.

In the second scenario, governments are increasingly viewing MNEs as a means by which they can advance the efficiency of their own resource usage, and sustain or improve their living standards, *vis-à-vis* those of their major foreign competitors (Vernon, 1983). This will occur when outward direct investment (relative to some other

Table 13.1 Illustrations of structural and endemic market imperfections and some possible government responses to them

Types of distortion	Possible government response
(A) Structural market distortions	
Barriers to entry,* legally restricted access to inputs or final goods markets, possession of proprietary rights (e.g. patents, trademarks) by encumbent firms, restrictive entry requirements (e.g. for some kinds of labor), scale economies, non-contestability of markets.	Disallow exclusive ownership of essential inputs, and/or exclusive dealing with customers; deregulate and/or encourage the contestability of markets, assist new (and small) firms to enter markets; revise patent laws to encourage more innovation.
Oligopoly/monopoly control of output* (leading, e.g. to price hiking) 'X' inefficiency, restrictive business practices, cartelization, higher transaction costs (through unreliability of delivery schedules), lack of pressure to innovate, etc.	Break up monopolies and outlaw restrictive business practices and cartels; in case of 'natural' monopolies, enforce accountability and monitoring procedures over performance, and/or introduce price controls.
Excessive product differentiation or market fragmentation (leading to higher unit costs, and/or cut throat competition and lower product standards), excessive marketing (including advertising) expenditure.	Sometimes legally imposed entry barriers may be desirable (e.g. to protect quality standards and/or reduce *excessive* competition) but mainly government action should be directed to encouraging more *effective* competition, e.g. by removing import barriers which may tend to a proliferation of foreign owned production units (as in Canada).
Interference with market mechanism by governments* (e.g. price controls, import quotas, output limitations, performance requirements, employment subsidies, inefficient imposition of health, safety and environmental regulations, immigration laws, discriminatory taxation, etc.)	Reduced government intervention to allow firms to perform more effectively and to encourage domestic competition.
(B) Endemic or intrinsic market failure	
Failure of markets to take account of costs and benefits of transactions which accrue to non-market participants. Results	A variety of actions which may increase (or reduce) demand and/or supply as the need arises. *A propos* R&D and the

in social consequences of markets being different than 'private' consequences. Especially noticeable in markets for knowledge, and human capital, and often leads to under-investment in creation of new assets (Brooks, 1982).

Failure of markets to adequately deal with risk and uncertainty. To a varying degree, uncertainty is inherent in most markets. Again, however, the social costs of risk may be greater than the private costs; and governments have a responsibility to reduce the private costs or increase the (expected) private benefits of risk taking to equate the social and private net returns of uncertainty bearing.

upgrading of human capital, action may vary from generic policies to improve educational standards and encourage basic research in universities (often in cooperation with local firms), and treatment of intellectual property rights, to more specific fiscal, labor market and innovation policies designed to promote more (or less) investment in asset creation. These may include the undertaking, or commissioning, of R&D, and the dissemination of its results by government itself, especially in sectors, which tend to be made up of small producers, that cannot economically perform these functions.

Encourage private institutions to 'socialize' uncertainty, e.g. by facilitating insurance and futures markets, and to protect buyers and sellers from some of the consequences of uninsurable risks (the breaking of commercial contracts). In cases of government-related risks, to foster or help finance investment, guarantee and/or insurance schemes, e.g. as set up by several governments to protect their overseas investors from adverse political actions of foreign governments. To encourage capital markets to be entrepreneurial in the financing of risk-intensive projects, particularly by small firms; where necessary (preferably jointly with the private sector) to help provide a fund of risk capital. To lessen politically related uncertainty by injecting more stability in economic policies. Governments should also encourage a positive ethos to (judicious) risk taking and not penalize rewards for successful risk taking by excessive taxation. Finally, governments may help reduce uncertainty by providing more information – again, especially to smaller firms, e.g. with respect to export markets, foreign investment regulations, etc.

Table 13.1 continued

Types of distortion	Possible government response
(B) Endemic or intrinsic market failure (continued)	
Failure of markets to cope with the public goods characteristics of some products, i.e. those which involve very high 'front end' or 'set-up' costs and low or zero marginal costs. Again, many public goods have characteristics of social intermediate or final goods. This uncertainty sometimes reflects a lack of knowledge or information, and in their cases from the difficulty of risk evaluation. Willingness to undertake risks also reflects the structure of rewards and the transaction costs of risk taking. Often, too, the pay-back period of such production is very long indeed (e.g. for highways and airports).	Allow consortia of companies, sometimes jointly financed by governments, even though these result in a monopolistic or oligopolistic market structure. The more socially generic the use of goods the more they should be funded by government. Note, however, that the presence or absence and the quality of some public goods facilitates or hinders production by firms. Hence, governments have a responsibility to increase the supply of these goods, whereas the social rate of return justifies it.
Failure of markets to ensure that all firms are price takers and, at the same time, to ensure they produce at the optimum level or output. Technological imperatives may require a concentrated market structure and/or alliances between firms, either along or across value-added chains. In some cases such alliances may be required to be cross-border.	Some positive response in respect to competition and anti-trust policies. This kind of market failure requires government to encourage delicate balance between too little and too much industrial concentration. A constant monitoring and redefining of the concept of workable competition, i.e. that which promotes the market structure, which best combines static efficiency and the dynamic upgrading of resource usage and product quality.
Insufficiency or inadequacy of institutional framework within which markets can operate efficiently. (A good example is the current situation in many Eastern European countries.) Lack	Responsibility of government to set up an institutional and legal framework so that markets can efficiently perform their function. Such a framework is more complicated with

of impetus or initiative of producers to innovate or upgrade resources, and of consumers to demand sophisticated and fault-free products.

technologically sophisticated and 'generic' intermediate goods and services than with simple consumer products. Governments can also do much by legislation, persuasion and example to help set the appropriate entrepreneurial and work ethos, and to upgrade consumption standards.

Failure of markets to adjust to changes demanded of them speedily and efficiently, due to extra-market structural rigidities.

To promote, encourage and financially assist in retraining and relocation schemes. Encourage, by tax credits, etc., firms to absorb redundant labor elsewhere in their organization by appropriately restructuring their portfolios of products and/or markets. Foster a positive attitude towards changes, while helping those who are adversely affected by change to help themselves.

---

* NB These practices are only structurally distorting if they result in a less than static or dynamic optimal market structure, and/or allow the supplying firms to exploit their privileged position by earning economic rent or engaging in anti-competitive practices for their own gain.

allocation of resources) advances the innovatory capacity and the efficiency of resource allocation of the investing country, and when inward direct investment increases the innovatory capacity and competitiveness of the resources of the recipient economy. In this scenario, governments and MNEs are seen to cooperate, rather than compete, with each other to promote their respective goals.

POLICIES AFFECTING MNEs: 1950–1980

With the above analysis in mind, let us now consider the changing role of governments as they have interacted with MNEs. We shall consider just two periods, viz. 1950 to (around) 1980 and 1980 to date. The final section will then speculate a little on the possible future direction of the interaction between governments and MNEs.

For the three decades up to 1980, and for most, but not all, countries, inward and outward direct investment were treated by policy makers as two quite separate and unrelated economic phenomena. In discussing government actions taken, either to influence, or as a result of, these two kinds of MNE activity, a distinction might usefully be made between (a) those specifically designed to affect the behavior of foreign direct investors and their affiliates and (b) those intended to affect the general conditions within which both domestic and foreign firms operate. Examples of the former include investment incentives and regulations, performance requirements and capital outflow controls. Examples of the latter include modifications in development, trade, industrial, innovatory or macro-economic policies, which influence either the locational attractions of countries to both domestic and foreign investment, or the ability of their domestic firms to become MNEs or increase their share of global markets.

Inward direct investment

While it is difficult to generalize about the actions of host governments towards, or as a result of, inward direct investment, for most of the three decades prior to 1980 it is possible to make two assertions. The first is that, in almost all cases, such actions that were taken were directed towards maximizing the benefits and minimizing the costs of inward direct investment, *given* the existing economic system and policies pursued by these same governments. The philosophy seemed to be that, if the net benefits were not as much as governments believed they could (or should) be, this reflected the structurally distorting behavior of the foreign investors and/or lack of bargaining power on their own part, rather than an inefficient or inappropriate economic system or set of policy instruments, which the host governments were either unable or unwilling to modify.

The second assertion is that, except in the case of a few East Asian economies, actions taken to affect the level and structure of inward direct investment and the behavior of foreign affiliates were rarely part of a systemic or holistic economic strategy of governments. Usually, action was directed towards achieving a particular set of objectives, with little understanding or appreciation of how inward investment might impact on this goal, or, indeed, of how government policies might, themselves, affect the unique contribution of inward direct investment. Only in the case of Japan and later of Korea, and, to a lesser extent, of Singapore and Taiwan, did administrators seek to incorporate inward investment into their broader economic planning. One of the consequences of this partial and fragmented approach was that the governance costs were higher than would otherwise have been – including the devising, administration and monitoring of inward investment policy *per se.*

Over the years, an extensive documentation has amassed on the various strategies and policies pursued by host governments towards inward direct investment, and on the agreements concluded with MNEs in a variety of sectors.[5] *Inter alia*, a reading of these studies reveals that the laws, regulations and policies towards MNEs have been frequently modified over the last 30 years, even by the same country. There has been an iterative learning process, both by MNEs of the economic conditions in host countries and of the expectancies of their governments, and by the latter of the costs and benefits of different kinds of MNE activity. By the 1980s, apart from the very poor developing countries, most countries had compiled a fairly sophisticated set of regulations and requirements towards inward investors, and most, too, offered a medley of incentives and controls that they considered best suited their particular needs. In addition, by drawing on the data, advice and training facilities of such international agencies as the UNCTC, the World Bank and Foreign Investment Advisory Service of the International Finance Corporation, and gleaning from the experience of other countries, governments have gradually learned to modify and refine their inward investment policies with respect to changes in environmental conditions, their own macro-management and technological capacity, and to the new opportunities opening up for MNEs.

We have suggested that most actions by governments to influence inward direct investment between 1960 and 1975 were intended to achieve two main objectives. The first was to remove, or re-dress, the perceived adverse affects of the behavior of MNEs or their affiliates. Examples include restrictions over sourcing of inputs and destination of exports by subsidiaries imposed by parent companies, the transfer of inappropriate technology, transfer pricing abuses, and so on. The second was to promote domestic economic policies which, themselves, were designed to modify the perceived imperfections of cross-border markets. While, in some cases, e.g. Japan, these could be justified insofar as they helped facilitate long term comparative advantages, in others, and especially in developing countries pursuing import substitution policies, e.g. India, the result was simply to distort (or further distort) market prices and make for a less efficient allocation of resources.

We have also mentioned that the reaction of host governments towards inward investment until the mid-1970s was often dependent on the political party in power. However, in the latter part of the decade, a series of events occurred which caused a shift in the perceptions and actions of most governments. Some of these, e.g. the world recession following the two oil price hikes, which led governments to reappraise the costs and benefits of inward investment, could well be of a cyclical nature. Likewise, it is too early to judge whether the contemporary disenchantment with socialist economic regimes and the liberalization and deregulation of many markets are a lasting phenomena. Each of these events has, however, fostered the belief by governments that MNEs, far from distorting *internal* market structures, may help coun-tries to 'tap into' the *international* division of labor, and to question the ability of central planning to allocate resources more efficiently than the market.

But, perhaps the most far-reaching, and for the most part we believe, irreversible change affecting host government attitudes and policies towards inward investment has been the tremendous techno-logical advances of the last two decades. These have brought about effects on the demand for particular factor endowments and capa-bilities, and on the organization of economic activity. In turn, these effects have both widened the options open to firms in the location of their value-adding activities, and have modified the relative signifi-cance of many of the parameters affecting locational decisions.

Together with the rapid growth of some industrializing economies, particularly in East Asia, these events have had two results. First, they have generally lessened the desire and the ability of both governments and MNEs to engage in practices and policies which add to structural market distortions. Second, they have increased the bargaining power of MNEs, relative to the governments of many host countries, simply because their locational options have widened. But, third, as the next section will show in more detail, the technological changes have caused a reevaluation by national authorities of their attitudes towards the internationalization of value-added activities.

Outward direct investment

To begin with, we would reiterate the point made earlier, that in the 1960s and 1970s, the attitudes and actions of most governments towards the foreign activities of their own MNEs were totally divorced from those towards inward investment by foreign MNEs. In some cases, different government departments (or sections of the same department) were responsible for the collection and analysis of data on outward and inward investment, and/or for the formulation and implementation of policies towards it.

In the two decades up to 1980, the US, UK, West Germany, Japan and France were the major outward investors, although, as Chapter 11 has shown, the relative significance of foreign investment to economies of some smaller developed countries, e.g. Switzerland, The Netherlands, Belgium and Sweden, was even greater. Nevertheless, only in the UK, the US and Japan was there any kind of coherent policy towards outbound MNE activity.

In the former two cases there were four points of concern. The first was to do with the comparative rates of return on foreign and domestic investment. Here the hypothesis was that since the former represented mainly the profits earned by companies, *net* of tax on capital invested, while the latter represented the total value-added by such investment, *gross* of the tax, there was a bias against outward investment. If correct, this hypothesis had certain implications for tax policies.

The second disquiet related to the perceived balance of payments consequences of outward investment; the third to its employment effects, particularly in stagnant and labor-intensive sectors; and the fourth to the technological capacity of the home country. Other concerns, e.g. the impact of foreign investment on industrial structure and anti-trust policy, were also voiced in the 1970s by economists (e.g. Musgrave, 1975; Bergsten, Horst and Moran, 1978).

The implicit assumption underlying most anxieties by home governments was that foreign and domestic investment were *substitutable* for each other, and that because of the loss of taxation to the home country, the social rate of return on foreign investment was normally less than the private rate of return. It was not surprising, then, that attention was primarily focused on export substituting, rather than on resource based investment, although, later in the 1970s the growing participation of MNEs in the export processing zones established by developing countries further added to the concerns of labor unions in capital exporting countries. Rarely, outside the resource based sectors, was outward investment perceived to be *complementary* to domestic investment, or as part and parcel of a restructuring of indigenous resource usage. The main exception was Japan, which, by the early 1970s, perceived outward investment in the manufacturing and service sectors as a way of exporting lower value-added activities, and redeploying the labor released in more high value-added activities.

In spite of the worries over outward direct investment, the policies of Western governments were largely confined to the introduction of selective controls on the capital exports of MNEs (which were rarely effective as most MNEs were able to raise the capital they needed from outside their home countries), and/or on the remission of dividends, and a variety of fiscal provisions, which were designed to neutralize any tax advantages on income earned from foreign investment *vis-à-vis* domestic investment![6] In addition, there were extraterritorial restrictions sometimes imposed by governments on the exports of certain types of products by the foreign affiliates of their own MNEs to unfriendly powers, and on the conclusion of crossborder mergers, alliances and business agreements, which, had they been undertaken in the home country, would have contravened antitrust regulations. Finally, in this period, home governments occasionally intervened to counteract intervention taken by foreign governments, which they perceived to be against their own interest;[7] or to negotiate with them to ensure a level playing field for the treatment of inward and outward direct investment.

GOVERNMENT POLICIES IN THE 1980S – AND BEYOND?

Perhaps the most striking development which has affected government attitudes and policies towards MNEs since the 1980s has been the globalization of the world economy. Such globalization is shown by the tremendous growth of all forms of international transactions, and especially that of MNE related activities. It has been coupled with a reaffirmation of the merits of a market economy, the most dramatic expression of which is currently being played out in Central and Eastern Europe. At the same time, a new generation of advantages in information and communications technology have brought about major consequences on both the location and organization of economic activity.

The increased participation of MNEs in almost all economies has forced governments to reappraise, not only their actions taken to influence the behavior of such firms, or that of their affiliates, but also their general macro-economic and organizational strategies which might directly affect, or be affected by, inward or outward investment. Moreover, the growing convergence in the structure of production of the advanced industrial economies and of cross-border intra-industry transactions has meant that most of these economies are now both major outward and inward direct investors. Within the Triad, the economic activities of MNEs are now becoming increasingly interdependent and influenced by similar economic factors.

The last decade or more has also seen a change in the economic focus of many nation states. Though domestic issues still dominate the thinking of the larger industrial countries, increasingly the need to be competitive in global markets, or with foreign firms in domestic markets, has become a major catalyst for action. Much of this shift in interest has reflected the recovery of Western Europe – now given an additional boost through the prospects of the completion of the internal market in 1992 – and the growth of newly industrialized developing countries, especially in East Asia. Such inroads into the markets of the leading industrial powers have led countries to re-evaluate the factors influencing their own competitiveness in international markets, and to judge the contribution of MNEs in this light.

These developments have also resulted in a change of emphasis in the role of domestic governments in an international oriented economy. From actions designed to remove structural distortions in domestic markets – especially in the production of goods and services based on natural factor endowments – governments are increasingly being required to examine how they might facilitate the supply capabilities of their own firms, by lowering transaction-related barriers, and by fostering the upgrading and structural redeployment of the assets within their jurisdiction.

Admittedly, this shift of interest is quite new, and, except in Japan, South Korea, Taiwan and Singapore, has not yet been translated into policy. Neither the US nor the UK administrations, for example, while acknowledging the need to improve industrial competitiveness, has shown any inclination to adopt a holistic or systemic approach to its long term micro-economic strategy, or to the role which outward or inward investment might play in the pursuance of this strategy. To be sure, both governments are quick to publicize particular actions they take to improve national competitiveness, and they frequently reiterate the need to rid markets of structural impediments. But, underlying the rhetoric and fragmentary policies, there seems little real appreciation of the activist role which governments – especially those of societies whose main competitive advantages have to be *created* – need to play in setting the conditions for hierarchies and market forces to operate efficiently, especially in the upgrading of resources and restructuring of economic activity. To sustain the efficient working of an established market, i.e. one in which the necessary supply and demand conditions for such a market are already in place, is one thing; to create entirely new markets, particularly of goods and services which are jointly demanded or supplied, and to ensure that existing hierarchies and markets can adjust speedily and efficiently to the changes required of them, is quite another.[8]

In Chapter 5, we analyzed the concept of the 'diamond of competitive advantage' introduced by Michael Porter (Porter, 1990) and suggested that a third exogenous influence, e.g. multinational business activity, should be incorporated into his framework along with 'government' and 'chance'. It is also possible to examine the interaction of these variables and the four facets of the diamond from a dynamic perspective. The result of the exercise – which is confirmed by a very different exercise on the kind of industrial sectors most likely to be affected by the reduction in market distortions as a result of Europe 1992 (Cecchini, Catinat and Jacquemin, 1988) – is that it is precisely the sectors in which MNEs are concentrated, or are increasing their concentration, which are those whose prosperity is linked to the role played by governments in affecting the structure and social efficiency of markets and, especially, the extent to which they are able to minimize the net costs of endemic market failure.

We may further hypothesize that this is likely to be the main battle ground for competition *between* countries in these and other industries in the 1990s. Such competition shows itself in the attempts by many governments both to attract inward direct investment to help upgrade their indigenous innovatory capacity,[9] and to improve the competitive capabilities of their own MNEs in foreign markets. To this extent – and this is the final piece of the jigsaw – inward and outward investment becomes *complementary* to, rather than *substitutable* for, domestic investment.

All of this suggests a very different scenario of the way in which

MNEs and governments may interact in the 1990s, compared with that in the 1960s and 1970s. Essentially we are suggesting that, whereas in the earlier period, the focus of interest was on the possible *conflicts* between governments and MNEs,[10] today it is much more on the ways in which the two parties might *cooperate* to promote their mutual economic goals, and, in the case of governments, to best promote the restructuring of their own resources and institutions to meet the challenges of the global marketplace. This is not to suggest that all is 'sweetness and light' between governments and MNEs, or that bargaining over the distribution of the benefits of MNE activity is any less important than it once was. Nor does it lessen the need for an internationally agreed regime, and/or rules of the game, in which inward and outward investment may flourish. Moreover, concern over some of the possible non-economic costs of cross-border production, the export of unacceptable, e.g. health, safety and environmental, standards, and the erosion of country-specific social norms and cultures, is as pronounced, or more pronounced, as it has ever been. But, in most industrial countries, at least, these have now taken second place to the more pressing need of advancing competitiveness in international markets. Moreover, most of the non-economic issues facing nation states today have little to do with the multinationality of firms, *per se*, even though MNEs may be transmitters of resources, values and behavioral patterns which may have a distinctive impact on these issues.

Let us now return to our main theme. The basic thesis of this chapter is that the task of governments, as custodians of the wealth creating capabilities of the institutions and citizens within their jurisdiction, is currently undergoing a fundamental reorientation as a result of six features associated with the modern world economy. First is the increasingly important role of 'created' factor endowments and capabilities in determining the economic prosperity of most nation states. Second is the fact that the markets for these endowments and capabilities is often intrinsically imperfect, and that, in many instances, their demand and/or supply is directly or indirectly influenced by governments. This especially applies to the markets for human capital and for knowledge-intensive intermediate products. Third is the increasing convergence in the economic structure of the advanced industrial economies, and the growing competitiveness between these economies in the markets they seek to serve. One sign of this competitiveness is revealed by the dramatic growth in cross-border intra-industry trade and investment (UNCTC, 1991). Fourth is the growing participation by multinational hierarchies in these same economies, and the mobility of resources, capabilities and inter-mediate products. Fifth is the increasingly significant role of government in influencing the location of production by MNEs, and particularly by affecting the transaction costs associated with high value-added activities (Dunning, 1991b and 1993). Sixth is the growing instability of, and growing interdependence between, the markets for intermediate products, and the complementarity between the role of governments, hierarchies and markets in creating and sustaining an orderly, flexible and efficient system of resource restructuring.

Added to these factors are others such as the growing liberalization of many political and economic systems, the learning experience of both home and host countries of the costs and benefits of FDI. But no less significant is the fact that whereas earlier government measures, intended to affect the behavior of MNEs, are *specifically* addressed to such firms, contemporary policies, while accepting that MNEs may be the most affected by such actions, are more general in their orientation. At the same time, there is need for a better understanding by governments that some markets need to be collectively organized and/or administered by hierarchies if other markets – and, indeed, the market system as a whole – are to operate at optimal or near optimal efficiency.

COMPARATIVE GOVERNMENT POLICIES

A review of the contemporary and changing attitudes and actions of governments, as they seek to come to terms with the globalization of production and markets, would seem to belie much of the analysis so far presented in this chapter. Few governments currently either adopt, or even acknowledge the necessity to adopt, a systemic strategy towards MNE-related activity, or to the upgrading or restructuring of indigenous resources and capabilities occasioned by this activity. Views as to the role of government as a resource creator or as a facilitator of competitiveness, differ considerably between countries (Dunning, 1993), as do ideas about the extent to which governments should be entrepreneurial, customer driven, or market-oriented in their strategic thinking. Until very recently, the philosophy of the UK government, for example, was that this task is almost the exclusive responsibility of the private sector, and that the onus on governments begins and ends with the removal of structural market distortions. By contrast, the Japanese philosophy, as, for example, described in the writings of Teretumo Ozawa (Ozawa, 1989) is that even if the market were completely free of structural distortions, it would not be capable, by itself, of upgrading resources and responding to the changes demanded of it at a societal optimal rate.

This philosophy is demonstrated by the very different policies and practices of the UK and Japanese governments, particularly as they affect international business. For many years, the Japanese government has viewed both outward and inward direct investment as an integral part of its broader micro-economic strategy. In turn, this strategy has been systemic in its objective of improving the long term competitive advantage of the Japanese economy by reducing the transaction costs facing its firms in their attempts to improve their capabilities and restructure the activities of their firms to meet the challenges of the global marketplace.

Such government interaction has been cohesive and comprehensive, and designed to achieve a set of well specified and clearly articulated economic goals. Specific policy measures include those directed to personal and corporate savings, education and training, R&D, taxation, environmental issues, transport and communications, the exchange rate, technology transfer and dissemination, and competition; but each is coordinated so as to achieve a similar set of objectives, and to do so in a way which captures the economies of governance.

The promotion of a well conceived, positive and systemic policy to reduce endemic market failure, and so improve the long term competitiveness of Japanese resources and of Japanese MNEs, is in marked contrast to the UK government, which, for most of the last decade, might be best described as neo-*laissez-faire*. This is not to say that, by its actions or policies, the UK government does not affect the ability of its own firms to compete in foreign markets or the propensity of foreign investors to set up factories in the UL. Indeed, taking a broad brush perspective, it could be argued that the Thatcher administration was one of the most interventionist of any administration since the Second World War (Dunning, 1990).

In each of the areas identified in the previous paragraphs, the UK government has a distinct, and well articulated, policy, but rarely is it possible to see a link between these policies – or the *raison d'être* for them. There seems to be little clear appreciation of the very positive and responsible role which the UK government can play in affecting the competitiveness of its resources and capabilities by helping individuals and firms to overcome the obstacles to that competitiveness which result from endemic market failure. For example, it is strange that, at the time when its major competitors were assigning relatively more resources to education, R&D, vocational training, transport and communications and the like, the UK government (in the belief that such public spending is inherently unproductive) was doing the reverse.

It would be wrong for me to give the impression that the UK administration of the 1980s did not do a great deal to improve the competitiveness of the UK economy or its attractions to foreign companies. In particular, its philosophy and policies have exerted a considerable influence on the ethos of the British people towards competition, work, incentives and entrepreneurship. But, at least until the change of leadership in the Conservative Party in November 1990, I for one found its faith in the invisible hand to solve all the economic problems of the UK both naïve and disturbing, and quite out of touch with the needs and realities of modern business. Even as this chapter is written (December 1992), one sees little evidence of any active coalition between the British government and the private sector in charting the future course of the UK economy. Nor is there little sense of any real cooperation between government and industry in charting the future course of the UK economy, and, except in particular situations,[12] a recognition that the kind of variables which most influence international companies in their investment decisions are transaction rather than production driven, and are critically determined by government policies towards market failure. If there was one particular piece of advice the present author would like to offer to the present (Conservative) administration, it is that it should adopt, and be seen to adopt, a holistic and systemic approach to the organization of economic activity, and to accept that governments, markets and hierarchies have a complementary and interactive role to play in upgrading the human and physical assets and the restructuring of resource allocation so as to best meet the continually changing challenges of the global marketplace. This, we would emphasize, is not government telling firms and markets what to do, or attempting to replace their functions, but government cooperating with firms and markets to achieve mutually beneficial goals.

SUMMARY AND CONCLUSIONS

This chapter has sought to demonstrate that the changing character of market imperfections, and the attitudes and actions of governments to these changes, have fundamentally affected both the ability and willingness of domestic firms to become MNEs, or increase their degree of multinationality, and the level and pattern of inward direct investment. It has suggested that, for much of the post-war period, governments have sought to negate the effects of structural market distortions, including those perceived to be created or practiced by MNEs or their affiliates, and to intervene in the workings of existing markets wherever the outcome is not in accord with their own political and economic expectations. In general, in the 1960s and 1970s, the actions taken by governments to achieve their goals were piecemeal and uncoordinated; and those directed to affect outward and inward direct investment were implemented quite independently of each other. There were few attempts to adapt or modify macro- or micro-economic strategies in the light of the growth of international direct investment or trade related to it. These strategies generally led to a confrontation between MNEs and governments, as, basically, the latter sought to affect the behavioral pattern of the former so as to increase their own share of the economic rent created by them.

In the early 1990s, the main cause of market imperfection in most industrialized countries is not that of structural distortion but of the transaction costs associated with unstable, integrated or interdependent markets. In particular, the costs associated with the uncertainty underlying demand and supply conditions, those which result from the externalities of transactions, those which arise from the segmentation of markets where the optimum size of production is very large, and those which stem from the need to ensure that the core competencies of firms are properly and efficiently exploited have each become a more important component of the total costs of economic activity.

The chapter has further argued that the exogenous variables affecting market structure and government behavior have led to a broad convergence of economic structures in the industrialized countries. This has been accompanied by a growth of intra-industry trade and investment, and an intensification of competition between countries in the production and marketing of a wide range of products. This, in turn, has led governments to reassess their portfolio of strategies to protect or promote their international competitive positions. One of the means by which this can be achieved is by helping to lower the transaction costs of hierarchies or markets over which they (i.e. the governments) have some influence, and by so doing to reduce systemic market failure. Another is to develop a systemic approach to a whole range of policies which, directly or indirectly, affect the competitiveness of their resources within their jurisdiction. Such a need is accentuated not only by the growing ease with which firms can move their activities across national boundaries, but also by their need to seek global sales in order to finance the upgrading of their competitive advantages.

All of these developments suggest the need for a *symbiotic*, rather than an *anti-symbiotic*, relationship between governments, hierarchies and markets (Ozawa, 1989). This idea has already been explored in the previous chapter. As yet, the shift away from confrontation, and towards cooperation, has only been fully manifested in some Asian economies, notably Japan. In the West, the 1980s has seen a reaction to the interventionist policies of previous left-wing administrations, and to a restatement of the virtues of the free market system. This, unfortunately, has led governments to the view that any intervention by themselves to affect market forces (apart from that designed to reduce structural distortions) is to be avoided.

No doubt, there are a host of historical, cultural and institutional reasons which explain the differences in the reaction of the Japanese and Western governments (especially the US and the UK) to the global technological and organizational changes affecting the ownership and location of cross-border economic activities. But, as things currently stand, for most countries, the age of an integrated competitiveness-led economic strategy, jointly fashioned by the government and the private sector, has not yet come.

Whether it will happen in the next decade, or indeed in the next century, we can only speculate upon. My own judgment is that although there will continue to be country-specific differences in the perceived organizational role of government, and its interaction with that of hierarchies and markets, all the major industrial economies will be forced to adopt – gradually or otherwise – more holistic and collaborative micro-economic strategies. This has already happened at a macro-level where cooperation between countries is much greater today than most people could have imagined two decades ago. Because of the intra-governmental transactional costs [sic] it has not yet occurred at a micro-level – and, if and when it does, it will be between governments and firms and hierarchies within a country rather than between governments in different countries.

In a variety of directions, there are signs of this happening. Certainly many Western governments have more explicit policies towards a whole variety of issues affecting competitiveness than they once had. But, a systemic approach is still lacking, and – what is no less important – is seen to be lacking. All too frequently, the market is regarded as the quintessence of the private enterprise system, rather than as a public good, which needs to be fostered and sustained if it is to fulfil the tasks demanded of it. Only, I suspect, the full force of international competition – not only from the Far East but from Eastern Europe, as well as from a revitalized Economic Community – will compel governments to realize that they, as well as the constituents they represent, will either swim or drown together! And, part of this force will, undoubtedly, be the influence on, or the response of MNEs to, the changing shape of our global village.

14 The political economy of MNE activity

INTRODUCTION

The interface between the strategy and behavior of multinational enterprises (MNEs) and that of the attitudes or policies of governments of the countries or regions in which they operate is a subject which has frequently engaged the attention of international business scholars.

For the most part, however, the political economy of MNEs, or MNE activity, has been studied from the viewpoint of a particular issue or set of issues. Examples include assessing the impact of outward foreign direct investment (FDI) on the welfare of a particular home country, the designing of an appropriate set of government measures towards inward direct investment, and evaluating the response of foreign or domestic MNEs to specific host or home government policies.[1] By contrast, there has been little or no attempt to study the political economy of MNEs as a subject in its own right.[2] This is the rather ambitious task of the present chapter.

The main thrust of the chapter will be to examine and explain the growing attention given by governments to the activities of MNEs over the past century or more, and especially within the last decade. We shall argue that this is partly due to the growing participation of MNEs in the economies of most nation states; partly to the changing perceptions of national governments of the contribution of MNEs to their economic and social goals; and partly because the strategies of governments, either in response to the presence of MNEs, or directly to affect their patterns of behavior, have been revised. We shall conclude that, as a result of these factors, the political economy of MNE activity in the early 1990s is very different from that in past years, and that, in spite of country- and sector-specific variations in the way in which MNEs interact with national economic and social policies, some general trends can be discerned.

THE DISTINCTIVE CHARACTERISTICS OF MNE ACTIVITY

First, however, it may legitimately be asked why should the political economy of MNE activity be any different than that of the activity of other business enterprises? The answer must rest in the specific attributes of multinationality and their distinctive impact on the goals and policies of governments. As these issues have been frequently addressed in the literature[3] we shall do no more than to highlight them here.

The distinctive impact of MNEs arises from the fact that, unlike international trading firms or multiplant domestic firms, they own or control value-added activities across national boundaries. In so doing, they internalize (i.e. integrate within their sphere of governance) cross-border intermediate product markets. It is the ownership, by MNEs, of intermediate products and the way in which these are used in combination with other resources which they may own or acquire, which results in an output, and the distribution of benefits arising from that output, different from that which might be produced or generated by uninational firms.

The consequences of these differences are shown in four main ways. The first is in the international pattern of production undertaken by MNEs in the home and host countries in which they operate. This embraces not only the types of products produced but also the stages of the value chain involved in the production of those products. The second is in the methods of production and the efficiency with which the products are produced. The third is in the impact on consumers, workers and other firms and/or on the region in which the MNEs or their affiliates are located. The fourth is in the influence exerted by MNEs on, or their response to, the actions of the governments of the countries in which they operate.

The combination of these effects is shown directly in the size and structure of output produced, and in the competitive position of particular firms and sectors. Indirectly, through any changes in government policies induced by the affects of MNEs on environmental, social and other objectives, the consequences are seen more broadly in the quality of life, on the political and economic sovereignty of nation states, and on the extent and pattern of intercountry economic integration.

Because of their unique and special characteristics, MNEs may react differently to government policies than their uninational counterparts. At the same time, MNEs may proactively affect the content and implementation of such policies, and the distribution of value-added between residents and non-residents. They may do so, either as a result of their own behavior, or by influencing the behavior of other firms, consumers, employees or other business groups. By their product, production and marketing strategies, MNEs may help advance a government's economic strategy; or they might inhibit the achievement of such strategy. At the same time, there are many areas of conflict, or potential conflict between the behavior of MNEs and the objectives of government. These include the extent, form and ownership of economic activity and the distribution of its benefits. Finally, for good or bad, MNEs are currently responsible for the great majority of economic linkages between countries. It is the creative tension between the private and social costs and gains of FDI and the way in which these tensions are resolved that is the essence of the political economy of MNEs.

THE POLITICAL ECONOMY OF MNEs: THE CHANGING SCENARIO

Up to 1939

For most of the period prior to the Second World War, the direct interaction between MNEs and governments was of two main kinds. First, there was the use of MNEs as an instrument of the territorial extension of government economic and/or political jurisdiction (Svedberg, 1981). In the nineteenth and early twentieth centuries, for example, most European governments looked upon their foreign owned possessions as a means of supplying the mother country with raw materials, foodstuffs and minerals, and as markets for products manufactured by it. In pursuance of these goals, governments often politically or economically supported their MNEs, even to the extent of providing them with military protection.

Second, some governments viewed foreign MNEs as potential suppliers of at least some of the resources and markets needed for their domestic development.[4] The main instruments used by them to attract entrepreneurship, technology and management skills in the nineteenth century were import restrictions, fiscal incentives and land grants. Fiscal inducements were also provided by both home and host governments to attract resource-based investment. There were few controls or requirements imposed by host governments on inward direct investors; indeed, most governments had yet to fashion any kind of policy towards such investment. Some home governments, however, – and particularly the UK in the first part of the nineteenth century – discouraged certain kinds of outbound MNE activity which they perceived would work to the disadvantage of their domestic economic welfare.

Indirectly, of course, the actions of MNEs considerably affected the ability of governments to achieve their economic and social goals, while the policies and development strategies implemented by governments affected the capabilities and willingness of their own firms to engage in outward investment, and that of foreign firms to invest in their countries.

1945 to c. 1980

The political economy of MNEs or of MNE activity has dramatically changed in the last half century. By the early 1980s, most countries had formulated explicit policies towards outward direct investment, while, on several fronts, attempts had been made to influence the conduct and behavior of MNEs by multilateral action. Several countries had also introduced legislation or policies to affect the level and direction of outward direct investment, albeit, in most cases, to achieve very specific objectives.

We might suggest five main reasons for the introduction and continuation of these policies. The first is the growing role of MNEs in the economies of most nations. By the mid-1970s, for example, inward direct investors accounted for more than 30 per cent of the production of goods and services in at least 25 countries (Dunning and Cantwell, 1987), while a rapidly increasing percentage of the output, employment and profits of MNEs was being accounted for by their foreign operations. Second, the kind of capabilities possessed by MNEs – notably, technological, organizational and managerial expertise and access to international markets – have become an increasingly important determinant of economic growth. Third, mention must be made of the growing role of the state in the management of national economies, both at a macro- and a micro-level. Fourth, many developing countries gained their political independence in the years following the Second World War. With such independence has come a sensitivity to any vestige of economic colonialization.

The fifth reason – which has become an increasingly important factor in recent years – has been the tendency of MNEs, especially those producing in developed countries, to pursue integrated organizational strategies and to view their foreign subsidiaries less as self-contained production units identified with the interests of host countries, and more as members of a global and regional network of value-added activities. In this way, MNEs, for good or bad, have become an increasingly important bridge between the economic and political environments of the countries in which they operate. While some governments have welcomed this, others have looked upon it as a challenge to their sovereignty.

An examination of the policies and regulations of governments of home and host countries reveals a large number of actions to affect both the level and structure of inward investment, and the distribution of the value generated by it.[5] These actions – which include the terms of entry and the performance requirements expected of foreign affiliates – vary enormously between countries and in the same country, over time, between economic sectors, and according to the extent of foreign participation. Such measures range from obtaining information about the operations of MNEs, through persuasion and a gamut of macro- and micro-organizational policies likely to affect their behavior, to mandatory controls and requirements of one kind or another.

Much research has been done in assessing both the conditions under which the different kinds of government action might be introduced, and the likely consequences of such action. Essentially, however, the policies of governments depend, first, on their perceptions of the extent to which MNEs help advance economic welfare and at what cost, and, second, on whether or not they believe that, by one means or another, they might increase the net benefit of such investment. Certainly, for much of the period under review, there was a strong feeling among the governments of most developing countries and some developed countries that, without some intervention on their part, inward direct investment would not provide them with the amount or kind of benefits which they perceived it should,[6] and consequently they chose to take action to affect it.

At this point, it is important to distinguish between two kinds of actions which governments might take towards MNEs and MNE activity. The first are those which are addressed specifically to modify the conduct of MNEs, given the exogenous economic and political environment in which they operate. The second are those taken to ensure that these latter conditions are changed in such a way that the response of the MNEs to them will improve the latter's contribution to national social and economic goals. For example, a MNE which enters a country in response to a high tariff on its exports, and is faced with a bevy of performance requirements, is likely to engage in different and, for the most part, lower value-added activities, than one which responds to the presence of a well motivated and trained labor force or a modern and efficient telecommunications and transportation infrastructure. While both sets of inducements may be strongly influenced by host government policies, the former will be in response to distorted market signals, while the latter is a reaction to the actions taken to facilitate the dynamic comparative advantage of the resources and capabilities for which they are responsible.

For the most part, in the period prior to the mid-1980s, governments expected MNEs to adapt to the economic environment in which they located their activities, as witnessed by the plethora of FDI regulations, requirements and incentives devised by countries. In many instances, this was bad political economy as it simply added one set of market impurities to another, with the result that nations either did not get the amount of MNE activity they wanted, or, when they did, it was of the wrong kind or they paid too high a price for it. It was to avoid incurring the unacceptable costs of inward direct investment that many governments in the 1960s and 1970s expropriated the assets of foreign subsidiaries, particularly in resource based sectors. But even this strategy frequently failed to achieve its objectives, as the countries still had to rely upon the nationalized firms for the kind of intermediate products and markets they previously supplied. Moreover, because it was these assets, together with the distorted markets in the host countries, which allowed the erstwhile foreign investors to earn above average profits in the first place, they continued to extract an economic rent, but without the risk attached to an equity investment.

The political economy of outward investment in the period 1950–1980 was even more *ad hoc* and pragmatic. For the first 20 years or so after the last World War, most countries, apart from the US, were faced with a difficult balance of payments situations. Because of this, and the belief that outward investment generally substituted for domestic investment,[7] efforts were made, particularly by European governments, to restrict the outflow of FDI. Even in the US, there was a vigorous debate in the 1960s, about the effect of the foreign operations of US MNEs on the American balance of payments (Snider, 1964; Hufbauer and Adler, 1968). Several countries instituted capital export controls at this time. Most of them failed to achieve their objectives, mainly because many MNEs, and particularly established MNEs, were able to raise the capital required for their foreign activities from other sources.

In the 1970s, attention switched to the effects of outward investment on employment in the home country. The question of the export of jobs by MNEs, especially to developing countries, was examined by analysts representing the interests of US management and labor as well as by several independent institutions and academic economists.[8] As might be expected, the effects identified crucially depended on the assumptions made about what might have happened to domestic employment in the absence of outward investment (the so called 'counter-factual' or 'alternative' position); but, in any event, the government made no real attempt to discourage the foreign operations of American owned MNEs.

Of the studies published in the 1970s on the political economy of MNE activity, two deserve special attention. The first was that by Bergsten, Horst and Moran on *American Interests and American Multinationals* (1978). The merits of this work were twofold. First, it presented a carefully argued case for a neutral policy towards outward investment *per se*. Whether or not this influenced US government policy it is difficult to tell; but the fact remains that, until the late 1980s, apart from some aberrations in the taxation of foreign earnings and extraterritorial legislations, US policy towards outward direct investment was generally neutral. Second, Bergsten, Horst and Moran argued that American policy towards its own MNEs needed to be systemic. While not favoring action specifically addressed to foreign direct investors, they argued that US policy makers should accept that, if outbound MNE activity was to make its optimum contribution to the home country's economic goals, this might require some modification to its own macro-economic and organizational policies. This recommendation made no impression on the US administration at the time; but, interestingly, it was entirely consistent with the policies then being pursued by the Japanese (Ozawa, 1989).

The second interesting study (or polemic would be a better word) of this time was that of Jacques Servan-Schreiber on *The American Challenge* (1968). This monograph asserted that without a coordinated policy towards the promotion of technological capacity and economic restructuring, Europe was in danger of being colonized by US owned MNEs, while European owned firms would be out-competed in world markets. Servan Schreiber vigorously argued for restrictions to be placed on the hostile acquisition of European firms by American MNEs, and for an increase in government spending on indigenous innovatory activities and manpower training. Yet, only seven years later, Robert Gilpin, an American political scientist, was putting together a similar case against outward US investment, because, as he saw it, US competitiveness and economic power were brought about by the export of cutting edge technology by US companies to their foreign subsidiaries elsewhere in the Triad (Gilpin, 1975). Gilpin suggested that part of the reason for the increase of this kind of US multinational activity in the 1960s and 1970s was the perceived need by US oligopolists, particularly in technologically advanced sectors, to protect their foreign markets against their domestic competitors and potential foreign rivals. This view was upheld by Knickerbocker's study of the timing of the establishment of American subsidiaries in several industries (Knickerbocker, 1973). It was also endorsed by Kiyoshi Kojima (Kojima, 1978) who regarded such outward investment as anti-trade, and likely to lead to a deterioration in the investing country's comparative trading advantage.

At the same time, Kojima asserted that Japanese investment abroad in the 1970s was trade-enhancing and consistent with Japan's economic interests. Certainly his views were supportive of the contemporary Japanese strategy towards the internationalization of its own firms. As Chapter 6 has described, like its British equivalent a century earlier, this strategy was primarily directed both to facilitating the developments of natural resources vital to its domestic industry, and/or to promoting manufacturing exports from Japan.[9] By the late 1970s, however, Japanese firms were increasingly being encouraged to engage in foreign based value-adding activities which required resources (e.g. low cost labour) in which Japan was losing its competitive advantage. At the same time, neither Gilpin nor Servan-Schreiber's recommendations were heeded by the US or French governments.

1980s to date

Several important developments in the world economic scenario since the late 1970s have substantially affected the political economy of international production. Foremost among these has been the renascence of the market philosophy by many – indeed most – countries of the world. Second, and scarcely less important, has been the growing competition among countries for resources and competences, and particularly those which enable firms to produce new or improved products, to exploit new markets, to produce existing products more efficiently, or to lower their organizational costs. Third, there have been quite staggering advances in technology – particularly in the production, dissemination and organization of all kinds of information and knowledge. These have affected not only the level and structure of FDI, but also the nature of the impact of MNEs on the countries in which they operate.

Together with the emergence of new industrializing nations on the world scene and moves towards regional economic integration in several parts of the world, these changes have affected not only the responses of nation states towards the activities of MNEs, but also the willingness and capabilities of governments to effect these activities (Dunning, 1991). Fourth, there has been the continued growth in the relative importance of FDI as a form of international economic involvement. By 1989, for example, the value of international production had exceeded that of international trade, while an increasing proportion of trade, both in intermediate and final products, is now being undertaken by and within MNEs (UNCTS, 1991).

Among the more significant consequences of these changes on the nature of the interaction between governments and MNEs, we would identify four. The first is that many countries have chosen to reassess the priority of some of their economic and social goals, and, in particular, to give more attention to the promotion of the competitiveness of their firms and industries in international markets. Current events in both Western and Eastern Europe amply testify to this realignment of interest. At the same time, several developing countries – including many in sub-Saharan Africa – have reoriented their development strategies towards export-led growth and a more active participation in the international division of labor. This has virtually forced such governments – and particularly those dependent on international aid – to rethink their general macro-economic and organizational policies to ensure that these strategies are best advanced.

MNEs are, then, increasingly being evaluated by both home and host countries in terms of their contribution towards upgrading the quality of indigenous resources and capabilities, and advancing long term comparative advantage. As we shall demonstrate later in this chapter, this change in philosophy is leading to a less adversarial and more symbiotic relationship between many governments and MNEs – much along the style of that which has been adopted by the Japanese and Korean governments for the past two decades or more.

The second consequence of the changing world economic scenario is the growing symmetry between outward and inward direct investment flows, particularly among advanced industrialized countries. At the same time, an increasing proportion of cross-border investment is of an intra-industry kind. More and more, the pattern of MNE activity is beginning to resemble that of trade; and just as the political economy of trade is multidimensional rather than undimensional, so increasingly policy makers are considering their strategies towards inward and outward direct investment as different sides of the same coin. For example, Japanese policy makers aim to encourage outward investment in sectors in which their own firms are perceived to have a comparative competitive or O specific advantage, but which require location bound resources in which Japan is comparatively disadvantaged. Such outward investment then releases resources, which are available to foreign owned MNEs[10] to use with their O specific advantages which they transfer from their home countries. In this way, outbound and inbound MNE activity play a complementary role in the restructuring of Japan's industries, to promote its dynamic comparative advantage.

Third, we would note that the changes earlier described have affected not only the cost structure of firms, but the options open to them in the location of their activities. Essentially, this reflects the reduced significance of natural and location bound resources, such as land and unskilled labor, and the increasing importance of created or 'improved' factor endowments,[11] e.g. human and physical capital, including all forms of information and knowledge. Previous chapters have already referred to these latter endowments as 'capabilities' or 'competences'. Three features about them should be re-emphasized. The first is that they are generally more mobile across national boundaries than are natural resources. The second is that their efficient creation and usage is increasingly determined by the ability of firms to organize them and the natural resources at their disposal so as to minimize both transaction and production costs. The third is that non-market forces, and particularly the actions taken by governments, are likely to be more important in affecting the former than the latter costs. Examples include the role of education, training, science and technology policies in the up-grading of human and physical capabilities, and of transport and communications, fiscal, competition and environmental policies in affecting the ability and willingness of firms to create value-added from these capabilities.

The fourth consequence we might identify is the restructuring of the value-added activities of MNEs, and a change in the governance of these activities. Though the majority of firms[12] will most surely continue to invest abroad mainly to supply goods to the markets in which their affiliates are located, an increasing number of the larger companies, particularly those operating in technology or information intensive sectors, have responded to the decreasing costs of organizing cross-border operations, and the liberalization of intraregional markets, by rationalizing their foreign production, and integrating their global organizational networks. Since, as several writers, e.g. Doz (1986), Bartlett and Ghoshal (1989), have pointed out, the impact of MNEs pursuing these kinds of strategies on the efficacy of national economic policies differs from those which treat their foreign affiliates as self-contained profit centers, it follows that the political economy of their activities requires some reappraisal.

Each of these four consequences on MNE activity has not only led to more international linkages. It has fundamentally changed, and is continuing to change, the nature of these linkages. In the early 1990s, a substantial proportion of cross-border transactions are internalized within MNEs, or between members of corporate networks located in different countries. Such linkages have dramatically reshaped both the character of economic interdependence between countries, and the ability of governments to frame macro-organizational or structural adjustment policies without taking account of the way in which these might effect MNE activity, and through that activity, the economic welfare of other countries. MNEs are, in fact, becoming a major instrument used by nation states in their quest to become more competitive in both domestic and world markets.

THE NEW POLITICAL ECONOMY OF MNE ACTIVITY

Nation states and MNEs: towards a congruence of interests?

Governments usually exhibit mixed feelings towards the activities of MNEs. On the one hand, governments acknowledge that they may help advance domestic competitiveness and economic growth. On the other hand, MNEs are viewed as adversaries whenever a conflict arises between corporate and national objectives. In the first scenario, there is assumed to be a complementarity of interests between the policies of governments and the strategies of MNEs. For example, to attract the kind of inward investment which is perceived to best advance their dynamic comparative advantage, governments will do their best to offer at least as favorable locational opportunities as those provided by other countries – and particularly those they regard as their main international competitors seeking the same kind of investment. We have argued elsewhere (Dunning, 1990) that, except in the case of resource-rich countries and those at the very early stage of their economic development, these attractions now rest increasingly on the extent to which firms or corporate groups of firms are able to organize their cross-border activities efficiently.

There is a similar mutuality of interest between firms engaging in outward direct investment and their home governments. Increasingly, it would seem that, to gain new markets, to acquire new competitive advantages, and to capture the systemic advantages of producing in several countries, firms need to increase the extent of their international production. At the same time, governments can do much to fashion the economic and business environment within which their own firms can create and sustain the necessary competitive advantages for foreign production. This is not to suggest that governments should play a direct interventionist role by distorting market signals, but rather, as Chapter 13 has suggested, that they may help facilitate markets and hierarchies to perform efficiently the tasks required of them; and that, where this is not possible (because of endemic or intrinsic market failure) that they, themselves, may counteract, or compensate for, such failure.[13]

An obvious example is where firms perceive that the level of output at which the private (marginal) costs of creating new knowledge or upgrading human capital (by various training schemes) is equal to the expected (net) marginal receipts of such investment is below that at which the government perceives marginal social costs will equal marginal social revenue. This might occur where private hierarchies believe that part of the output of research and development expenditures or training costs 'leaks out' of the firm to the rest of the economy. In such an event, the government, on behalf of society, may be justified in incurring costs of the firm equal to the output it loses. Another example is where the insurance market cannot fully compensate for the political (or other non-commercial risks) which a particular economic activity might involve. In such an event, it may be entirely appropriate that, either unilaterally or multilaterally, nation states should facilitate the setting up of insurance guarantee schemes.

A third instance of market failure is the case of a product, the innovating costs of which are high but the costs of reproducing it (once it is supplied) are zero or very low. In such circumstances, a firm may be dissuaded from engaging in R&D because competitors can so easily appropriate the economic rent from any successful innovations. This kind of market failure cannot be easily corrected by action taken by the participants in the market. More often than not, it can only be reduced or circumvented by governments taking action either to offer some temporary protection to the innovating firm, or to devise some system by which firms may be induced to engage in worthwhile innovatory activities without their having the exclusive rights to the output of these activities.

An examination of these and other market failures suggests that they are not only increasing in the modern world, but that the actions taken by governments to help overcome them affects the capacity and willingness of foreign and domestic MNEs to advance the competitiveness of the resources and competences under their jurisdiction. Yet, except for Japan, and to a lesser extent some newly industrializing countries, e.g. Singapore and South Korea, few countries have embraced this aspect of the new political economy of the MNE. We shall return to this point later in this chapter.

Nation states and MNEs: a new bargaining relationship?

However much MNEs may aid the objectives of nation states, there remain a number of potential conflicts between MNEs and home and host governments. These arise because of the differences in the goals of corporations and those of the country in which they operate. Three of these – which are primarily the concern of host governments – require a special mention.[14] The first relates to the type of value-added activities in which they are engaged. In their efforts to promote an efficiency seeking production strategy, MNEs may not always engage in as stable or as high value activities in particular countries as the governments of those countries would like, while some developing countries have long since argued that the type of technology transferred by First World MNEs may not always be suitable to their needs. The second cause for conflict concerns the sourcing and marketing policies pursued by MNEs. In their attempt to reap the economies of scope and scale of cross-border activities, and to reduce environmental volatility, MNEs may pursue strategies which result in less sourcing from domestic firms or less selling to export markets than host countries would like.

The third area of concern surrounds the distribution of the economic rents between the MNE and the host country. This has always caused much controversy, particularly in developing countries where foreign MNEs own or control natural resources or groups of resources in which the recipient country has a marked comparative advantage. The conflict is likely to be particularly pronounced in cases when no provision is made for the obsolescence of a bargain struck at the time of the entry of a foreign firm. Moreover, over the years, it has become increasingly obvious that ownership is not the only, and sometimes not even the main, factor affecting the negotiating power of MNEs. Control of the use of resources and the distribution of value-added to them may no less be affected by a variety of cooperative arrangements; and, as Chapter 9 has suggested, it is the terms of these arrangements – and, in the case of joint equity ventures, the allocation of corporate responsibility and rewards –

which are the crucial variables determining the share of this rent. Moreover, it is worth observing that cost and revenue manipulating tactics, e.g. by such means as transfer pricing, may also affect the sharing of the gains of MNE activity.

The contemporary political economy of the distribution of income arising from MNE activity is broadly the same as it has ever been, and essentially reduces to the extent of the bargaining power of the two parties. But the structure of this power has changed. Partly, this is because, as they better understand their own objectives, their ability to obtain these objectives, and the contribution of MNEs to them, governments are able to bargain more effectively. On the other hand, there can be no doubt, and this especially applies to MNEs which pursue global or regional strategies in technology-intensive industries, and to those producing goods and services for international markets, that the information asymmetry between MNEs and governments (or local firms) has increased in favor of the former. In general, such companies have wider options than previously, particularly in export generating activities; and, although it is true that host countries often have more choice in their sources of technological and managerial capabilities, the global shortage of these capabilities, together with a plentiful supply of natural resources and unskilled labor, has meant that host countries have not been able to capture these advantages of the growing competition among MNEs as much as they would have wished (Stopford, 1990).

But the main difference in the current response of governments to MNEs, and/or their affiliates, relates to the policies they adopt towards them. In spite of the increasing influence of MNEs in the world economy, the main emphasis of economic strategy has switched from regulations and measures specifically directed to MNEs and more to macro- and micro-policies, which essentially attempt to set the economic environment in which both foreign and domestic enterprises operate.[15] At the same time, the increasing regionalization or globalization of economic activity is causing governments to revise their *general* macro-organizational strategies, so as best to exploit the benefits of inbound and outbound FDI.

This major shift in policy dates back to the early 1980s when it became increasingly evident that measures directed specifically to affect the behavior of MNEs were not achieving the success hoped for by governments. At that time, there were a plethora of incentives, regulations, controls and requirements directed towards inward investors, and, to a lesser extent, towards outward investors as well. These policies were introduced and sustained at a time when governments across the world were influenced by Keynsian economic thinking, and were pursuing highly interventionist micro-organizational strategies. While welcomed for the capabilities and markets they provided, MNEs, and particularly those from the larger market economies, were viewed with concern wherever they were able to thwart or reduce the effectiveness of government policies.[16] Moreover, as we have mentioned earlier, if MNEs responded to government policies in an unacceptable way, the responsibility for this fact was always put at the door of the MNEs, and not of the policies *per se.*

Changes in attitude towards the efficacy of the market economy have not only resulted in governments upgrading the role of monetary policy, coupled with attempts (rather less successful) to introduce more disciplined fiscal policies. No less important has been the widespread liberalization and deregulation of markets, and the reduction of direct government participation in the production of goods and services. Finally, at a supra-government level, the move towards reducing trade and investment barriers, as illustrated by the North American Free Trade Agreement and the completion of the EC's internal market by the end of 1992, have led to a reduction in both domestic and cross-border market imperfections.

As both domestic and international market signals have become less distorted, so governments have discovered that the behavior of the MNEs (along with those of domestic firms) has become more acceptable. As a result, they have found it less necessary or desirable to address specific policies towards inward direct investors. This has been particularly the case when, in reviewing the effectiveness of such policies, governments have judged their success not by the amount of new inward investment attracted or additional employment on exports generated by it, but by the contribution of such investment to the real output of the community, given the opportunity cost of the resources used.

We accept that the above scenario has not yet widely come to pass. Progress towards it is currently most marked in Europe and in some East Asian economies. It is accelerating in North America, while there is a growing acceptance of the need for a change in both general economic policy and that towards FDI in particular in the case of a large number of African countries (especially those in Southern and East Africa). At the same time, it cannot be denied that elements of protectionism are still very much alive, especially within the Triad, and noticeably between Japan and the EC and between the EC and the US; and should this get out of hand, it would undoubtedly harm the cross-border efficiency and competitiveness of MNE activity.

To conclude this section, we would observe that the political economy of MNEs varies considerably between countries and firms. Some of the ways in which different forms of MNE organization affect government policy and *vice versa* have been explored by Doz (1986) and others. In this chapter, we shall confine ourselves to a brief examination of policies of two countries, viz. Japan and the UK.[17]

Japan

For most of the post-war period, although the Japanese government has operated a market system framework, her macro-, micro- and foreign investment policies have been different from that of her Western neighbors in a number of ways. First, from the start, she has pursued a holistic and comprehensive economic strategy which has been primarily directed to advancing the long term industrial growth and competitiveness of its firms. Within this strategy, various sub-strategies involving resource usage and development may be identified.

Second, at a macro-economic level, the Japanese have placed great store on an interest rate and fiscal policy which encourages domestic savings and an exchange rate which favors domestic production and exports. Third, at a macro-organizational level, the government has devoted substantial resources to education and/or encouraging private firms to invest in training schemes. Within a series of five-year plans, each of which has been designed to upgrade the industrial productivity and restructure the allocation of domestic resources towards higher value activities, firms have been guaranteed a favorable investment climate, while the suppliers of capital have been encouraged to take a long term view of the return on their investments. Though in the 1960s and 1970s, the government, through the Ministry of International Trade and Industry (MITI), did attempt some specific targeting of industries (and, it might be added, without any great success), and although there were a host of import barriers, the main thrust of Japanese industrial strategy has been to ensure that it's corporations are provided with the appropriate legal, commercial and communications infrastructure, and the necessary incentives to perform in a way consistent with national economic goals.

For the last three decades, policy towards both outward and inward investment has been an integral part of the Japanese government's overall economic design. As Chapter 6 has described, to begin with, investment was encouraged (e.g. by insurance guarantee schemes and the like) to developing countries in Asia to ensure the supply of minerals and raw materials for Japanese industry. Later, investment was made in labor-intensive offshore manufacturing production. In more recent years, the quality of value-added activities of Japanese firms has been stepped up as their competitive advantages in such sectors as motor vehicles and electronics have increased, while protectionist measures have made it difficult to export to the large markets of the US and the EEC. In the 1990s, Japanese firms are becoming acutely aware of the need to develop an innovatory presence in both the US and the EC, and when this is perceived by the Japanese government to assist the competitiveness or restructuring of the domestic industry, it is likely to be actively encouraged.[18] At the same time, as the Japanese economy has moved towards maturity, policies affecting MNE activity have become less specific and more general.

Although there has been some relaxation of restrictions placed on inward investment in recent years, there have been few attempts explicitly to foster a welcoming climate for foreign companies. Certainly, the practice and regulations of the Japanese stock exchange, and the difficulties faced by foreign firms in concluding acquisitions and mergers with Japanese companies, does little to advance this kind of investment. Furthermore, there are a plethora of (what are in effect) non-tariff barriers facing foreign firms. These include differences in business customs, language and technical standards, and the difficulty of breaking into existing or establishing new, distribution channels. Whatever the truth in the assertion that foreign firms are not prepared to make the effort required to penetrate and understand the Japanese market, there can be no question that the costs of initial entry into Japan are high. Yet as Ohmae (1985, 1989) has shown, foreign corporations producing in Japan are generally profitable, and some have carved out quite substantial shares of the domestic market.

The United Kingdom

As of December 1992, there was no UK policy specifically directed towards inward and outward investment, although this, in itself, is quite deliberate. While the present authorities see each as a vehicle for upgrading the productivity of UK resources and capabilities, it believes that the market should determine the amount and pattern of MNE activity. On inward investment, most government action is confined to providing information to non-resident investors, of trying to ensure that the local content of the output of foreign subsidiaries is kept to an acceptable level, and to minimizing the possibility of anti-competitive tactics on the part of the investing companies. In addition, the UK government has provided foreign firms with generous regional subsidies, investment grants and tax incentives. The fact that indigenous firms are also offered similar inducements does not entirely satisfy the critics, who argue that foreign firms (particularly *de novo* foreign firms) have much more opportunity to take advantage of such schemes.

Where the political economy of MNE activity in the UK does differ from that in Japan, is first in respect of the macro-organizational setting within which both the subsidiaries of foreign firms and home country MNEs operate, and second the extent to which the globalization of the economic activity is perceived to require modification to domestic economic policies. The privatization and deregulation of markets has generally led to a more 'hands off' attitude towards the allocation of indigenous resources and capabilities, and to the contribution of inbound and outbound MNE activity. It has also led to a compartmentalization of organizational strategies which is in total contrast to the situation in Japan. The UK government appears to have no overall strategy towards improving industrial competitiveness, apart from that which arises from its belief in the free market.

The role of government as an active participant in factor and intermediate product markets is not one which generally appeals to the current UK administration, nor is there much evidence that it acknowledges its responsibility to ensure the provision of the right kind of technological, transport and communication infrastructure necessary for UK owned enterprises to be competitive in world markets.[19] At the same time, many of the government's actions in course of the last decade have positively affected the ethos of entrepreneurship, the work ethic and the climate of industrial relations; and these, much more than any specific policies directed towards foreign investors, have attracted the presence of Japanese and other foreign firms to the UK since the early 1980s.

CONCLUSIONS

Let us now briefly summarize the main conclusions of this chapter. First, the political economy of MNE activity is likely to vary according to the interaction between two sets of interrelated forces. The first is the macro-economic and organizational strategies of the governments of both home and host countries; and indeed, as this chapter has argued, the contribution of FDI is more likely to depend on these strategies than on policies specifically addressed to such investment. The second force influencing the interplay between MNE activity and governments is the kind of value-added activity generated by MNEs and the kind of governance they exercise over their foreign affiliates.

Second, over the last two decades, this political economy of MNE activity has undergone substantial changes. Foremost among these has been the learning experience of both MNEs and governments on the likely consequences of FDI, and the movement away from centrally administered economic policies towards market-oriented strategies.

Third, there has been a growing recognition that, as countries seek to compete with each other for resources and markets, MNE activity and cross-border corporate alliances can play an important role in advancing or inhibiting national competitiveness. Increasingly, the capabilities and markets provided by MNEs are perceived to be synergistic or complementary to the needs of governments, and are especially welcomed by countries whose trade and investment patterns are characterized by intra- rather that an interindustry transactions.

Fourth, the last 20 years has seen a growth in the importance of created capabilities or competences rather than natural resources as variables influencing the competitiveness of firms. At the same time, to be translated into final products, created capabilities or competences often involve many more transactions along the value chains, while the way in which these transactions are organized is becoming an increasingly significant determinant of the cost effectiveness of producers. Two other features about created capabilities is that they tend to be more mobile across national boundaries than natural endowments, and their availability, price and quality is often critically influenced by government policy.[20]

Fifth, the chapter has argued that the political economy of MNE activity is likely to be most welfare enhancing when (a) governments pursue a holistic and integrated strategy towards advancing national competitiveness, and regard FDI as an integral part of that strategy; (b) cross-border transactions involving MNE activity are conducted under competitive market conditions; and (c) governments are prepared to take the necessary action to reduce transaction costs (or market failure) in circumstances where both markets and/or hierarchies fail.[21]

Sixth, the chapter has suggested that, *de facto,* the political economy of MNE activity is strongly country-specific. At the same time, it has argued that there are a number of essential components for an optimal strategy towards (and in consequence of) MNE activity which are common to all governments. The chapter concluded by suggesting that some countries – noticeably Japan – have been more successful in implementing such a strategy than others.

15 Multinational investment in the EC: some policy implications

INTRODUCTION

This chapter seeks to analyze some of the implications of European economic integration, and particularly the completion of the internal market in 1992, for the policies adopted, both by the leading EC nations and by the European Commission, towards inward and outward direct investment, and the activities of multinational enterprises (MNEs).

We shall limit our analysis to two main time periods: first, the early post-war years through the establishment of the European Economic Community (EC) on 1 January 1958, to around 1975, and second, from that date to the present day. While the first period was mainly characterized by an inflow of US MNE activity into Europe, the latter saw both a widening of the sources of inward investment and a shift in its nature from both primarily import substituting to efficiency or strategic asset seeking. In addition, the latter years of the second period saw a marked increase in inward investment in anticipation of EC 1992, and a liberalization and harmonization of both national and regional policies towards such investment.

FDI AND THE MACRO-ECONOMIC ORGANIZATION OF NATION STATES: SOME CONCEPTUAL ISSUES

The issues identified

Until recently, the ways in which individual European countries organized their economic activities had little to do with the presence or absence of foreign owned firms in their midst or with the outward investment of their own MNEs. Essentially, the macro-organizational policies of governments were addressed to fostering their macro-economic and social objectives, and primarily reflected the political ideology and the value judgments of alternative modes of organization of the governments in power. All the Western (but not the Southern) European countries, which are now members of the EC, operated mixed economies in which the role of the state in affecting the workings of the free market varied along a spectrum from near centralized planning to near *laissez-faire*. However aware governments may have been of the impact on their economic and political gaols of outbound or inbound MNE activity, there is no evidence that it had any direct effect on the macro-organization of economic activity.[1]

This is not to say that governments had no policies towards MNE activity, or that, in certain areas of micro-organization (such as anti-trust legislation, regional development and investment incentives) their strategies were not modified in the light of the special features of MNEs or their affiliates. But, in general, government actions specifically directed to foreign direct investors were designed to ensure that the latter's conduct and performance enhanced rather than inhibited the success of *existing* macro-economic and organizational policies. It then follows that, as long as MNEs were perceived to affect national objectives no differently than national firms, government policy would be neutral. If, for good or bad, their behavior was distinctive, then measures might be taken either to encourge or to discourage their activities – or, more likely, to discourage the adverse micro-organizational impacts, while encouraging (or not deterring) the beneficial impacts.

For the most part, the philosophy of all European governments led either to no specific macro-organizational policies to MNE activity, or to a number of very specific measures designed to achieve quite particular micro-organizational or macro-economic objectives. Before considering these actions, however, it is worth observing that there are several different kinds of motives for FDI, and the economic consequences of each of these is quite distinctive.

The literature[2] identifies four main types of FDI: *natural resource seeking, market seeking, rationalized* (or *efficiency*) *seeking* and *strategic asset and capability seeking*. For the most part, EC countries have attracted and continue to attract direct investment of the three latter types.[3] Outward direct investment from EC countries is of all four kinds.

Inward direct investment

Each kind of MNE activity has its distinctive policy implications. Let us take inward investment first. *Market seeking* investment, as its name implies, is investment designed to produce goods for the market in which the investment is made. Essentially, it occurs because foreign firms perceive that they can best service a particular market by being physically present in that market, rather than by exports from their home countries (or other host countries), or by licencing local producers to manufacture the products being sold on their behalf. Historically, the main impetus for market seeking investment has been the restrictions imposed by host governments on imports of foreign made goods. In this event, there is a deliberate attempt by governments to switch the location of production and/or to protect their indigenous sectors against foreign imports.

The distinctive consequences of such market seeking investment arise from the resources and capabilities transferred by the investing company and the way in which these resources and capabilities are utilized and managed. This resource-providing and organizational function of MNE activity may impinge upon both the host country's macro-economic goals – for example, employment, interest rates, balance of payments, inflation – and its macro- or micro-organizational goals, such as industrial restructuring, competition, the environment, industrial relations, research and development (R&D) strategy, and so on.

Governments usually tried to protect themselves against the possible adverse consequences of inbound investment by imposing certain conditions of entry on the investing firms, and by insisting on certain patterns of behavior from them. Thus, a country in balance of payments difficulty might require a foreign subsidiary to buy a high proportion of its inputs from local sources or to export a certain proportion of its output. Another country which is suffering from regional unemployment may steer its foreign investors to the areas most seriously affected. FDI in particular sectors may be welcome in some countries but not in others, according to its industrial structure, and the competitiveness of its indigenous firms. Because, then, of the different differential impact of FDI on host countries, and because of differences in the perceived needs and concerns of governments, it follows that the policies will also vary. Such policies may also vary according to whether the inward MNE activity takes the form of a greenfield investment or an acquisition or merger of an existing domestic company.

The purpose of *rationalized* or *efficiency seeking* investment is primarily to restructure – and sometimes expand – existing MNE activities so as to enhance the efficiency or global competitiveness of the investing corporation. Such investment is amost always 'sequential', that is, additional to existing investment.[4] Its impact on the host country is likely to be different from market seeking investment (which it often complements) in that rather than, or in addition to, providing its affiliates with resources, technology and management capabilities, it provides them with cross-border organizational direction. Indeed, sequential investment captures much of the distinctive characteristics of modern day MNE activity. While initially a firm's main ownership specific advantages tend to lie in its privileged possession of, or access to, particular assets (which it makes available to its affiliates),[5] sequentially, it is the cross-border organization of these assets, i.e. the advantages of (efficient) multinationality *per se*, which may predominate. At the same time, these organizational advantages[6] may enable a firm to sustain or enhance the kind of proprietary rights which made possible the initial investment.[7]

Nevertheless, rationalized production affects the structure of economic activity of the host country by locking it into the international corporate strategy of the investing companies. Whether or not this is to the benefit of the host nation depends on (a) how far its interests are best served by being part of an international division of labor, which implies some delegation of sovereignty – either to foreign markets or hierarchies, and (b) how far the ownership and control of that division of labor by MNE hierarchies benefits the host country *vis-à-vis* some alternative organizational pattern.

The more the government of a country perceives its interests to be similar to those of the world economy (and especially to those of the countries with whom it trades), and the more MNEs are forced to behave as if they were operating in a competitive environment, the more it is likely to welcome MNEs for the cross-border organizational direction they provide. The more a government wishes to pursue a policy of economic autonomy and is concerned lest inbound MNE activity forces on it an unacceptable division of labor, and/or reduces its bargaining or negotiating capabilities, the more it will seek to introduce specific policy instruments to control the level, direction or behavior of foreign MNEs.

Unlike market seeking investment, cross-border rationalized investment can occur only where there is relatively free trade between the countries which are host to the subsidiaries of MNEs. While market seeking investment often responds to government-imposed market distortions and/or is undertaken to counteract the actions of competitiors, rationalized investment flourishes where there are no structural market distortions but where, because of endemic market failure, the benefits of the common governance of economic activities and the transactions arising from these are substantial.

From the perspective of the investing company, rationalized investment is a response to the imperative of technological developments on the one hand, and the liberalization of cross-border markets on the other. It tends to occur in capital- or technology-intensive sectors in which the advantages of both intra-industry and intrafirm trade are the most prevalent. These are the sectors in which the economies of scale, scope and geographical specialization can best be reaped, and where firms tend to differentiate their products as a form of competitive advantage. They include motor vehicles, consumer electronics, pharmaceuticals and telecommunications in the manufacturing sector, and finance, banking and insurance, consultancy and construction in the services sector. These are also the sectors which tend to be among the most footloose in their value-added activities and which, in a Western European context at least, are less influenced in their location strategies by the availability of national resources and size of local markets, and more by that of technological, educational, transport and communications infrastructure. Each of these latter variables has been shown to be critical to minimizing the costs of governance and maximizing the benefits of cross-border corporate integration (Dunning, 1991b).

Partly because rationalized investment is sequential – even though, currently, Japanese MNEs setting up subsidiaries in Europe are pursuing market seeking FDI as part of a regionally integrated strategy – partly because its output is not primarily destined for the local market, and partly because the product and production configuration of rationalized affiliates is likely to be different from that of their local competitors, not only does government policy need to be different than in the case of market seeking investment, but governments require to recognize that the responsiveness by rationalized or efficiency seeking affiliates to any set of policy instruments is also likely to be unique.

In a seminal contribution, Yves Doz (1986) distinguished between three types of foreign affiliates which might operate in Western Europe. The first he classified as *nationally responsive* affiliates. These are entities which are similar to their indigenous competitors in all major respects, except for their privileged access to the assets and capabilities of the foreign corporations of which they are part. They tend to be truncated versions of their parent companies, which treat them as part of a polycentric organization. These are also the foreign affiliates, the conduct of which host governments are most easily able to influence, although the nature and direction of such influence varies according to the structure of the host economies and their objectives, while their power to influence the behavior of the affiliates, or extract the maximum economic rent from them rests on their bargaining capabilities.[8]

The second kind of affiliate identified by Doz is one which is part of an MNE which pursues a regionally or globally rationalized strategy. In such cases, host governments perceive the benefits to be those which arise from integration; but the costs are a reduction in the flexibility to enforce certain policies to ensure that affiliates behave in the national interest. Doz refers to a trade-off between the MNE not exploiting all the benefits of integration to be a good citizen, whereas the government accepts that the benefits of integration may not be achieved without some costs. Such costs may include the MNE purchasing a higher percentage of its inputs from foreign sources in order for it to maintain the quality standards on output destined for international markets.

The rationalized affiliate is likely to be part of a geocentrically oriented investing company, and to engage in a considerable amount of intrafirm trade. Because they are less tied to a particular location, MNEs can (and often do) react to unwelcome government policies by relocating their activities. MNEs are usually more anxious to retain full equity control of efficiency seeking affiliates than they are of market seeking affiliates. *Inter alia*, this is shown by their greater reluctance to conclude joint equity ventures in the latter than in the former.[9] Consequently, the leeway for action by governments is likely to be less than in the case of market seeking investments, although, much again, will depend on the balance between the rents earned on the resources transferred, on the one hand, and the benefits which arise from cross-border integration on the other.

Doz classifies most value-added activities by MNEs as being some kind of balance between the degree of national responsiveness (or local citizenry) on the one hand, and international integration (or worldwide citizenry) on the other. He acknowledges that most foreign MNEs operating in Western Europe fall somewhere in the middle. Such companies, he suggests, pursue a multifocal strategy, by which management assess the appropriate trade-off between responsiveness and integration for each decision taking (or functional) area separately. Thus an MNE may behave as a nationally responsive company in the arena of labor relations, or where (within a country) it locates its plant; but, as far as its sourcing, marketing and R&D strategy is concerned, it may operate as a regionally or globally integrated company.

Certainly, too, the balance between integrated and nationally responsive MNEs will depend on the countries in which they locate their activities, and the countries from which they originate. As we have already seen, it will also vary between sectors. Thus, even within a regionally integrated area, one might expect there to be a higher proportion of nationally responsive MNEs in countries which have large and prosperous markets, good supply capabilities, and whose governments exercise a critical and selective eye on the costs and benefits of economic interdependence. By contrast, in smaller countries which practice an export-oriented industrial strategy, one might find the ratio of efficiency to market seeking investments rather higher. Examples of the latter group of EC countries are Belgium, Luxembourg, The Netherlands, Portugal, Ireland and Denmark. Examples of the former are West Germany, Italy and France. Spain and the UK, each for very different reasons, fall between these groups.

We now turn to consider the fourth kind of FDI in Western Europe, which has only recently been given explicit attention by economists and business analysts.[10] This investment we have called *strategic asset seeking* investment. Its purpose is essentially to protect, sustain or advance the *global* competitive position of the investing company *vis-à-vis* its major national and international competitors. Such investment has been almost solely concentrated within Western Europe and in the US. It is directed chiefly to globally oriented sectors,[11] whether these be growing or stagnating. European firms have acquired assets in the US mainly to strengthen their competitive position *vis-à-vis* US and Japanese MNEs and US firms have acquired European firms to strengthen their position *vis-à-vis* European and Japanese MNEs, and to reconfigure their investments in preparation for EC 92. Meanwhile, Japanese firms have tended to use this strategy to acquire assets in international sectors in which they are comparatively disadvantaged, such as pharmaceuticals, or in those in which there is surplus capacity in the world markets (for example, Sunitomo's acquisition of Dunlop), or in those which offer complementary technologies or market access, such as Fujitsu's take-over of ICL. We have suggested that the intended effect of asset acquiring investment is to benefit the global portfolio of the investing company. Often, this will mean a restructuring of the acquired firm's value-added activities. This may take various forms, including a divestment of resources and capabilities unrelated to the core assets of the business, a slimming-down of the operations and a change in the organization of production.

The consequences of asset acquiring investment for the host country are not easily predictable. Much depends on the characteristics of the firms involved, and their positioning in international markets. The benefits include the injection of new capital, technology, markets, entrepreneurship and ideas, and perhaps the rescusitation of a declining industry. In others, there is a strengthening of the international posture of the acquired firm, even if it is now foreign owned and integrated into the global network of activities. The costs are that the locus of control may be changed to the disadvantage of the host country. A company which was nationally responsive and integrated into the domestic economy may now become more responsive to global corporate objectives. There may even be a hollowing-out of the assets and markets of the acquired firm. This is most likely to be the case where its innovatory capabilities are transferred back to the new foreign owners and absorbed into their domestic R&D facilities.

Governments often have much less leeway to control or influence the outcome of an inward investment after it has been made, except where the effects are so widespread and far-reaching that it pays them to modify their general macro- or micro-organizational policies. Generally speaking, until the mid-1980s, European governments were generally skeptical about the benefits of foreign acquisitions or takeovers, primarily because they feared that these might increase the concentration of foreign ownership, reduce indigenous and technological capacity, or close particular foreign markets (which the acquiring firm may prefer to service from one of its other subsidiaries). For many years now, the main policy instrument used by governments to thwart hostile takeovers has been monopoly and anti-trust legislation, which has been implemented with greater or lesser vigor by all European administrations.

In the last decade, however, attitudes towards cross-border mergers and acquisitions have become more relaxed even though both individual, national governments and the EC still view as unacceptable certain types of 'restrictive business practices'. This is due partly to the opening up of domestic European markets to outside competition, and partly to the increasing belief that inward direct investment (or alliances involving foreign partners) can, by the provision of new assets, capabilities and organizational direction, aid the competitiveness of the host countries. This latter claim is yet to be substantiated. Certainly, in some instances, it has dubious validity, as exactly the same argument is advanced by home countries about the benefit of some kinds of outward direct investment.

In summary, depending on the type of inward direct investment, the extent of the existing foreign investment stake, the sectors in which it is made, the conditions under which it is made, and the home and host countries involved, its policy implications are likely to differ. However, one generalization is, perhaps, permissible. Over the last 20 years or more, the economic significance of inward direct investment to most EC countries has steadily risen (UNCTC, 1991; Dunning, 1993). So indeed, has that of outward direct investment. The result is that the MNE intensity of economic activity (measured as the percentage of inward plus outward investment stake to GNP) has risen from being generally of marginal significance to being of very considerable significance. In 1990, for example, in the UK and The Netherlands the MNE intensity was over 40 per cent, in Belgium it was 30 per cent and in Germany, Greece and Ireland it was more than 15 per cent. Most of these percentages are at least double those of 20 years ago. This index alone (and there are others which tell a similar story)[12] suggest that the time is coming when governments will need to take account more explicitly of the specific role of both domestic and foreign MNE activity in the formulation of their micro- and macro-per cental policies (and, indeed, some of their macro-economic policies as well)[13] and the very specific contributions made by such companies to national economic objectives.

But as Section 3 (on the EC dimension) of this chapter will suggest, there is little evidence that this is being done – at least not in an EC context. Indeed, early in 1991, the author of this chapter was informed by a senior official of the EC Secretariat that the nationality of the owners of firms producing in the EC was of little or no interest to the European Commission. This is in stark contrast to the Japanese perception of the significance of inward and outward direct invest-ment, where, since the mid-1960s, it has not only been explicitly incorporated into their industrial, trade and technology policies, but in recent years has come to dominate increasingly these policies[14] (Ozawa, 1989). But before taking these comparisons further, we turn to consider some effects of outward investment on the policy forma-tion of the capital exporting countries.

Outward direct investment

For much of the twentieth century, most Western European MNEs have been actively involved in both *resource* and *market seeking* outward investments. Because of intra-European tariff barriers (including cultural and political barriers), and their inability or unwillingness to exploit the economies of cross-border activities, they have lagged behind US MNEs in developing both horizontal and vertical *rationalized* investments.[15] There are signs that Europe 1992 is producing a major change in the attitude of European MNEs, who, at the same time, are engaging in more aggressive *strategic asset acquiring* investment both within Western Europe and in the US and Japan. However, rather than repeat (in mirror fashion) the approach of the previous section, to analyzing the policy implications of outward investment, we shall examine two or three of the major policy areas by which such investment has been evaluated. We shall then relate the shift in priority given to these areas to the changes in the international economic scenario, and in the attitudes of home governments towards the costs and benefits of outbound MNE activity.

The national output and the balance of payments of the home country

As the previous chapter has demonstrated, the initial post-1945 concern of most European governments was about the effects of outward MNE activity on the balance of payments. Many European currencies, including sterling were not fully convertible until the early 1960s, while, for most of the rest of that decade, the (current) balance of payments of European countries with the exception of Germany was in deficit, and much macro-economic policy was directed to correcting this deficit. In addition, governments of the era (and particularly that of the UK) were concerned about the consequences of outward investment on the real national output, as, at the time, academic research was showing that the *direct* social rate of return on foreign direct investment was less that the social rate of return on domestic investment.[16] However, outbound investment sometimes led to *indirect* benefits to the home country. Among the most important of these identified by economists in the 1960s were the additional demand for the goods produced by the home country and a feedback of technical knowledge resulting from foreign production (Reddaway, Potter and Taylor, 1968; Hufbauer and Adler, 1968).

As with inward investment, the effects and policy implications of outward investment rest crucially on the kind of investment being made and the assumptions made about what would have happened in the absence of such investment – the so-called 'counterfactual' or 'alternative' position. For example, most *market seeking* FDI is likely – to some extent at least – to be export replacing. However, if, in the absence of such FDI, MNEs from other countries had made the investment, it is possible that exports would have fallen even more. Moreover, if government macro-economic policy is successful in filling the investment 'gap' opened by the capital exports, this will have very different consequences for the national output and the balance of payments than if there is no compensatory investment.[17]

By contrast, *resource seeking* outward investment is less likely to be substitutable for domestic investment or exports from the investing country; indeed, it may be complementary to them. Much resource-based investment by developed industrialized countries is undertaken to safeguard sources, lower the prices, or improve the quality of minerals, energy supplies, raw materials and agricultural products used by domestic manufacturing firms, and to protect or advance their supply capabilities *vis-à-vis* those of their competitors. At the same time, the extent to which such investment benefits the capital exporting country is likely to depend, first, on whether or not, in its absence, some other firms would have made the investment, and second, on how far it is at the expense of other kinds of domestic capital formation, or indeed, of the efforts of the purchasing companies, to seek alternative sources of primary products, or to economize on their use. It may also partially rest on the extent to which home governments are prepared to protect their investors from the uninsurable risks of FDI (for example, the possibility of national-ization or expropriation of their foreign assets), by some kind of investment insurance or guarantee schemes.

Governments' strategic options may differ according to their perception of the likelihood and the costs and benefits of these alternative scenarios. But one thing is clear: the opening-up of opportunities for FDI in resource-based sectors implies some kind of policy response on the part of the home government – even though this may result in no action being taken!

The attractions of *rationalized* outward investment to capital-exporting countries rest largely on the extent to which the *raison d'être* for such investment is consistent with the economic goals of the home countries. In general, assuming that the home country accepts the benefits of economic interdependence, and that MNEs are operating within a (reasonably) competitive international environment, it is to be expected that they are. A division of labor forged by MNEs from West Germany or the UK, provided it is in response to market forces rather than to government-imposed distortions, is likely to create structural changes, and secure an economic rent which will accrue to the benefit of the home country. The main policy challenge posed by rationalized investment is how best to minimize the costs of structural adjustment arising from it. Such fragmentary research as has been undertaken on this subject (OECD, 1985) suggests that MNEs tend to respond to changes in the external business environment more speedily that their uninational competitors, and that this could exacerbate the short-run problems of resource reallocation. Certainly, outward investment, which is designed to take advantage of low labor costs (a form of resource-based investment but one which is motivated by efficiency seeking considerations) by US MNEs in Mexico and some Asian industrializing countries, has been loudly condemned by those in the home countries who attribute to it their loss of jobs. At the same time, it is likely that, in the absence of such investment, European, and latterly Japanese, MNEs would have captured at least some of the markets supplied by US firms.

If rationalized investment is broadly consistent with the long-term output and trading goals of home countries, the effects of *strategic asset acquiring* investment are more difficult to assess, simply because the conditions for such investment and the rationale behind it are so firm-specific. And yet, in some ways, since very large capital exports are involved, this kind of investment is directly substitutable for domestic investment; indeed, for reasons which we shortly discuss, it has the potential to be the most socially costly form of FDI. At the same time, the possible social benefits are also quite significant. Much again depends on whether other kinds of domestic or inward foreign investment can fill (or would have filled) the gap vacated by the outward investments.

Long term competitiveness and technological capability

The last two decades have seen a noticeable change of emphasis in the evaluation of outward direct investment by most countries. Except in the case of some Asian countries, however, it is still too early to identify the policy changes which can be specifically attributed to this reconfiguration of values. Basically, however, attention has switched from judging outward investment by its direct effects (for example, the profits it earns) to assessing its wider consequences on the resources and capabilities of the investing country, and the efficiency at which these resources and capabilities are organized. This explicitly or implicitly assumes that FDI, like trade, can (depending on the conditions in which it is made) either advance or retard a nation's competitive advantages. Action taken to further this objective may range from eliminating internal structural market distortions, to introducing or strengthening a variety of measures designed to facilitate domestic resources and competences better to deal with and react to market forces, including those requiring changes in the direction of resource allocation and the organization of resource usage.

However, national policy might go well beyond that specifically directed to outbound MNEs. It could, for example, encompass actions taken against other countries which pursue strategic trade (and/or other) policies to protect or advance the interests of their national champions (Stegemann, 1989). Domestic policy may also extend to other areas of macro-organization which are affected by, or affect, the ability and willingness of domestic companies to be competitive in global markets. Of these, education and training, science and technology, transport and communications and environmental policies are perhaps most important. These directly affect the willingness and ability of a country's firms to upgrade the quality of indigenous resources, and the way in which these are organized, both at home and abroad.

Using this criterion, outward direct investment is assessed by the way in which it contributes to the long term competitiveness of a nation, not only by advancing the efficiency of its own resources, but by accomplishing this goal more effectively than its competitors. To this extent, governments, and particularly governments of advanced industrial nations which are at a similar stage of economic development and producing broadly similar products, are increasingly implementing organizational strategies not unlike those pursued by their own firms.

Such a strategic or holistic approach to outbound MNE activity tends to require a very different set of policy measures than those described earlier. Moreover, ideally, governments should adopt policies which take domestic investment by indigenous firms, domestic investment by foreign firms, and foreign investment by indigenous firms as part of the same package of resource usage and allocation.

We have not the space to take this argument much further. It has, in any case, been partially dealt with elsewhere in this volume.[18]

However, it may be useful to illustrate our contentions by reference to the contemporary debate on the role of MNEs and generators, organizers and utilizers of technological capacity. To what extent is outward direct investment likely to assist or inhibit the achievement of this goal?

There seem to be a number of arguments both in favor of and against government intervention in outbound MNE activity. The main arguments in favor of such activity is that (whether it be *market, resource, efficiency* or *strategic asset seeking*) it may help the investing firms to acquire resources, capabilities or markets which will help them sustain or advance their competitiveness in world markets and to engage in more higher-value-added activity in their home countries. R&D is becoming increasingly expensive and needs either global markets to help finance it or for its costs to be shared with other firms.[19] According to the protagonists, foreign and domestic investment are complementary ingredients of the global competitive strategy of firms and of the upgrading of domestic resources, and, as such, should be supported rather than discouraged by home governments.

The main arguments put forward against FDI – especially in high technology sectors – are twofold. First, firms may be transferring technology to foreign countries at too low a social price. This is thought particularly likely where the importing countries are potential competitors to the exporting country. This argument is sometimes coupled with another, which is that, in pursuance of their defensive oligopolistic strategies, MNEs may transfer some of their ownership specific advantages to a foreign location, at the cost of eroding the competitive advantage of domestic resources. Second, the strategic or security-related concern is that, having assisted a foreign country to become economically strong – particularly in defence-sensitive sectors – should that country then become unfriendly, it could rebound to the detriment of the home nation. The validity of both these arguments depends on the extent to which the host countries are able to obtain the technology being exported by the MNE either from other countries or by other routes, for example, export, licensing arrangements and so on. They also tend to assume that there would be no retaliations from the country adversely affected by restrictions on technological exports and to underestimate the technological gains it may be receiving from *inward* investment.

While it would be difficult to deny that there are some cases where FDI is to the long term technological disadvantage of the investing country, in general, a combination of the convergence in the technological abilities of the major investing countries, and the two-way flow of MNE activity in high-technology sectors, seems to suggest that the case for a neutral – if not a (market) supportive – government policy towards outward direct investment and the complementary restructuring and upgrading of domestic resources and capabilities, is more desirable than a restrictive policy.[20]

POLICY MEASURES

With these analytical underpinnings in mind, let us review the evolving national and regional (that is to say, EC) policies towards inbound and outbound MNE activity in the EC. Because some of the important issues surrounding the impact of contemporary events on intra-EC investment patterns have been dealt with elsewhere (Cantwell, 1992), we shall refer only to past policies insofar as they help us understand the current policies, and the changes which have occurred in the actions of governments over the past three or more decades.

Phase I: the post-war period up to *c.* 1975

Prior to the establishment of the European Economic Community, there was no policy harmonization of governments of the future member states towards inward or outward direct investment. Almost all the inward investment until the late 1950s was *market seeking,* although in some cases, investment in one country was used to service other European countries and, in the case of the UK, the non-Commonwealth markets. Outbound MNE activity was predominantly *resource seeking* and mainly directed to the rich Commonwealth or developing countries. The exception was some *market seeking* investment in the US, and in other parts of Europe.

Most countries used foreign exchange control measures to ensure that both inward and outward MNE activity did as little damage as possible to their balance of payments; while, especially in countries which pursued or had pursued socialist economic policies and promoted the state ownership of industry (such as France and the UK), there were strict limitations on the participation of foreign firms in 'key' or strategically-sensitive sectors. The identification of these key sectors varied between countries,[21] as did the attitude of the authorities to the acquisition of local firms by foreign MNEs, the access of foreign investors to local capital markets, the restriction of official aid, subsidies and public purchasing to nationally owned firms, and discriminatory legal treatment of foreign affiliates.[22] Outward investment was disallowed or discouraged to hard-currency areas. At the same time, apart from the UK, Switzerland, Sweden and The Netherlands, MNEs generally lacked the ability or the incentive to engage in new foreign value-added activities – apart from those which were export promoting.

Of the European countries, France had the most explicit general policies towards inward investment which, after the publication of Jacques Servan-Schreiber's treatise, *Le Défi American* in 1968, became more restrictive. It is also fair to say that, by this time, France had evolved the most aggressive and distinctive policies towards technological development, as most noticeably witnessed by its efforts to maintain a French presence in the computer and related high-technology sectors. The French authorities also much preferred greenfield to foreign investment, and generally resisted proposals for new investment (which had to be registered with the Ministry of Economics and Finance) which were likely to be highly competitive with those of local firms, or interfered with their own plans to restructure industry (Safarian, 1983).

At the other end of the policy spectrum was the Federal Republic of Germany. Even in the early years of the post-war period, few sectors were closed to foreign participation, although until recently, a number of sectors, e.g. telecommunications, have been subject to strong governmental control. Neither has there ever been any authorization or screening of forms of entry or of foreign takeovers, although Germany currently operates one of the most stringent anti-trust policies in Europe. In the 1950s and 1960s, the UK occupied a midway position between Germany and France in its attitudes towards MNE activity. Generally taking a welcoming stance, the main policy instruments used by successive UK governments were foreign exchange control regulations[23] and such agencies as the Industrial Reorganization Corporation set up in the 1960s to help rationalize and restructure some key industrial sectors. Debates in the House of Commons, recorded by Hansard[24], suggest that, on frequent occasions, there were calls for more control on both inbound and outbound capital movements. In addition, certain sections of the UK community, such as the Trades Union Congress, were particularly critical of certain kinds of MNE activity. At the same time, despite its liberal stance, the UK government has, from time to time, intervened to support indigenous firms in competition with foreign affiliates, noticeably in the motor vehicles, microelectronic and computer industries. Other critical measures by which the UK government was able to influence FDI were the Monopolies and Restrictive Practices Act (1965) and the City Panel of Takeovers and Mergers. However, these facilities were not *specifically* directed to foreign companies, and there is no reason to suppose that they were used in a discriminatory way either in favor of or against such companies.

The Italian attitude to FDI was similar to that of Germany. However, the 1956 law on foreign investments stated that such participation in Italian industry was welcome only insofar as it might be expected to lead to the establishment of new 'productive' corporations or help existing productive corporations to expand. The result of the law is that, since 1956, such designated or approved foreign owned firms have, to all intents and purposes, been treated as domestic firms. The only exception is that foreign firms do not have complete freedom of access to Italian financial and capital markets. Italy, like France, also has a substantial public sector, in which in the 1960s and 1970s foreign firms were not allowed to invest. Finally, for many years, the government of Italy has reserved the right (infrequently used) to block an acquisition of a major Italian firm by a foreign MNE (after 1958 a non-EC MNE), but, to the best of our knowledge, this prerogative has never been used!

Until the 1950s, the policy of the Irish authorities was to keep control of its industry and to discourage inward foreign investment. This policy was dramatically reversed in the 1960s. Since that time Ireland, along with Belgium, has developed a very extensive range of incentives to foreign investors, some of which have since drawn the critical attention of the European Commission. Both Belgium and Ireland are examples of countries which, from the start, have tried to attract rationalized or export-oriented inward investment; but both countries have also used such MNE activity as a means of fostering regional development. In both countries, too, the foreign-owned manufacturing sector has recorded impressive productivity and growth performances, although in the case of Ireland, at least, not all scholars agree that the impact of inward investment has been an unalloyed benefit (O'Hearn, 1990). Finally, for many years, the foreign sector has played such a dominant role in both Belgium and Ireland, that the macro-organizational policies of these countries cannot but have been strongly influenced by their presence. These have included anti-cyclical policies, bearing in mind that, in years of domestic economic strain, foreign firms tend to cut back their foreign investments earlier than their domestic investment.[25]

Like Ireland and Belgium, The Netherlands is also heavily reliant on inward investment. Nonetheless, for many years past, The Netherlands has been an important capital exporter.[26] It is not surprising then, that in spite of the export orientation of her major inward investors, Dutch policies towards MNE activity have been generally comparable to the UK, which *par excellence*, is the world's leading international investor.[27] Except in broadcasting, military production and aviation, foreign owned affiliates are treated exactly the same as domestic firms. The rules on acquisitions and mergers are also non-discriminatory. As with other governments, the Dutch have tried to steer foreign firms into areas suffering from above-average unemployment. They were one of the first European countries to stimulate both foreign and domestic investors in energy conservation and to make use of alternative energy sources and pollu-tion preventatives. The Dutch have never operated any screening mechanism for foreign investment.

Portugal, Spain and Greece did not join the EC until the 1980s. In the mid-1960s and 1970s, they took a somewhat more selective, though generally welcoming, attitude to foreign investment. In Spain, for example, there was no democratically elected government until 1975, and, prior to that date, the economy was highly protectionist. Even in the late 1970s, FDI was vetted in most high-technology sectors and those with approved industrial conversion plans (for example, cars, shipbuilding, household appliances and textiles). The Spaniards also had quite complex administrative procedures for inward investors, and several government ministries, including the Council of Ministers (the Spanish cabinet) were usually to be consulted. The authorities also exercised dividend limitations up to early 1981.

In the past, Portugal has imposed quite extensive requirements on foreign investors. As recently as the early 1980s, not only were some sectors barred to foreign MNEs altogether, but in others, such as mining and quarrying, fishing and international road transport, only a 49 per cent foreign shareholding was permitted. The conditions under which acquisitions were authorized were also laid down. Repatriation of dividends and profits required Bank of Portugal approval, while Portugal's main watchdog on foreign investments (The Foreign Investment Review Agency) carefully evaluated and monitored all technology transfer agreements, and was apt to view unfavorably any efforts by a foreign firm to integrate the production and marketing strategy of its Portuguese affiliates with that of the parent company. To a greater extent than in Spain, FDI in Portugal was encouraged towards sectors in which Portugal had, or was striving to achieve, a comparative trading advantage (Simoes, 1985).

Although Spain and Portugal were not major outward investors prior to the mid-1980s, both countries operated fairly strict exchange control regimes. Of all the current members of the EC, perhaps Greece has historically viewed inward investment with the greatest caution. Though the attitude of successive governments has been generally cordial, since 1953, foreign investment has been expected to meet certain conditions not required of domestic firms. Like several developing countries, it has valued MNE activity as a means of importing technology, creating jobs and promoting exports: such investments are classified as productive investments. Along with quite generous investment incentives, the Greek authorities also laid down fairly stringent performance requirements which foreign firms were expected to meet before they could freely remit any profits and dividends earned.

Acquisitions of Greek companies were generally not eligible for investment incentives. All investments had to be approved by the Minister of National Economy on the recommendation of the appropriate consultative committee. In general, the Greek attitude towards inward investment, which was a mixture of *resource* and *market seeking*, was similar to that of many developing countries of the time.

In summary, in the period prior to, and during the early years of, European integration, there was no harmonization of national policies towards MNE activity. Attitudes and actions varied according to the political complexion of the government in power, the macro-organization policies it pursued, and its attitude towards economic interdependence. Policies tended to be most liberal in the smaller industrialized countries which relied heavily on international transactions for their prosperity and least liberal in the less-developed and less-integrated economies. In the larger developed countries, much rested on their role as international investors in the world economy, and the extent to which governments intervened in the management of their economies.

Phase II: the later years and preparing for EC 1992

The new economic climate for MNE activity

With the increasing integration of Western European economies, and as MNEs have come to view the EC as a single market, the geographical distribution of FDI between the member countries has become increasingly based on an *efficiency seeking* rather than (national) *market* or *resource seeking* kind. The restructuring of MNE activity in the EC between 1957 and the mid-1980s has been well documented, for example by Cantwell (1989, 1992), and the UN (1992b); and there is considerable evidence to suggest that at least the larger and more experienced US foreign investors are engaging in a regional division of labor in the EC. Foremost among this evidence is the quite dramatic increase in intra-firm EC trade undertaken by US MNEs (US Department of Commerce, v.d.; UNCTC, 1991). As Chapter 7 has shown, in 1985, 56.1 per cent of the sales of US subsidiaries in the EC were sold to other US affiliates,[28] compared with 21.5 per cent in 1966. Between 1985 and 1988, these sales rose by 74.7 per cent compared with local sales of 37.4 per cent.

Yet coupled with this efficiency seeking investment, since the early 1980s there has been a surge of 'first time' MNE activity by medium and smaller US firms, by Japanese firms, by some Third World MNEs, and, perhaps most interestingly of all, by EC MNEs in other EC countries (that is, intra-EC direct investment). Much of this investment, at least since 1986, has been 'pulled in' by expectancies about EC 1992. It is, in part, defensive or protective and, in part, aggressive and opportunistic. Part too – especially that undertaken by the Japanese MNEs – can be thought of as traditional *market seeking* investment – most certainly so if one takes the EC as a single market in its own right; while part – and one suspects this particularly applies to intra-European investment – has more the characteristics of *strategic asset acquiring* investment, as firms aim to sustain and advance their global competitive positions. One response of EC firms to this new thrust of inbound MNE activity has been to step up their own intra-EC direct investments and strategic alliances. Indeed, apart from Asian FDI, this is the fastest growing form of cross-border value-added activity now being undertaken within the EC.

Quite apart from the changes in the motives for, and character of, MNE activity in and out of the EC, governments of EC countries have also been reappraising their economic objectives, and reevaluating the means by which they can best achieve these objectives. In particular, there has been a wholesale revamping of macro-organizational policies, as witnessed, for example, by the liberalization and privatization of many markets and the reduced role of government as an organizer of economic activity. The liberalization and reform of financial markets has also led to a spectacular increase in the cross-border mobility of capital. It has also resulted in a phasing out of all forms of exchange control. At the same time, added to national government policies, there are now EC policies on a whole range of economic matters, including those specifically directed to MNE activity.

A review of national policies recently undertaken by OECD (1991) reveals a general removal of obstacles to both outward and inward MNE value-added activity and a relaxation in the performance expectations of foreign affiliates. At the same time, it is clear that some sharp differences are emerging as to the *kind* of inward investment that is most welcome. These differences are particularly marked as between the smaller and larger, and between the more-and less-developed EC. There is also a growing divergence of attitude – particularly on the part of France and Italy – towards inward investment according to its country of origin. Japanese inward investment, for example, is often viewed more as a Trojan Horse than is either intra-EC investment or North American investment.

At the same time, the kind of FDI policies now being pursued by European governments are best considered as part and parcel of macro-organization strategies, which, directly or indirectly, are being increasingly influenced by the globalization of economic activity. But before discussing these broader strategies, let us identify the main changes in the attitudes and actions of EC governments towards inward and outward investment.

Inward investment

The changing attitudes and actions towards inbound MNE activity may be summarized under eight headings.

1 There has been a general warming of attitudes and relaxation of policies towards inward direct investment and the removal of restrictions and obstacles to most kinds of capital imports. Foremost among the liberalizing countries in the later 1980s have been France, Spain and Portugal; and, in the early 1990s, Greece is following a similar path.

2 Many countries have replaced fairly detailed and multifaceted authorization procedures for inward investment by simple notification or verification devices. Authorization procedures are now normally confined to very large transactions and/or acquisitions, and, in most cases, only one authorizing ministry or agency is involved. The greatest progress towards liberalization has been made by Portugal, Spain and France.

3 Many sectoral restrictions have been lifted or greatly reduced. Sectors which used to be wholly denied to foreign investors have now been opened up. However, most EC countries still limit and/or regulate conditions for non-EC foreign investment in the finance and insurance sectors (see (5) below); basic telecommunications services (Spain); broadcasting (Spain, the UK and France); publishing (France); nuclear power and oil related activities (France); airlines (Spain, Italy, the UK, Ireland, Luxembourg); maritime transport, and particularly the registration of ships and the access of foreign owned vessels to cabotage (most EC countries); fishing (Italy, Ireland, Denmark and France); and armaments manufacturers (Denmark, Spain, France and The Netherlands).

4 There has been a reduction or elimination of all exchange controls on inward investment. Here the most radical reforms have occurred in France, Spain, Portugal and Greece. There is now a virtually free international capital market in the EC, although there are still some restrictions imposed on non-EC investment by France, Portugal and Greece.

5 Restrictions on the local financing of capital expenditure by non-residents have also been markedly reduced. Those which remain relate mainly to some general provisions on the access by non-residents to local capital markets, currently imposed by Italy, Portugal and Spain.

6 Provisions maintained by member countries on essential national security and public-order grounds, however, continue to be extensive and some have even been strengthened, especially in the strategic economic and 'cutting edge' technology sectors.

7 There has been rather less progress made on the liberalization of FDI in services. Reciprocity conditions, linking the recipient country's treatment of a foreign investor to that granted to the recipient country MNEs in the investor's country of origin are still frequently imposed – particularly on US and Japanese MNEs. For example, in the banking sector, reciprocity conditions are being applied by Belgium, Germany and the UK; in the insurance sector, by Luxembourg and Portugal; and in other financial services, by Denmark and Portugal.

8 In spite of the general loosening of controls on inbound MNE activity, many countries, including those which otherwise adopt a most welcoming stance, still encourage, or even insist that, foreign investors should accept certain performance requirements. Often, the adherence to these requirements is the price

extracted by host governments for tax concessions and other incentives. To this extent – unwisely in the views of some economists – EC countries have taken a leaf out of the books of developing countries by intervening in the normal market process. The two requirements[29] most widely imposed – even by the most liberal-minded governments – are, first, that over a certain period of time, a certain pre-agreed proportion of the value of a good sold by a foreign subsidiary in an EC country will be produced in the EC (the local-content requirement), and second (and this is linked to the first), that an investing firm will, by an agreed date, undertake at least some of its higher-value-added activities in its European subsidiaries. Both these provisions are particularly directed to Japanese investors. The particular concern is lest Europe should simply become a low-value-added base servicing the higher-value-added activities of Japanese firms in their home country.

Outward investment

According to the OECD (1991), there are practically no restrictions on outward direct investment currently imposed by EC countries, either in authorization procedures or in financing. It would seem that as the balance of payments constraints of the leading investing countries have become less severe (or the measures taken to influence outward investment for this reason have proved ineffective or inappropriate), policy towards outbound MNE activity has become more relaxed. Moreover, the liberalization of both exchange and capital markets, together with a more congenial climate towards inward investment, has mellowed the attitude of most authorities towards capital exports.

At the same time, over the past decade or more, domestic unemployment has risen in all EC countries, while the need to increase investment in competitive enhancing domestic activities has become more urgent. Certainly, labor unions have continued to be vocal against the export of capital in labor-intensive sectors to developing countries; while some commentators believe the large outflows of capital by MNEs conglomerates to acquire US assets do little to help the restructuring and wealth-creating activities of domestic industry.

However, in general, there would appear to be much less concern in most European countries than there is in the US about the possible adverse effects of outward investment on domestic competitiveness and technological capacity. Partly this may be because most EC MNE activity (outside the EC) is not made to exploit a cutting edge technology in countries lower down the innovating 'pecking order'; nor is it directed to potential competitors. There is comparatively little EC high-technology investment in Japan, while that undertaken in the US is intended more to acquire a competitive advantage rather than to exploit an existing one. Any concern of national governments over exporting Europe's technological heritage to its competitors would seem to be outweighed by the belief that both *efficiency* and *strategic asset seeking* by European firms are ways of strengthening their global competitive positions; while, in the US and Japan, *market seeking* investment, along with exports and a range of co-operative agreements, are intended to gain an entrance to the two wealthiest countries in the world.

Contemporary national policies of EC governments towards inward and outward investment are being increasingly dominated by the perceived need for their firms and resources to benefit from the liberalization of world markets on the one hand, and from EC 1992 and the exciting opportunities opening up in Central and Eastern Europe on the other. The outcome has been not only a general unshackling of controls over all forms of MNE activity, but a more positive recognition of the benefits likely to arise from such activities.

At the same time, we would observe that such a change in national policies towards FDI has resulted in a shift from being one of 'negative' interventionism to one of 'no' interventionism. Positive interventionism to use inbound or outbound MNE activity, in the restructuring or upgrading of domestic resources, is generally absent throughout EC countries. Since any kind of government interventionism in macro-organization is generally out of keeping with the current philosophy of most European governments, this should come as no surprise. Certainly, all EC governments have a long way to go before they approach the holistic approach of the Japanese government as it seeks to incorporate its policies towards both outward and inward direct investment into its wider macro-organizational strategy.[30]

Elsewhere in this volume, we have argued the case for a new macro-organizational approach by Western governments which is directed not specifically to MNE activity, but rather to all areas of policy germane to determining the competitiveness of a country's resources and firms in the global market place (Dunning, 1991a, 1991b, 1991c). As suggested earlier in this chapter, it is our contention that governments, like firms, need to take a strategic perspective to the organization of the resources under their jurisdiction or influence. At the very least, this means monitoring the macro-organizational strategies of foreign governments, particularly those micro-organizational policies which either facilitate markets or distort market signals. While some of the arguments for strategic trade policies are not as persuasive as was first thought (Stegemann, 1989), there is still an important complementary role for governments to play in assisting the market economy and encouraging the response of their firms to be effective.

This indeed is the central message of the World Bank in its latest development report (World Bank, 1991). Though addressed mainly to developing countries, it is no less applicable to developed countries. The Bank hypothesizes that the countries which most efficiently manage this particular form of co-operation or complementarity are those most likely to prosper over the next decade or more. And, since the interaction between governments and MNEs is becoming more important all the time, the need to devise positive and constructive policies which optimize the benefits from such activity are an integral part of this task.

THE EC DIMENSION

The completion of the internal market by the end of 1992 is the second of the major efforts of the European Commission to achieve economic integration among its member states. The first, which marked the initiation of the Community in 1958, was the removal of intra-EC tariff barriers and import controls. The second, which began in the mid-1980s, and is described in the Cecchini Report (1988), is to remove the major non-tariff barriers by 1 January 1993.

The European Commission does not have a policy towards MNE activity *per se*. As described earlier, the 'revealed' philosophy of its Secretariat is to downplay the significance of the nationality of ownership as a factor influencing the efficiency of intra-EC resource organization and utilization.[31] But through its various economic and social programmes, as agreed by the member countries, it can and does greatly influence the conditions affecting MNE activity.

Considerable research has already been done in assessing the impact of the first phase of European integration on the volume and direction of MNE activity,[32] while, elsewhere in this chapter, we have examined how it affected both the motives for, and organization of, such activity. Much less work has been done on the impact of pre-1992 EC integration on the policies of individual member states towards inward or outward investment. In its recent study, the OECD (1991) identified the EC as one of the factors making for a more liberalized climate towards MNE activity, although it observes that the main changes in policy have occurred only in the last quarter of the Community's existence (that is, over the last eight years or so).[33] However, although the formation of the EC has not dramatically changed the FDI policies of national governments, it has affected the costs and benefits of different kinds of MNE activity and the opportunity costs of that activity. This has forced national governments, particularly those of smaller countries, to be more competitive in their bidding for inbound investment and to shape their general economic policies accordingly.[34]

The more pronounced competitive environment for MNE activity so far fostered by European integration is likely to be reinforced by EC 1992 which liberalizes even further both markets and opportunities open to MNEs. Since, too, EC directives and regulations have led to a harmonization of many national policy instruments and measures, which otherwise might have affected the locational decisions of firms, purely commercial considerations, particularly those to do with the underlying supply capabilities offered by individual countries – many of which are strongly government influenced (Porter, 1990) – will be of greater importance (Dunning, 1991a). It is, then, the way in which countries respond to regional integration in their resource organization and utilization policies, as much regional integration *per se*, that will determine their success or failure both in attracting new inward investment, and in providing the opportunities and incentives for competitive enhancing outward investment.

But there are also other aspects of European integration which affect the intra-EC distribution of MNE activity. One of these is the social programme of the European Commission[35] which, in the 1960s and 1970s, considerably affected the attitudes of foreign MNEs towards investing in the EC. Another is the attempt by the Community to help the poorer regions of the Community to develop their resource potential and also assist in the restructuring of other regions suffering from above-average unemployment. To promote these latter two objectives, the Community provides grants or loans, known as 'fiscal transfers', which are financed by the more-prosperous member states.

Such fiscal transfers are, quite intentionally, discriminatory in their consequences. They are used by the recipient countries in various ways, some of which are likely to affect their relative attractions to foreign investors. Thus structural adjustment funds may be used to upgrade infrastructure of less-prosperous EC countries in such a way as will attract *efficiency seeking* MNE activity which might otherwise have been located in more-prosperous EC countries. Or they might be used to assist domestic firms in the upgrading of their technological capabilities, which may help to improve their competitiveness *vis-à-vis* other European firms in the markets in which they both compete.

Thus, by a variety of means designed to help the poorer regions of the EC to become more productive, the Commission can affect the level and geographical composition of both inward and outward direct investment. But other policies – such as those which aim to stimulate the innovatory capacity of EC-based firms in cutting edge technologies – are likely to favor the wealthier member states, as it is from these countries that MNEs in advanced-technology sectors are most likely to come. A study of the membership of government-funded research-based consortia, and of the recipients of grants from the various EC-funded science and technology initiatives (Mytelka and Delapierre, 1988) reveals that these are mainly located in the high-income EC nations. Such subsidies, then, will tend to enhance the ability of countries to be outward investors, and, by the upgrading of domestic resource capability, add to their locational attractions for inward investment.

More generally, the completion of the internal market will most certainly affect the relative competitiveness of EC firms *vis-à-vis* non-EC firms and the attractions of a European location for investment by all kinds of firms. Because some of the main beneficiaries of the removal of non-tariff barriers are likely to be in the service sectors, one would expect an increase in *efficiency seeking* and *strategic asset seeking* MNE investment in the years to come. Also, through the increase in intra-European competition, one might also expect to see the emergence of a leaner and fitter group of European MNEs, better equipped than their predecessors to penetrate global markets.

At the same time, the policy of the Community towards import barriers to non-EC countries is as yet unclear. This will clearly affect the amount of EC market seeking investment, particularly of newer Japanese MNEs. Here, of course, the policy of the Community is intimately tied up with the progress of the GATT negotiations; but it is this area of policy which the Community *qua* Community is most likely to influence.

At a micro-organizational level, the European Commission, through the provisions of the Rome Treaty, can and does impact on the actions of both domestic- and foreign-based MNEs. Foremost among these are a wide range of regulations designed to reduce monopolistic practices and encourage competition in the Community as for example, laid down in Article 85 of the Treaty, the EC's labor law programme, which is especially directed to advancing employment protection and worker participation[36] (as outlined in the Fifth Directive of the Commission: the directives on corporate responsibility and group accounts, the harmonization of aids to inward investment – Articles 92–94 of the Treaty) and a variety of directives and rulings on environmental, safety and health matters. One particularly good example of a regional ruling directly affecting inward investment is that made by the Commission in July 1991 about the local content of a 'European-made' car produced in the Community by Japanese owned firms. Cars with that amount of local (EC made) content can then trade freely in the EC without any barriers. At the same time, the Community pegged the level of imports of Japanese cars at the 1990 level until 1998 when all quotas are to be abolished. It is by such decrees or directive measures that the EC may have a direct impact on MNE activity, on the level and direction of MNE activity and on the policies of individual member states.

In summary, although the European Commission may have few distinctive policies towards MNE activity *per se*, many of their macro-organizational strategies affect, for good or bad, both the total amount of foreign direct investment in the EC and its distribution among member states. Take, for example, environmental standards and regulations. If these are kept at too high a level, they will not only divert MNE activity to non-EC countries (as an EC location will become less competitive), but, within the EC, they will redirect it from low-wage, low-productivity countries, to high-wage, high-productivity countries. These latter countries are also those which tend to have high tax rates and social expenditures along with more stringent environmental standards (Sweeney, 1991). By contrast, a reduction in domestic content requirements, or in other non-tariff barriers, is likely to lead to more foreign investment in the EC, in which all EC countries should benefit to a greater or lesser extent.

More generally, the EC can opt for two contrasting mixes of policies. The one is to force poorer EC members to adopt a Maastricht-type social charter, for example, in respect of wages, welfare and environmental standards, closer to the levels of the higher-income members. This is likely to put poorer countries at a disadvantage and divert the flow of inward investment from them to their wealthier neighbors, as well as possibly reducing the total amount of FDI in the EC.[37] At the other extreme, the EC may choose to implement policies that do not attempt to keep investment from being diverted from high- to low-income member states. The outcome of this strategy might be that high-income countries would unilaterally reduce their tax rates or lower their social transaction costs, so as to make themselves more competitive with the rest of the EC – and, indeed, the rest of the world. In this event, the net result would be an increase in both domestic and foreign investment and a reduction in structural employment (Sweeney, 1991).

CONCLUSIONS

In the future, it is likely that the European Commission will play a more active role on setting the ground rules which member states will be expected to follow in their policies towards MNE activity.

However, notwithstanding a likely trend towards more-harmonized policies, we believe that the role of national governments in influencing both the locational attractions of their countries to foreign direct investors and the competitive advantages of their own MNEs is likely to become more, rather than less, important.

Moreover, there is a world of difference between a convergence of national policies (Safarian, 1991) and that of the ability of governments to organize efficiently and monitor these policies. In their attempts to promote the economic wellbeing of their citizens, individual EC governments are likely to be paying more attention to their macro-organizational policies because central to these policies is the role played by international direct investment and cross-border collaborative alliances. In this respect, it may be that the 1990s will see a new era of cooperation between governments and firms, as the role of the former is steered increasingly towards compensating for market failures that inhibit the latter from achieving their full economic potential.

All this is not to ignore the economic powers ceded to the European Community or the Commission by the individual member states. These will not only have the affect of largely neutralizing intercountry, structurally distorting, national policies, but will also considerably influence patterns of individual development, particularly those of peripheral regions. The EC is also likely to play a more important role in the harmonization of intra-EC technical standards and of sectoral regulations and restrictions, particularly in the service sectors.

Finally, perhaps, most importantly, in the light of the strategically-oriented trade and investment policies of the US and Japan, the EC *qua* EC is likely to strengthen the negotiating hand of individual

European governments, in international fora. Barring completely unforeseen events, by the year 2000, for most practical economic purposes, the economic space of Western Europe, and particularly the EC, will be very similar to that of the newly established North American Free Trade Area. Yet, within these regional blocs, national governments and regional authorities (for example, US states) will continue to devise strategis both to promote their own national champions and to encourage the appropriate investment by firms from outside their countries or regions. Competition between countries and regions will coexist with cooperation between countries and regions. Each will both affect and be affected by the level, structure and geographical distribution of MNE activity; and it is this interaction and the opportunities and tensions it brings which is likely to offer a fruitful area of research for international business scholars for many years to come.

Notes and references

1 STUDY OF INTERNATIONAL BUSINESS

Notes

1 This chapter contains a full version of the author's Presidential Address to the Academy of International Business in October 1988. In general, the first tense has been retained, but some of the material has been updated to take account of events since that date.
2 Though there were many institutions who taught business studies in the UK and other parts of Europe. IMI in Geneva was set up in 1948 specifically to teach international management. Others of more recent origin include: IMEDE in 1957; INSEAD, established by the French Chamber of Commerce in 1958; the London Business School in 1965; and the Manchester Business School in 1965. However, most of the European business schools were initially staffed by US (and often Harvard) trained faculty and even today the US influence on teaching and research methodology remains very strong. For a comprehensive list of schools engaging in international business study see McNulty, 1986 and Thanapoulos, 1986.
3 See, for example, Dunning, 1958 (UK); Stonehill, 1965 (Norway); Kidron, 1965 (India); Safarian, 1966 (Canada); Brash, 1966 (Australia); Deane, 1970 (New Zealand); Stubenitsky, 1970 (The Netherlands).
4 See, for example, Vernon, 1966, 1974, 1979, Wells, 1972, Vaupel and Curhan, 1969, 1974.
5 Some of which have been summarized in Dunning, 1988.
6 Such attention as was given to market failure was usually confined to the chapter on welfare economics.
7 See, for example, Chandler, 1962 and Williamson, 1964, 1970, 1971.
8 See particularly Nehrt, 1987, Daniels and Radebaugh, 1974, Grosse and Perritt, 1980 and Thanapoulos, 1986.
9 This is explored in more detail in Part IV of this book.
10 It is possible that some costs may be considered as transaction costs by consumers but production costs by producers. The costs of travel and communications are essentially a transaction cost as far as intermediate and final consumers are concerned, but a production cost as far as the producer of these services is concerned.

11   Mainly producers, it should be said!
12   This part is taken up in more detail in Chapter 2.
13   Though a new survey is due to be published later in 1993.
14   This indeed, was the subject of a landmark conference, organized by the University of Carolina in May 1992. See Toyne and Nigh, 1993.
15   While accepting that scholars such as Alfred Chandler and Douglass North as professional historians, Seymour Rubin and Daniel Vagts as lawyers, Herbert Simon and Oliver Williamson as organizational theorists, Joseph Nye as a political scientist, Ronald Coase and Kenneth Arrow as economists, have offered theoretical insights of considerable relevance to our understanding of IB, I would submit that it is not necessary to have their background and training to appreciate the basic message they are intending to convey.
16   See, for example, Teece, 1987.

References

Bartlett, C. A. and Ghoshal, S. (1989) *Beyond Global Management*, Boston: Harvard Business School Press

Blake, D. (1987) *International Competitiveness and Educational Insularity*, Presentation at a Congressional Panel Discussion on International Trade and Competitiveness Sponsored by the American Assembly of Collegiate Schools of Business, September 17

Boddewyn, J. J. (1988) Political aspects of MNE theory, *Journal of International Business Studies 19*: 341–364

Boddewyn, J. J. (1993) 'The conceptual domain of international business: territory, boundaries and levels' in Toyne, B. and Nigh, D. (eds) *Perspectives on International Business Theory, Research and Industrial Arrangements*, Westport Ct: Greenwood

Brash, D. T. (1966) *American Investment in Australian Industry*, Canberra: Australian University Press

Chandler, A. D. Jr. (1962) *Strategy and Structure: The History of American Industrial Enterprise*, Cambridge, Mass.: MIT Press

Daniels, J. D and Radebaugh, L. E. (1974) *International Business Curricula Survey*, Cleveland: Academy of International Business

Deane, R. S. (1970) *Foreign Investment in New Zealand Manufacturing*, Wellington, N.Z.: Street and Maxwell

Doz, T. and Prahalad, C. K. (1987) *The Multinational Mission*, New York: Free Press

Dunning, J. H. (1958) *American Investment in British Manufacturing Industry*, London: Allen and Unwin

Dunning, J. H. (1988) *Explaining International Production*, London: Unwin Hyman

Dunning, J. H. (1993) 'The global economy, domestic governance strategies and transnational corporations: interactions and policy implications', *Transnational Corporations 1*, No. 3, December: 7–46

Fayweather, J. (1986) 'A history of the Academy of International Business from infancy to maturity: The first 25 years', *South Carolina Essays in International Business*, No. 6, November

Freeman, E. and Gilbert, D. (1988) *Corporate Strategy and the Search for Ethics*, Englewood Cliffs, NJ: Prentice Hall

Grosse, R. and Perritt, G. W. (1980) *International Business Curricula: A Global Survey*, Cleveland: Academy of International Business

Kidron, M. (1965) *Foreign Investments in India*, Oxford: Oxford University Press

McNulty, N. (1986) *International Directory of Executive Education*, Oxford: Pergamon

Nehrt, J. C. (1981) *Case Studies of Internationalisation of the Business School Curriculum*, St. Louis American Assembly of Collegiate Schools of Business

Nehrt, J. C. (1987) 'The internationalization of the curriculum', *Journal of International Business Studies 18*: 83–90

Porter, M. (ed.) (1986) *Competition in Global Industries*, Boston: Harvard Business School Press

Porter, M. (1990) *The Competitive Advantages of Nations and Firms*, New York: Free Press

Robbins, J. A. (1985) 'Organisations and economics: Some topical problems of transaction costs analysis', *Academy of Management Proceedings*: 181–185

Safarian, A. E. (1966) *Foreign Ownership of Canadian Industry*, Toronto: McGraw-Hill

Stonehill, A. (1965) *Foreign Ownership in Norwegian Enterprises*, Oslo: Central Bureau of Statistics

Stubenitsky, F. (1970) *American Direct Investment in Netherlands Industry*, Rotterdam: Rotterdam University Press

Teece, D. J. (1985) 'Transaction cost economics and the multinational enterprise: An assessment', *Journal of Economic Behaviour and Organisation 7*: 21–45

Teece, D. J. (1987) 'Profiting from technological innovation: Implications for integration, collaboration, licensing and public policy', in Teece, D. J. (ed.) *The Competitive Challenge*, Cambridge, Mass.: Ballinger

Thanapoulos, J. (1986) *International Business Curricula: A Global Survey*, Cleveland: Academy of International Business

Thanapoulos, J. and Vernon, I. R. (1987) 'International business education in the AASCB schools', *Journal of International Business Studies 18*: 91–98

Toyne, B. and Nigh, D. (1993) *Perspectives on International Business: Theory, Research and Institutional Arrangements*, Westport Ct. Greenwood

UNCTC (1988) *Transnational Corporations and World Development*, New York: UN E.88. II. A.7

UN (1992) *World Investment Report 1992, Transnational Corporations and Engines of Growth*, New York: Transnational Corporations and Management Division of Department of Economic and Social Development

Van Tulder, R. and Junne, G. (1988) *European Multinationals in Core Technologies*, Chichester and New York: Wiley

Vaupel, J. W. and Curhan, J. P. (1969) *The Making of Multinational Enterprise*, Cambridge, Mass.: Harvard Business School

Vaupel, J. W. and Curhan, J. P. (1974) *The World's Multinational Enterprises*, Cambridge, Mass.: Harvard Business School

Vernon, R. (1966) 'International investment and international trade in the product cycle', *Quarterly Journal of Economics 80*: 190–217

Vernon, R. (1974) 'The location of economic activity', in Dunning, J. H. (ed.) *Economic Analysis and the Multinational Enterprise*, London: Allen and Unwin

Vernon, R. (1979) 'The product cycle hypothesis in a new international environment', *Oxford Bulletin of Economics and Statistics 41*: 255–267

Wells, L. (ed.) (1972) *The Product Life Cycle and International Trade*, Cambridge, Mass.: Harvard University Press

Westney, E. and Ghoshal, S. (eds) (1992) *Organizing the Multinational Corporation*, Basingstoke and London: Macmillan

Williamson, O. E. (1964) *The Economics of Discretionary Behaviour: Managerial Objectives in the Theory of the Firm*, Englewood Cliffs, N.J.: Prentice Hall

Williamson, O. E. (1970) *Corporate Control and Business Behaviour*, Englewood Cliffs, N.J.: Prentice Hall

Williamson, O. E. (1971) 'The vertical integration of production; market failure considerations', *American Economic Review 61*: 112–123

World Bank (1991) *World Development Report, 1991*, Oxford: Oxford University Press

2 MICRO- AND MACRO-ORGANIZATIONAL ASPECTS OF MNEs AND MNE ACTIVITY

Notes

1 For recent reviews of these different approaches see Cantwell, 1991 and Dunning, 1992b.

2 A point made at some length, but from a somewhat different perspective to that taken in this chapter, by Strange (1988), Behrman and Grosse (1990), Eden and Hampson (1990), Yarbrough and Yarbrough (1990), Schmidtchen and Schmidt-Trenz (1990) and Grosse and Behrman (1992).

3 For an analysis of the various approaches to identifying and evaluating the interaction between the strategies of MNEs and those of governments see Boddewyn, 1988, 1991 and 1993.

4 The concept of the territoriality of law resulting in a heightened amount of risk specific to international transactions is developed by Schmidtchen and Schmidt-Trenz (1990). In this paper, the authors argue that many of the specific properties of cross-border transaction can be traced to constitutional uncertainty caused by the different national legal and regulatory systems.

5 Using the term in the sense defined above or taking Webster's definition as the 'skills, arts, etc. of a given people at a given period of time'.

6 As recently discussed by Hedlund and Rolander (1991) and Hedlund and Kogut (1992).

7 Other approaches include that of Hedlund and Kogut (1992), who suggest that the modern MNE is better received as a professional organization than as a bureaucracy; and that rather than thinking of the headquarters of the firm as being the brain with its subsidiaries being the

links, it would be more helpful to conceive of the firm as a brain where all parts of the organization contribute to the thinking as well as the action.

8   The literature on this subject is vast. But, for a contemporary examination of such practices, especially as they affect intrafirm organizational costs, see several essays in Kogut, 1992.

9   As we shall explain later, we prefer the term relational costs, as many intra- and interfirm costs have only a distant hearing on specific trans-actions. Indeed, much more work is needed on the different kinds of costs arising from the establishment, substance and implementation of ongoing commercial relationships.

10 See, for example, Dunning, 1986 and 1993c, Schmitter, 1988, Gustafs-son and Williamson, 1989, Weiermair, 1990, Fruin and Nishiguchi, 1993, Lindberg, Campbell and Hollingsworth, 1992 and Lincoln, 1993.

11 These differences are similar to those suggested by William Ouchi in 1977 in distinguishing two measures of administrative control, viz. behavioral and output control. Ouchi argued that the former was necessary to ensure that the performance expected of people was actively achieved, whereas the control of output was less dependent on idio-syncratic human behavior, and could be adjusted, by some kind of mechanical or electronic device, to achieve expected performance.

12 The decline in hierarchical integrated mass production and mass distri-bution systems, and a labor-capital accord in the form of tacit informal understandings and collective bargaining practices between large in-dustrial oligopolies and no less bureaucratic trades unions, has been fashioned by a series of events over the last 30 years. These have included a rebellion by labor unions against the monotonous and repetitive character of narrowly defined tasks; a rise in the educational qualifica-tions and expectations of many workers; the world economic recession of the 1970s; the introduction of new and flexible techniques of manu-facturing and information systems; the greater attention paid by consumers to the quality and variety of goods and services purchased; the demobilization of national oligopolies as competition has become global, and the greater the pressure on firms to engage in cross-border joint ventures and strategic alliances, e.g. to exploit unfamiliar markets and/or to gain technological synergies, or exploit scale economies. All these events have necessitated a reconceptualization of the nature of pro-duction, and have dramatically affected the form of intra- (and interfirm) relations. Toyotaism is one attempt to get to grips with these environ-mental changes, although, in turn, it is requiring several modifications to meet the new technical, organizational and environmental challenges of the 1990s (Weiermair, 1990; and Fruin and Nishiguchi, 1993).

13 For an excellent account of these differences, see Fruin and Nishiguchi (1993). In particular, the authors emphasize the importance attached to the mutuality of networking relationships, the specificity of transaction rights being separated from the residual rights of ownership, and the concept of embeddedness, which refers to the accumulation of the relational goodwill arising from the continuous interaction of people, institutions and institutional environments over time. For an explanation of differences in US and Japanese corporate structure in terms of economics of trust see Casson and Nicholas, 1989.

14 Data of these kind are contained in US Department of Commerce, 1993 and UN, 1992.
15 Defined as costs of producing a good or service in a perfect market.
16 See, e.g. some excellent contributions in Contractor and Lorange, 1988 and Buckley, 1993.
17 See those identified in note 10.
18 Again, examples can be found to the contrary, particularly in sections in which there is a strong Japanese presence.
19 It will be observed that in the first part of the chapter we dealt with only organizational issues except in so far as these were affected by the location of value-added activities; we did not deal with location issues *per se.*
20 We use the word restructuring to cover the 'development' of already industrially developed countries (which embrace mostly the OECD countries).
21 According to Dierickx and Cool (1989), the sustainability of a firm's accumulated assets depends on how easily assets may be substituted or imitated. This, in turn, is linked to the characteristics of the asset accumulation process, e.g. the extent to which there are asset mass efficiencies, interconnectedness between assets and the speed of erosion, e.g. by obsolescence, of asset values. In the light of the argument set out earlier in this chapter, we might add the form and content of relational assets to these characteristics.
22 Resource-based theory is also relevant to this discussion (Wernerfelt, 1984; Barney, 1991; Mahoney and Pandian, 1992), but the concepts of rent yielding resources needs to be broadened out to incorporate rents which may arise from the accumulation of relational competitive advantages.
23 For a further elaboration of this concept see Dunning, 1990, 1991a, 1991b.
24 See also Part IV of this volume.
25 Since writing these paragraphs, I have come across an extremely interesting contribution by Eden and Hampson (1990) which identifies several different kinds of failures specific to cross-border markets. Some of these are economic; others relate to distributional conflicts and security dilemmas. All are relevant to the kind of arguments I am making in this chapter.

References

Barney, J. (1991) 'Firm resources and sustained competitive advantage', *Journal of Management 17*: 99–120

Behrman, J. N. and Grosse, R. (1990) *International Business and Governments,* Columbia: University of South Carolina Press

Boddewyn, J. (1988) 'Political aspects of MNE theory', *Journal of International Business Studies 19*: 341–363

Boddewyn, J. (1991) *International Business Political – Behavior Research: Assumptions, Categories and Propositions,* New York: Baruch College (CUNY), mimeo

Boddewyn, J. (1993) 'The conceptual domain of international business territory boundaries and level', in Toyne, B. and Nigh, D. (eds) *Perspectives on International Business: Theory, Research and Institutional Arrangements*, Westport Ct.: Greenwood

Buckley, P. J. (ed.) (1993) *Cooperative Forms of TNC Activity*, UN Library on Transnational Corporations, London and New York: Routledge

Buckley, P. J. and Casson, M. C. (1991) 'Multinational enterprises in less developed countries: cultural and economic considerations', in Buckley, P. J. and Clegg, J. (eds) *Multinational Enterprises in Less Developed Countries*, Basingstoke and London: Macmillan

Cantwell, J. C. (1989) *Technological Innovation and Multinational Corporations*, Oxford: Basil Blackwell

Cantwell, J. C. (1990) *The Technological Competence Theory of International Production and its Implications*, Reading: University of Reading Discussion Papers in International Investment and Business Studies, Series B. No. 149, November

Cantwell, J. C. (1991) 'A survey of theories of international production', in Pitelis, C. and Sugden, R. *The Nature of the Transnational Firm*, London and New York: Routledge

Casson, M. C. (1990) *Enterprise and Competitiveness*, Oxford: Clarendon Press

Casson, M. C. (1991a) 'Internationalization theory and beyond', in Buckley, P. J. (ed.) *Recent Research on the Multinational Enterprise*, Cheltenham: Edward Elgar

Casson, M. C. (1991b) *The Economics of Business Culture: Game Theory, Transaction Costs and Economic Performance*, Oxford: Clarendon Press

Casson, M. C. (1993) 'Economic theories of international business', in Toyne, B. and Nigh, D. (eds) *Perspectives on International Business: Theory, Research and Institutional Arrangements*, Westport Ct.: Greenwood

Casson, M. C. and Nicholas, S. (1989) *The Economics of Trust: Explaining Differences in Corporate Structure Between the US and Japan*, Reading: University of Reading Discussion Papers in Economics Vol. II No. 219

Chenery, H., Robinson, S. and Syrquin, M. (1986) *Industrialization and Growth*, Oxford: Oxford University Press

Contractor, F. J. and Lorange, P. (eds) (1988) *Cooperative Strategies in International Business*, Lexington, Mass: Lexington Books

Dierickx, I. and Cool, K. (1989) 'Asset stock accumulation and sustainability of competitive advantage', *Management Science 35*: 1504–1511

Dunning, J. H. (1986) *Japanese Participation in British Industry*, London: Croom Helm

Dunning, J. H. (1988) *Explaining International Production*, London and Boston: Unwin Hyman

Dunning, J. H. (1990) *The Globalization of Firms and the Competitiveness of Nations*, Lund: University of Lund, The Crafoord Lectures 1989

Dunning, J. H. (1991a) 'Governments – markets – firms: towards a new balance', *CTC Reporter 31*: 2–7

Dunning, J. H. (1991b) 'Governments and multinational enterprises: From confrontation to cooperation?', *Millennium 20*: 225–244

Dunning, J. H. (1993a) 'The governance of Japanese US manufacturing affiliates in the UK: Some country specific differences', in Kogut, B. (ed.)

Country Competitiveness: Technology and the Organization of Work, Oxford: Oxford University Press

Dunning, J. H. (1993b) 'Japanese and US manufacturing investment in Europe: Some comparisons and contrasts', Reading: University of Reading Discussion Papers in International Investment and Business Studies, *V*, No. 171

Dunning, J. H. (1993) *Multinational Enterprises and the Global Economy*, Reading: Addison-Wesley

Eden, L. and Hampson, F. O. (1990) *Clubs are Trumps: Towards a Taxonomy of International Regimes*, Ottawa: Carleton University Centre for International Trade and Policy Studies Working Paper 90-02

Franke, R. H, Hofstede, G. and Bond, M. H. (1991) 'Cultural roots of economic performance: a research note', *Strategic Management Journal* *12*: 165–173

Fruin, M. and Nishiguchi, T. (1993) 'Supplying the Toyota production system: Making a molehill out of a mountain in Japan', in Kogut, B. and Van den Bulcke, D. (eds) *Country Competitiveness: Technology and the Organizing of Work*, Oxford: Oxford University Press

Gittleman, M. and Dunning, J. H. (1992) 'Japanese multinationals in Europe and the United States: some comparisons and contrasts', in Klein, M. W. and Welfens, P. J. (eds) *Multinationals in the New Europe and Global Trade*, Berlin and New York: Springer-Verlag

Grosse, R. and Behrman, J. N. (1992) 'Theory in international business', *Transnationals 1*: 93–126

Gugler, P. (1991) *Les Alliances Strategiques Transnationales*, Fribourg: Editions Universitaires

Gustafsson, B. and Williamson, O. (eds) (1989) *The Firm as a Nexus of Treaties*, London: Sage Publications

Hedlund, G. and Kogut, B. (1992) 'Managing the MNC: The end of the missionary era', in Hedlund, G. (ed.) *Transnational Corporations and Organization*, UN Library on Transnational Corporations, London and New York: Routledge

Hedlund, G. and Rolander, D. (1991) 'Action in heterarchies – new approaches to managing the MNC' in Bartlett, C. A., Doz, Y. and Hedlund, G. (eds) *Managing the Global Firm*, London and New York: Routledge

Kogut, B. (1990) 'The permeability of borders and the speed of learning across countries', in Dunning, J. H., Kogut, B. and Blomstrom, M. (eds) *Globalization of Firms and the Competitiveness of Nations*, Lund, Sweden: Lund University Institute of Economic Research

Kogut, B. (ed.) (1993) *Country Competitiveness and the Organization of Work*, Oxford: Oxford University Press

Kogut, B. and Parkinson, D. (1993) 'The diffusion of American organizing principles to Europe', in Kogut, B. (ed.) *Country Competitiveness and the Organization of Work*, Oxford: Oxford University Press

Lincoln, J. R. (1993) 'Work organization in Japan and the United States', in Kogut, B. (ed.) *Country Competitiveness and the Organization of Work*, Oxford: Oxford University Press

Lindberg, L. N., Campbell, J. L. and Hollingsworth, J. R. (1992) 'Economic governance and the analysis of structural change in the American economy', in Campbell, J. L., Hollingsworth, J. R. and Lindberg L. N.

(eds) *The Governance of the American Economy*, New York: Cambridge University Press

Lipsey, R. (1991) *Economic Growth: Science and Technology and Institutional Change in the Global Economy*, Toronto: Canadian Institute for Advanced Research CIAR Publication No. 4, June

Mahoney, J. T. and Pandian, J. R. (1992) 'The resource based view within the context of strategic management', *Strategic Management Journal 13*: 363–380

Okada, Y. (1991) *Cooperative Sectoral Governance Strategies of Japanese Automobile Multinationals in Asian Countries*, Niigata-Ken: International University of Japan (mimeo)

Ouchi, W. C. (1977) 'The relationship between organizational structure and organizational control', *Administrative Science Quarterly 22* (1) March: 95–113

Ozawa, T. (1992a) 'Foreign investment and economic development', *Transnational Corporations 1*: 27–54

Ozawa, T. (1992b) *Images, Economics of Concentration and Animal Spirits: Dependency vs. Emulation Paradigm*, Paper presented at Conference on *Perspectives on International Business: Theory Research and Institutional Arrangements*, Columbia, South Carolina, May 20–23

Pavitt, K. (1987) 'International patterns of technological accumulation', in Hood, N. and Vahlne, J. (eds) *Strategies in Global Competition*, Chichester and New York: John Wiley

Porter, M. E. (1990) *The Competitive Advantages of Nations*, New York: Free Press

Rostow, W. W. (1959) *The Stages of Economic Growth*, Cambridge: Cambridge University Press

Schmidtchen, D. and Schmidt-Trenz, H. J. (1990) 'New institutional economics of international transactions', in Boettcher, E., Harder-Dorneich, [no initials available], Schenk, K. E. and Schmidtchen, D. (eds) *Jahruch für Neve Politische Ökonomie* Vol. 9, Tübingen: J. C. B. Mohr

Schmitter, P. C. (1988) 'Sectors in modern capitalism: modes of governance and variations in performance', Paper presented at a Conference in honor of Evio Tarantelli on *Markets, Institutions and Cooperation: Labor Relations and Economic Performances*, Venice, October 20–22, 1988

Stowsky, J. (1987) *The Weakest Link: Semiconductor Production Equipment, Linkages and the Limits to International Trade*, BRIE Working Paper No. 27, Berkeley: University of California

Strange, S. (1988) *States and Markets*, Oxford and New York: Basil Blackwell

UN (1992) *World Investment Report 1992: Transnational Corporations as Engines of Growth*, New York: United Nations, Transnational Corporations and Management Division of Department of Economic and Social Development

US Department of Commerce (1993) *US Direct Investment Abroad. 1991 Benchmark Survey*, Washington: Bureau of Economic Analysis, US Department of Commerce

Weiermair, K. (1990) *Globalization, the Diffusion of Technology and New Forms of Organization*, Toronto: York University (mimeo)

Wernerfelt, B. (1984) 'A resource based view of the firm', *Strategic Management Journal 5*: 171–180

Yarbrough, B. V. and Yarbrough, R. M. (1990) 'International institutions and the new economics of organization', *International Organization 44*: 235–260

3 CHANGING DYNAMICS OF INTERNATIONAL PRODUCTION

Notes

1 Some parts of this chapter were first presented at the Annual Conference of the European International Business Association, which was held at Helsinki in December 1989.
2 As surveyed, for example, by Cantwell (1990 and 1993).
3 As summarized by Root (1987).
4 Note that country strategy may be an exogenous variable as far as explaining the international production of a particular MNE is concerned, but an endogenous variable as far as explaining the inter-national production of all MNEs is concerned.
5 For some illustrations of the way the strategies of firms may affect the strategies of governments, see Rugman and Verbeke (1989).
6 For a review of the literature on the global strategy of firms, see Ghoshal (1987).
7 But see an interesting research paper by Cainarca, Colombo and Mariotti (1990).
8 As discussed in detail in Cantwell (1989), Aydalot and Keeble (1988), Dosi *et al.* (1988) and Grandstrand *et al.* (1992).
9 The substantial investments by the Japanese auto producers Nissan, Toyota and Honda in the late 1980s and early 1990s are dramatically changing the situation and, by the mid-1990s, the UK is expected to be a net exporter of motor vehicles again.
10 Between 1978 and 1986, the new pharmaceutical patents registered by the world's largest firms in the US by UK companies, as a percentage of those of the world's largest 727 industrial firms, was 2.56 greater than the percentage of all patents registered by UK companies. The respective percentage of patents registered by UK motor vehicle companies was 49 per cent of the average percentage of registered patents.
11 The implicit assumption in this argument is that both domestic and foreign owned companies are competing for world (not just UK) markets.
12 For a discussion of the impact of these and other events on the pattern of international direct investment and MNE activity, see Part 3 of this volume.
13 For example, World Bank data suggest that between 1976 and 1989 the share of services to the total gross domestic product of the leading developed countries rose from 52 per cent to 63 per cent. The corresponding percentages for some 82 developing countries were 43 per cent and 45 per cent.
14 In France, West Germany, Japan, the UK and the US.
15 This does not mean that such activities will automatically be located in their home countries.
16 For the period 1969–1972, 9.8 per cent of the patents registered by the

world's largest firms in the US were attributable to innovatory activities in foreign locations (i.e. outside the home country of the parent company). By the period 1983–1986 this percentage had risen to 10.6 per cent.
17   This idea is explored more fully in Dunning, 1988a and 1993.
18   One such example of the influence of large multinational companies is that of the Chairmen of Philips of Eindhoven and Volvo of Sweden in their lobbying of European politicians to speed up the completion of the internal market of the EC (Franko, 1989).
19   See Chapter 11 for more details.
20   See especially Chapters 3, 5 and 6.
21   See especially Chapters 3, 5 and 6.
22   See, for example, the volumes of Bartlett and Ghoshal (1989), Hedlund (1986), Kogut (1990), Bartlett, Doz and Hedlund (1990), Westney and Ghoshal (1992) and Kogut (1993).

References

Anderson, E. and Gatignon, H. (1986) 'Modes of foreign entry: a transaction cost analysis and propositions', *Journal of International Business 17*, Fall: 1–26

Aydalot, P. and Keeble, D. (eds) (1988) *High Technology Industry and Innovative Environments*, London: Routledge

Bartlett, C. A. and Ghoshal, S. (1989) *Managing Across National Borders: The Transnational Solution*, Boston: Harvard Business School Press

Bartlett, C. A., Doz, Y. and Hedlund, G. (eds) (1990) *Managing the Global Firm*, London and New York: Routledge

Buckley, P. (1988) 'The limits of explanation; tests of the theory of the multinational enterprise', *Journal of International Business Studies 20*: 181–193

Buckley, P. and Casson, M. C. (1981) 'The optimal timing of a foreign direct investment', *Economic Journal 91*, March: 75–87

Cainarca, G. C., Colombo, N. G. and Mariotti, S. (1990) 'Agreement between firms and the technological life cycle of industry', Milano (mimeo)

Cantwell, J. (1989) *Technological Innovation and the Multinational Corporation*, Oxford: Basil Blackwell

Cantwell, J. (1990) 'A survey of theories of international production', in Pitelis, C. N. and Sugden, R. (eds) *The Nature of the Transnational Firm*, London: Routledge

Cantwell, J. (ed.) (1993) *Transnational Corporations and Innovatory Activities*, UN Library on Transnational Corporations, Routledge: London and New York

Cantwell, J. and Hodson, C. (1991) 'Global R&D and British competitiveness', in Casson, M. C. (ed.) *Global Research Strategy and International Competitiveness*, Oxford: Basil Blackwell

Casson, M. C. (1987) *The Firm and the Market*, Oxford: Basil Blackwell

Davidson, W. H. and McFeteridge, D. G. (1985) 'Key characteristics in the choice of international transfer mode', *Journal of International Business Studies, XVI*, Summer: 5–23

Dosi, G., Freeman, C., Nelson, R.R., Silverberg, G. and Boete, L.G. (eds) (1988) *Technical Change and Economic Theory*, London: Frances Pinter

Doz, Y. (1986) *Strategic Management in Multinational Companies*, Oxford: Pergamon Press

Doz, Y. (1987) 'International industries: fragmentation versus globalization', in Guile, H. (ed.) *Technology and Growth*, Washington: National Academy of Sciences

Dunning, J. H. (1972) *The Location of International Firms in an Enlarged EEC*, An exploratory paper, Manchester: Manchester Statistical Society.

Dunning, J. H. (1988a) *Explaining International Production*, London: Unwin Hyman

Dunning, J. H. (1988b) *Multinationals, Technology and Competitiveness*, London: Unwin Hyman

Dunning, J.H. (1991) 'Governments, organization and international competitiveness', in Mattson, L. G. and Stymne, B. (eds) *Corporate and Industrial Strategies for Europe*, Amsterdam: Elsevier Science Publishers

Dunning, J. H. (1993) *Multinational Enterprises and the Global Economy*, Wokingham, Berks: Addison-Wesley

Dunning, J. H. and Cantwell, J. (1990) 'The changing role of multinational enterprises in the international creation, transfer and diffusion of technology', in Arcangeli, F., David, P. A. and Dosi, G. (eds) *Technology Diffusion and Economic Growth: International and National Policy Perspectives*, Oxford: Oxford University Press

Dunning, J. H. and Robson, P. (1988) *Multinationals and the European Community*, Oxford: Basil Blackwell

Flowers, E. B. (1976) 'Oligopolistic reaction in European and Canadian direct investment in the US', *Journal of International Business Studies* 7: 43–55

Franko, L. (1989) *Europe 1992: The Impact of Global Corporate Competition and Multinational Corporate Strategy*, Boston: University of Massachusetts (mimeo)

Ghoshal, S. (1987) 'Global strategy: An organizing framework', *Strategic Management Journal 8*: 425–440

Graham, E. M. (1975) *Oligopolistic Imitation and European Direct Investment in the United States*, D. B. A. Dissertation, Harvard University, unpublished

Graham, E. M. (1986) *Internal Economies, Oligopoly Reaction and Dynamic Contestability in Global Industries: A First Cut at a Synthesis* (mimeo)

Graham, E. M. (1991) 'Strategic management and transnational behavior: a formal approach', in Pitelis, C. and Sugden, R. (eds) *The Nature of the Transnational Firm*, London: Routledge

Grandstrand, O., Håkanson, L. and Sjölander, S. (eds) (1992) *Technology Management and International Business: Internationalization of R&D and Technology*, Chichester: John Wiley

Haude, D. (1991) *Domestic Agribusiness in Peripheral Countries: A Challenge to Established International Firms*, Nijmegen: Third World Centre University of Nijmegen (mimeo)

Hedlund, G. (1986) 'The hypermodern MNC – A heterarchy', *Human Resource Management 25*: 9–25

Hill, C. and Kim, W. C. (1988) 'Searching for a dynamic theory of the multinational enterprise: a transaction cost model', *Strategic Management Journal 9*: 93–104

Hirsch, S. (1976) 'An international trade and investment theory of the firm', *Oxford Economic Papers 28*: 258–270

Japan Update (1990) 'Direct investment in Japan: new developments', Winter

Knickerbocker, F. T. (1973) *Oligopolistic Reaction and the Multinational Enterprise*, Cambridge, Mass.: Harvard University Press

Kogut, B. (1983) 'Foreign direct investment as a sequential process', in Kindleberger, C. P. and Audretsch, D. (eds) *The Multinational Corporation in the 1980s*, Cambridge: MIT Press

Kogut, B. (1985a) 'Designing global strategies: corporate and competitive value added chain', *Sloan Management Review 26*, Fall: 27–38

Kogut, B. (1985b) 'Designing global strategies: profiting from operational flexibility', *Sloan Management Review 26*, Fall: 27–38

Kogut, B. (1987) *International Sequential Advantages and Network Flexibility*, mimeo

Kogut, B. (1990) *The Permeability of Borders and the Speed of Learning Among Countries*, University of Lund, Lund: The Craford Lectures, 1989.

Kogut, B. (ed.) (1993) *Country Competitiveness: Technology and the Organizing of Work*, Oxford: Oxford University Press

Kojima, K. (1978) *Direct Foreign Investment: A Japanese Model of Multinational Business Operations*, London: Croom Helm

Kojima, K. (1982) 'Macro economic versus international business approaches to foreign direct investment', *Hitosubashi Journal of Economics 23*: 1–19

Kojima, K. (1990) *Japanese Direct Investment Abroad*, Tokyo: Social Science Research Institute, International Christian University

McGee, J. and Thomas, H. (1986) 'Strategic groups: theory, research and taxonomy', *Strategic Management Journal 7*: 141–60

Magee, S. P. (1981) 'Information and the multinational corporation: and appropriability theory of foreign direct investment', in Blagwati, J. N. (ed.) *The New International Economic Order*, Cambridge, Mass.: MIT Press, 123–35

Matalini, R. J. (1989) 'Capital expenditures by majority owned affiliates of US Companies, 1990', *Survey of Current Business*, September, 21–27

National Science Foundation (1991) *Science and Engineering Indicators – 1991*, Washington: National Science Board

Ozawa, T. (1989) *Japan's Strategic Investment Policy Towards the Developing Countries. From an Ad Hoc to a New Comprehensive Approach*, Fort Collins: Colorado State University (mimeo)

Perlmutter, H. V. (1969) 'The tortuous evolution of the multinational corporation', *Columbia Journal of World Business 4*: 9–18

Porter, M. (1990) *The Competitive Advantages of Nations*, New York: Free Press

Prahalad, C. K. and Doz, Y. (1987) *The Multinational Mission*, London and New York: Free Press

Prahalad, C. K. and Hamel, G. (1990) 'The core competence of the corporation', *Harvard Business Review 68*: 79–91

Root, F. R. (1987) *Entry Strategies for International Markets*, Lexington/Toronto, DC: Heath

Rugman, A. (1989) *Globalization and Industrial Policy: An Assessment of the Report of the Premier's Council of Ontario*, Toronto: University of Toronto (mimeo)

Rugman, A. and Verbeke, A. (1989) 'Strategic management and trade policy', *Journal of International Economic Studies 3*: 139–152

Stopford, J. M. and Baden Fuller, C. (1992) *Rejuvenating the Mature Business*, London and New York: Routledge

UN (1993) *From the Common Market to EC 92. Regional Integration in the European Community and Transnational Corporations*, New York: UN Transnational Corporations and Management Division

UNCTC (1981) *Transnational Corporation Linkages and Developing Countries*, New York: UNCTC, E83 II, A 19

US Department of Commerce (1992) *Highlights in Patent Activity*, Washington: US Department of Commerce, Patent and Trademark Office

Vernon, R. (1966) 'International investment and trade in the product cycle', *Quarterly Journal of Economics 86*: 90–207

Westney, E. and Ghoshal, S. (1992) *Organizing the Multinational Enterprise*, Basingstoke and London: Macmillan

Wilkins, M. (1974) *The Maturing of the Multinational Enterprise*, Boston: Harvard University Press

4 GLOBAL STRATEGY AND THEORY OF INTERNATIONAL PRODUCTION

Notes

1 See, for example, the work of Doz (1986), Ghoshal (1987), and Kogut (1985, 1989, 1990), Kogut and Singh (1988) and Porter (1980, 1985, 1986, 1990).

2 For an analysis of the state of the art of this latter theory, see a special issue of the *Strategic Management Journal*, Vol. 12, 1991.

3 See Knickerbocker (1973), Graham (1978), Lessard (1977) and Rugman (1979).

4 These are compared and contrasted more fully in Dunning (1993).

5 Business scholars, however, do well to acquaint themselves with macroeconomic theories of foreign direct investment, of which that of Kiyoshi Kojima (Kojima, 1978, 1982) is the best known. The particular merit of Kojima's approach is that it looks at the issue of outward and inward investment from a *country's* viewpoint, and attempts to argue that it is the *comparative* locational or competitive advantages of countries which should determine the amount, form and structure of international business operations. To this extent, there is some parallel between the attributes of competitiveness identified by Porter in his latest book (1990), and those analyzed by Kojima. However, Kojima pays only limited attention to the market replacing, or systemic advantages of multinational firms, as his whole analysis if strongly neoclassical, and based on the principle that cross-border markets are (or should be) (near) perfectly competitive.

6 For reviews of this literature see especially Buckley and Casson, 1985, Casson, 1987, Hennart, 1986, Teece, 1985 and Rugman, 1986.

7 For example, with respect to the behavior of suppliers, customers or

competitors of the investing firm (Vernon, 1983) and of environmental volatility (Kogut, 1985).

8   For example, both Stuckey (1983), in his study of vertical integration in the aluminum industry, and Hennart (1988), in his comparison of the organization of the international aluminium and tin industries, discuss the alternative strageties which MNEs may adopt towards minimizing their cross-border transaction costs. For a more general analysis of the choice of organizational strategies within hierarchies when market failure exists, see Anderson and Gatignon, 1986 and Kogut, 1988.

9   See especially Chapters 3 and 6 of Dunning, 1988.

10 As explained more fully in Dunning, 1993.

11 These include both firm specific variables (e.g. attitude of decision takers to risk, time profile of earnings, innovation, age, segments of market served, long term objectives) and exogenous factors (e.g. corporation taxes, R&D subsidies, training grants, presence of related industries, and demand patterns).

12 Cf. Caves (1980a), who argues that the concept of strategic groups and mobility barriers 'do not add up to a tight formal model ... but serve as a dynamized add-on to the traditional structure–conduct–performance paradigm'.

13 For recent surveys of some of these findings, see Clegg, 1987, Kumar, 1990, Dunning, 1993 and UNCTC 1992.

14 Although they vary, classification of different types of international production itself requires careful research and analysis.

References

Anderson, E. and Gatignon, H. (1986) 'Models of foreign entry: A transaction cost analysis and propositions', *Journal of International Business Studies 17*, Fall: 1–16

Bartlett, C. A., and Ghoshal, S. (1990) *Managing Across Borders: The Transnational Solution*, Boston: Harvard Business School Press

Buckley, P. J. and Casson, M. C. (1981) 'The optimal timing of a foreign direct investment' *Economic Journal 91*, March: 75–87

Buckley, P. J. and Casson, M. C. (1985) *The Economic Theory of the Multinational Enterprise*, London: Macmillan

Cantwell, J. (1989) *Technological Innovation and Multinational Corporations*, Oxford: Basil Blackwell

Cantwell, J. (1991) 'Theories of international production' in Pitelis, C. and Sugden, R. (eds) *The Nature of the Transnational Firm*, London: Routledge

Casson, M. C. (1987) *The Firm and the Market*, Oxford: Basil Blackwell

Casson, M. C. (1988) *Entrepreneurship as a Cultural Advantage*, University of Reading Discussion Papers in International Investment and Business Studies No. 124, November

Caves, R. E. (1980a) 'Industrial organization, corporate strategy and structure', *Journal of Economic Literature XVIII*: 64–92

Caves, R. E. (1980b) 'Investment and location policies of multinational companies', *Schweiz Zeitschrift für Volkwirtschaft und Statistik 116*: 321–327

Clegg, J. (1987) *Multinational Enterprises and World Competition*, London: Macmillan

Contractor, F. J. (1990) 'Ownership patterns of U.S. joint ventures abroad and the liberalization of foreign government regulations in the 1980s. Evidence from the bench mark surveys', *Journal of International Business Studies 21*: 55–74

Contractor, F. J. and Lorange, P. (eds) (1988) *Cooperative Strategies in International Business*, Lexington, Mass.: Lexington Books

Douglas, S. P. and Rhee, Dong Kee (1989) 'Examining generic strategy types in US and European markets', *Journal of International Business Studies 20*: Fall: 437–463

Doz, Y. (1986) *Strategic Management in Multinational Companies*, Oxford: Pergamon Press

Doz, Y. (1988) 'International industries: fragmentation versus globalization', in Guile, B. R. and Brooks, H. (eds) *Technology and Global Industry*, Washington: National Academy Press

Dunning, J. H. (1977) 'Trade location of economic activity and the multi-national enterprise: A search for an eclectic approach', in Ohlin, B., Hesselborn, P. O., and Wikman, P. M. (eds) *The International Allocation of Economic Activity*, London: Macmillan: 395–418

Dunning, J. H. (1981) *International Production and the Multinational Enterprise*, London: Allen and Unwin

Dunning, J. H. (1988) *Explaining International Production*, London: Unwin Hyman

Dunning, J. H. (1989) 'The theory of international production', in Fatemi, K. (ed.) *International Trade*, New York: Taylor and Francis

Dunning, J. H. (1990) 'The eclectic paradigm of international production: A personal perspective', in Pitelis, C. and Sugden, R. (eds), *The Nature of The Transnational Firm*, London: Routledge

Dunning, J. H. (1992) *The Theory of Transnational Corporations*, Vol. 1 of UN Library on Transnational Corporations, London and New York: Routledge

Dunning, J. H. (1993) *Multinational Enterprises and the Global Economy*, Reading, Mass.: Addison-Wesley

Flowers, E. B. (1976) 'Oligopolistic reaction in European and Canadian direct investment in the U.S.', *Journal of International Business Studies 7*: 43–55

Ghoshal, S. (1987) 'Global strategy: An organizing framework', *Strategic Management Review 8*: 425–440

Giersch, H. (ed.) (1989) *Services in World Economic Growth*, Tubingen: J. C. B. Mohr

Graham, E. M. (1978) 'Transatlantic investment by multinational firms: A rivalistic phenomenon', *Journal of Post Keynesian Economics 1*: 82–99

Graham, E. M. (1990) 'Strategic interaction among multinational firms and foreign direct investment', in Pitelis, C. and Sugden, R. (eds) *The Nature of the Transnational Firm*, London: Routledge

Hamel, G. and Prahalad, C. K. (1987) 'Creating global strategic capability', in Hood, N. and Vahlne, J. E. (eds) *Strategies in Global Competition*, London: Routledge

Hedlund, G. (1986) 'The hypermodern MNC: A heterarchy human resource',

Human Resource Management, Spring: 9–35

Hennart, J. F. (1986) 'What is internalization?', *Weltwirtschaftliches Archiv,* *122*: 791–804

Hennart, J. F. (1988) 'Upstream vertical integration in the aluminum and tin industries: A comparative study of the choice between market and intra-firm coordination', *Journal of Economic Behavior and Organization 9*(3): 281–300

Knickerbocker, F. (1973) *Oligopolistic Reaction and the Multinational Enterprise,* Cambridge, Mass.: Harvard University Press

Kogut, B. (1983) 'Foreign direct investment as a sequential process', in Kindleberger. C. P. and Audretsch, D. (eds) *The Multinational Corporation in the 1980s,* Cambridge, Mass.: MIT Press

Kogut, B. (1985) 'Designing global strategies: profiting from operational flexibility', *Sloan Management Review,* Fall: 27–37

Kogut, B. (1989) 'A note on global strategies', *Journal of International Business Studies 10*: 383–389

Kogut, B. (1990) *The Permeability of Borders and the Speed of Learning Among Countries,* Lund: The Crafoord Lectures, 1989

Kogut, B. and Singh, Harbir (1988) 'The effects of national culture on the choice of entry mode', *Journal of International Business Studies,* Fall: 411–432

Kojima, K. (1978) *Direct Foreign Investment: A Japanese Model of Multi-national Business Operations,* London: Croom Helm

Kojima, K. (1982) 'Macro economic versus international business approach to foreign direct investment', *Hitosubashi Journal of Economics 23*: 1–19

Kumar, K. (1990) *Multinational Enterprises in India,* London: Routledge

Lessard, D. G. (1977) 'International diversification and foreign direct investment', in Eitman, D. and Stonehill, A. (eds) *Multinational Business Finance,* 4th Edition, Reading, Mass.: Addison-Wesley

McGee, J. and Thomas, H. (1986) 'Strategic groups: Theory research and taxonomy', *Strategic Management Journal 7*: 141–160

Porter, M. E. (1980) *Competitive Behavior,* New York: Free Press

Porter, M. E. (1985) *Competitive Advantage,* New York: Free Press

Porter, M. E. (ed.) (1986) *Competition in Global Industries,* Boston: Harvard Business School Press

Porter, M. E. (1990) *The Competitive Advantage of Nations,* New York: Free Press

Robbins, L. (1928) 'The Representative Firm', *Economic Journal 38*: 387–404

Rugman, A. M. (1975) 'Motives for foreign investment: The markets imperfection and risk diversification hypothesis', *Journal of World Trade Law 9*: 567–573

Rugman, A. M. (1979) *International Diversification and the Multinational Enterprise,* Lexington, Mass.: Lexington Books

Rugman, A. M. (1986) 'New theories of the multinational enterprise: An assessment of internalization theory', *Bulletin of Economic Research 38*: 101–118

Stuckey, J. (1983) *Vertical Integration and Joint Ventures in the Aluminum Industry,* Cambridge, Mass.: Harvard University Press

Teece, D. J. (1984) 'Economic analysis and strategic management', *California*

Management Review, XXVI: 87–110

Teece, D. J. (1985) 'Transaction cost economics and the multinational enterprise: An assessment', *Journal of Economic Behavior and Organization* 7: 21–45

Teece, D. J. , Pisano, G. and Shuen, A. (1990) *Firm Capabilities, Resources and the Concept of Strategy*, Berkeley: University of California (mimeo)

UN (1993) *From the Common Market to EC 92. Regional Integration in the European Community and Transnational Corporations*, New York: UN Transnational Corporations and Management Division

UNCTC (1988) *Transnational Corporations and World Development*, New York: United Nations, No. E88 II A8

UNCTC (1992) *The Determinants of Foreign Direct Investment*, New York: United Nations

Vernon, R. (1966) 'International investment and international trade in the product cycle', *Quarterly Journal of Economics 80*: 90–207

Vernon, R. (1979) 'The product cycle hypothesis in the new international environment', *Oxford Bulletin of Economics and Statistics 41*: 255–267

Vernon, R. (1983) 'Organizational and institutional responses to international risk', in Herring, R. J. (ed.), *Managing International Risk*, Cambridge: Cambridge University Press

5 COMPETITIVE ADVANTAGE OF NATIONS

Notes

1 Defined as production financed by foreign direct investment or controlled by foreign owned multinational firms.

2 We say renewed attention as some of the earlier explanations of the foreign value-added activity of firms focused largely on their ability to engage in such activities (e.g. Vernon, 1966; Caves, 1971).

3 Amit and Schoemaker (1990) distinguish between resources and capabilities in the following way.

> Resources consist of proprietary know-how (e.g. patents and trade secrets), financial or physical assets (e.g. property, plant and equipment), human capital, government licenses, etc. Capabilities, in contrast, are tangible or intangible (invisible) assets that are firm-specific and are created over time through complex interactions among the firm's resources. They can be thought of as 'intermediate goods' generated by the firm to provide enhanced productivity of its resources as well as flexibility and protection for its final product or service. Capabilities are based on developing, carrying, and exchanging information through the firm's human capital.

4 For a distinction between the theory of the MNE and the theory of MNE activity see Dunning, 1992.

5 At least as an explanation of the growth of the MNE.

6 More particularly that part which enters into international transactions.

7 *Natural* factor endowments are defined as the stock of unimproved resources and the uneducated labor force of a country. *Created* factor

    endowments or capabilities are the difference between these and the actual wealth creating assets of a community. These include not only its *ability* to create wealth, but also its *willingness* to do so.

8   Even though Porter's approach is essentially Schumpeterian.

9   For an elaboration of the ESP paradigm see, for example, Koopmans and Montias, 1971.

10 Seven from developed and one from a relatively advanced developing country (Korea). It is interesting to speculate on the relevance of Porter's analysis and conclusions to the great majority of developing economies. For a recent analysis of the interaction between the international competitiveness of developing country firms and government policies, see Agarwal and Agmon, 1990.

11 To give one (admittedly a rather extreme) example, 95 per cent of the sales of Nestlé is accounted for by their foreign subsidiaries. It follows that the diamond(s) of competitive advantage of foreign countries within which Nestlé operates may be more important to determining the contribution of Nestlé to the Swiss GNP than the equivalent diamond within which Nestlé operates in Switzerland. The point is further explored in an MNE detailed study of the competitive advantages of Sweden (Solvell, Porter and Zander, 1991).

12 To give an illustration, first at an industry level, inward investment in the UK motor industry might rise (fall) with outward investment, or inward investment might rise (fall) as outward investment falls (rises). Second, at a meso-level, inward investment in the UK industry might rise (fall) with outward investment in *other* sectors, or the total outward investment might fall (rise) in sympathy with outward investment. The net effect on competitiveness of all these movements is highly ambiguous and dependent upon the precise configuration of the components of the UK's diamond of competitive advantage.

13 Although the two are not necessarily exclusive alternatives.

14 This is not to say that the investment may not be beneficial as it could stimulate domestic rivalry and raise efficiency in the production of low cost chocolates!

15 Either directly or by affecting the demand of consumers. In India, for example, the priority of the Indian government has been to encourage self-sufficiency of output rather than raise the quality of domestic demand.

16 We accept that part of the stimulus to foreign demand may come from exports.

17 Rather than indirectly by domestic rivalry or innovation.

18 For example, by driving out competition and making possible monopoly pricing.

19 Similarly, if the US airways were open to foreign competition, almost certainly the quality of air travel would improve.

20 For further details, see Dunning 1993.

21 For example, is it prompted by market distortions, or a response to market forces? Is it part of a defensive oligopolistic reaction or a result of the increased efficiency of cross-border hierarchies?

22 A somewhat more sophisticated argument is that, rather than investing overseas to protect or advance their competition in high technology

products, it might have more productivity in the long run if the US firms had devoted more resources to product innovation or improving production efficiency in their domestic plants.

23 See especially those contained in Dunning, 1985 and Reddaway, Potter and Taylor, 1968.

24 To quote from Lawrence: 'An industry needs to experience rigorous competition if it is to be economically strong. Either too little or too much competitive pressure can lead an industry to a predictably weak economic performance characterized by its becoming inefficient and/or non-innovative' (Lawrence, 1987: 102).

25 For example, it is possible to envisage multinationalization leading to international cartelization, or helping to inject competition into markets dominated by a single or few producers.

26 Where a new science city at Tsukuba already has the reputation as a world-class center for R&D (*Japan Update*, 1990).

27 For an analysis of this interaction, see Chapters 12 and 13 and Behrman and Grosse, 1990.

28 Witness, for example, the strenuous efforts by state legislatures in the US to attract inward direct investment. On the interaction between the strategy of resource usage by governments and MNEs, see an interesting paper by Stopford (1990).

29 For an analysis of the interaction between the politically oriented strategies of firms and the likely response of governments, see Rugman and Verbeke (1990).

30 See Stegemann (1989) for a review of the literature on this subject.

31 Some further thoughts on the appropriateness of Porter's focus on a country's 'domestic' diamond of competitive advantage are contained in a special issue of Management International Review, edited by Alan Rugman, in the Spring of 1993.

References

Agarwal, R. and Agmon, T. (1990) 'The international success of developing country firms role of government-directed comparative advantage', *Management International Review 30*

Amit, R. and Schoemaker, P. J. (1990) *Key Success Factors: Their Foundation and Application*, Evanston, Ill.: Northwestern University Working Paper

Aydalot, P. and Keeble D. (eds) (1988) *High Technology and Industry and Innovatory Environment: The European Experience*, London: Routledge

Behrman, J. and Grosse, R. (1990) *International Business and Governments*, Columbia: University of Carolina Press

Boisgontier, P. and de Bernardy, M. (1986) *Les Enterprises de 'micro' et la Technopole*, Grenoble CEPS: Université des Grenobles

Buckley, P. and Casson, M. (1985) *The Economic Theory of the Multinational Enterprise*, London and Basingstoke: Macmillan

Caves, R. E. (1971) 'International corporations: the industrial economics of foreign investment', *Economica 38*: 1–27

Cowling, K. (1986) 'The internationalization of production and deindustrialization' in Amin, A. and Goddard, J. (eds) *Technological Change, Industrial Restructuring and Regional Development*, London: Allen and Unwin

Dunning, J. H. (ed.) (1985) *Multinational Enterprises, Economic Structure and International Competitiveness*, Chichester: John Wiley

Dunning, J. H. (1990) *The Globalization of Firms and the Competitiveness of Countries: Some Implications for the Theory of International Production*, Lund: Institute of Economic Research, Lund University

Dunning, J. H. (1991a) 'Governments, economic organization and international competitiveness' in Mattson, L. G. and Stymne, B. (eds) *Corporate and Industry Strategies for Europe*, Amsterdam: Elsevier Science Publishers, B.V.

Dunning, J. H. (1991b) 'Governments and multinational enterprises: from confrontation to cooperation?', *Millenium (Journal of International Studies) 20*: 225–243

Dunning, J. H. (1992) 'The theory of transnational corporations' in UNCTC Library on Transnational Corporations, London and New York: Routledge

Dunning, J. H. (1993) *Multinational Enterprise and the Global Economy*, Wokingham, Berks: Addison-Wesley

Dunning, J. H. and Morgan, E. V. (1971) *An Economic Study of the City of London*, London: Allen and Unwin

Dunning, J. H. and Steuer, M. (1969) 'The effects of US direct investment on British technology', *Moorgate and Wall Street*, Autumn: 1–30

Gilpin, R. (1975) *US Power and the Multinational Corporation*, London: Macmillan

Gilpin, R. (1987) 'Trade investment and technology policy', in Giersch, H. (ed.) *Emerging Technologies: Consequences for Economic Growth, Structural Change and Employment*, Tübinger: J. C. B. Mohr

Hall, P., Breheny, M., McQuaid, D. and Hart, D. (1987) *Western Sunrise*, London: Allen and Unwin

Japan Update (1990) 'Direct investment in Japan: new developments', *Japan Update*, Winter: 12–15

Julius DeAnne (1989) *Global Companies and Public Policies: The Challenge of the New Economic Linkages*, London: Chatham House

Knickerbocker, F. T. (1973) *Oligopolistic Reaction and the Multinational Enterprise*, Cambridge, Mass.: MIT Press

Kogut, B. (1985) 'Designing global strategies: profiting from operational Flexibility', *Sloan Management Review 26*, Fall: 27–38

Koopmans, K. and Montias, J. M. (1971) 'On the description and comparison of economic systems' in Eckstein, A. (ed.) *Comparison of Economic Systems*, California: University of California Press

Lawrence, P. R. (1987) 'Competition: a renewed focus for industrial policy', in Teece, D. J. (ed.) *The Competition Challenge*, Cambridge, Mass.: Ballinger

Lipsey, R. and Dobson, W. (1987) *Shaping Comparative Advantage*, Ontario: Prentice Hall for C. D. Howe Institute

Malerba, F. (1990) 'The Italian system of innovation', Paper presented at the Workshop on The Organization of International Competitiveness, Brussels, May–June 1990

Ozawa, T. (1989) *Japan's Strategic Policy Towards Outward Direct Investment*, Fort Collins: Colorado State University (mimeo)

Porter, M. E. (1990) *The Competitive Advantage of Nations*, New York: Free Press

Reddaway, W. B., Potter, S. T. and Taylor, C. T. (1968) *The Effects of UK Direct Investment Overseas*, Cambridge: Cambridge University Press

Rugman, A. and Verbeke, A. (1990) *Global Corporate Strategy and Trade Policy*, London and New York: Routledge

Safarian, A. E. (1989) 'Firm and government strategies in the context of economic integration', Paper presented to a round-table on *Multinational Firms and European Integration*, Geneva, May 1989

Scott, A. J. and Angel, D. P. (1987) 'The US semi-conductor industry: a locational analysis', *Environment and Planning A 19*: 875–912

Solvell, O., Porter, M. E. and Zander, I. (1991) *Advantage Sweden*, Stockholm: Norstedts

Stegemann, K. (1989) 'Policy rivalry among industrial states: what we can learn from models of strategic trade policy?', *International Organization 43*, Winter: 73–100

Stopford, J. (1990) 'Global strategic change and resource usage', Paper presented at International Symposium on *MNEs and 21st Century Scenarios*, organized for the studies of Multinational Enterprise, Tokyo

Vernon, R. (1966) 'International investment and international trade in the product cycle', *Quarterly Journal of Economics 80*: 190–207

6 JAPANESE MNEs IN EUROPE AND US

Notes

1 e.g. through the failure of subcontractors to keep to delivery dates or to supply agreed product quality, and the inability or unwillingness of industrial customers or distributors to maintain the reputation of the contracting firm.

2 As explored in more detail in Chapter 10 of Dunning, 1993.

3 As, for example, explored in Chapter 4.

4 Real wages tripled in Japan between 1950 and 1970, evidence that productivity gains were not fast enough to keep up with the desired rate of upgrading (Dunning and Narula, 1992).

5 For some implications of the differences between Fordism and Toyotaism see Chapter 2, especially notes 12 and 13 (p. 408).

6 Exceptions are the quite high ratios of intragroup local sales of Japanese affiliates in the US car industry and in the EC electrical and electronic industry.

7 For a recent assessment of Japanese MNE activity in Central and Eastern Europe, see Ozawa, 1992.

8 In the US, at least, 100 Japanese affiliates had R&D facilities in 1988 (*Research Management*, 1990).

9 For a recent examination of the alternative organizational strategies which MNEs might pursue, see Bartlett and Ghoshal, 1990. According to the authors, a transnational strategy is one in which there is a regular

interchange of knowledge and ideas between the different parts of the organization, which better enable decisions to be taken for the benefit of the system as a whole.

10 Examples include high savings ratios, a dedicated work ethic and highly personalized transactional relationships.

References

Baldwin, R. (1989) 'The growth effects of 1992', *Economic Policy*, 9 November

Bartlett, C. and Ghoshal, S. (1990) *Managing Across National Boundaries: The Transnational Solution*, Harvard: Harvard University Press

Cecchini, P., Catinat, M. and Jacquemin, A. (1988) *The European Challenge 1992: The Benefits of a Single Market*, Aldershot, Hants/Wildwood House

Dunning, J. H. (1988) *Explaining International Production*, London: Unwin Hyman

Dunning, J. H. (1989) 'The theory of international production', in Fatemi, K. (ed.) *The Theory of International Trade*, New York: Taylor and Francis

Dunning, J. H. (1990) *The Globalization of Firms and the Competitiveness of Countries*, Lund: University of Lund, Crafoord Lectures 1989

Dunning, J. H. (1993) *Multinational Enterprises and the Global Economy*, Wokingham, Berks: Addison-Wesley

Dunning, J. H. and Cantwell J. A. (1990) 'Japanese manufacturing direct investment in the EEC, post 1992: some alternative scenarios', in Burgenmeir, B. and Mucchielli, J. L. (eds) *Multinationals and Europe 1992*, London and New York: Routledge

Dunning, J. H. and Narula, R. (1992) *Transpacific Foreign Direct Investment and the Investment Development Path: The Record Assessed*, Rutgers University, February (mimeo)

Financial Times (London) (1990) *World Industrial Review* (Special Survey) 8 January: 4

Industrial Bank of Japan (1989) 'Factors behind Japanese direct investment abroad, *Quarterly Survey of Japanese Finance and Industry 80*, IV: 13–24

Japan Economic Journal (1990) 'M & A activity shifting to Europe', July 28: 1

Japanese External Trade Organization (JETRO) (1988, 1990) *Current Situation of Business Operations of Japanese-Manufacturing Enterprises in Europe*, Fourth and Sixth Survey Reports, March

Kirkland, R.I. (1990) 'The big Japanese push into Europe', *Fortune*, 2 July: 94–98

Kogut, B. and Parkinson, D. (1993) 'The diffusion of American organizing principles to Europe', in Kogut, B. (ed.) *Country Competitiveness, Technology and the Organizing of Work*, Oxford: Oxford University Press

Ministry of International Trade and Industry (MITI) (1990) *1987 Survey of Overseas Activities of Japanese Enterprises*, March

Ozawa, T. (1989a) *Japan's 'Strategic' Policy Toward Outward Direct Investments*, University of Colorado, July (mimeo)

Ozawa, T. (1989b) *Japan's Strategic Investment Policy Toward the Devel-*

oping Countries: from the Ad Hoc to a New Comprehensive Approach, University of Colorado, October (mimeo)

Ozawa, T. (1989c) *The EC and Japan as Investment Partners: A Case Study*, University of Colorado, July (mimeo)

Ozawa, T. (1992) 'Japanese MNCs as potential partners in East Europe's economic reconstruction', in Buckley, P. J. and Ghauri, P. N. (eds) *The Liberalization of Eastern Europe and the Impact of International Business*, London: Edward Elgar

Porter, M. E. (1990) *The Competitive Advantages of Nations*, New York: Free Press

Research Management (1990) 'R&D by Japanese manufacturing subsidiaries in the US', *Research Management*, 1989

Tokyo Business Today (1989) 'Rapid increase in Japanese overseas M & A', January: 20–24

United Kingdom Central Statistical Office (annual) *Business Monitor* MA4. (various editors)

UNCTC (1989) *The Process of Transnationalization and Transnational Mergers*, UNCTC Current Studies Series A No. 8, United Nations

United States Department of Commerce (1990) US International Sales and Purchases of Services, *Survey of Current Business 70*: 37–73

7 TRANSATLANTIC FOREIGN DIRECT INVESTMENT AND THE EUROPEAN ECONOMIC COMMUNITY

Notes

1 I am grateful to Rajneesh Narula of Rutgers University for his statistical assistance in the preparation of this chapter.

2 Defined as production financed by foreign direct investment (FDI) and undertaken by multinational enterprises (MNEs).

3 See Chapter 4 for further details.

4 It is worth pointing out that in conditions of imperfect competition firms may not only lower their transactional costs by internalizing markets but reap positive transactional benefits.

5 For recent reviews see Casson, 1987 and Hennart, 1990.

6 i.e. $1.35 billion compared with $2.2 billion. The corresponding percentage for manufacturing industry alone was 35.5 per cent.

7 The figure in brackets next to EC indicates the number of countries in the Community at the time (6 between 1957 and 1972, i.e. Belgium, France, Italy, Luxembourg, The Netherlands, and West Germany); 9 between 1973 and 1985 (the 6 plus Denmark, Ireland and the UK); 10 between 1986 and 1987 (the 9 plus Greece), and 12 since 1988 (the 10 plus Portugal and Spain).

8 These include the cost of tariff discrimination and the potential economic growth of the member countries.

9 Including exports by US manufacturing subsidiaries in the EC.

10 Data derived from those published by the US Department of Commerce and UN Statistical Year Book (various editions).

11 Little sectoral data are available on EC investment in the US over these

years. However, for manufacturing industry alone, taking the EC to mean all Europe less the UK and Switzerland, the value of the direct investment in the US rose from $406 million in 1959 to $1,715 million in 1972 (i.e. by nearly four times).

12   The sales of European affiliates in the US, less those of the UK and Switzerland, in 1959, were $1.25 billion, 3.1 times the value of the foreign investments. Applying this same sales/asset ratio in 1972, we come up with a sales estimate in that year of $5.96 billion.

13   To give just one example. In 1972 10 German marks would have brought 3.13 dollars; in 1985 they brought 3.40 dollars.

14   Unfortunately the assumption of *ceteris paribus* is not always a realistic one as firms may sometimes manipulate the charges to their subsidiaries for the intermediate services they supplied to them. This is exactly what seems to have happened between 1982 and 1986 when the royalties and fees received from EC affiliates of US firms actually fell by 4.1 per cent at a time when those received from other EC firms rose by 36.2 per cent.

15   Between 1981 and 1984 there was a net disinvestment by US firms in the EC of $11.2 billion.

16   The ratio between the value of output of EC manufacturing subsidiaries and exports from the EC to the US rose marginally from 1.40 in 1972 to 1.55 in 1985.

17   Later figures released in 1992 suggest that in 1989, the proportion of goods exported by US affiliates in the EC fell from 35.1 per cent to 25.9 per cent. The increase in the exports of intra-affiliate services to other than the US rose by 221.2 per cent between 1985 and 1989.

18   European affiliates less Swiss affiliates.

19   Even accepting the fact that EC direct investment in the US is generally of newer vintage, a revaluation of the assets of both European corporations in the US and US corporations in Europe, to reflect their replacement value, would still suggest that the EC is a net direct investor in the US.

20   As discussed in the following chapter.

21   For a speculation of the possible shape of triadic relationships between the US, the EC and Japan in the 1990s see a fascinating and highly perceptive article by Bergsten (1990).

References

Balassa, B. (1966) 'American direct investments in the Common Market', *Banco Nazionale del Laroro Quarterly Review*, June: 121–146

Bergsten, C. F. (1990) 'The world economy after the Cold War', *Foreign Affairs 69*: 96–112

Casson, M. C. (1987) *The Firm and the Market*, Oxford: Basil Blackwell

Dunning, J. H. (1970) 'Foreign capital and economic growth in Europe', in Denton, G. C. (ed.) *Economic Integration in Europe*, London: Weidenfeld and Nicolson

Dunning, J. H. (1972) *The Location of International Firms in an Enlarged EEC: An Exploratory Paper*, Manchester: Manchester Statistical Society

Dunning, J. H. (1988) *Multinationals, Technology and Competitiveness*, London: Unwin Hyman

Dunning, J. H. (1989) 'The theory of international production', in Fatemi, K. (ed.) *International Trade: Existing Problems and Prospective Solutions*, New York: Taylor and Francis

Dunning, J. H. (1991) 'European economic integration and transatlantic foreign direct investment: The record assessed', in Yannopoulos, G. (ed.) *Europe and America 1992: US–EC Economic Relations and the Simple European Market*, Manchester: Manchester University Press

Dunning, J. H. (1993) *Multinational Enterprises and the Global Economy*, Wokingham, Berks: Addison-Wesley

Edwards, A. (1964) *Investment in the European Economic Community*, New York: Praeger

Franko, L. (1989) *Europe 1992: The Impact of Global Corporate Competition and Multinational Corporate Strategy*, University of Massachusetts at Boston (mimeo)

Hennart, J. F. (1990) 'Internalization analysis', in Pitelis, C. N. and Sugden, R. (eds) *The Nature of the Transnational Firm*, London: Routledge

Krause, L. B. (1968) *European Economic Integration and the United States*, Washington: The Brookings Institution.

Mataloni, R. J. (1990) 'Capital expenditures by majority owned foreign affiliates of US companies, 1990', *Survey of Current Business* September: 30–36

Robson, P. (1993) *TNCs and Economic Integration*, UN Library on Transnational Corporations, London and New York: Routledge

UN (v.d.) *Commodity Trade Statistics*

UN (1992) *From the Common Market to EC 92. Regional Economic Integration in the European Community and Transnational Corporations*, New York: United Nations

US Department of Commerce (1959) *US Overseas Direct Investment in 1957*, Washington: Bureau of Economic Analysis

US Department of Commerce (v.d.) *Survey of Current Business*

US Department of Commerce (1963) *oreign Direct Investment in the US 1950–61*, Washington: Bureau of Economic Analysis

US Department of Commerce (v.d.) *Foreign Direct Investment in the United States, Operation of US Affiliates, 1977–80, 1982, 1984, 1985, 1986, and 1987* (preliminary), Washington: Bureau of Economic Analysis

US Department of Commerce (v.d.) *Foreign Direct Investment of the U.S., Bench Mark Surveys for 1972, 1977, 1982 and 1989*, Washington: Bureau of Economic Analysis

Walter, I. (1992) 'Patterns of mergers and acquisitions 1985–1990', in Oxelheim, L. (ed.) *The Global Race for Foreign Direct Investments in the 1990s*, Berlin and New York: Springer-Verlag

8 TECHNOLOGY-BASED CROSS-BORDER ALLIANCES

Notes

1 Some of these are reviewed in Buckley, 1993. See also Hennart, 1988, 1991.

2 Based on an earlier estimate by *The Economist*, 1990.

3 These, and other examples, have been culled from *The New York Times*, *The Financial Times*, *Wall Street Journal* and *Business Week*.

References

Agmon, T. and Hirsch, S. (1979) 'Multinational corporations and the developing economies: potential gains in a world of imperfect markets and uncertainty', *Oxford Bulletin of Economics and Statistics 41* (4) November: 333–334

Anderson, E. and Gatignon, H. (1986) 'Modes of foreign entry: a transaction cost analysis and propositions', *Journal of International Business Studies 17*, Fall: 1–26

Aumann, R. J. and Maschler, M. (1964) 'The bargaining set for cooperative games', *Annals of Mathematics Studies 52*: 443–476

Axelrod, R. (1984) *The Evolution of Cooperation*, New York: Basic Books

Axelsson, B. (1987) 'Supplier management and technological development', in Hakansson, H. (ed.) *Industrial Technological Development: A Network Approach*, Croom Helm

Beamish, P. W. and Banks, J. C. (1987) 'Equity joint ventures and the theory of the multinational enterprise', *Journal of International Business Studies 19*, Summer: 1–16

Buckley, P. E. (1988) 'The limits of explanation: testing the internalization theory of the multinational enterprise', *Journal of International Business Studies 19* (2) Summer: 184, 181–193

Buckley, P. E. (1993) 'TNCs and cooperative agreements', *UN Library on Transnational Corporations*, London and New York: Routledge

Buckley, P. J. and Casson, M. (1988) 'A theory of cooperation in international business', in Contractor, F. J. and Lorange, P. (eds) *Cooperative Strategies in International Business*, Lexington, Mass.: Lexington Books

Buckley, P. J. and Davies, H. (1979) *The Place of Licensing in the Theory and Practice of Foreign Operations*, University of Reading Discussion Papers in International investment and Business Studies No. 47, November

Buigues, P. and Jacquemin, A. (1989) 'Strategies of firms and structural environments in the large internal market', *Journal of Common Market Studies XXVIII* (1) September: 65

Business Week (1989) October 23: 110

Business Week (1990) February 19: 38

Cainarca, G. C., Colombo, M. G. and Mariotti, S. (1988) *Cooperative Agreements in the Information and Communication Industrial System*, Milan: Politechnico de Milano

Cainarca, G. C., Colombo, M. G., Mariotti, S., Ciborra, C., De Michelis, G. and Losano, M. G. (1989) *Tecnologie Dell'Informazione E Accordi Tra Imprese*, Milano: Fondazione Adriano Olivetti, Edizioni di Comunità

Cantwell, J. C. (1987) *Technological Advantage as a Determinant of the International Economic Activity of Firms*, University of Reading Discussion Papers in International Investment and Business Studies 105, October: 3

Chandler, A. D. (1962) *Strategy and Structure: Chapters in the History of the American Industrial Enterprise*, Boston: MIT Press: 7–17

Clarke, C. and Brennan, K. (1988) 'Allied Forces', *Management Today*, November: 128

Coase, R. (1937) 'The nature of the firm', *Economica* IV, New Series: 386–405

Commission des Communautés européennes (1989) *Dix-huitième Rapport sur la Politique de Concurrence*, Bruxelles-Luxembourg

Commission des Communautés européennes (1990) *Dix-neuvième Rapport sur la Politique de Concurrence*, Bruxelles-Luxembourg

Contractor, F. (1989) *Contractual and Cooperative Modes of International Business: Towards A Unified Theory of Model Choice*, Graduate School of Management Working Paper 89–15, Rutgers University, August, 13–14

Contractor, F. and Lorange, P. (eds) (1988) *Cooperative Strategies in International Business*, Lexington, Mass.: Lexington Books

Cook, K. S. and Emerson, R. M. (1978) 'Power, equity, and commitment in exchange networks', *American Sociological Review 43*: 725

Davidson, W. H. (1988), 'Ecostructures and international competitiveness', in Negandhi, A. R. and Arun, S. (eds) *International Strategic Management*, Lexington, Mass.: Lexington Books: 20

Drucker, P. F. (1989) 'From dangerous liaisons to alliances for progress', *The Wall Street Journal*, September 8: 14

Dunning, J. H. and Narula, R. (1992) *Foreign research and development expenditures by US MNEs and by foreign MNEs in the US*, Newark: Rutgers University (mimeo)

ECE/UNCTC Joint Unit on Transnational Corporations (1987) *Recent Developments in Operations and Behavior of Transnational Corporations: Towards New Structures and Strategies of Transnational Corporations*, Genera: ECE/UNCTC Joint Unit Publications Series 7, 19

ECE/UNCTC Joint Unit on Transnational Corporations (1991) *Les sociétés transnationales japonaises en Europe: structures, stratégies et nouvelles tendances*, Geneva and New York: ECE/UNCTC Joint Unit Publications Series 7

Economist (The) (1990) February 3: 66

Electronic Business (1989) August: 50

Electronic Business (1990) March: 58

Engwall, L. and Johanson, J. (1989) *Banks in Industrial Networks*, Working Paper 2, Uppsala University, 4–5

Ferné, G. (1989) 'Programmes for Information Technology', *The OECD Observer*, August–September: 10

Financial Times (1991) March 11

Fortune (1989) March 27: 50; August 28: 70

Geringer, J. M. (1988) 'Partner selection criteria for developed country joint ventures', *Business Quarterly 53* (1), Summer: 61

Geringer, J. M. (1991) 'Strategic determinants of partner selection: criteria in international joint ventures', *Journal of International Business Studies 22*: 44–61

Gugler, P. (1991) *Les alliances stratégiques transnationales*, Fribourg: Editions Universitaires Fribourg Suisse

Hagedoorn, J. and Schakenraad, J. (1990) *Leading Companies and the Structure of Strategic Alliances in Core Technologies*, Limburg: University of Limburg, MERIT

Hakansson, H. (1987) *Industrial Technological Development: A Network Approach*, London: Croom Helm: 3

Haklisch, C. S. (1986) *Technical Alliances in the Semi-conductor Industry*, New York: New York University (mimeo)

Hamel, G., Doz, Y. L. and Prahalad, C. K. (1989) 'Collaborate with your competitors – and win', *Harvard Business Review*, January–February: 136

Harsanyi, J. C. (1977) *Rational Behavior and Bargaining Equilibrium in Games and Social Situations*, Cambridge, Mass.: Cambridge University Press: 273–288

Hawk, B. E. (1988) 'La recherche-développement en droit communautaire et en droit anti-trust américain', in Alexis, J. and Bernard, R. (eds) *Coopération entre enterprises: Enterprises conjointes, stratégies industrielles et pouvoirs publics*, Brussels: De Boeck/Editions Universitaires: 230–231

Hawkins, R. G. (1982) 'Technical cooperation and industrial growth: a survey of the economic issues', in Fusfeld, H. I. and Haklisch, C. S. (eds) *Industrial Productivity and International Technical Cooperation*, Oxford: Pergamon Press

Hennart, J. F. (1988) 'A transaction costs theory of equity joint ventures', *Strategic Management Journal 9*: 361–374

Hennart, J. F. (1991) 'Control in multinational firms: the role of price and hierarchy', *Management International Review 31*: 71–96

Hill, C. W. L. and Kim, W. C. (1988) 'Searching for a dynamic theory of the multinational enterprise: a transaction cost model', *Strategic Management Journal 9*: 93–104

Hill, C. W. L., Wang, P. and Kim, W. C. (1990) 'An eclectic theory of the choice of international entry mode', *Strategic Management Journal 11*: 117–118

Hirsch, S. (1976) 'An international and trade investment theory of the firm', *Oxford Economic Papers (New Series) 28* (2): 258–270

Hladik, K. J. (1985) *International Joint Ventures*, Lexington, Mass.: Lexington Books

Hladik, K. J. and Linden, L. H. (1989) 'Is an international joint venture in R&D for you?', *Research Technology Management 32* (4) July–August: 12

Hull, F. and Slowinski, G. (1987) *Strategic Partnerships between Small and Large Firms in High Technology: A Theoretical Framework for Analysis*, Rutgers University (mimeo)

Hull, F., Slowinski, G., Wharton, R. and Azumi, T. (1988) 'Strategic partnerships between technological entrepreneurs in the United States and large corporations in Japan and the United States', in Contractor, F. J. and Lorange, P. (eds), *Cooperative Strategies in International Business*, Lexington, Mass.: Lexington Books, 451

Inman, B. R. and Burton, D. F. (1990) 'Technology and competitiveness: the new policy frontier', *Foreign Affairs*, Spring: 122–125

International Management (1984) December: 58

Jacquemin, A. (1988) 'Cooperative agreements in R&D and European antitrust policy', *European Economic Review 32*: 552

Jacquemin, A., Lammerant, M. and Spinoit, B. (1986) *Compétition Européenne et Coopération entre Enterprises en Matière de Recherche-développement*, Luxembourg: Commission des Communautés européennes (document)

Johanson, J. and Mattson, L. (1987) 'Interorganizational relations in industrial systems: a network approach compared with the transaction-cost approach', *International Studies of Management and Organization XVII* (1): 35

Kalai, E. and Smorondinsky, M. (1975) 'Other solutions to Nash's bargaining problem', *Econometrica 43* (3) May: 513–518

Kamman, D. F. and Strijker, D. (1989) 'Concept of dynamic networking in economic and geographical space and their application', in GREMI, *Innovative Milieux and Transnational Firm Networks: Towards a New Theory of Spatial Development*, International Workshop, Barcelona, March

Knickerbocker, F. T. (1973) *Oligopolistic Reaction and Multinational Enterprise*, Cambridge, Mass.: Harvard University Press

Kogut, B. (1988) 'Joint ventures: theoretical and empirical perspectives', *Strategic Management Journal 9*: 319–332

Kraar, L. (1989) 'Your rivals can be your allies', *Fortune*, March 27: 58

Kuentz, P. (1990) 'Expériences réalisées en matière de coopération technologique européenne', *Vie Economique*, June: 13

Lewis, J. D. (1990) *Partnerships For Profit: Structuring and Managing Strategic Alliances*, New York: Free Press

Lynch, R. P. (1990) 'Building alliances to penetrate European markets', *The Journal of Business Strategy*, March–April: 8

Mariotti, S. and Ricotta, E. (1986) *Diversification, Agreements Between Firms and Innovative Behavior*, Paper presented at the Conference on Innovation Diffusion, Venice: 39

Moffatt, S. (1991) 'Picking Japan's research brains', *Fortune*, March: 54–59

Mowery, D. C. (1989) 'Collaborative ventures between US and foreign manufacturing firms', *Research Policy 18*: 23, 26

Nash, J. F. (1950) 'The bargaining problem', *Econometrica 18*, No. 2, April: 152–162

Nash, J. F. (1953) 'Two-person cooperative games', *Econometrica 21*, No. 1, January: 128–140

New York Times (1990) February 2: D1, D9

OECD (1986) *Technical Cooperation Agreements Between Firms: Some Initial Data and Analysis*, Paris: OECD (DSTI/SPR 86.20)

Ohmae, K. (1989) *Beyond National Borders: Reflections on Japan and the World*, Homewood, Illinois: Dow Jones-Irwin

Penrose, E. T. (1958) *The Theory of the Growth of the Firm*, Oxford: Basil Blackwell

Perlmuter, H. V. and Heenan, D. A. (1986) 'Cooperate to compete globally', *Harvard Business Review*, March–April: 142

Porter, M. E. (1990) *The Competitive Advantage of Nations* New York: Free Press

Porter, M. E. and Fuller, M. B. (1986) 'Coalitions and global strategy', in Porter, M. E. (ed.) *Competition in Global Industries*, Boston, Mass.: Harvard Business School Press: 316

Reich, R. B. and Mankin, E. D. (1986) 'Joint ventures with Japan give away our future', *Harvard Business Review*, March–April: 78–86

Richardson, G. B. (1972) 'The organization of industry', *Economic Journal 82* (327) 883–96

Rubinstein, A. (1982) 'Perfect equilibrium in a bargaining model', *Econometrica 50* (1) January: 97–109

Rubinstein, A. (1985) 'A bargaining model with incomplete information about time preferences', *Econometrica 53* (5) September: 1151–1172

Rugman, A. (1981) *Inside the Multinationals*, New York: Columbia University Press: 54–60

Sapienza, A. M. (1989) 'R&D collaboration as global competitive tactic – Biotechnology and the ethical pharmaceutical industry', *R&D Management 19* (4) October: 285

Shan, W. (1990) 'An empirical analysis of organizational strategies by entrepreneurial high-technology firms', *Strategic Management Journal 11*: 129–131

Shapley, L. S. (1953) 'A value for n-person games', *Annals of Mathematical Studies 28*: 307–371

Shubik, M. (1970) 'Game theory, behavior, and the paradox of the Prisoner's Dilemma: Three solutions', *Journal of Conflict Resolution XIV* (2): 181–93

Teece, D. J. (1981) 'The multinational enterprise: market failure and market power considerations', *Sloan Management Review 22* (3): 7–10

Teece, D. J. (1985) 'Multinational enterprise, internal governance, and industrial organization', *American Economic Review 75* (2) May: 233–8

Teece, D. J. (1986) 'Profiting from technological innovation: Implications for integration, collaboration, licensing and public policy', *Research Policy 15* (1) February: 288–290

Teece, D. J. (1989) 'Inter-organizational requirements of the innovation process', *Managerial and Decision Economics*, Special issue, Spring: 35–42

Van Tulder, R. and Junne, G. (1988) *European Multinationals in Core Technologies*, Chichester: John Wiley/IRM

Vernon, R. (1966) 'International investment and international trade in the product cycle', *Quarterly Journal of Economics LXXX*: 190–207

Von Neumann, J. and Morgenstern, O. (1947) *Theory of Games and Economic Behavior*, Princeton: Princeton University Press

Walker, G. and Weber, D. (1984) 'A transaction cost approach to make-or-buy decisions', *Administrative Science Quarterly 29* (3): 373–391

Zenthen, F. (1930) *Problems of Monopoly and Economic Warfare*, London: Routledge and Kegan Paul

9 THE PROSPECTS FOR FOREIGN DIRECT INVESTMENT IN CENTRAL AND EASTERN EUROPE

Notes

1 An earlier version of this chapter first appeared in the June 1991 issue of *Development and International Cooperation*. Readers interested in the subject of FDI in Central and Eastern European countries will find the contents of that issue especially interesting.

2 For the purposes of this chapter, we shall not consider Yugoslavia (as it then was) as part of Eastern Europe, although there are many similarities between that country and those dealt with in this chapter. In fact, of

course, until its segmentation Yugoslavia had many institutional advantages over the rest of Eastern Europe, and, between the mid-1960s and the end of the 1980s, had made considerable progress in the introduction of market-oriented economic reforms, and the development of a cadre of managers and entrepreneurs. For further details, see Rojec, 1991.

3   About one-half of operative joint ventures involving foreign firms in the former USSR are also in the service sector.

4   For example, in the decade before the political reforms, some 700 foreign enterprises were set up in Poland (June, 1990).

5   The precise date varies between January 1990 for Hungary and Poland to March 1991 for the Czech and Slavic Republics.

6   Ozawa asserts that this miniscule presence of Japan as an investor in Central and Eastern Europe closely parallels its relatively insignificant position as a trade partner. He quotes a survey undertaken by MITI in 1990 in which, while 51.8 per cent of European owned firms assessed Central and Eastern Europe as a very or somewhat attractive potential production base, only 11.6 per cent of Japanese firms so opined. Unfamiliarity with local economic conditions, language difficulties and greater investment attractions in other parts of the word were the main reasons given for the lack of investment by potential Japanese investors.

7   Further details of recent acquisitions and newly established joint ventures are given in McMillan, 1991 and in Samuelsson, 1992.

8   Examples quoted by Ozawa (1992) include an agreement between Nissho Iwai Corporation and Metall Gesselschaft to develop markets in the former Soviet Bloc countries in five key fields, viz. non-ferrous metals, chemicals, machinery, steel and finance, and that between the Murebeni Corporation and Austrian Industries in product and market development in the area of plant exports and electronic home products to Eastern Europe. It may also be worth observing that some of the investments classified to Germany are in fact undertaken by foreign owned subsidiaries located in that country.

9   These include the decision of the Mitsubishi group to switch a new manufacturing plant from Spain to Eastern Europe; Suzuki, which initially planned to set up an assembly plant for motor cycles in Portugal and subsequently opted for Eastern Europe; and Foundation Publishing, which decided to expand its typesetting operations by establishing a joint venture in Budapest rather than in Greece.

10 In early 1991, for example, monthly wages were $140 in Hungary and $45 in Poland as compared with $235 in Portugal and $400 in Spain.

11 These include the sale of over 8,000 state owned companies in Poland (in which foreign firms may acquire up to a 10 per cent equity stake), and the public auctioning of up to 100,000 small and medium-size trading and service firms in Czechoslovakia.

12 Although much of this expenditure was directed to defence and space related activities.

13 For an interesting critique of the economic role of the US government which could well be applied to the Central and Eastern European situations see Osborne and Gaebler, 1992.

14 See, for example, Chapter 5 of Dunning 1988. The investment development cycle suggests that, as countries develop, their propensities

to be invested in, or to engage in, outward investment proceeds through various phases with the inward/outward ratio being at its highest as countries approach full industrialization.

15 For a more critical view of the role of MNEs in economic development – particularly the nations newly exposed to international competition – see O'Hearn, 1990.

16 *European Bank for Reconstruction and Development*, which has been set up with a capital of ECU 10bn to help finance market oriented projects in Central and East Europe.

17 For a review of these programmes, see Commission of the European Communities, 1990.

18 As summarized in *International Economic Insights*, 1991.

19 As put forward in a six point plan designed primarily to promote the trade of, and provide technical assistance to, the former Soviet Union, agreed at the G7 Summit of Heads of Governments, held in London in July 1991. For details of this plan, see *Financial Times*, July 18, 1991.

References

Bornschier, V. (1980) 'Multinational corporations and economic growth: A cross-national test of the decapitalization thesis, *Journal of Development Economies* 7: 191–210

Cantwell, J. C. (1990) *East–West Business Links and the Economic Development of Poland and Eastern Europe*, Reading: University of Reading (mimeo)

Commission of the European Communities (1990) *Industrial Cooperation with Central and Eastern Europe: Ways to Strengthen Cooperation*, Brussels (Communication from the Commission to the Council and European Parliament): SEC (90) 1213, July

Dunning, J. H. (ed.) (1985) *Multinational Enterprises, Economic Structure and International Competitiveness*, Chichester and New York: John Wiley

Dunning, J. H. (1988) *Explaining International Production*, Unwin Hyman

Dunning, J. H. (1993) *Multinational Enterprises and the Global Economy*, Reading, Mass.: Addison-Wesley

Gutman, P. (1990) *From Joint Ventures to Foreign Direct Investment: New Perspectives in Eastern Europe and the Soviet Union*, Revised version of paper presented at a Conference on Opportunities and Contracts for East West Soviet Ventures, Moscow, December: 7–16

International Economic Insights (1991) Vol. 2, March–April

McMillan, C. (1991) *Foreign Direct Investment Flows to Eastern Europe and the Implications for Developing Countries*, paper prepared for Department of Economic and Social Affairs, UN, April

Mikhail, A. D., Nandola, K. N. and Prasad, S. B. (1990) *Perceptions of US Exeutives in Doing Business in Eastern Europe and the USSR: Testing the International Exchange Framework*, Paper presented at the 16th Annual Conference of *European International Business Studies Association*, Madrid, December

O'Hearn, D. (1990) 'TNCs intervening mechanisms and economic growth in Ireland: A longitudinal test and extension of the Bornschier model', *World Development 18*: 417–429

Osborne, D. and Gaebler, E. (1992) *Reinventing Government: How the Entrepreneurial Spirit is Transforming the Public Sector*, Reading, Mass.: Addison-Wesley

Ozawa, T. (1991a) 'Europe 1992 and Japanese multinationals transplanting a subcontracting system in the expanded market', in Bürgenmeier, B. and Mucchielli, J. (eds) *Multinationals and Europe 1992*, London and New York: Routledge

Ozawa, T. (1991b) 'Japan in a new phase of multinationalization and industrial upgrading: Functional integration of trade growth and FDI', *Journal of World Trade 25*: 43–60

Ozawa, T. (1992) 'Japanese MNEs as potential partners in East Europe's economic reconstruction', in Buckley, P. J. and Ghauri, P. N. (eds) *The Liberalization of Eastern Europe and the Impact of International Business*, London: Edward Elgar

Palmer, M. (1991) *A Plan for Economic Growth in Central and Eastern Europe*, Luxembourg (mimeo)

Radice, H. (1991) *Transnational Corporations and Eastern Europe*, Leeds: University of Leeds School of Business and Economics Discussion Paper G91/108

Rojec, M. (1991) 'Liberalization of foreign investment legislation in Yugoslavia', *Development and International Corporations 12*: 69–83

Samuelsson, H. F (1992) *Foreign Direct Investments in Eastern Europe: Current Situation and Potential*, Geneva: ECE/UNCTC

UNCTC (1989) *CTC Reporter 28* Fall

World Bank (1990) *World Development Report 1990*, Oxford: Oxford University Press

10 THE GLOBALIZATION OF SERVICE ACTIVITIES

Notes

1 Examples include the work of Johanson and Vahlne (1977) and Anderson and Gatignon (1986). For a general review of entry strategies of firms into foreign markets, see Root, 1987.

2 For example, it has been estimated that about three-quarters of the value of ethical drugs produced by pharmaceutical companies represents non-manufacturing, i.e. service activities. Yet, since these activities are largely internalized by the drug companies, they are classified as part of goods finally produced. More generally, if the value of internalized production of services was added to the externalized value of services, then the significance of MNE related services production would be of overwhelming importance.

3 See also Seev Hirsch's paper presented at this Conference, and his previous writings on the subject, e.g. Hirsch, 1988.

4 *Inter alia*, this is shown by the fairly stable share of services in the GNP of countries. Although this varies from 32 per cent in low-income developing countries, to 55 per cent in developed countries, the spread is far smaller than in manufacturing industry and even more so in particular manufacturing industries.

5 The argument here is that sales in at least some of the major markets of the world are necessary to finance the ever increasing fixed costs of R&D which, in turn, are required to generate the innovations upon which dynamic competitiveness rests.

6 Except, we repeat, those which are internalized by MNE goods producing firms.

7 Normally high value activities are service-intensive; the best example is research, development and design, which tends to be one of the last activities undertaken by goods producing affiliates of MNEs.

8 Foreign production is defined as production financed by foreign direct investment and undertaken by MNEs.

9 For example, some 75 per cent of exports of US manufacturing affiliates from EC countries are to US affiliates in other EC countries.

10 For some recent analyses, see Hennart, 1990 and Casson, 1990.

11 Although such gains arise only as a result of the common governance of *both* existing and newly created or acquired advantages.

12 The argument being that the O advantages of MNEs may not arise from the fact that they are multinationals, and may be no less possessed by firms who choose to exploit such advantages by routes other than foreign direct investment.

13 See especially Dunning, 1988 and 1993.

14 Chapters 3 and 4.

15 As measured by the percentage of the sales of their foreign affiliates to their global sales.

16 While the eclectic paradigm considers all OLI variables affecting international production separately, it fully acknowledges that, over time, these variables are inextricably interlinked. Thus, the O advantage of a firm in time $t + 1$ may be related to how it responds to the advantages in time t. And, indeed, the O advantage of firms may influence their ability to affect L advantages (by, for example, their impact on government behavior).

17 In all, 286 firms provided data.

18 The authors define these new technologies as those including all information technologies and other systems operations, software or hardware technologies developed specifically for or applied in service functions. Examples include diagnostic techniques, treatment devices and specialized procedures for health care, advanced cargo handling or passenger movement for transportation, automatic teller machines or satellite communications systems for banking, and so on (Quinn, Doorley and Pacquette, 1990).

19 Often the advantages just described were built up in the domestic market. Because of its widely spread borders and size and prosperity of the US, US hoteliers, car rental companies, industrial laundries all gained experience from a multiplant network of activities within the US, which could fairly readily be transplanted abroad.

20 Such service intensity might relate either to pre- or post-production, e.g. after sales activities.

21 For further details see Chapter 13.

22 Environment, systems and policies. See Koopman and Montias (1971) and Chapter 10 of Dunning (1988).

23 A good example are the economies associated with the clustering of banking, finance, insurance and shipping firms in the City of London (Dunning and Morgan, 1971).
24 At the same time, others may be shedding their service activities. An example includes Uniteven's opting out of owning its own shipping fleet.
25 For example, the removal of intra-EC non-tariff barriers is likely to affect the strategy of both EC and non-EC pharmaceutical MNEs towards the location and organization of the service-intensive stages of their value-added chain, e.g. R&D and marketing activities, just as the earlier removal of tariff barriers dramatically affected the location of the goods intensive stages of the value chain, e.g. the production of the drug ingredients and dosage preparation activities.
26 For example, in the early 1980s, about 30 per cent of the hotels managed by the leading US hotel chains were owned by them, about 40 per cent managed by them and the balance were managed by local hotels under franchise to the US chains.
27 See, for example, Dunning, 1993.
28 Although earlier, Yair Aharoni (1966) had taken a behavioral perspective to examining the foreign investment decision taking process.
29 But see an interesting article by Enderwick (1990) on the kind of service sectors in which the Japanese are developing a competitive advantage.

References

Aharoni, Y. (1966) *The Foreign Investment Decision Process*, Boston: Harvard University Press

Aliber, R. Z. (1970) 'A theory of foreign direct investment', in Kindleberger, C. P. (ed.) *The International Corporation*, Cambridge, Mass.: MIT Press

Aliber, R. Z. (1971) 'The multinational enterprise in a multiple currency world', in Dunning, J. H. (ed.) *The Multinational Enterprise*, London: Allen and Unwin

Aliber, R. Z. (1983) 'Money, multinationals and sovereigns' in Kindleberger, C. P. and Andresch, D. B. (eds) *The Multinational Corporation in the 1980s*, Cambridge, Mass.: MIT Press

Anderson, L. and Gatignon, H. (1986) 'A transaction cost approach to modes of market entry', *Journal of International Business Studies 17*, Fall: 1–21

Bartlett, C. and Ghoshal, S. (1989) *Managing Across National Boundaries: The Transnational Solution*, Boston: Harvard Business School Press

Boddewyn, J. J., Halbrich, M. B. and Perry, A. C. (1986) 'Service multinationals: conceptualization, measurement and theory', *Journal of International Business Studies 16*: 41–57

Boyd-Barrett, O. (1989) 'Multinational news agencies', in Enderwick, P. (ed.) *Multinational Service Firms*, London and New York: Routledge

Buckley, P. J. (1987) 'An economic transaction analysis of tourism', *Tourism Management 8*, September

Buckley, P. J. (1990) 'Problems and developments in the core theory of international business', *Journal of International Business Studies 21*: 657–666

Campayne, P. (1990) *The Impact of Multinational Banks on the International*

Location of Banking Activity, Reading: University of Reading (mimeo)

Cantwell, J. A. (1992) 'The effects of integration on the structure of multinational corporation activity in the EC', in Klein, M. W. and Welfens, P. J. (eds) *Multinationals in the New Europe and Global Trade*, Berlin and New York: Springer-Verlag

Casson, M. (1982) 'Transaction costs and the theory of the multinational enterprise', in Rugman, A. M. (ed.) *New Theories of the Multinational Enterprise*, New York: St Martins Press

Casson, M. (1987) *The Firm and the Market*, Oxford: Basil Blackwell

Casson, M. (1989) 'An economic theory of multinational banking', Paper presented to a Conference on *Banks as Multinationals*, University of Reading

Casson, M. (1990) *Enterprise and Competitiveness*, Oxford: Clarendon Press

Casson, M. (1992) 'Internalization theory and beyond', in Dunning, J. H. (ed.) *The Theory of Transnational Corporations*, London and New York: Routledge

Caves, R. E. (1974) 'Causes of direct investment: foreign firms' shares in Canadian and UK manufacturing industries', *The Review of Economics and Statistics 56* (3): 279–293

Caves, R. E., Porter, M. and Spence, M. (1980) *Competition in the Open Economy: A Model Applied to Canada*, Cambridge, Mass.: Harvard University Press

Chandler, A. D. J. (1962) *Strategy and Structure: The History of American Industrial Enterprise*, Cambridge, Mass.: MIT Press

Chandler, A. D. J. (1977) *The Visible Hand: The Managerial Revolution in American Business*, Cambridge, Mass.: Harvard University Press

Cho, K. R. (1985) *Multinational Banks: Their Identities and Determinants*, Michigan: Ann Arbor

Contractor, F. J. and Lorange, P. (eds) (1988) *Cooperative Strategies in International Business*, Lexington, Mass.: D. C. Heath

Daniels, P. W., Thrift, N. J. and Leyshon, A. (1989) 'Internationalization of professional producer services: accountancy conglomerates', in Enderwick, P. (ed.) *Multinational Service Firms*, London and New York: Routledge

Douglas, S. and Dong Kee Rhee (1989) 'Examining generic competitive strategy types in US and European markets, *Journal of International Business Studies 20*: 437–464

Dunning, J. H. (1988) *Explaining International Production*, London: Unwin Hyman

Dunning, J. H. (1989) *Transnational Corporation and the Growth of Services: Some Conceptual and Theoretical Issues*, New York: UN, Sales No. E89:A.5

Dunning, J. H. (1990) 'The theory of international production', in Fatemi, K. (ed.) *International Trade*, New York: Taylor and Francis

Dunning, J. H. (1993) *Multinational Enterprises and the Global Economy*, Reading, Berkshire: Addison-Wesley

Dunning, J. H. and McQueen, M. (1981) 'The eclectic theory of production: a case study of the international hotel industry', *Managerial and Decision Economics 21*: 197–210

Dunning, J. H. and Morgan, E. V. (1971) *An Economic Study of the City of London*, London: Allen and Unwin

Dunning, J. H. and Norman, G. (1987) 'The location choice of offices of international companies', *Environment and Planning*, A, 19: 613–631

Enderwick, P. (ed.) (1989) *Multinational Service Firms*, London: Routledge

Enderwick, P. (1990) 'The international competitiveness of Japanese service industries, a cause for concern?', *California Management Review* 32: 22–37

Erramilli, M. K. and Rao, C. P. (1990) 'Choice of foreign entry modes by service firms: role of market knowledge; *Management International Review 30*: 135–150

Fatemi, K. (ed.) (1989) *International Trade*, New York: Taylor and Francis

Feketekuty, Geza and Hauser, G. (1985) 'Information technology and trade in services', *Economic Impact 52*: 22–28

Flowers, E. G. (1976) 'Oligopolistic reaction to European and Canadian direct investment in the US', *Journal of International Business Studies 7*: 43–55

Ghoshal, S. (1987) 'Global strategy: an organizing framework', *Strategic Management Journal 8*: 425–440

Giersch, H. (ed.) (1988) *Services in World Economic Growth*, Tubingen: J. C. B. Mohr

Graham, E. M. (1978) 'Transatlantic investment by multinational firms: a rivalistic phenomenon', *Journal of Post-Keynesian Economics 1* (1) Fall: 82–99

Gray, H. P. (1990) 'The role of services in global change', in Dunning, J. H. and Webster, A. (eds) *Structural Change in the World Economy*, London and New York: Routledge

Gray, H. P. and Gray, J. (1981) 'A multinational bank: a financial MNC?', *Journal of Banking and Finance 5*: 33–63

Grubel, H. (1968) 'Internationally diversified portfolios: welfare gains and capital flows', *American Economic Review 58* (5) Part 1: 1299–1314

Grubel, H. (1977) 'A theory of multinational banking', *Banca Nazionale del Lavoro Quarterly Review* (123): 349–364

Grubel, H. (1989) 'Multinational banking', in Enderwick, P. (ed.) *Multinational Service Firms*, London and New York: Routledge

Hedlund, G. (ed.) 1993) *Transnational Corporations and Organizational Management, United Nations Library on Transnational Corporations*, London: Routledge

Hennart, J. F. (1990) 'The transaction cost theory of the multinational enterprise', in Pitelis, C. and Sugden, R. (eds) *The Nature of the Transnational Firm*, London and New York: Routledge

Hergert, M. and Morris, D. (1988) 'Trends in international cooperative agreements', in Contractor, F. and Lorange, P. (eds) *Co-operative Strategies in International Business*, Lexington, Mass.: D. C. Heath

Hirsch, S. (1988) 'International transactions involving interactions: a conceptual framework combining goods and services', in Giersch, H. (ed.) *Services in World Economic Growth*, Tubingen: J. C. B. Mohr

Hymer, S. H. (1976) *The International Operations of National Firms: A Study of Direct Foreign Investment*, Cambridge, Mass.: MIT Press

Johanson, J. and Vahlne, J. E. (1977) 'The internationalization process of the firm: a model of knowledge, development and increasing foreign commitments', *Journal of International Business 8*, Spring/Summer: 23–32

Johnson, H. G. (1970) 'The efficiency and welfare implications of the international corporation', in Kindleberger, C. P. (ed.) *The International Corporation*, Cambridge, Mass.: MIT Press

Kay, N. M. (1991) 'Multinational enterprise as strategic choice: some transaction cost perspectives', in Pitelis, C. and Sugden, R. (eds) *The Nature of the Transnational Firm*, London and New York: Routledge

Knickerbocker, F. T. (1973) *Oligopolistic Reaction and the Multinational Enterprise*, Boston, Mass.: Harvard University Press

Kogut, B. (1983) 'Foreign direct investment as a sequential process', in Kindleberger, C. P. and Audretsch, D. (eds) *The Multinational Corporation in the 1980s*, Cambridge, Mass.: MIT Press

Kogut, B. (1985) 'Designing global strategies: profiting from operational flexibility', *Sloan Management Review 26*, Fall: 27–38

Kogut, B. (1987) *International Sequential Advantages and Network Flexibility* (mimeo)

Kogut, B. and Kulatilaha, N. (1988) *Multinational Flexibility and the Theory of Foreign Direct Investment*, Reginald H. Jones Center for Management Policy, University of Pennsylvania

Kojima, K. (1978) *Direct Foreign Investment*, New York: Praeger

Kojima, K. (1982) 'Macroeconomic versus international business approach to direct foreign investment', *Hitotsubashi Journal of Economics 23* (1) June: 1–19

Kojima, K. (1990) *Japanese Direct Investment Abroad*, Tokyo: International Christian University

Koopman, K. and Montias, J. M. (1971) 'On the description and comparison of economic systems', in Eckstein, A. (ed.) *Comparison of Economic Systems*, California: University of California Press

McGee, J. and Thomas, H. (1986) 'Strategic groups: theory research and taxomony', *Strategic Management Journal 7*: 141–160

Magee, S. (1977) 'Information and multinational corporations: an appropriability theory of direct foreign investment', in Bhagwati, J. (ed.) *The New International Economic Order*, Cambridge, Mass.: MIT Press

Mintzberg, H. (1978) 'Patterns in strategy formation', *Management Science 24*: 934–948

Nicholas, S. J. (1983) 'Agency contract, institutional modes, and the transaction of foreign direct investment by British manufacturing multinationals before 1939', *Journal of Economic History 43*: 675–686

Ozawa, T. (ed.) (1987) *The Role of General Trading Firms in Trade and Development: Some Experiences*, Tokyo: Asian Productivity Organization

Perlmutter, H. (1969) 'The tortuous evolution of the multinational enterprise', *Columbia Journal of World Business*: 9–18

Porter, M. E. (1980) *Competitive Strategy: Techniques for Analyzing Industries and Competitors*, New York: Free Press

Porter, M. E. (ed.) (1986) *Competition in Global Industries*, Boston, Mass.: Harvard Business School Press

Porter, M. E. (1990) *The Competitive Advantages of Nations*, New York: Free Press

Quinn, J. F. and Pacquette, P. C. (1990) 'Technology in services: creating organization revolutions', *Sloan Management Review*, Winter: 67–78

Quinn, J. F., Doorley, T. L. and Pacquette, P. C. (1990) 'Technology in services: rethinking strategic focus', *Sloan Management Review*, Winter: 79–87

Rimmer, P. J. (1988) 'The internationalization of engineering consultancies' problems of breaking into the club', *Environment and Planning*, A *20*: 761–788

Roche, E. M. (1992) *Managing Information Technology in Multinational Corporations*, New York: Macmillan

Root, F. R. (1987) *Entry Strategies for International Markets*, Lexington, Mass.: D. C. Heath

Rugman, A. (1979) *International Diversification and the Multinational Enterprise*, Lexington, Mass.: Lexington Books

Rugman, A. (1981) *Inside the Multinationals: The Economics of Internal Markets*, New York: Columbia University Press

Sagari, S. B. (1992) 'United States foreign direct investment in the banking industry', *Transnational Corporations* 1, No. 3, December: 93–124.

Sauvant, K. G. (1986) *International Transactions in Services*, Boulder, Colorado and London: Westview Press

Seymour, H. (1987) *The International Construction Industry*, London: Croom Helm

Sharma, D. D. and Johanson, J. (1987) 'Technical consultancy in internationalization', *International Marketing Review*, Winter: 20–29

Stevens, M. (1981) *The Big Eight*, London: Macmillan

Teece, D. J. (1984) 'Economic analysis and strategic management', *California Management Review XXCI*: 87–110

Teece, D. J. (1986) 'Transaction cost economics and the multinational enterprise: an assessment', *Journal of Economic Behavior and Organization 1*: 21–45

Terpstra, V. and Yu, Chwo-Ming (1988) 'Determinants of foreign investment of US advertising agencies', *Journal of International Business Studies 19*: 33–46

UNCTC (1979) *Transnational Corporations in Advertising*, New York: United Nations, Sales No. E.79.II.A.2

UNCTC (1981) *Transnational Banks: Operations, Strategies and their Effects in Developing Countries*, New York: UN, Sales No. E81.IIA.7

UNCTC (1984) *Transnational Corporations and Transborder Data Flows: Background and Overview*, Amsterdam and New York: Elsevier-North Holland

UNCTC (1988) *Transnational Corporations and World Development*, New York: UN, Sales No. E88.II A.7

UNCTC (1989) *Transnational Corporations in the Construction and Design Engineering Industry*, New York: UN, Sales No. E89.II A.6

Vernon, R. (1966) 'International investment and international trade in the produce cycle', *The Quarterly Journal of Economics 80* (2) May: 190–207

World Bank (1987) *World Development Report, 1987*, Washington: The World Bank

World Bank (1990) *World Development Report 1990*, Oxford: Oxford University Press

Yannopoulos, G. (1983) 'The growth of transnational banking', in Casson, M. (ed.) *The Growth of International Business*, London: Allen and Unwin

11 INTERNATIONAL DIRECT INVESTMENT PATTERNS IN THE 1990s

Notes

1   A report by the UNCTC (UN, 1992a) suggests that, in contrast to world recession in the early 1990s when flows of FDI declined substantially, between 1989 and 1991, the three most recent years of recession or low growth, it continued to rise; *inter alia*, this reflected the propensity of MNEs to engage in the cross-border acquisition of assets to maintain their global competitive advantages.

2   Between 1988 and 1990, Japanese outward direct investment (excluding reinvested earnings) amounted to $126 billion, compared with the UK and US, which included reinvested earnings of $94 million and $72 billion, respectively (UNCTC, 1992a).

3   The Japanese year end for all their FDI data is 31 March.

4   In 1991, the stock of FDI in Eastern and Central Europe probably amounted to only about 0.5 per cent of the total stock of FDI. Between 1989 and 1991, however, flows of new investment were running at about 2 per cent of the world total.

5   Which consist of the EC, the US and Japan.

6   Further details are set out in UNCTC, 1992a. The corresponding figure for 1980 was 58 per cent. However, in terms of investment *flows*, French capital exports between 1986 and 1990 amounted to 2002 billion francs compared with capital imports of 427.5 billion francs (Mucchielli, 1992).

7   As expressed, for example, in Casson, 1990 and a volume of readings edited by Bartlett, Doz and Hedlund (1990).

8   In the case of new foreign direct investment in the US, between 1988 and 1990 some 87.3 per cent took the form of A&Ms by foreign MNEs; the comparable figure for 1982 and 1983 was 64.8 per cent (Graham, 1991).

9   Described at some length in Pearce, 1990 and Casson, 1991.

10 Of course, there are exceptions, e.g. market seeking investment in large countries like China, India and Russia, is likely to grow.

11 See Cantwell and Hodson, 1991 and Dunning, 1992.

12 For further details of the R&D activities of Swedish MNEs, see Hakanson and Nobel, 1989.

13 For example, ozone depleting chloroflurocarbons (CFCs) are (or were) produced almost exclusively by TNCs, while they are involved in activities which generate more than half the greenhouse gases emitted by the six industrial sectors with the greatest impact on global warming (UNCTC, 1991b).

14 At the same time, FDI is likely to continue to be an important source of investment for some sectors in some developing countries.

15 According to the UNCTC (1992a), intra-regional investment flows in East, South and South-East Asia expanded rapidly during the second half of the 1980s, and now account for a quite substantial share of inward investments of some recipient countries, noticeably Malaysia, Thailand and China.

16 For a recent interesting analysis of the internationalization of New Zealand firms, see Akoorie and Enderwick, 1992.

17 For a brief discussion of the ways in which globalization may impinge on developing countries through investment, trade and technology linkages, see UNCTC, 1992a.

References

Akoorie, M. and Enderwick, P. (1992) 'The international operations of New Zealand companies', *Asia Pacific Journal of Management 9*: 51–69

Bartlett, C. A., Doz, Y. and Hedlund, G. (eds) (1990) *Managing the Global Firm*, London and New York: Routledge

Bergsten, C. F. (1990) 'The world economy after the cold war', *Foreign Affairs 60*: 96–112

Cantwell, J. and Hodson, C. (1991) 'Global research and development and UK competitiveness', in Casson, M. C. (ed.) *Global Research Strategy and International Competitiveness*, Oxford: Basil Blackwell

Casson, M. C. (1990) *Enterprise and Competitiveness*, Oxford: Clarendon Press

Casson, M. C. (ed.) (1991) *Global Research Strategy and International Competitiveness*, Oxford: Basil Blackwell

Contractor, F. (1990) 'The changing form of US international business', *Journal of International Business Studies*

Dunning, J. H. (1988) *Explaining International Production*, London: Unwin Hyman

Dunning, J. H. (1991) 'The prospects for foreign direct investment in Eastern Europe', *Development and International Cooperation VII*: 21–40.

Dunning, J. H. (1992) 'Multinational enterprises and the globalization of innovatory capacity', in Grandstand, O., Sjölander, S. and Hakanson, L. (eds) *Technology Management and International Business*, Chichester: John Wiley

Dunning, J. H. (1993) *Multinational Enterprises and the Global Economy*, Reading: Addison-Wesley

Eatwell, J. (1982) *Whatever happened to Britain?*, London: Duckworth

Graham, E. M. (1991) 'Foreign direct investment in the United States and U.S. interests', *Science 254*: 1740–1745

Gugler, P. (1991) *Les Alliances Stratégiques Transnationales*, Friborg: Editions Universitaires Friborg Suisse

Hakanson, L. and Nobel, R. (1989) 'Overseas research and development in Swedish multinationals', Stockholm Institute of International Business, Research Paper 89/3

Hedlund, G. and Rolander, D. (1990) 'Action in heterarchies: New approaches to managing the MNE', in Bartlett, C. A., Doz, Y. and Hedlund, G. (eds) *Managing the Global Firm*, London and New York: Routledge

Julius, DeAnne (1990) *Global Companies and Public Policy*, London: Pinter Publishers

McMillan, C. (1991) *Foreign Direct Investment Flows to Eastern Europe and their Implications for Developing Countries*, New York: UN

Moller, J. O. (1991) 'Visions of the New Europe', *Economic Integration v. Cultural Diversity*, Copenhagen: Business and Economic Studies on European Integration Working Paper 18–91

Morss, E. R. (1991) 'The new global players; how they compete and collaborate', *World Development 19*: 55–64

Mucchielli, J. L. (1992) *European Policies to Attract Foreign Investment: The French Case Favoring Japanese Manufacturing FDI*, University of Paris (mimeo)

Pearce, R. D. (1990) *The Internationalization of Research and Development*, Basingstoke: Macmillan

UN (1992a) *World Investment Report 1992*, New York: UN Transnational Corporations and Management Division

UN (1992b and 1993) *World Investment Directory* (various volumes), New York: UN Transnational Corporations and Management Division

UNCTC (1991a) *World Investment Report 1991*, New York: UNCTC

UNCTC (1991b) *Transnational Corporations and Issues Relating to the Environment*, Report of Secretary-General presented at seventeenth session of Commission on Transnational Corporations, New York: E/C.10/1991/3

UNCTC (1992a) *Trends in Foreign Direct Investment*, paper prepared by UNCTC for eighteenth session of Commission on Transnational Corporations, January, New York, E/C.10/1992/3

UNCTC (1992b) *Globalization and Developing countries: Investment Trade and Technology Linkages in the 1990s* (Proceedings of a symposium at The Hague, March 1992), New York: UN

US Department of Commerce (1991) *US Direct Investment Abroad, 1989 Benchmark Survey, Preliminary Results*, Washington, DC: US Department of Commerce

Van Tulder, R. and Junne, G. (1988) *European Multinationals in Core Technologies*, Chichester: John Wiley

World Bank (1991) *World Development Report, 1991*, Washington, DC: World Bank

12 GOVERNMENTS, HIERARCHIES AND MARKETS: TOWARDS A NEW BALANCE?

Notes

1 Intermediate products are defined as goods and services other than those which are sold directly to final customers.

2 For further details, the reader is invited to consult Bartlett and Ghoshal 1990, Casson, 1987, 1992, Dunning, 1988, 1990, 1993, Ohmae, 1987, 1989, Ozawa, 1987, Porter, 1986, 1990, Stopford, 1990 and UNCTC, 1991.

3 Again, this is partly a function of technological advance and the fact that so many markets are now transnational. Compare, for example, the changing character of the market for telecommunications equipment over the last 100 years. Compare too, the cost of operating efficient markets for (say) a pharmaceutical ingredient between firms within the US, and firms located in the US and (say) Tanzania.

4 Essentially, a country's capabilities at time t will determine the pro-

ductivity of its natural resources at time t and the added value to its natural resources (through upgrading human and physical capital) in time t + 1.

5 As evidenced, for example, by the rising proportion of intrafirm trade as a proportion of all trade.

6 These comments should be read in conjunction with those set out in Chapter 2.

7 These issues are further explored in Dunning, 1992 and in Eden and Hampson, 1990.

8 To quote from Charles Perrow (1986) who, himself, was drawing upon some thoughts of Sidney Winter, 'the distinction between markets and hierarchies is greatly overdrawn. The continuum from market to hierarchy is less like a ruler than a football, with a vanishingly small pure type at each end and a swollen middle that mixes the two' (Perrow, 1986: 255).

9 In terms of Figure 12.1, for economic activity as a whole, the aim of each government in respect of the goals it seeks to achieve must surely be to organize economic activity in such a way as to make optimum use of the three organizational modes. For any particular economic activity, the perspective contribution of governments, hierarchies and firms is likely to vary a great deal. Similarly, the optimum macro-organizational structure is likely to be different between countries or within the same country over a period of time. For a more detailed discussion on this issue, see Dunning (1993b).

References

Bartlett, C. A. and Ghoshal, S. (1990) *Managing Across Borders: The Transnational Solution*, Boston: Harvard Business School Press

Casson, M. C. (1987) *The Firm and the Market*, Oxford: Basil Blackwell

Casson, M. C. (1992) *Internalization Theory and Beyond*, in Dunning, J. H. (ed.) *The Theory of Transnational Corporations*, UN Library on Transnational Corporations, London and New York: Routledge

Dunning, J. H. (1988) *Explaining International Production*, London: Unwin Hyman

Dunning, J. H. (1990) *The Globalization of Firms and the Competitiveness of Countries: Some Implications for the Theory of International Production*, Lund: University of Lund, The Crafoord Lectures

Dunning, J. H. (1992) *Multinational Enterprise and the Global Economy*, Reading, Berkshire: Addison-Wesley

Dunning, J. H. (1993) 'The global economy, domestic governance strategies and transnational corporations: interactions and policy implications', *Transnational Corporations 1*, No. 3, December: 7–46

Eden, L. and Hampson, F. O. (1990) *Clubs are Trumps: Towards a Taxonomy of International Regimes*, Ottawa: Norman Patterson School of International Affairs, CITIPS Working Paper 90-02.

Ohmae, K. (1987) *Triad Power: The Coming Shape of Global Competition*, New York: Free Press

Ohmae, K. (1989) *The Borderless World*, New York: Free Press

Osborne, D. and Gaebler, T. (1992) *Re-inventing Government: How the*

Entrepreneurial Spirit is Transforming the Public Sector, Reading, Mass.: Addison-Wesley

Ostrey, S. (1990) *Governments and Corporations in a Shrinking World*, New York: Council on Foreign Relations Press

Ozawa, T. (1987) 'Can the market alone manage structural upgrading? A challenge posed by interdependence', in Dunning, J. H. and Usui, M. (eds) *Structural Change, Economic Interdependence and World Development*, Vol. 1, Economic Interdependence, Basingstoke: Macmillan

Perrow, C. (1986) *Complex Organizations*, New York: McGraw-Hill

Porter, M. (ed.) (1986) *Competition in Global Industries*, Boston: Harvard Business School Press

Porter, M. (1990) *The Competitive Advantage of Nations*, New York: Free Press

Scott, B. R. and Lodge, G. R. (eds) (1985) *US Competitiveness in the World Economy*, Boston: Harvard Business School Press

Stopford, J. (1990) *Multinationals, Strategy: Competition for Resources*, London: London Business School (mimeo)

UNCTC (1991) *World Investment Report. The Triad in Foreign Direct Investment*, New York: UN

Wade, R. (1988) 'The role of government in overcoming market failure in Taiwan, Republic of Korea and Japan', in Hughes, H. (ed.) *Achieving Industrialisation in East Asia*, Cambridge: Cambridge University Press

13 GOVERNMENTS AND MULTINATIONAL ENTERPRISES: FROM CONFRONTATION TO COOPERATION?

Notes

1 Although, in this chapter, we shall be primarily concerned with the role of central or federal governments, the term government should be taken to embrace subnational and supranational administrations as well.

2 In the economist's language, the ratio of marginal productivity of each input is proportional to its price, while in the case of each input, its marginal productivity will be equal to its price.

3 They may also confer power on the buyers, but in this chapter we shall concentrate on seller power.

4 As described in standard industrial organization textbooks.

5 These include those compiled by national and regional governments, private consultancies and banks; but perhaps the most comprehensive source is that of United Nations Centre on Transnational Corporations. See especially UNCTC, 1989, and Sections III and IV of the *List of Sales Publications of the UNCTC*, 1973–1989, issued by the United Nations in October 1989.

6 Sweden was an exception, and by 1974 had enacted fairly comprehensive legislation in an attempt to ensure that foreign investment by Swedish MNEs was in the national interest of the home country.

7 Bergsten, Horst and Moran (1978) give examples of the US reacting to the policies of some European governments giving exemption from domestic taxation of export income and direct support in their oil MNEs.

8 A good example of the costs of creating (or recreating) a market system is now being played out in Eastern Europe. Here the transitional costs from a centrally planned to a market-oriented system seem so huge that only by united international financial support (rather akin to the US Marshall Plan for Western European recovery after the last World War) can this change in the macro-governance of economic activity be accomplished relatively smoothly and within a reasonable period of time.

9 And, by implication, depict their competition of such opportunities. Good examples include those countries comprising the EC and States in the USA, and some East Asian economies.

10 The quotation (from Goldberg and Kindleberger, 1970) that 'reduced to its simplest terms, there is an inherent conflict between the objectives of the international corporation and the nation-state' does not ring as true today as it did 20 years ago. Nevertheless, the idea of a general agreement on an international framework in which FDI can play its full and proper role is now being reexamined. See, e.g. Bergsten and Graham, 1992.

11 See, for example, various reports on these issues published by the UNCTC.

12 The paper on which this chapter is based was first written prior to the resignation of Mrs Thatcher in November 1990.

13 This view is developed in a recently published report (EAG, 1993) of which I was the main author.

References

Bergsten, F. and Graham, E. M. (1992) 'Needed: new rules for foreign direct investment', *International Trade Journal* 7: 15–44

Bergsten, F., Horst, T. and Moran, T. (1978) *American Multinationals and American Interests*, Washington DC: The Brookings Institution

Brooks, H. (1982) 'Towards an efficient public technology policy criteria and evidence', in Giersch, H. (ed.) *Emerging Technologies: Consequences for Economic Growth, Structural Change and Employment*, Tubingen: J. C. B. Mohr

Cecchini, P., Catinat, M. and Jacquemin, A. (1988) *The European Challenge: The Benefits of a Single Market*, Aldershot: Wildwood House

Drucker, P. (1986) 'The changed world economy', *Foreign Affairs 64*: 768–791

Dunning, J. H. (1971) Studies in International Investment, London: Allen and Unwin

Dunning, J. H. (1990) *The Globalization of Firms and the Competitiveness of Countries. Some Implications for the Theory of International Production*, Lund: University of Lund, The Crafoord Lectures, 1989

Dunning, J. H. (1991a) 'Governments, economic organization and international competitiveness', in Mattson, L. and Styme, B. (eds) *Corporate and Industry Strategies for Europe*, Amsterdam: Elsevier Science Publishers, B.V.

Dunning, J. H. (1991b) 'Multinational enterprises and the globalization of innovatory capacity', in Grandstrand, O., Håkanson, L. and Sjölander, S. (eds) *Technology Management and International Business: Internalization of R&D and Technology*, Chichester and New York: John Wiley

Dunning, J. H. (1992) 'The competitive advantage of countries and the activities of transnational corporations', *Transnational Corporations 1*: 135–168

Dunning, J. H. (1993) *Multinational Enterprises and the Global Economy*, Wokingham, Berks: Addison-Wesley

Dunning, J. H. and Cantwell, J. (1987) *The IRM Directory of Statistics of International Investment and Production*, Basingstoke: Macmillan

Dunning, J. H. and Norman, G. (1987) 'The location choice of offices of international companies', *Environment and Planning A* (19) 613–631

EAG (1993) *Sharpening the Competitive Edge*, London: Economists Advisory Group

Ergas, H. (1987) 'Does technology policy matter?', in Guile, B. R. and Brooks, H. (eds) *Technology and Global Industry*, Washington: National Academy Press.

Fagre, N. and Wells, L. T. (1982) 'Bargaining power of multinationals and host governments', *Journal of International Studies 13*: 9–23

Fishwick, F. (1976) *Multinational Companies and Economic Concentration in Europe*, Aldershot, Hampshire: Gower

Goldberg, P. M. and Kindleberger, C. K. (1970) 'Towards a GATT for investment. A proposal for supervision of the international corporation', *Law and Policy in International Business 2*: 295–323

Lall, P. and Streeten, P. (1977) *Foreign Investment, Transnationals and Developing Countries*, London and Basingstoke: Macmillan

Lawrence, P. (1987) 'Competition: a renewed focus for industrial policy', in Teece, D. (ed.) *The Competitive Challenge*, Cambridge, Mass.: Ballinger

Lecraw, D. J. and Morrison, A. (1990) 'Transnational corporation – host country relations: a framework for analysis, South Carolina Essays in International Business 9

Lipsey, R. and Dobson, W. (1987) *Shaping Comparative Advantage*, Ontario: Prentice Hall for C. D. Howe Institute

Musgrave, P. B. (1975) *Direct Investment Abroad and the Multinationals: Effects on the US Economy*, Washington: Senate Foreign Relations Committee – Subcommittee on Multinational Corporations

North, D. (1985) 'Transaction costs in history', *Journal of European Economic History 42*: 566–576.

Ohmae, K. (1985) *Triad Power*, New York: Free Press

Ozawa, T. (1987) 'Can the market alone manage structural upgrading: a challenge posed by economic interdependence', in Dunning, J. H. and Usui, M. (eds) *Structural Change, Economic Interdependence and World Development* Vol. 4, *Economic Interdependence*, Basingstoke and London: Macmillan

Ozawa, T. (1989) *Japan's Strategic Policy Towards Outward Direct Investment*, Fort Collins, Colorado (mimeo)

Porter, M. (1990) *The Competitive Advantage of Nations*, New York: Free Press

Reddaway, W. B., Potter, S. J. and Taylor, C. T. (1968) *The Effects of UK Direct Investment Overseas*, Cambridge: Cambridge University Press

Servan Schreiber, J. (1978) *The American Challenge*, New York: Hamish Hamilton

Stegemann, K. (1989) 'Policy rivalry among industrial states: what can we learn from models of strategic trade policy?', *International Organization 43*, Winter: 73–100

Steuer, M. D., Abell, P., Gennard, J., Perlman, M., Rees, R., Scott, B. and Wallis, K. (1973) *The Impact of Foreign Investment in the United Kingdom*, London: HMSO

Teece, D. J. (1985) 'Transaction cost economics and the multinational enterprise: an assessment', *Journal of Economic Behavior and Organization 7*: 21–45

UNCTC (1989) *National Legislation and Regulations Towards Transnational Corporations* (Volume VII), New York: United Nations Sales No. E.89.II.A.9

UNCTC (1991) *World Investment Report 1991*, New York: United Nations

Vernon, R. (1983) 'Organizational and institutional responses to international risk', in Herring, R. J. (ed.) *Managing International Risk*, Cambridge: Cambridge University Press

Wells, S. J. (1964) *British Export Performance: A Comparative Study*, London: Cambridge University Press

14 THE POLITICAL ECONOMY OF MNE ACTIVITY

Notes

1   For the purpose of this chapter, government embraces all forms of political authority be it exercised at a multinational, regional, national or local level.

2   One exception is a recently published book by Behrman and Grosse (1991) which the author came across only after he had written this chapter.

3   See, for example, Dunning, 1993 and a variety of contributions in Casson, 1990.

4   However, generally speaking, development resources were provided by way of intragovernment loans or through the international capital or technology market.

5   See especially UNCTC, 1989.

6   Examples include the desired amount, kind or price of technology transferred from abroad; the taxable profits earned; the employment and training of the local labour force; the access to foreign markets, and the extent to which parts and components are bought from local producers.

7   For some of the arguments put forward at the time, see Dunning, 1971.

8   For analysis of these, see Hawkins, 1972.

9   In the words of Teretumo Ozawa

> Although no requirements for approval (to invest abroad) were officially made public, it was generally understood that:
>
> 1 Direct foreign investment must either promote exports from Japan or lead to the overseas development of natural resources vital to Japanese industry;
>
> 2 Foreign investment must not jeopardize the competitive position of other Japanese firms at home;

3 Foreign investment must not interfere with the effectiveness of domestic monetary policy.

These requirements, particularly the first two, clearly specified the trade supportive, domestic-production-enhancing function of overseas investment: overseas investment was construed only as augmenting home based industrial activities

(Ozawa, 1989)

10 And, of course, by domestic firms as well.
11 Representing value added to natural resources and new assets created from these resources.
12 Which currently are estimated at between 17,500 and 20,000 (Dunning, 1993). The UNCTC (UN, 1992) estimate the figure to be 35,000, but they include subsidiaries of subsidiaries in their calculations.
13 For example by the provision or support of insurance or investment guarantee schemes. Some of the different roles which governments may play in reducing or circumventing market or hierarchical failure are sent out in Dunning, 1991.
14 Other areas of friction (e.g. to do with taxation, information provision, extraterritoriality, anti-trust, environmental protection) are identified in Vernon, 1991.
15 Consider the analogy of a price demand curve. When price changes, consumers demand moves up and down along the curve. When the conditions of demand change, the consumers move to a new demand curve.
16 For an examination of the impact of MNEs on various macro-policies, see Wilson and Scheffer, 1974. Examples include the lack of responsiveness of MNEs to devaluation or anti-spending measures, and the greater responsiveness in their locational policies.
17 For a more extended treatment of this subject, see Dunning, 1990.
18 For an elaboration on this issue, see Chapter 6 and Ozawa, 1989.
19 There are signs that this is beginning to change; witness the setting up of an industrial competitiveness unit at the Department of Trade and Industry at the end of 1992.
20 Or, put another way, the extent and ease at which the failure of markets to organize transactions can be overcome or compensated.
21 More correctly, governments should intervene only insofar as the marginal reduction in transaction costs (or increase in transactional benefits) exceeds the marginal costs in that particular action by governments, and the overall net benefits of government action exceed or at least are as great as any alternative organizational route to achieve the same purpose.

References

Bartlett, C. A. and Ghoshal, S. (1989) *Managing Across Borders: The Transnational Solutions,* Boston: Harvard Business School Press
Behrman, J. and Grosse, R. (1991) *International Business and Governments,* Columbia: University of South Carolina Press

Bergsten, C. F., Horst, T. and Moran, T. (1978) *American Interests and American Multinationals*, Washington D.C.: The Brookings Institution

Casson, M. C. (ed.) (1990) *The Multinational Enterprise*, London: Edward Elgar

Doz, Y. (1986) *Strategic Management in Multinational Companies*, Oxford and New York: Pergamon Press

Dunning, J. H. (1971) *Studies in International Investment*, London: Allen and Unwin

Dunning, J. H. (1990) *The Globalization of Firms and the Competitiveness of Countries: Some Implications for the Theory of International Production*, Lund: University of Lund, The Crafoord Lectures

Dunning, J. H. (1991) 'Governments, organization and international competitiveness', in Mattsson, L. G. and Stymne, B. (eds) *Corporate and Industrial Strategies for Europe*, Amsterdam: Elsevier Science Publications

Dunning, J. H. (1993) *Multinational Enterprises and the Global Economy*, Reading, Berkshire: Addison-Wesley

Dunning, J. H. and Cantwell, J. A. (1987) *The I.R.M. Directory of Statistics on International Investment and Production*, Basingstoke: Macmillan Reference Books

Gilpin, R. (1975) *U.S. Power and the Multinational Corporation*, London: Macmillan

Hawkins, R. G. (1972) *Job Displacement and the Multinational Firm: A Methodological Review*, Washington D.C.: Center for Multinational Studies, Occasional Paper No. 3, June

Hufbauer, G. C. and Adler, M. (1968) *U.S. Manufacturing Investment and the Balance of Payments*, Washington D.C.: U.S. Treasury Department, Tax Policy Research Study No. 1

Knickerbocker, K. (1973) *Oligopolistic Reaction and the Multinational Enterprise*, Cambridge, Mass: MIT Press

Kojima, K. (1978) *Direct Foreign Investment*, London: Croom Helm

Ohmae, K. (1985) *Triad Power*, New York: Free Press

Ohmae, K. (1989) *The Borderless World*, New York: Free Press

Ozawa, T. (1979) *Multinationalization, Japanese Style: The Political Economy of Outward Dependency*, Princeton: Princeton University Press

Ozawa, T. (1989) *Japans 'Strategic' Policy Towards Outward Direct Investment*, Fort Collins, University of Colorado (mimeo)

Servan-Schreiber, J. J. (1968) *The American Challenge*, London: Hamish Hamilton

Snider, D. A. (1964) 'The case for capital controls to relieve the U.S. balance of payments', *American Economic Review 84*: 346–358, reprinted in Dunning, J. H. (ed.) *International Investment*, Harmondsworth: Penguin Books, 359–374

Stopford, J. (1990) *Competition for Global Resources*. Paper presented to Workshop on *MNEs and the 21st Century*, Tokyo, June 1990

Svedberg, P. (1981) 'Colonial enforcement of foreign direct investment', *Manchester School of Economic and Social Studies 50*: 21–38

UN (1992a) *World Investment Report 1992*, New York: UN Transnational Corporations and Management Division

UN (1992b) *The World Investment Directory*, New York: UN Transnational Corporations and Management Division

UNCTC (1988) *Transnational Corporations and World Development, Trends and Prospects,* New York: United Nations Sales No. E.88.II.A.7

UNCTC (1989) *Legislation and Regulations Towards Investment Regulations, Transnational Corporations and Inward Direct Investment,* New York: United Nations

UNCTC (1991) *World Investment Report 1991,* New York: United Nations

Vernon, R. (1991) 'Sovereignty at bay: twenty years after', *Millennium 20*

Wilson, J. S. G. and Scheffer C. F. (eds) (1974) *Multinational Enterprises – Finance and Monetary Aspects,* Leide: Sijthoff

15 MULTINATIONAL INVESTMENT IN THE EC: SOME POLICY IMPLICATIONS

Notes

1   By macro-organization policy, we mean the instruments available to and chosen by governments to affect the overall organization of the production and transactions of resources. As compared with macro-economic policy, it is designed to bring about a certain system of resource allocation (i.e. a means towards an end) rather than to achieve certain goals (employment, stable exchange rates, economic growth, etc). We shall use the term micro-organization to refer to specific aspects of macro-organization policy as subsidies to assist training grants, R&D subventions, patent regulations, anti-trust legislation, environmental controls, investment incentives, etc.

2   As set out most recently in Chapters 4 and 5 of Dunning, 1993.

3   The exception is in Southern Europe where some investment is undertaken to take advantage of a plentiful and cheap supply of labour.

4   For analysis of the distinctive characteristics of sequential investment, see Kogut, 1983.

5   Elsewhere referred to as O_a (the ownership of specific assets) advantages (Dunning, 1988).

6   Elsewhere referred to as O (the ownership of the ability to organise assets to minimise transaction costs and maximise productive efficiency).

7   For example, efficient organization may lead to cost reducing in the price of products, which may lead to an increase in sales, which may raise profits and which may enable a firm to spend more on R&D to create new products or production methods.

8   Which, in turn, rested on the balance between the respective opportunity costs of the bargaining parties.

9   Though there is less reluctance by foreign MNEs to conclude some kinds of non-equity ventures, e.g. strategic alliances, for specific purposes.

10   See Dunning, 1991d and 1992a.

11   That is, those who record an average proportion of their sales (whether by export or FDI) outside their national boundaries.

12   Such as the percentage of domestic corporate profits accounted by the foreign activities of domestic MNEs plus those of foreign subsidiaries, the percentage of domestic output and employment accounted for by the

same two groups of activities. Ratios on these are currently being calculated by the UNCTC and will appear in UN, 1992a.

13 For example, the effects of a currency devaluation orrevaluation which fails to take account of the (likely) very different pricing policies of domestic firms and foreign subsidiaries may fail to achieve its purpose.

14 See also Ozawa 1992.

15 With the notable exception of a few large MNEs, e.g. Philips of Eindhoven and Electrolux of Sweden.

16 Defined as the average income earned on FDI less taxes paid to foreign governments, as compared with the earnings on domestic investment gross of tax. For an analysis of the UK situation, see Chapters 2 and 3 of Dunning, 1970 entitled 'The costs and benefits of foreign direct investment to the investing country: the UK experience' and 'Further thoughts on foreign investment'.

17 For analysis of the likely impact of outward direct investment on the UK and US balance of payments according to the assumptions made, see Dunning, 1969.

18 See also Dunning, 1991a, 1991b, 1991c.

19 Hence the growth of joint ventures and strategic alliances particularly in high-technology sectors. See Chapter 9 for further details.

20 We do, however, accept the argument that, in some cases, firms contemplating FDI (or an expansion in FDI) as a means of promoting their competitive position might be better advised to use the resources to improve the efficiency of their domestic activities, and/or engage in more R&D.

21 Usually they tended to be defence and related high-technology sectors, those which were nationalized or closely regulated (e.g. transport and banking) and those which were identified with the maintenance of national culture (e.g. newspapers and broadcasting). For further details, see Safarian, 1983 and OECD, 1982.

22 Including denial of work permits or professional cards to technical and managerial staff and restriction of shareholder voting rights to nationals.

23 The Exchange Control Act gave the Treasury wide powers to influence the amount and pattern of both inward and outward investment. Exchange control permission was, for example, required for any change in the control of a UK company passing to a foreign resident. So far as the Treasury was concerned, the main objective of the Exchange Control Act was that FDI should have a favorable impact on the foreign currency reserves.

24 Some of these are summarized in Hodges, 1974.

25 For some examples of plant closures in Ireland and Belgium in the 1970s, see OECD, 1985 and Van den Bulcke, 1985.

26 For example, some 33.0 per cent of manufacturing employment in Belgium in 1985 and 42.8 per cent of that in Ireland in 1987, was accounted for by foreign owned firms.

27 As measured, for example, by the ratio between the accumulated inward and outward direct capital stake and the GNP of the country.

28 The exact proportion sold to other EC affiliates is unknown, but it is believed to be very substantial indeed.

29 It is not always easy to distinguish between a request, a tacit agreement

and a contractual obligation imposed on a foreign direct investor, as, *de facto*, very rarely do negotiated settlements between national governments and foreign MNEs have any binding force.

30 For a somewhat different view which argues that Japanese policy – at least towards inward investment – was more influenced by the actions and bargaining power of foreign MNEs, see Encarnation and Mason, 1990.

31 For example, hardly any mention is made of the role of outward or inward direct investment in the Ceccini report.

32 For a review of this work, see Dunning and Robson, 1988, Yannopolous, 1990 and UN, 1992b.

33 In particular, it is possible that countries like the UK, Germany and Italy would have adopted less-liberal policies towards inward investment in the absence of their membership of the EC. This is simply because MNEs would have had less opportunity to engage in efficiency seeking investment. In other words, their affiliates would most likely have been more responsive to domestic government policies.

34 For a discussion of the impact of different kinds of MNE activity on the framing of national economic policies, see Panic, 1991. An interesting perspective on the (positive) role played by US MNEs on the (limited) liberalization of inward investment policy in Japan is contained in Encarnation and Mason, 1990.

35 As described, for example, in Robinson, 1983.

36 Which included the contentious Vredling initiative which, *inter alia*, was designed to force foreign MNEs to disclose information about their worldwide operations to labor representatives bargaining with their European affiliates.

37 This diversion might be prevented if the wealthier countries, through such institutions as the Regional Development Fund, help the poorer countries to upgrade their standards.

References

Cantwell, J. A. (1988) 'The reorganisation of European industries after integration', in Dunning, J. H. and Robson, P. (eds) *Multinationals and the European Community*, Oxford: Basil Blackwell

Cantwell, J. A. (1989) *Technological Innovation and Multinational Corporations*, Oxford: Basil Blackwell

Cantwell, J. A. (1992) 'The effects of integration on the structure of multinational corporation activity in the EC,' in Klein, M. and Welfens, P. J. J. (eds) *Multinationals in the New Europe and Global Trade*, Berlin and New York: Springer-Verlag

Cecchini, P., Catinat, M. and Jacquemin, A. (1988) *The European Challenge 1992; The Benefits of a Single Market*, Aldershot, Hants: Wildwood House

Doz, Y. (1986) *Strategic Management in Multinational Corporations*, Oxford: Pergamon Press

Dunning, J. H. (1969) 'The Reddaway and Hufbauer/Adler Reports', *Bankers Magazine*, May, June and July

Dunning, J. H. (1970) *Studies in International Investment*, London: Allen and Unwin

Dunning, J. H. (1988) *Explaining International Production*, London and Boston: Unwin Hyman

Dunning, J. H. (1991a) 'Governments – markets – firms: towards a new balance?' *CTC Reporter 31*: 2–7

Dunning, J. H. (1991b) 'Governments and multinational enterprises: from confrontation to co-operation', *Millineum Journal of International Studies 20*: 223–244

Dunning, J. H. (1991c) 'Governments organization and international competitiveness', in Mattson, L. G. and Stymne, B. (eds) *Corporate and Industry Strategies for Europe*, Amsterdam: Elsevier Science Publishers

Dunning, J. H. (1991d) 'The eclectic paradigm of international production: a personal perspective', in Pitelis, C. N. and Sugden, R. (eds) *The Nature of the Transnational Firm*, London and New York: Routledge

Dunning, J. H. (1992) 'The political economy of international production', in Buckley, P. (ed.) *New Directions in International Business*, London: Edward Elgar

Dunning, J. H. (1993) *Multinational Enterprises and the Global Economy*, Reading, Mass. and London: Addison-Wesley

Dunning, J. H. and Robson, P. (eds) (1988) *Multinationals and the European Community*, Oxford: Basil Blackwell

Encarnation, D. J. and Mason, M. (1990) 'Neither MITI nor America; the political economy of capital liberalisation in Japan', *International Organisation 44*: 25–54.

Gugler, P. and Dunning, J. H. (1992) 'Technology based cross-border alliances', in Culpan, R. (ed.) *Multinational Strategic Alliances*, New York: Haworth Press

Hodges, M. (1974) *Multinational Corporations and National Governments: A Case Study of the United Kingdom Experience*, London: D. C. Heath

Hufbauer, G. and Adler, F. M. (1968) *Overseas Manufacturing Investment and the Balance of Payments*, Washington, DC: US Treasury Department, Tax Policy Research Study No. 1

Kogut, B. (1983) 'Foreign direct investment as a sequential process', in Kindleberger, C. P. and Audretsch, D. (eds) *The Multinational in the 1980s*, Cambridge, Mass.: MIT Press

Mytelka, L. K. and Delapierre, M. (1988) 'The alliance strategies of European firms in the information technology industry and the role of ESPRIT', in Dunning, J. and Robson, P. (eds) *Multinationals and the European Community*, Oxford: Basil Blackwell

OECD (1982 and 1987) *Controls and Impediments Affecting Inward Direct Investment in OECD Countries*, Paris: OECD

OECD (1985) *Structural Adjustment and Multinational Enterprises*, Paris: OECD

OECD (1991) *Measures Affecting Direct Investment in OECD Countries*, Paris: OECD

O'Hearn, D. (1990) 'TNCs, intervening mechanisms and economic growth in Ireland: a longitudinal test and extension of the Bornschier model', *World Development 18*: 417–429

Ozawa, T. (1989) *Japan's Strategic Policy Towards Outward Investment*, Fort

458   Notes and references

Collins: Colorado State University (mimeo)

Ozawa, T. (1992) 'Cross-investments between Japan and the EC: income similarities, technological congruity and the economies of scope', in Cantwell, J. (ed.) *Multinational Investment in Modern Europe*, Aldershot, Hants and Brookfield, Mass.: Edward Elgar

Panic, M. (1991) 'The impact of multinationals on national economic policies', in Bürgenmeier, B. and Mucchielli, J. L. (eds) *Multinationals and Europe 1992*, London and New York: Routledge

Porter, M. (1990) *The Competitive Advantage of Nations*, New York: Basic Books

Reddaway, W. B., Potter, S. J. and Taylor, C. T. (1968) *Effects of UK Direct Investment Overseas*, Cambridge: Cambridge University Press

Robinson, J. (1983) *Multinationals and Political Control*, Aldershot, Hants: Gower

Safarian, A. E. (1983) *Governments and Multinationals: Policies in the Developed Countries*, Washington DC: British-North American Committee

Safarian A. E. (1991) 'Firm and government strategies', in Bürgenmeier, B. and Mucchielli, J. L. (eds) *Multinationals and Europe 1992*, London and New York: Routledge

Servan-Schreiber, J. J. (1968) *Le Défi American (The American Challenge)*, London: Hamish Hamilton

Simoes, V. (1985) 'Portugal', in Dunning, J. H. (ed.) *Multinational Enterprises, Economic Structure and Competitiveness*, Chichester and New York: John Wiley

Stegemann, K. (1989) 'Policy rivalry among nation states: what can we learn from models of strategic trade policy', *International Organisation 43*: 1

Sweeney, R. J. (1991) *The Competition for Foreign Direct Investment*, Washington DC: Georgetown University (mimeo)

UN (1992a) *World Investment Directory*, Vols 1 and 2, New York: UN Transnational Corporations and Management Division

UN (1992b) *From the Common Market to EC 1992. Regional Integration in the European Community and Transnational Corporations*, New York: UN Transnational Corporations and Management Division

UNCTC (1991) *World Investment Report, The Triad in foreign direct investment*, New York: UN Transnational Corporations and Management Division

US Department of Commerce (v.d.), *Survey of Current Business*.

Van den Bulcke, D. (1985), 'Belgium', in Dunning, J. H. (ed.) *Multinational Enterprises, Economic Structure and International Competitiveness*, Chichester: John Wiley

World Bank (1991) *World Development Report*, Washington DC: World Bank

Yannopoulus, G. N. (1990) 'Foreign direct investment and European integration: the evidence from the formative years of the European Community', *Journal of Common Market Studies 28*, 235–259

Young, S., Hood, N. and Hamill, J. (1988) *Foreign Multinationals and the British Economy*, London and New York: Croom Helm

Index